Gibbon for Moderns

GIBBON FOR MODERNS

The History of
the Decline and Fall
of the Roman Empire
With Lessons for America Today

Edited with commentary by

Peter P. Witonski

ARLINGTON HOUSE·PUBLISHERS
NEW ROCHELLE, N. Y.

Second Printing, March 1974

Library of Congress Catalog Card Number 73-10710

MANUFACTURED IN THE UNITED STATES OF AMERICA

Library of Congress Cataloging in Publication Data

Gibbon, Edward, 1737–1794.
Gibbon for moderns.

Includes Bibliographical references.
1. Rome—History—Empire, 30 B.C.—476A.D.
2. Byzantine Empire—History. I. Witonski, Peter, ed. II. Title.
DG311.G55 1974 937'.06 73–10710
ISBN 0–87000–198–1

TO

Frank S. Meyer, 1909–72

Patriot, Historian, Philosopher of Freedom

"He did not loosely, through silence, allow things to pass away, as in a dream."

Contents

An Acknowledgment

History, wrote Pieter Geyle, is an active force in the struggles of every generation, and the historian, by reason of his vocation, invariably takes an active part in these struggles, for his judgment of the past is a reflection of his understanding of the present. There will, as a result, always be a connection between the way in which men contemplate the past and the way they contemplate the present; for history, even in its humblest guise, is a great conversation between the past and the present in which the historian is the mediating spirit. History is thus an enterprise to be reckoned with in every age, and because of this it will be *used* and *abused* for the best and worst of reasons. This inescapable fact was more than understood by Edward Gibbon, who was nothing if he was not a child of his troubled age; and it was well appreciated by the late Frank S. Meyer, the singular man to whom this abridged edition of Gibbon's masterpiece is dedicated.

Meyer's devotion to the study of history, like Gibbon's, was largely motivated by his understanding of the terrible problems of his age. This does not mean that he was a *presentist* in the vulgar sense; his sense of history was too strong to allow for concessions to anything even vaguely resembling historical relativism. While his entire life was devoted to trying to fathom the great political struggles of the present day, he was, like Friedrich Meinecke before him, capable of valuing the study of history as an end in itself. Indeed, he rejected the fashionable prejudices of twentieth-century historiography, and approached history, in Johan Huizinga's sense, from an *indeterminist* point of view, always placing his analysis, as he developed it, at a point in the past from which the available evidence allowed for different outcomes. Thus, when he spoke, for example, of the American Civil War, he did so in such a way as to convince his listeners that the South might still be able to win. The result of this method was highly instructive, and invariably led to a better understanding of the phenomenon under discussion. This was important because Frank Meyer was at heart a great teacher, and his intellectual life was dominated by this fact, as those of us who profited from his teaching will attest. He belonged to no university faculty, but those who knew him—either in person, or through his books and articles—thought of him first as a teacher, as a man whose teaching helped to inspire and form the intellectual renaissance of conservatism in America.

In the early stages of my work on the *Decline and Fall,* I freely availed myself of Frank Meyer's counsel, which was, as ever, generous and abundant. Many of his suggestions have been incorporated into the present volume. He knew and loved Gibbon's writings, and he understood the kind of difficulties I would confront in attempting to abridge a work as vast as the *Decline and Fall.* Without his suggestions on what should be retained and what should be edited out, my labor would have been far more difficult. But this work is dedicated to Frank Meyer's memory for other reasons, reasons which, I think, Gibbon would have approved. Without wishing to compare their talents and interests, I find both men to be strikingly similar. Both men, for example, rejected the orthodoxies of their respective nations in their youth, only to return to those orthodoxies in their later lives; both men were driven by a passionate love of liberty; and both were moved in their intellectual labors by the muse of history. Such similarities, for me, make their obvious differences unimportant, for these are rooted in the realities of two different epochs.

Unlike Gibbon, Frank Meyer left no magnum opus behind him, although he often spoke of such a work, his "philosophy of history," as he called it. Some of his best thoughts manifested themselves in his spontaneous but vehement conversation, which, alas, is not recorded. Had he systematized his almost casual wisdom, he would have left us an enduring legacy. As things stand, we must be satisfied with his slender literary corpus, which was no real measure of his intellect. As a conservative who had espoused radicalism in his youth, he could say, with St. Augustine, "Sero Te amavi, pulchritudo Tam Antiqua"; but history had taught him that Augustine was wrong about the passing of Antiquity: Rome may have died, but Roman civilization survived in the spirit of the Christian West, which Frank Meyer devoted his waning years to defending. Here he differed with Gibbon, for he truly believed in the eternality of Rome. Frank Meyer was one of those rare creatures who had learned through the course of his life to think, in Max Cary's phrase, "beyond yesterday," and thus, like Gibbon, he could see Rome in its proper perspective, as the focusing-point of Western history; and on this central point, he and Gibbon would have agreed.

Peter P. Witonski

INTRODUCTION

1

The Historiographical Background

Truth, naked, unblushing truth, the first virtue of . . . serious history . . .

Edward Gibbon

I

No event in Western history has been as painstakingly pondered and debated as the collapse of the Roman Empire. The theories and interpretations endeavoring to account for Rome's decline are virtually unlimited in their number and variety, surpassing all other themes in the annals of historical literature. Since Roman times, thoughtful men have desired to discover the reason or reasons for Rome's death; for even then—despite the Augustan poet Tibullus' vainglorious prophecy, "Roma aeterna"—it was clear that Rome was to be less than eternal.

Indeed, it is striking to discover the extent to which contemporary witnesses of Roman decadence appreciated their own plight. One need only contemplate the debauchery satirized by such knowing observers as Juvenal and Martial for telling examples of how contemporaries saw Rome's decline. The great historian Dio Cassius, coming to the end of Marcus' rule, bitterly noted that his history "now descends from a kingdom of gold to one of iron and rust." St. Augustine bewailed the fact that "the seductions of evil-minded devils had more influence with [the Romans] than the precautions of prudent men," such as Scipio, who saw "how easily prosperity would corrupt and destroy [Rome]." Anticipating Vico and Toynbee, Gregory of Tours—who saw what he perceived to be the shadows of barbaric darkness descending over the remains of the Empire—summed up his feelings with the words, "Mundus senescit" ("The world grows old").

With the rise of more modern historiographical techniques during the Renaissance, interpretations of Rome's fall became less metaphoric and more sophisticated. Petrarch maintained that Rome was the victim of her own internal problems; Marsilio Ficino argued that the eclipse of learning was to blame; and Machiavelli placed all the fault on the shoulders of Rome's barbarian invaders. These great Italians saw themselves as heirs to the greatness of Rome, identifying their renascent civilization with the best and worst aspects of Roman life. This is especially true of Machiavelli, who sought to derive lessons from Rome's fall that might aid the fortunes of Florence, which he correctly saw to be in danger. Indeed, it is interesting to note that most of those who have tried to discover the reasons for Rome's decline have invariably started with the assumption that their own historical situation mirrored that of ancient Rome. This is as true in our own time as it was in fifteenth- and sixteenth-century Italy and eighteenth-century England. It is not surprising to learn that even Hitler, who thought he knew all the answers, is reported to have said, "I often wonder why the Ancient World collapsed." He answered his own query by tentatively suggesting that racial impurity was the cause, and proceeded to "purify" his own incipient empire so that it would not go the way of Rome.[1]

II

The achievements of such Renaissance historians as Machiavelli, Guicciardini, Lorenzo Valla, and Erasmus, were marked improvements, in scholarship as well as technique, over the biased ecclesiastical chronicles of the Middle Ages. Nonetheless, before historians could deal with a problem as complex as the fall of Rome with the kind

1. Hugh Trevor-Roper, *The Rise of Christian Europe* (New York: Harcourt, Brace and World, 1965), pp. 25–26. "The fact that even Hitler condescended to wonder [about the collapse of Rome]," writes Trevor-Roper, ". . . illuminates the permanence of the problem."

of rigorous objectivity and authenticity we have come to value in our modern histories, the craft of history had to advance beyond the brilliant but rude studies of these early practitioners. During the fifteenth and sixteenth centuries historical studies made major strides in this direction, progressing far beyond the teleological constructions of the encyclopedic medieval historians; but it was not until the seventeenth century that the discipline of history came, as it were, into its own as a full-fledged intellectual enterprise.

It is in particular from two seventeenth-century historical enterprises, Bollandism and Maurism, that the modern historical ethos derives much of its professionalism.[2] Both of these early ventures in cooperative scholarship were to profoundly influence subsequent generations of historians, and Gibbon is most effusive in acknowledging his debt to them for their diligent study and compilation of authentic historical source materials. The Bollandists (whose great work continues to the present day) were Jesuits from what is now Belgium, who, under the leadership of Heribert Roswede (1569–1629) and John Bolland (1596–1665), applied the techniques developed by Renaissance humanist scholars to the study of hagiography and Church history, pioneering in the development of such vital scholarly skills as paleography and diplomatic (the study of manuscript charters and official letters and documents).[3] The work of the Bollandists was augmented and, in sheer bulk and quality of scholarship, excelled, by the Benedictine monks of the Congregation of St. Maur at the ancient abbey of St. Germain-des-Prés in Paris. So impressively solid was the Maurist achievement that contemporary scholars continue to avail themselves of it.[4] In particular, one must mention the work of Mabillon, the greatest of the seventeenth-century Maurists, whose masterpiece, *De re diplomatica* (1681), revolutionized the science of manuscript criticism, engendering whole libraries full of books which could not have been written without it. Gibbon, among others, was liberal

2. Dom David Knowles, *Great Historical Enterprises* (London: Nelson, 1963), especially pp. 1–62. Professor Knowles' book is a monument to the little-studied history of historical scholarship, and certainly the best account of Bollandism and Maurism in the English language.

3. There is no definitive history of the Bollandists. Of great interest are R. Aigrain's chapters on the Bollandists in *L'Hagiographie* (Paris, 1953), and A. Poncelet's *Histoire de la Compagnie de Jésus dans les Pays-Bas* (Brussels, 1928).

4. Like the Bollandists, the Maurists also lack a complete accounting. The classic work is Dom E. Martène's *Histoire de la Congrégation de Saint-Maur*, 9 vols. (Ligugé, 1928–43). Also of importance are Dom P. Tassin's *Histoire littéraire de la Congregation de Saint-Maur* (Brussels, 1770), and Dom H. Leclercq's *Mabillon*, 2 vols. (Paris, 1953–57).

in his praise of what he called "the Benedictine workshop of St. Germain-des-Prés," lamenting only that he had mastered the theory of Mabillon's treatise on diplomatic without attaining the art.

For all the historiographical accomplishments of the Bollandists and Maurists, seventeenth-century historians retained certain prejudices about history that we nowadays associate with the Renaissance. Ancient Authority was considered to be superior to that of modern scholarship, and history was generally taught in the form of a commentary on ancient historians. While this preference for the Ancients over the Moderns did not pose a great problem to the historian interested in what was then called "modern history," it presented a great problem to the historian of antiquity.[5] The very idea of a modern historian writing, say, a work on ancient Rome that might equal or surpass the works of Sallust, Livy, or Tacitus, was quite alien to the historiographical thought of the seventeenth century. Classical Authority remained as supreme for the seventeenth-century historian as it did for the seventeenth-century natural scientist, who was reluctantly beginning to shed his Ptolemy and Galen to lay the foundations of modern science.

With the onset of the eighteenth century, and the first accompanying rumblings of the Enlightenment, historians, like natural scientists, began to shake loose the bonds of Classical Authority. Already in 1713, the Abbé Lenglet du Fresnoy, writing in the preface to his *Méthode pour étudier l'Histoire,* could boast of the accomplishments of post-medieval historians, emphasizing the advantages they had over the Ancients. During the eighteenth century, mere narrative history began to give way to a more analytical and philosophical form of historical explanation; and historians began to take a more detached view of their vocation, seeing themselves, as Srbik has noted, as creatures of their own historical period, performing a function that was itself a manifestation of the historical process.[6]

To the eighteenth century mind, *true* history was, in Lord Bolingbroke's characteristic phrase, "philosophy teaching by examples." A good piece of historical writing, as Dr. Johnson observed, had to be

5. See A. Momigliano's "Ancient history and the Antiquarian" in *Contributo alla Storia degli Studi Classici* (Rome, 1955), pp. 75–76.
6. H. R. von Srbik, *Geist und Geschichte vom deutschen Humanismus bis zur Gegenwart* (Munich and Salzburg, 1950), 1:i.

more than a summary of famous speeches and battles; it had to have "some tincture of philosophy and criticism"; it had to go beyond telling us, as Voltaire wrote in the *Encyclopedia,* "that one barbarian succeeded another barbarian on the banks of the Oxus and the Jaxartes." The most notable quality of eighteenth-century historiography, however—even more notable than its penchant for philosophizing—was its emphasis on style at the expense of detail. The seventeenth-century fascination with detail—exemplified in the work of Mabillon—gave way to an almost inordinate attraction to style. "Woe to details," declared Voltaire: "they are a sort of vermin that destroys great works." Style, observed Gibbon with typical modesty, in the opening page of his *Memoirs,* "is the image of character." This is not to say that Gibbon and his contemporaries—despite their assiduous cultivation of literary eloquence—thought of style as an end in itself. As representatives of the best the Enlightenment had to offer they were far too sophisticated to submit to any such vulgarization of their method. The times quite simply *demanded* well-written histories, if for no other reason than to accommodate the tastes of the reading public to Clio's pleasures. The best historians of the Enlightenment were true Cliosophs; they conceived history *not* as a science, but as a branch of literature, albeit *philosophical* literature; and the elevation of style was a manifestation of their artistic aspirations.

III

"Any fool can make history," Oscar Wilde declared, "but it takes a genius to write it." This dictum was fully appreciated by the philosophers of the Enlightenment. Never before or since have so many brilliant minds labored in the service of history. Good histories were in demand, and historians received vast sums of money for writing them. Gibbon, of course, was the century's premier historian, the only one whose work is still read as much for its historical value as its philosophic and stylistic excellence, but he had many gifted rivals. David Hume and William Robertson—the two Scots who, with Gibbon, formed the great triumvirate of eighteenth-century British historians—were widely read all over Europe. Indeed, Hume was better known in his own day for his history than his philosophy; his great history of England made his fortune, while his *Treatise on Human Nature* went largely ignored by the history-hungry reading public. Robertson, a Presbyterian divine who was to become the moderator of the General Assembly of the Church of Scotland, achieved world fame for his best-selling *History of Charles V,* and his monumental works on the history of Scotland and America during the epoch of European discovery and expansion.

Both Robertson and Hume were profoundly influenced by the studies of Continental historians and philosophers, particularly Voltaire and Montesquieu. Being products of the University of Edinburgh, both men escaped the narrow pedantry that dominated Oxford and Cambridge during the eighteenth century. Their education was fully in keeping with the spirit of the Enlightenment. Gibbon, for his part, was forced to endure one unhappy year at Oxford, which proved, in his words, to be "the most idle and unprofitable [period] of my whole life." His real education took place in Lausanne, and was, perforce, grounded in the prejudices of the French Enlightenment. For an eighteenth-century Englishman his education was unique: he eluded the "barbarous science" of Oxford without actually losing his Englishness (although he thought he had lost it), and mastered the rigorous Gallicism of his Swiss Protestant mentors at the same time.[7]

It is impossible to hypothesize how Gibbon might have developed had he remained at Oxford. Clearly eighteenth-century Oxford was no place for a prodigy of Gibbon's standing. He himself delighted in speculating on how a prolonged stay at Oxford might have affected his intellectual growth, and concluded that he quite probably would have succumbed to the spirit of torpid idleness that permeated the atmosphere of his rejected alma mater. His Swiss education did not transform him into a great philosophic historian; it merely *equipped* him for his future vocation, introducing him to writers and sources not much studied in Oxford's pleasant confines. The "port and prejudice" of Oxford simply could not compare to the "rigid course of discipline

7. In his *Autobiography* Gibbon thanked fate for delivering him from his masters at Oxford. "The schools of Oxford . . . ," he wrote, "were founded in a dark age of false and barbarous science; and they are still tainted with the vices of their origin." Had he been forced to remain in England, he would have "grown to manhood ignorant of the life and language of Europe," but his banishment to Lausanne had rendered him, he claimed, more Swiss than English. This may have been true at first, especially during the period when he wrote in French, but the author of the *Autobiography* and the *Decline and Fall*—despite protestations to the contrary—was a true Englishman, albeit a *well-educated* Englishman.

and abstinence" that were the marks of his Lausanne experience. Not only did his Swiss education open the doors of Continental historiography to him, but it allowed him to become a part of that historiographical tradition.

IV

Gibbon's education was essentially classical, an "enlightened" version of the *trivium* and *quadrivium;* but it allowed for a great deal of reading in the literature of his day. His thought, as Christopher Dawson wrote, became moulded by the vices and virtues of the Enlightenment to the point where he could recognize no other intellectual values.[8] On occasion the values Gibbon had absorbed in Lausanne were to hinder his judgment and distort his clarity of vision, as in the case of his celebrated inability to understand the significance of the rise of Christianity. Like his Enlightened colleagues, he early fell under the spell of Rousseau and Voltaire; but he also explored the rigorous studies of Lodovico Muratori, the father of Italian history. Indeed, it was because of Muratori that he came in time to reject Voltaire's hatred of facts. While he remained a philosophical stylist, in keeping with the spirit of his age, he learned from Muratori that facts were not necessarily the "sort of vermin that destroys great works." "All sciences are founded on reasoning and facts," he wrote. "Without the latter, our studies would be chimerical; deprived of the former, they are blind."

Among the historians of his century, he valued some above all others. One was the Neapolitan lawyer and scholar, Pietro Giannone, whose *Civil History of Naples* (1723) critically examined the impact of the Catholic Church on the history of Naples. Giannone was excommunicated for his efforts and died in prison in Turin, a fate that doubtless helped to raise his standing in Gibbon's eyes. "In Giannone's *Civil History . . .,*" Gibbon wrote, "I observed with a critical eye the progress and abuse of sacerdotal power, and the revolutions of Italy in the darker ages." He greatly admired the writings of the German Lutheran theologian, J. L. von Mosheim, again because of his

8. See Dawson's introduction to the Everyman's Library edition of *The Decline and Fall of the Roman Empire* (London: Dent, n.d.), p. ix.

critical interpretation of early Church history. Mosheim saw the Church as a human institution, subject to the needs of human society, rather than as the repository of the Truth.

For Gibbon and his contemporaries, two very philosophic historians overshadowed everyone else: those two diligent arbiters of Enlightenment standards, Voltaire and Montesquieu. Voltaire saw himself as the embodiment of a new type of history that totally rejected the supernatural in favor of the new spirit of secularism and naturalism. His own historical writing, he thought, was the embodiment of truth. Of his *Essay on the Manners and Customs of Nations* (1757), he wrote, "Mankind dictated it and truth acted as the scribe." His massive and eloquent *Age of Louis XIV* (1752) is full of witty vituperation against older historians, for whom the great skeptic had nothing but scorn and contempt. Montesquieu, on the other hand, was far less partisan in his writing. The father of modern sociology had far more respect for facts than the "truth-seeking" Voltaire—or many *present-day* sociologists for that matter. His brilliant masterpiece, *De l'Esprit des lois* (1748), treated history in a truly new manner, regarding all human activities as proper subjects for historical investigation. In many ways, he paved the way for the great Annales school, which has dominated French historiography in our own day. His early *Considérations sur les causes de la grandeur des Romains et de leur décadence* (1734), which adumbrated the methodological scope of *De l'Esprit des lois,* was to influence Gibbon more than any work of the day.

Both Voltaire and Montesquieu shared the fundamental ideals of the Enlightenment, but they differed strongly on certain basic issues. Montesquieu was essentially a reformer with conservative inclinations. He conceived society as being organic, and believed that societal changes ought to proceed in a limited, gradual manner if they were to take root. This was a position that was to appeal to the Burkean Whigs in Britain and the Federalist Founding Fathers in America. Voltaire and his Encyclopedist disciples advocated more radical societal reforms. The society of the Old Regime was, for them, *not* a living organism, but, in Voltaire's supremely confident analysis, "dead tissue" resistant to the new Voltairean *truth.* Ultimately, the Encyclopedists paved the way for Jacobinism and the modern revolutionary ethos, while Montesquieu foreshadowed the spirit of modern conservatism.

Gibbon was initially captivated by Voltaire, and even sought him out at Ferney. "Before I was recalled from Switzerland," he wrote, "I had the satisfaction of seeing the most extraordinary man of the age; a poet, an historian, a philosopher, who has filled thirty quartos, of prose and verse, with his various productions, often excellent, and always entertaining. Need I add the name Voltaire?" Later, however, he came to reject Voltaire in favor of Montesquieu. He had, he confessed, rated Voltaire above his magnitude. Voltaire's crass modernism, coupled with his cavalier treatment of facts that conflicted with his own opinions, disgusted the young Gibbon. Lord Byron properly perceived the differences between Gibbon and Voltaire, when he wrote of Gibbon:

> The other deep and slow, exhausting thought,
> And hiving wisdom with each passing year,
> In meditation dwelt, with learning wrought,
> And shaped his weapon with an edge severe,
> Sapping a solemn creed with solemn sneer; . . .

Indeed, Gibbon's French masterpiece, the *Essai sur l'etude de la littérature,* was full of hostility toward Voltaire. He sided with Montesquieu, as he was to side with Burke when the French Revolution came. His *Essai,* as he himself later admitted, was impaired by his overly enthusiastic imitation of Montesquieu's thought, and even of his prose style. The *Essai* is important not simply because it underlines Gibbon's debt to Montesquieu. It also articulated his philosophy of history. Initially written as an attack on the relativism of the Voltairean school, Gibbon managed to turn a youthful polemic into a statement of philosophy. Juxtaposing Tacitus and Livy, he rejected Livy in favor of Tacitus because of his failure properly to understand the complex relationship between the laws of the Roman Republic—Montesquieu's "spirit of the laws"—and the Romans themselves. Tacitus, however, appreciated how "these laws, made for a small, poor, half-civilized republic, overturned it when the power of its institutions had carried it to the highest pitch of grandeur."

V

Gibbon was a true son of the Enlightenment, but one can also detect the rumblings of Romanticism in his *Essai.*[9] The Voltairean school had carried the rationalism of the Enlightenment too far, and Gibbon, like

9. See R. G. Collingwood, *The Idea of History* (New York: Oxford University Press, 1956), p. 79.

other members of his generation, recognized this fact. Voltaire had depicted history in a consistently rational manner; excluded from his analysis were the irrational elements in history, which Gibbon recognized as being vital parts of the historical experience. In his early studies he had absorbed the rationalism of the day, and while he never rejected that rationalism, as the Romantics were to reject it, he allowed it to coexist, as it were, with an incipient Romanticism that in many ways was quite irrational in its subjectivism. This coexistence of two seemingly conflicting trends was not unique in the *siècle des lumières:* it can be clearly seen in Montesquieu's writing, in the antirationalist *Another Philosophy of History for the Education of Humanity* (1774) of Johann Gottfried von Herder, in Adam Ferguson's *Essay on the History of Civil Society* (1767), in Bishop Butler's ethical discourses (1726), in Count Henri de Boulainvilliers' *History of the Ancient Government of France* (1727), and even in the anti-Cartesianism of Giambattista Vico's *New Science* (1725).[10] There was even something irrational about Denis Diderot's blind faith in liberty, even when he masked it with rationalistic jargon. It is noteworthy that in Montesquieu, Gibbon chose a mentor whose theories on society and history failed to conform to those advocated by the most influential intellectual leaders of the Enlightenment. The prevailing view that the past was personified by the ever-advancing progress of man and his institutions; that this *progress* was no mere accident, but a *law of history* that would continue indefinitely into the future; and that this *fact* of progress would inexorably lead to an expansion in man's happiness and understanding—was firmly *rejected* by Gibbon in his *Essai* and his subsequent writings.

What Gibbon learned from the *philosophes* had more to do with the *form* of their doctrine than its content. The chapter on "The Philosophy of History," in Voltaire's *Essay on the Manners and Spirit of Nations,* meant more to Gibbon than anything else in the Voltairean corpus. Nevertheless, he refused to accept Voltaire's philosophy of history as being *authoritative.* There were limits to his admiration, and

10. The Romantic movement in historiography was, quite simply, a reaction to the "philosophizing" of Enlightenment historians. For the Romantics, there were no "constant and universal principles of human nature"; on the contrary, human nature differed for different individuals, nations, and periods. This was Herder's point when he argued that the historian could only learn to understand the past through "empathy" *(Einfühlung).* See Peter Burke's *The Renaissance Sense of the Past* (New York: St. Martin's Press, 1969), pp. 142–45.

he wisely rejected most of Voltaire's pet prejudices. Indeed, he was cautious about all ideas that tended to conflict with his Tory orthodoxy —a result, no doubt, of his unorthodox youthful conversion to Catholicism. He was even selective in his adherence to that great symbol of Enlightenment virtue, the Voltairean motto, *"Écrasez l'infâme!"*— "Crush the infamous thing!"—which he applied to some issues, such as the slave trade, and ignored in the face of other equally controversial circumstances. The *philosophes* of the later Enlightenment—that is, the period dominated by Voltaire and the Encyclopedists—tended, with a few notable exceptions, to be radicals, and hence one-sided and sectarian. Sectarianism did not appeal to Gibbon, even though he was himself one-sided and sectarian on certain matters. His sectarianism had less to do with the philosophy of the Enlightenment than his own idiosyncratic predilections. He was far less one-sided and sectarian, for example, than that formidable enemy of the Enlightenment, Dr. Johnson.

Although he lived in the later Enlightenment, Gibbon clearly felt more at home with the philosophers of the early Enlightenment, especially Montesquieu. He had, typically, sided with the Ancients in the *quérelle des anciens et des modernes.* He did not equate evil with the environment, nor did he believe that man was born innately good, corrupted only by the evils of society. His prejudice in favor of the early Enlightenment, as opposed to the later Enlightenment, may be attributed, perhaps, to the Englishness he thought he had lost, and to the somewhat retarded doctrines of the Swiss scholars who helped to shape his youthful mind. In terms of practical ideas, it must be remembered, he preferred the antediluvian solutions of Lord North, the arch-Tory Prime Minister, to the nostrums of the Encyclopedists. Just as he rejected Christianity, he also rejected what Carl Becker called the "heavenly city of the eighteenth-century philosophers," with its materialistic eschatology. Nevertheless,—despite his fastidious rejection of certain fundamental conceptions of the Enlightenment—he remained a child of his age; and what he got out of the Enlightenment was exactly what he needed to complete his *Decline and Fall.* The art of history, as we have already noted, had not developed sufficiently before the eighteenth century to allow historians to tackle a subject as difficult as the collapse of Rome with any degree of rigor; and it is doubtful whether the monograph-oriented historiography of the nineteenth and twentieth centuries would have easily tolerated a work of such huge scope, a development that was lamented by both Niebuhr and Mommsen.

Gibbon came into his own at the right moment for his great work to be written. With the apotheosis of the Enlightenment philosophy of history, the way was set for historians to contemplate themes as vast as the one selected by Gibbon. The historians of the Renaissance reawakened the sense of *historical perspective,* which had been lost in the darkness of what Petrarch called the *aetas nova,* which succeeded the brilliant *aetas antiqua* of pre-Constantinean Rome; they rescued Clio from the clutches of the moribund historiography of the Middle Ages, at the same time reviving the historical methods of the ancient Greeks and Romans. The seventeenth century was a time of transition, of historiographical gestation, during which learned scholars, such as the Benedictine monks of the Congregation of St. Maur, advanced the science of manuscript criticism, organized the first *modern* archival techniques, codified methods for determining the authenticity of sources, and provided future historians with tools that would help to revolutionize the study of history. But it was during the eighteenth century that historians as diverse as Muratori, Giannone, and Gibbon—girded with the spirit of the Enlightenment, with its fascination for philosophical and social history—wedded the revived historical perspective of the Renaissance to the vigorous scholarly exactitude of the seventeenth century, to produce modern historiography. The historians of the Enlightenment sought to make historical events conform to certain general "laws." "The chief use of history," Hume wrote, "is to discover the constant and universal principles of human nature." In Gibbon the age found its perfect historian: a philosophical scholar who, in his own words, struggled to select from "the vast chaos of events" the facts that explain the "general causes" that have helped "to change the face of the earth." In his great study of what he called "the fabric of human greatness," he took history away from the antiquarians, setting standards that were to be part of his legacy to future generations of historians.

2

Gibbon: The Man and His Work

Gibbon is a kind of bridge that connects the ancient with the modern ages. And how gorgeously does it swing across the gloomy and tumultuous chasm of these barbarous centuries.

Thomas Carlyle

I

Writing in the preface to the first edition of his monumental *Römanische Geschichte,* the great Danish historian Barthold Georg Niebuhr elaborated on his reasons for ending his work where Gibbon had begun—for not daring to venture onto Gibbon's turf. "The book," he said of his own history, "if fate allows me to complete it, will terminate where Gibbon's history commenced. His work surely renders a new treatment superfluous and foolhardy; and as for the more remote period, where Gibbon's work was and could afford to be deficient, the gaps can be filled without presuming to compete with him."[1] This judicious statement explains why so few of the great post-Gibbonian historians of Rome have been willing to tamper with what H. St. L. B. Moss has called "the magnificent architecture of Gibbon's *Decline and Fall,*" save for the humble purpose of making factual emendations.[2] Gibbon's formidable position was even recognized by the incomparable Theodor Mommsen, a fact which may serve to explain why the most widely acclaimed historian of the late nineteenth century mysteriously concluded his own Roman history with the *rise* of the Empire.[3] The Empire in its decline was, for Mommsen, Gibbon's territory, it literally *belonged* to him by virtue of his genius; and

1. B. G. Niebuhr, "Vorrende zu der ersten Ausgabe," *Römanische Geschichte* (Berlin, 1811–12). See Fritz Stern's partial translation of this preface in his *Varieties of History* (Cleveland and New York: Meridian Books, 1956), p. 47.

2. H. St. L. B. Moss, *The Birth of the Middle Ages* (Oxford: Oxford University Press, 1935), p. iii.

3. Mommsen's *Römanische Geschichte,* for which he received the Nobel Prize for Literature in 1902, ended with Julius Caesar, whom he wrongly saw as the founder of the Empire, rather than the last of the *nobilis.* He never wrote a fourth volume to his history, but in 1885 he skipped past the unwritten fourth volume and published a fifth volume, devoted to the Roman provinces from Augustus to Diocletian.

Gibbon's supremacy as *the* historian of Rome's decline and fall remains virtually unchallenged—despite the helpful corrections and additions of the monographists—to this day.

II

History, it has been duly noted, is what historians write about; and to fully appreciate the Gibbonian achievement we must know something of the historian. He himself recognized the significant relationship between his life and work when he wrote his *Autobiography,* a masterpiece that is hardly less important than his history, in that it is mainly devoted to the intellectual preparation for what was to be his life's work.[4] Indeed, the *Memoirs of My Life and Writings,* which has always been known simply as the *Autobiography of Edward Gibbon,* is, perhaps, the greatest autobiographical work ever written by a great historian. It is, as more than one student of Gibbon has noted, the best available introduction to the *Decline and Fall.*

By his own confession, Gibbon was "a puny child, neglected by my mother, starved by my nurse, and of whose being very little care or expectation was entertained." His childhood ill health was providential in that it allowed him to indulge his taste for "vague and multifarious reading." "From the ancients," he wrote, "I leaped to the modern world; many crude lumps of Speed, Rapin, Mézéray, Davila, Machiavel, Father Paul, Bower, etc. I devoured like so many novels; and I swallowed with the same voracious appetite the descriptions of India and China, Mexico and Peru." His early reading had more in common with early eighteenth-century English taste than with the Enlightenment. John Kirkby's *Life of Automathes* (1745) impressed him, not so

4. The best edition of the *Autobiography* is the one in the World Classics series (Oxford: Oxford University Press, 1907, reprinted in 1962), with an introduction by J. B. Bury. At his death, Gibbon left several drafts, which his friend and executor, Lord Sheffield, posthumously published. Sheffield reconstructed the book and gave it its final shape, a development which many scholars have long regretted. From the six versions which Gibbon left behind, Sheffield pasted together a narrative, adhering, he wrote, "with scrupulous fidelity to the very words of the author." Bury noted several of the interesting changes Sheffield made. Writing of his absences from Oxford, Gibbon commented, "I was too young and bashful to enjoy, like a manly Oxonian, the taverns and bagnios of Covent Garden." Sheffield euphemistically changed the last words to read "the pleasures of London." Describing the *pension* of M. de Mesery at Lausanne, Gibbon notes that "the boarders were numerous." Sheffield altered this to "the boarders were select." There are many other examples of Sheffield's desire not to offend contemporary English prejudices with Gibbon's often un-English frankness. Fortunately, however, the World Classics edition provides us with an authentic Gibbon, warts and all.

much for its depth of thought or elegance of style, as for its "entertainment and instruction." He learned, "at the expense of many tears and some blood," his Latin syntax, and delighted in "the dirty volumes of Phædrus and Cornelius Nepos, which I painfully construed and darkly understood." The elegant simplicity of Cornelius Nepos' *Lives* was to influence his own style and inspire his early interest in Greek and Roman history. He was well acquainted with Pope's *Homer* and the "specious miracles" of the *Arabian Nights' Entertainments;* he derived much pleasure from Ovid's *Metamorphoses,* "especially in the fall of Phæton, and the speeches of Ajax and Ulysses"; and he diligently devoured the works of Herodotus, Xenophon, and Tacitus.

The eccentricity of his entire education provided him with an excellent vantage point for observing and criticizing eighteenth-century British education. "Our seminaries of learning," he wrote, "do not exactly correspond with the precept of a Spartan king, 'that the child should be instructed in the arts which will be useful to the man'; since a finished scholar will emerge from the head of Westminster or Eton, in total ignorance of the business and conversation of English gentlemen." Gibbon was not advocating a kind of proto-utilitarianism, nor was he railing against the Classical Education in its purest form. Rather he recognized the public schools of England (i.e., the private schools, in the American sense) to be in a state of intellectual and moral decline; and he saw his beloved classical languages debased by self-righteous pedants intent only on flogging their charges into an "appreciation" of Horace. Too many lesser intellects, he rightly thought, were forced to submit to the rigors of the seven liberal arts. For his part he was content "with a very small share of the civil and literary fruits of a public school," and he thanked God for the debility that rescued him from the clutches of Winchester College and allowed him to pursue his studies at the hands of a single skillful master who helped him to acquire a love for Latin and the rudiments of Greek. "Instead of audaciously mingling in the sports and quarrels, and connections of our little world," he concluded, "I was . . . cherished at home under the maternal wing of my aunt."

III

Before his fifteenth year he unexpectedly recovered his health, and matriculated as a gentleman commoner at Magdalen College, Oxford, where his chief pleasure seems to have been the flowing academic gown that his rank allowed him. His short stay at Oxford was not to be a happy one. Unlike Bishop Lowth before him, he derived little pleasure from "breathing the same atmosphere that the Hookers, the Chillingworths, and the Lockes had breathed before"; he was, as he himself well knew, devoid "of capacity or application"; his preparation for Oxford had been excellent in some respects, but faulty in other important ways. He had brought to Oxford "a stock of erudition that might have puzzled a doctor and a degree of ignorance of which a schoolboy would have been ashamed." He found no solace in his instruction. His tutor, Dr. Waldgrave, led him through the comedies of Terence, and those Latin plays, he concluded, were the sum of his literary improvement while at Oxford. "No plan of study was recommended for my use," he lamented; "no exercises were prescribed for [my tutor's] . . . inspection; and, at the most precious season of youth, whole days and weeks were suffered to elapse without labor or amusement, without advice or account."

In a short time, he succumbed to the fashionable dissipations of the day. A penchant for extracurricular reading led him to the controversial writings of Conyers Middleton, a Cambridge clergyman famous both for the elegance of his style and for his skepticism. Middleton's reputation was derived, in particular, from three works, his *Letter from Rome* (1729), which drew parallels between Roman Catholic religious practice and paganism; his *Life of Cicero* (1741), which freely availed itself of Cicero's writings; and his disputatious *Free Inquiry into the Miraculous Powers Which Are Supposed to Have Subsisted in the Christian Church* (1749). This latter work was to have a profound influence on the young Gibbon. The book made Middleton very unpopular with Gibbon's mentors, a fact that led the rebellious student to pursue Middleton's writings, and those of his antagonists. Middleton's criticism, which Gibbon described as approaching the very precipice of infidelity, exposed the Protestant notion that dubbed the miracles of the early Christian centuries genuine, but rejected the corrupt, monastic, cult-and-relic-ridden miracles of later Christianity as false. Gibbon drew his own conclusions from Middleton's "bold criticism." He still believed in the saints "exposed" by Middleton; he still believed in the miracles of the early Church; and he "was unable to resist the weight of historical evidence, that within the same period most of the leading doctrines of Popery were already introduced in theory and practice." The marvelous tales attested to by the great saints compelled him, he declared, "to embrace the superior merits of celibacy, the institution of monastic life, the use of the sign of the cross, of holy oil, and even of images, the invocation of saints, the worship of relics, the rudiments of purgatory in prayers for the dead, and the tremendous mystery of the sacrifice of the body and blood of Christ, which insensibly swelled into the prodigy of transubstantiation."

Along with a college companion, a certain Mr. Molesworth, he began to read explicitly "Popish" books. He read the *Exposition of Catholic Doctrine* and the *History of the Protestant Variations* by Bossuet, Bishop of Meaux; and after reading these works he was prepared to embrace Rome. On June 3, 1753, when he was only sixteen, he was received into the Roman Catholic Church by the chaplain to the Sardinian Minister.[5] He later wrote that Bossuet, for all his speciousness, was an impressive apologist for Catholicism and a master of pseudo-candor. Still, Gibbon's adolescent reading fails to explain his uncharacteristic sudden conversion to Roman Catholicism. We may never know the full reason for his conversion, since he was reticent about his youthful Catholicism; but we may be sure that the reasons were far more complex than he would have us believe. His unhappiness at Oxford, the result, perhaps, of his isolated and pampered childhood, and his intellectual precocity, may have led him to rebel against Oxford by rejecting the Church of England, which, in the eighteenth century, was identified with that university. Whatever the specific cause of his act of conversion and rebellion, his reception into the Roman Church achieved basically what he may have wanted it to achieve: it led to his banishment from Oxford, and brought down the wrath of his irate father, who shipped him off to Lausanne, where it

5. Sheffield wrote, in a note to the *Autobiography,* that "Gibbon never talked with me on the subject of his conversion to Popery but once: he imputed his change to the works of Parsons the Jesuit, who lived in the reign of Elizabeth, and who, he said, had urged all the best arguments in favor of the Roman Catholic religion."

was hoped that he would eventually abjure papism in favor of the Calvinist nostrums of his Swiss tutor, Monsieur Pavilliard.

IV

Gibbon *did* reject Catholicism, but he adopted Calvinism in name only. Rather, he converted to the Calvinism of Monsieur Pavilliard, which bore little relationship to that of the great Geneva Reformer. Lausanne, at the time of Gibbon's arrival, had become a center of the French Enlightenment—tinged ever so slightly with the philosophy of the German *Aufklärung;* and it was to this movement that Gibbon was to convert. At the very moment that Gibbon was preparing to reject Catholicism in favor of the "enlightened" Calvinism of Monsieur Pavilliard, an even more celebrated Catholic convert, Jean-Jacques Rousseau, was renouncing the Mother Church in nearby Geneva. As if to symbolize Switzerland's status as a center of the Enlightenment, Gibbon's arrival coincided with that of Voltaire, who in 1755 established his headquarters—which was to become a mecca to the *philosophes* —in a house close to Lausanne. Thanks to the teaching of Monsieur Pavilliard, whose own philosophy was formed in the days before the Voltairean hegemony, Gibbon never fully accepted the teachings of the greatest of the Enlightenment's philosophers. For personal as well as intellectual reasons, he found the Protestant rationalism of Bayle, Le Clerc, and Barbeyrac more to his liking. One fancies, from what he says in his memoirs, that he actually identified with these writers, particularly Pierre Bayle, whose ephemeral conversion to Catholicism at Toulouse was not unlike his own. Bayle's *Nouvelle de la république des lettres,* with its evocation of the literary craft, had more to offer a literary man like Gibbon than the Party of Humanity. Bayle's hatred of superstition applied both to the churches of his day and to the great *social religion* of the Enlightenment. Voltaire, who thought that religion was necessary to hold society together, attacked Bayle for atheism in the *Encyclopedia.* Ultimately, Gibbon found the crypto-atheism of the Protestant rationalists to be less pernicious than the "religion" of the Voltaireans.

Under Monsieur Pavilliard's rigorous teaching, Gibbon's love of reading, which had been chilled at Oxford, returned. He came to speak the French of the *Pays de Vaud* with such perfection that it became, he wrote, more familiar to him than English. He began to come out of his shell, and moved in the elegant society of Lausanne. He even became somewhat proficient in the arts of fencing and dancing, and he "idly wasted" some months learning horseback riding. Pavilliard harnessed Gibbon's love of learning and led him through the works of modern history and geography, the French and Latin classics, and philosophy, theology, and logic. As soon as Pavilliard felt that his young student had advanced beyond his own speed and measure, he wisely left him to his genius. Young Gibbon even found time to fall in love with Susan Curchod, a local girl; but his father would not hear of such a strange alliance, and so Susan married the French statesman Jacques Necker, and Gibbon remained single for the rest of his life.[6] When he returned to England, he was certainly a more well-rounded man than he had been at the time of his departure for Switzerland. He had not become a good Christian, but, as Christopher Dawson has observed, he had become a good European, to whom one could apply the verse of the Christian poet concerning Emperor Julian, "Perfidus ille Deo, quamvis non perfidus Urbi."

It was in England that Gibbon penned his first important work, the *Essai sur L'étude de la littérature.* Provoked by Jean d'Alembert's statement in the *Discours préliminaire à l'Encyclopédie* that at the end of each century various *érudits* should make a selection of such knowledge as was worth conserving, leaving everything else to be

6. Rousseau thought that Mlle Curchod was well rid of Gibbon, whose cold nature, he said, would have rendered her life miserable. Gibbon was profoundly shocked and mortified by the ease with which she accepted losing him. Although she wrote him of her devotion, he did not believe her, noting in his diary that her "amusements convict her of the most odious dissimulation, and if infidelity is sometimes a weakness, duplicity is always a vice. This episode," he added, "curious throughout, has been of great use to me; it has opened my eyes to the character of love." Although he often spoke of finding a wife, he clearly never seriously contemplated matrimony again. To Lady Sheffield he wrote, in 1784: "Should you be very much surprised to hear of my being married? Amazing as it may seem, I do assure you that the event is less improbable than it would have appeared to myself twelvemonth ago. . . . [A] house like ours would be regulated, and graced, and enlivened, by an agreeable female Companion. . . . Since my residence here I have lived much in women's company; and to your credit be it spoken, I like you better the more I see of you. Not that I am in love with any particular person. I have discovered about half a dozen *Wives* who would please me in different ways, and by various merits: one as a mistress; a second, a lively entertaining acquaintance; a third, a sincere good-natured friend; a fourth, who would represent with grace and dignity at the head of my table and family; a fifth, an excellent economist and housekeeper; a sixth, a very useful nurse. Could I find all these qualities united in a single person, I should dare to make my addresses, and should deserve to be refused." Some years later he fell under the charms of a certain Madame de Montolieu, who would have none of him. Indeed, it was reported by Madame de Genlis, Madame de Montolieu's mother, that the fat historian proposed on his knees, and was not able to rise to a standing position after being turned down.

destroyed, Gibbon decided to defend past erudition. "I was ambitious," he wrote, "of proving by my own example, as well as by my precepts, that all the faculties of the mind may be exercised and displayed by the study of ancient literature." The *Essai* took him six weeks to write and was published in London in 1761. He received the first copy two days before he was called-up by the Hampshire militia. He was not happy with what he had written. "The most serious defect of my Essay," he wrote, "is a kind of obscurity and abruptness which always fatigues, and may often elude the attention of the reader. Instead of a precise and proper definition of the title itself, the sense of the word *Littérature* is loosely and variously applied: a number of remarks and examples, historical, critical, philosophical, are heaped on each other without method or connection; and if we except some introductory pages, all the remaining chapters might indifferently be reversed or transposed. The obscurity of many passages is often affected, 'brevis esse laboro, obscurus fio'; the desire of expressing perhaps a common idea with sententious and oracular brevity: alas! how fatal has been the imitation of Montesquieu!"

Gibbon's brief, bloodless, and inglorious experience as a soldier in the Hampshire militia often made him think of Cicero's complaint while commanding a provincial militia: "Clitellae bovi sunt impositae. Est incredibile quam me negoti taedeat. Non habet satis magnum campum ille tibi non ignotus cursus animi; et industriae meae praeclara opera cessat. Lucem, *libros,* urbem, domum, vos desidero. Sed feram, ut potero; sit modo annuum. Sit prorogatur est." Although he believed that he could have retired from the militia without disgrace, his father convinced him to accept the yoke of military servitude, which, he noted, was far more protracted than Cicero's. Upon being mustered-out, he decided that he would erect an altar to Clio, that he would write a history, although he was not sure what his subject would be. He played with the idea of writing a history of liberty in Switzerland and a study of Florence under the Medicis. To make up his mind, he went on a European tour. He hoped to converse with the greatest intellects of his age. Montesquieu and Fontenelle were no more, but he did meet with d'Alembert and Diderot. On his return to Switzerland "the good Pavilliard shed tears of joy as he embraced a pupil whose literary merit he might fairly impute to his own labors."

V

It was during his return to Lausanne that he met both the greatest friend of his life, John Baker Holroyd, later Lord Sheffield, and William Guise, the son of a Gloucester baronet, with whom he was to make his famous visit to Rome. The visit to Rome set Gibbon on his life's work. "It was at Rome," he wrote in his apologia for the benefits of foreign travel, "on the 15th of October, 1764, as I sat musing amidst the ruins of the Capitol, while the barefooted friars were singing vespers in the Temple of Jupiter, that the idea of writing the decline and fall of the city first started to my mind. But my original plan was circumscribed to the decay of the city rather than the empire: and, though my reading and reflections began to point towards that object, some years elapsed, and several avocations intervened, before I was seriously engaged in the execution of that laborious work."

While his visit to Rome aroused his interest in the subject that was to develop into his great history, it was some years before he began work on his *Decline and Fall.* He wrote many short essays and reviews, and continued to play with the idea of writing the histories of Swiss freedom and Medicean Florence. Indeed, it was not until the death of his implacably domineering father in 1770 that he was able to devote his energies to serious historical studies. "At the outset," he declared, "all was dark and doubtful; even the title of the work, the true era of the *Decline and Fall of the Empire,* the limits of the introduction, the division of the chapters, and the order of the narrative; and I was often tempted to cast away [my] labor . . ."

The style of a historian, he noted, should be the image of his mind, but his writing—that is, his prose style—is the result of much labor. Gibbon could not decide the correct tone between writing a dull chronicle and a piece of rhetoric, and, as a result, he wrote and rewrote his early chapters many times. His work was further delayed by his election to the House of Commons at the beginning of the American Revolution, during which time he "supported with many a sincere and silent vote, the rights, though not, perhaps, the interest, of the mother-country." He apologized for his silence during the great debates over the Revolution by declaring that the government's cause was ably vindicated by Lord North, whom he believed to be "a statesman of spotless integrity, a consummate master of debate, who could wield, with equal dexterity, the arms of reason and ridicule." His time in Parliament had impaired his progress on the *Decline and Fall,* but he viewed it as educative, in that it taught him the meaning of civil prudence, which he judged to be the most essential virtue of a good historian. He managed to complete the first volume of the history during this period, and to arrange for its publication. The book was destined to be an instant popular success.

"History," he explained, "is the most popular species of writing, since it can adapt itself to the highest and lowest capacity. I had chosen an illustrious subject. Rome is familiar to the school-boy and the statesman; and my narrative was deduced from the last period of classical reading. I had likewise flattered myself, that an age of light and liberty would receive, without scandal, an inquiry into the human *causes* of the progress and establishment of Christianity." While the approbation of the public was music to his ears, the candid praise of his two Scottish peers, Robertson and Hume, gave him more serious satisfaction. "Whether I consider the dignity of your style, the depth of your matter, or the extensiveness of your learning," wrote Hume in a letter to Gibbon, "I must regard the work as equally the object of esteem; and I own that if I had not previously had the happiness of your personal acquaintance, such a performance from an Englishman in our age," he added, with a Scotsman's pride, "would have given me some surprise."

Nearly two years elapsed between the publication of the first volume of the *Decline and Fall* and the commencement of the second volume. During this time Gibbon had busied himself with studies of a different nature, mainly in the natural and biological sciences, and had spent more time than he should have studying the Arian controversy and the age of Constantine. He had also been slowed down by the criticism of the clergy, who were unhappy with his anti-Christian views. His Christian critics, he wrote, presumed to attack, not the faith, but the fidelity of a serious historian. With the exception of the Rev. Richard Watson, a Cambridge clergyman, he treated his religious critics with disdain. Finally, under great pressure, he responded to the parsons with one of the most brilliant scholarly rejoinders of all time, the *Vindication.* In that work, Dean Milman wrote, "Gibbon, with a single discharge from his ponderous artillery of learning and sarcasm, laid prostrate the whole disorderly squadron." "My *Vindication,"*

Gibbon wrote, "[was] expressive . . . less [of] anger than contempt . . . [It] amused for a moment the busy and idle metropolis [of London]; and the most rational part of the laity, and even of the clergy, appear to have been satisfied of my innocence and accuracy." Having vindicated himself, he returned to his serious writing, and by 1783 he had published three volumes of the *Decline and Fall.*

He was well into the fourth volume when he decided to leave London and return to Lausanne, where he could live less expensively, thanks to his Swiss friend George Deyverdun, who had invited him to share his large house, La Grotte. Gibbon accepted, for, he confessed, he had "always cherished a secret wish that the school of my youth might become the retreat of my declining age." His English friends were shocked by his move. Lord Sheffield declared it to be just a little short of insanity; but Gibbon remained determined to finish his work in Lausanne, despite the protestations of those who could not imagine him living and working in "such an obscure nook in Switzerland." In Lausanne, he discovered, his style, which he thought to be crude in the first volume, had ripened into ease, due to the necessity of speaking in one language and writing in another; and it was in the school of his youth that he completed his history, during the evening of June 27, 1787. "After laying down my pen," he wrote, "I took several turns in a . . . covered walk of acacias . . . I will not dissemble the first emotions of joy on recovery of my freedom, and perhaps, the establishment of my fame. But my pride was soon humbled, and a sober melancholy was spread over my mind, by the idea that I had taken an everlasting leave of an old and agreeable companion, and that whatsoever might be the future date of my *History,* the life of the historian must be short and precarious."

He never contemplated another significant historical work. In 1787 he went to London to supervise the printing of the final volume of the *Decline and Fall.* In 1788 he returned to Lausanne as the most celebrated historian of his age. The following year Deyverdun died, and Gibbon secured title to their house. He busied himself with his *Autobiography,* which he never completed. His *History* had been his life, and there was nothing of great importance left for him. With the advance of the French Revolution into Switzerland, he decided, in 1793, to return to London, primarily to visit Lord Sheffield, whose wife had died from tuberculosis while caring for French refugees. Although he was in ill health, he greatly enjoyed London society, which lionized him. He died suddenly on January 16, 1794, and was given a Christian burial in Lord Sheffield's family church in Sussex.

VI

Gibbon was not an easy man to get on with, and it is a wonder that he possessed so many devoted friends. Genius alone does not explain his many friendships. He was, by all accounts, arrogant, over-sensitive, and exceedingly vain. He was physically ugly, but, at the same time, terribly scrupulous about his dress, adorning himself with expensive velvet coats and "ruffles of My Lady's choosing." He was, as Bury has noted,[7] the antithesis of his great contemporary, Dr. Samuel Johnson. George Colman, who met Gibbon in his youth, described the external historian in his *Random Records* (London, 1830):

> On the day I first sat down with Johnson, in his rusty brown, and his black worsteds, Gibbon was placed opposite to me in a suit of flower'd velvet, with bag and sword. Each had his measured phraseology, and Johnson's famous parallel between Dryden and Pope might be loosely parodied in reference to himself and Gibbon. Johnson's style was grand and Gibbon's elegant; the stateliness of the former was sometimes pedantic, and the polish of the latter was occasionally finical. Johnson march'd to kettle-drums and trumpets; Gibbon moved to flutes and hautboys; Johnson hew'd passages through the Alps, while Gibbon levell'd walks through parks and gardens. Maul'd as I had been by Johnson, Gibbon pour'd balm upon my bruises, by condescending once or twice, in the course of the evening, to talk with me; the great historian was light and playful; suiting his matter to the capacity of the boy; but it was done *more suo;* still his mannerism prevail'd; still he tapp'd his snuff-box, still he smirked and smiled; and rounded his periods with the same air of good breeding, as if he were conversing with men.—His mouth, mellifluous as Plato's, was a round hole, nearly in the centre of his visage.[8]

Gibbon was, in short, an insufferable fop, capable of being nice when Johnson was rude, but so deplorably vain as to make us prefer the person of the bigoted and boorish Dr. Johnson, bad manners, food-stained clothing, and all; for the meticulous sensibilities of Gib-

7. In the World Classics edition of the *Autobiography,* p. vii.
8. Quoted by R. Prothero in his edition of Gibbon's *Correspondence* (London, 1896), 1:213.

bon's age have little in common with the harsh egalitarianism of the twentieth century, which is incapable of tolerating *true* eccentricity. It is little wonder that Gibbon was never close, in the way he was *close* to Lord Sheffield, with any of the major intellects of his day. Thanks to his time in the militia, his travels, his membership in the House of Commons, and his literary fame, he came to know all the great men of his day, even if they did not particularly like him. When he left England in 1783, he could say with confidence that "there were few persons in the literary or political world to whom I am a stranger." He belonged to all of the most fashionable gentlemen's clubs, including Boodle's and White's; and at the intellectual Literary Club he regularly shared the conversation of Burke, Johnson, Adam Smith, Sir Joshua Reynolds, Garrick, Goldsmith, Fox, and Sheridan, among others.

His character was such that many of those who knew him did not suspect his true genius, and were surprised beyond belief by the brilliance of the first volume of the *Decline and Fall.* Horace Walpole was typical of those who failed to suspect Gibbon's genius due to his external behavior. To the Rev. William Mason, he wrote in 1776:

> Lo, there is just appeared a truly classic work: a history, not majestic like Livy, nor compressed like Tacitus; not stamped with character like Clarendon; perhaps not so deep as Robertson's "Scotland," but a thousand degrees above his "Charles"; not pointed like Voltaire . . . ; modest as he is *tranchant* and sly as Montesquieu without being so *recherché*. The style is as smooth as a Flemish picture, and the muscles are concealed and only for natural use, not exaggerated like Michael Angelo's to show the painter's skill in anatomy . . . This book is Mr. Gibbon's *History of the Decline and Fall of the Roman Empire.* He is the son of a foolish alderman, [and] is a Member of Parliament . . . a whimsical one . . . I know him . . . [and] never suspected the extent of his talents . . .[9]

Still, for all his genius he did not win the love and respect of his literary peers. Indeed, it was often suggested by members of Dr. Johnson's circle that Gibbon should be shunned for "the sneering infidelity", as Boswell put it, of his historical writing. On one occasion Boswell told Johnson that he had informed Burke that he objected to keeping company with Gibbon, the "notorious infidel." Johnson agreed that men could be "corrupted by evil communications," add-

9. Horace Walpole, *Selected Letters* (London: Dent, n.d.), pp. 210–11. Gibbon's father was never an alderman.

ing that if the profane find themselves accepted by the pious, "one of the checks upon an open declaration of their infidelity . . . is removed."[10] Boswell added that "Gibbon is an ugly, affected, disgusting fellow [who] . . . poisons our literary club for me . . . with his usual sneer." As if to punctuate his antipathy towards Gibbon, he mentions, with mock surprise, that the historian resented "Johnson's having talked with some disgust of his ugliness, which one would think a philosopher would not mind."

On the subject of the *Decline and Fall* and its author, Boswell wrote:

> We talked of a work much in vogue at that time, written in a very mellifluous style, but which, under pretext of another subject, contained much artful infidelity. I said it was not fair to attack us thus unexpectedly; [Gibbon] . . . should have warned us of our danger, before we entered his garden of flowery eloquence, by advertising, "Spring-guns and men-traps set here." [Gibbon] . . . had been an Oxonian, and was remembered there for having "turned Papist." I observed, that as he had changed several times—from the Church of England to the Church of Rome,—from the Church of Rome to infidelity,—I did not despair yet of seeing him a methodist preacher. Johnson, laughing, responded, "It is said, that his range has been more extensive, and that he has once been a Mahometan. However, now that he has published his infidelity, he will probably persist in it.[11]

Not all of Gibbon's critics were as harshly personal in their dislike as Boswell and Johnson. His clerical critics, whom he dealt with in his *Vindication,* devoted their criticism to his anti-Christian views, and not to his person. For his part, he had enough respect for "the parsons" to answer their criticisms in some detail, something he did not bother to do with Johnson, who is mentioned in the *Decline and Fall* only as an example of scholarly wrongheadedness. In Johnson's writings, he observed, one could detect "the workings of a bigoted though vigorous mind, greedy of every pretence to hate and persecute those who dissent from his creed." Still, it must be admitted—the immoderate praise and damnation of his champions and critics to the contrary—that Gibbon was not well liked by the intellectual and political elite of eighteenth-century Britain. Even the saintly Robertson had reservations about his gifted colleague. The liberal Burke, who tried vainly to

10. James Boswell, *Life of Johnson,* Oxford Standard Authors Edition (London: Oxford University Press, 1966), p. 1038.
11. *Ibid.,* p. 695.

sympathize with Gibbon, was forced eventually to agree with the judgment of his political rival, Fox, who detected the "oddness and vulgarity" of Gibbon's features even in the refined and flattering portrait by Reynolds that hung over Gibbon's chimney-piece in Lausanne. Gibbon was at home with the London intelligentsia, but he was not *of* them, a fact which may explain why he chose the course of "voluntary banishment" in Lausanne.

Just as he failed to appeal to the standards of his own day in many ways, Gibbon the man does not appeal to the standards of the modern world; and yet, as Bury has wisely commented, we cannot separate the history from the historian, or the historian from his own time. Gibbon, as we have noted, was not really at home in eighteenth-century Britain, despite his very English Toryism. He was more at home on the continent, where his intellect had been moulded by the philosophy of the French Enlightenment, but he never *belonged* to the continent in the way he belonged to England, despite his mastery of French prose. This was the paradox of his life, the fact that made his life less happy than it might have been had he developed in a more normal setting; it also, however, enabled him to write a history that could have been written by no other European of his age. The *Decline and Fall* was only recently finished when his own world, as symbolized by the Enlightenment, came crashing down around him in the form of the French Revolution. He did not live to enjoy the "autumnal felicity" he fully expected. He died, at the age of fifty-six, with his era. "His age was finished," wrote Christopher Dawson, "and his work was done, and nothing he might have added to it could have increased his fame."[12] In his youth he had thought himself inferior to the other historians of his period; he died knowing himself to be the supreme historian of the Enlightenment.

12. Dawson, *op. cit.,* p. vii.

3

The Decline and Fall of the Roman Empire

The decline of Rome was the natural and inevitable effect of immoderate greatness. Prosperity ripened the principle of decay; the causes of destruction multiplied with the extent of conquest; and, as soon as time or accident had removed the artificial supports, the stupendous fabric yielded to the pressure of its own weight. The story of its ruin is simple and obvious; and instead of inquiring why the Roman Empire was destroyed, we should rather be surprised that it had subsisted so long.

Edward Gibbon

I

After reading the *Decline and Fall,* Horace Walpole confessed he was more than a little confounded by Gibbon's propensity for "leaping backwards and forwards"; he could not, he complained, "recollect all those *fainéant* emperors of Constantinople who came again and again, like the same ships in a moving picture."[1] But it should be remembered that Gibbon's history covers approximately thirteen hundred years, and ranges over the geography of Europe, North Africa, and Asia; and because of this the historian must be forgiven the gaps and occasional juxtapositions that mark the basically coherent structure of his work. He apologized for the lack of unity in Chapter XLVIII. "Should I persevere [with the historical continuity that has marked the previous chapters] . . . a prolix and slender thread would be spun through many a volume, nor would the patient reader find an adequate reward of instruction or amusement. At every step," he continued, "as we sink deeper in the decline and fall of the Eastern empire, the annals of each succeeding reign would impose a more ungrateful and melancholy task. These annals must continue to repeat a tedious and uniform tale of weakness and misery; the natural connection of

1. Walpole, *op. cit.,* p. 209.

causes and events would be broken by frequent and hasty transitions, and a minute accumulation of circumstances must destroy the light and effect of those general pictures which compose the use and ornament of a remote history." His solution was simple, even though it troubled Walpole and others. He abandoned the uniform pattern of the earlier chapters, which presented a consecutive history of the Empire from the Antonines to Heraclius (a period of five centuries), and adopted a method by which the succeeding eight centuries, from the rise of Islam to the fall of Constantinople, were surveyed in a series of episodes. His rejection of chronological order enabled him to tie a vast proliferation of heterogeneous events into a massive, orderly unity.

Gibbon has also been criticized, by Lytton Strachey among others, for superficially confining his researches to published literary sources, ignoring such evidence as might be found in such incunabula as Roman coins and inscriptions. Gibbon, these critics argued, was essentially a literary or classical historian, whose narrative was based on the compilations of other scholars. As if to emphasize the weakness of this approach, they quoted Gibbon's own criticism of Voltaire's *Age of Louis XIV,* where he described the great philosopher as a man incapable of turning "over musty monkish writers to instruct himself," varnishing his history over "with the magic of his style" to produce "a most agreeable, superficial, inaccurate performance." Gibbon apologized for his weak grounding in what we nowadays call "grubby" scholarship, explaining that he had been inspired by his superficial visits to the Academy of Medals and the great public libraries of Paris to study the works of Mabillon, but the intricacies of Greek and Roman abbreviations and the Gothic alphabet remained a near mystery to him. Besides, he declared, he had no real interest in original manuscript criticism; he was a philosophic historian employing the anthropology of the Enlightenment to give new understanding and meaning to the scholarly data uncovered by those historians who had gone before him. "To Gibbon," Hugh Trevor-Roper has written, "history was never merely narrative—it was always explanation."[2]

This is not to say that Gibbon was a sedentary scholar, or an "armchair historian," to use Samuel Eliot Morison's telling phrase. While he

2. See Trevor-Roper's introduction to his edition of *The Decline and Fall of the Roman Empire and Other Selected Writings* (New York: Twayne Publishers, 1963), p. xxii.

had not visited the territories that had comprised the Byzantine Empire, or availed himself of the archaeological data that was being unearthed in his day, he traveled extensively, and through secondary sources his intellect ranged over the entire world. Under the influence of Montesquieu he took account of such nonliterary elements as the weather in ancient times, agriculture, and the distribution of human population. And while he never became a master of primary sources, he *did* study them, as his elaborate notations demonstrate.

II

Gibbon's devotion to the philosophy of the Enlightenment has been the source of the major criticism against his work. As we have noted, he was formed by the Enlightenment and its values, and found it difficult to comprehend other systems of values. His defense of antiquity in the *Essai* led him to denigrate the centuries that lay between it and his own age as an era of darkness and disorder. This was particularly true in his analysis of the Byzantine world, which, for him, was nothing more than the pale shadow of a vanished glory, and even more true of his opinion of the rise of Christianity, which he related to the triumph of barbarism. Gibbon could not understand religious values, which were quite alien to his fundamental philosophy. For him religion was another form of dogmatic superstition. He saw the Church purely as a social institution, subject to the caprices that influenced other nonspiritual social institutions. This was fully in keeping with the philosophy of the Enlightenment, but it is not good history or sociology. In his case, moreover, an understanding of Christianity was further thwarted by his almost fanatical hatred of Catholicism; and his diaries and *Autobiography* are full of references to monkish superstition and the profuse ostentation of the monasteries. While he fancied himself, on one occasion, as standing on the same intellectual ground as Huldrich Zwingli in his antipathy to Catholicism, he was, in truth, far closer to Voltaire.

Like many other eighteenth-century intellectuals, Gibbon was a deist; and like his fellows he allowed that since the Church was a social institution, it might, under "enlightened" conditions, advance the social good. It was, however, more likely to instigate social wrongs, to impede the progress of all good men and true. He anticipated the twentieth-century disciples of the Social Gospel by calling for a synthesis of society, as he knew it, and Christianity. He knew that such a synthesis would secularize and eventually destroy the "superstitious" aspects of Christianity, for the Church would be assimilated by society, and cease to function as a religious institution. This, at least, was the *desideratum* for Gibbon. Unfortunately for his history, he always approached religious issues in terms of his contemporary judgment, and *not* in terms relevant to the religious understanding of the early Christian centuries. He even boasted of his indifference to the theological disputes that plagued early Christianity.

For these sins of prejudice he has been justly criticized by both his admirers and his critics. His prejudice led to an inability to recognize that Christianity was a radically new force in human history, a revitalizing influence on an already collapsing Empire, and *not* the source of further decline. As a result, he failed to understand the most essential aspect of early medieval history. By maintaining that Christianity was a social and *not* a religious force, he found it impossible to convey the historic significance of the proliferation of creeds and sects that dominated the Byzantine and Western consciousness during the crucial centuries covered by his *History.* He is even reduced at times to sneering at the Christian martyrs. His antipathy and lack of sympathy with the spiritual influence of religion is the most serious defect in his otherwise great work, for it vitiates his judgment on problems that were central to the period it treats. Even J. B. Bury, who was himself a positivist, was forced to recognize that on religious matters "neither the historian nor the man of letters will any longer subscribe, without a thousand reserves, to the theological chapters of the *Decline and Fall,* and no discreet inquirer would go there for his ecclesiastical history."[3] Gibbon's prejudices led to a superficial and false impression of the Empire after Heraclius, Bury sadly concluded.

Nevertheless, the *Decline and Fall,* for all its weaknesses and occasional defects, remains not only a sound history, but a brilliant history; and not simply because of its magnificent literary merits. Its standards, in terms of both structure and fundamental accuracy, are exceedingly high. This is a point not often noticed by those who view Gibbon

3. *The Decline and Fall of the Roman Empire* (London, 1897), ed. J. B. Bury, 1: xxxix.

strictly as a literary historian, or by those who concentrate on his prejudices and factual errors, but it was understood by Niebuhr, and indeed by all historians who have ventured into the field of Roman and medieval history. No other historian, as Dawson has remarked, has so successfully identified himself with his subject, for "this somewhat absurd little man—'Monsieur Pomme de Terre'—with his pug of a face and his pot belly, was possessed and obsessed by the majestic spirit of Rome," to the point where he came to believe himself to be the Roman Empire.[4] In Gibbon we find the essence of Rome, both in its glory and in its decline; and this is the true genius of his history. He did not, as Bury noted, attempt to do what historians of the nineteenth century were to attempt—to judge his subject by the standards of its day, to acquire what we today call the "sense of history"; he tried, rather, to embody and personify Roman history, and the extent to which he succeeded in this act is the sense that makes his history the great work it is.

III

Gibbon did not believe in compartmentalizing history, which he saw to be a great unity. Indeed, his concept of historical continuity was central both to his "idea of progress" and to his philosophy of history. History was, for him, indivisible. In choosing the phrase "decline and fall" for his title he was not suggesting anything more than a metaphor to explain the way the complex groupings of peoples, laws, and customs—the components of ancient Rome—*developed* during the later Empire. He did not view the Empire as a vast, uniform structure that *suddenly* began to disintegrate, and eventually toppled. Rather, he understood Rome's "decline and fall" to be a process of transformation and evolution, ending in what were, for him, the dark centuries of the Middle Ages. The evolution was a slow, almost tedious one, leading from the Roman Pantheon to the cathedrals of Gothic Europe.

For all his deficiencies, Gibbon has remained the standard for all historians who have sought to inquire into the reasons for Rome's decline and fall. Some have held that the adoption of Christianity in the fourth century temporarily arrested the decline of the Empire; others have held, with Gibbon, that the Christians undermined the

4. Dawson, *op. cit.*, p. xi.

Empire. Most modern historians maintain that the decline began in the military anarchy of the third century, thus invalidating the thesis that it was engendered by the rise of Christianity. These historians argue that, even in the West, there were two Empires; the Empire of Augustus and the Antonines, with its glorious *Pax Romana*, which extended from the Atlantic to Persia and from the Danube to the Upper Nile and the Sahara; and the Empire after the third century, presided over by such Emperors as Diocletian, Constantine, Julian the Apostate, and Theodosius. The first Empire was one of order and expansion, untroubled by either barbarians or Christians; the later Empire was always under some threat, always on the defensive against Gibbon's "innocent barbarians." To date, however, no historian has been able to give the exact date of the Empire's demise. Did it die in the wake of the Lombard invasions of the sixth century? Did it survive until the fall of Constantinople? Or does it still survive in the institutions of the Christian West?

In our own day many historians have shed ink on the subject. Henri Pirenne rejected the traditional view that the ancient world ended and the Middle Ages began with the triumphs of the barbarians and of Christianity, and the disappearance of Roman government in the West.[5] Pirenne argued that the Roman world, in the economic, political, and cultural senses, survived and even prospered throughout the period of the barbarian invasions. It was the rise of Islam in the seventh and eighth centuries which, by destroying the unity of the Mediterranean and turning it into a Moslem lake, ended the Empire and ushered in the Carolingian era. "Without Islam," he wrote, in a phrase that has become famous, "the Frankish Empire would probably never have existed and Charlemagne, without Mahomet, would be inconceivable." Pirenne's thesis created a storm at the time of its publication, and forced historians to ask questions that Gibbon had failed to emphasize as strongly as he might have. Specifically, *what* in fact distinguishes Antiquity from the Middle Ages? *How* did the Arabs influence the West? And *how* did the Islamic influence differ from the German influence?[6]

Michael Rostovtzeff, the brilliant Russian historian whose interest in

5. Henri Pirenne, *Mohammed and Charlemagne* (London: George Allen and Unwin, 1939); and *Medieval Cities: Their Origins and the Revival of Trade* (Princeton, 1925).

6. For a succinct account of the debate over the Pirenne thesis, see Alfred Havighurst's *The Pirenne Thesis: Analysis, Criticism, and Revision* (Boston: D. C. Heath, 1958).

the collapse of Rome was inspired by his own unhappy experiences during the Russian Revolution, skillfully elaborated on Pirenne's theme. In endeavoring to explain what the Gibbonian terms "decay" and "decline and fall" represented in the historical context, he concluded that they did not properly apply to what happened in the ancient world in the time of the late Roman Empire and the beginning of, in his phrase, "the so-called Middle Ages." "Historians," he wrote, "do not recognize that there was anything like 'decay' of civilization in these periods. What happened was a slow and gradual change, a shifting of values in the consciousness of men." What seemed important to the educated men of Roman times, he emphasized, ceased to be important to the majority of men. The late Empire was a period during which the great standards of the Republic were barbarized, but not totally destroyed. Even after the disintegration of the unified Empire they survived, in simplified forms, in the institutions of the new national states that emerged from the ashes of the Empire's "fall." Even the unity of the Empire survived in the ecumenic powers of the *Roman* Catholic Church. "To apply to the events in the ancient world in the centuries after Diocletian and Constantine the term 'decay' or 'decline and fall,' " he concluded, "is unfair and misleading. . . . If, however, in the formula 'decay of ancient civilization' we lay stress on 'ancient' and not on 'civilization,' the formula hits the point. No doubt 'ancient' . . . civilization . . . was gradually simplified, barbarized, reduced . . . and the bearers of this civilization . . . gradually disappeared or changed their aspect almost completely."[7]

In a later work, Rostovtzeff revealed the extent to which his own experience in "classless" Soviet Russia had influenced his analysis of the collapse of Rome. "The main phenomenon which underlies the process of decline," he wrote, "is the gradual absorption of the educated classes by the masses and the consequent simplification of all functions of political, social, economic, and intellectual life which we call the barbarization of the ancient world."[8] The absorption of the higher classes by the lower classes led to a gradual leveling of the standards that personified Rome. The gradual penetration of the lower

7. M. I. Rostovtzeff, "The Decay of the Ancient World and Its Economic Explanations," *Economic History Review* 2 (January, 1930).

8. M. I. Rostovtzeff, *Social and Economic History of the Roman Empire* (Oxford: Oxford University Press, 1957), 1:532 ff.

classes into the higher, which were unable to assimilate these new elements, caused social, cultural, and civil conflict, with the lower classes coming out on top. Why, Rostovtzeff asked, was the Greco-Roman civilization unable to assimilate the masses? Why did it remain a civilization of the elite? Why was it incapable "of creating conditions which should secure the ancient world a continuous, uninterrupted movement along the same path of urban civilization?"

There have been many tentative answers to Rostovtzeff's questions. Professor Frank W. Walbank of the University of Liverpool has suggested that Rome's decline cannot be blamed on any single factor, including social and political factors, but rather must be attributed to a fault in the structure of Roman society. The City State, he argues, was a minority culture, and for that reason it tended to be aggressive and predatory, "its claim to autonomy sliding over insensibly, at every opportunity, into a claim to dominate others."[9] This quality manifested itself in numerous wars, and the consequent growth of the institution of slavery. As slavery insinuated itself into the various aspects of Roman life it led to a diminution of learning, to an emphasis on the importance of class, and to the isolation of the elite from the rest of the Empire. "Extremes of wealth and poverty became more marked, the internal market flagged, and ancient society suffered a decline of trade and population and, finally, the wastage of class warfare." This in turn led to a dispersion of industry and a reversion to agrarianism. The declining fortunes of the Roman Empire can be traced, Walbank concluded, to "the premises upon which classical civilization arose, namely an absolutely low technique and, to compensate for this, the institution of slavery. Herein lies the real cause of the decline and fall of the Roman Empire."

In a famous monograph, A. E. R. Boak, drawing from demographic data, attributed the collapse of Rome to a manpower shortage, especially in the rural areas.[10] By A.D. 235, he maintained, the Empire was showing definite symptoms of impoverishment in material and human resources. He blamed this impoverishment, in part, on both the increase in taxation, which consumed the capital resources of the popu-

9. F. W. Walbank, *The Decline of the Roman Empire in the West* (New York: Lawrence and Wishart, 1953), pp. 21 ff.

10. A. E. R. Boak, *Manpower Shortage and the Fall of the Roman Empire* (Ann Arbor: University of Michigan Press, 1955).

lation, and the rise of slavery. The decrease in population, in turn, led to a stagnation of industry and agriculture, and a corresponding decrease in public revenues. This caused a further decline in population. The late Empire did nothing to reverse this condition. As a result, by the fifth century the area of untilled land had reached astonishing proportions, and many cities were reduced to the status of ghost towns. "And so, with declining manpower and increasing impoverishment, the Roman Empire in the West, unable to defend itself against disintegration from within and invasion from without, staggered slowly on its inevitable dissolution."

Such shortsightedness on the part of Rome's leaders—a fact attested to by Marcus Aurelius in his *Meditations*—led the distinguished French historian, André Piganiol, to declare: "Roman civilization did not die a natural death. *It was murdered.*"[11] Piganiol argued that Rome, as a result of her declining fortunes, had, as it were, fallen asleep, allowed liberty to die, placed herself in the hands of barbarian defenders, and ceased to operate along civilized lines. She became, in Norman Baynes' phrase, "crippled" by her pitiful poverty, which rendered impossible the continuation of the civil and military order upon which the Empire was founded.[12] By the third and fourth centuries, Tenny Frank noted in a controversial paper, Rome had succumbed to the rabble; even the aristocracy at Rome was almost completely foreign, and "the people who had built Rome had given way to a different race."[13]

Such are some of the diverse and occasionally farfetched theories concerning the collapse of Rome. In truth, as J. B. Bury, Gibbon's greatest editor, has commented, it is virtually impossible to assign a general cause for Rome's decline and fall. The disintegration of the Roman Empire was the consequence of a series of contingent events —some of which cannot even be accounted for due to the paucity of evidence—of which the slavery system, the rise of Christianity, the decline in population, the bastardization of the race, the drain of natural resources, and the infiltration of barbarians, are most often blamed. Yet in the Eastern Empire, as Bury has reminded us, the same

11. André Piganiol, *L'Empire Chrétien* (Paris: Presses Universitaires de France, 1947), p. 422. Emphasis added.

12. N. H. Baynes, "The Decline of the Roman Empire in Western Europe: Some Modern Explanations," *Journal of Roman Studies* 33 (1943): 29–35.

13. Tenney Frank, "Race Mixture in the Roman Empire," *American Historical Review* 21 (July, 1916): 689–708.

conditions existed, and yet that Empire managed to survive.[14] Historians, no doubt, will continue to debate these questions. Those who derive satisfaction from asking the question, "What if . . . ?" will continue to wonder how things might have turned out if the Western Empire, during the crucial years of its decline, had been governed by Emperors as tough and powerful as Theodosius II and Anastasius in the East; or if Attila the Hun had been less competent; or if the Vandals had been defeated . . . But such questions are of no interest to Clio.

IV

It is to Gibbon, however, that the historians of Rome's decline and fall always return. Indeed, in a certain sense it is to Gibbon that *all* historians worth their salt return in the end. For Gibbon had *reasons* for studying the decline and fall of Rome, just as other historians—as opposed to mere antiquarians and historical pedants—have ulterior reasons for their individual studies. Gibbon, like those who continue to be fascinated with his subject, believed that there were lessons in Rome's fate that were directly relevant to his own age, and to the future. "This awful revolution," he wrote, "may be usefully applied to the instruction of the present age . . . Europe is still threatened with a repetition of those calamities which formerly oppressed the arms and institutions of Rome . . . The Romans were ignorant of the extent of their danger, and the number of their enemies . . . Cold, poverty, and a life of danger and fatigue, fortify the strength and courage of Barbarians. In every age they have oppressed the polite and peaceful nations of China, India, and Persia, who neglected, and still neglect, to counterbalance these natural powers by the resources of military art . . . [Roman] superiority . . . declined with their laws and manners; and the feeble policy of Constantine and his successors armed and instructed, for the ruin of the empire, the rude valor of the Barbarian mercenaries . . . Yet the experience of four thousand years should enlarge our hopes, and diminish our apprehensions; we cannot determine to what height the human species may aspire . . . Every age of the world has increased, and still increases, the real wealth, the happiness, the knowledge, and perhaps the virtue, of the human race."

Rostovtzeff, though he did not share Gibbon's faith in the "idea of

14. J. B. Bury, *History of the Later Roman Empire,* 2 vols. (London, 1923).

progress," profoundly believed that our civilization could learn from the fate of Rome. Violent attempts at leveling, he concluded, have never helped to uplift the masses. Such ventures have only succeeded, as in the case of Rome, in destroying the upper classes, and accelerating the process of barbarization. With great pessimism, he asked: "Is it possible to extend a higher civilization to the lower classes without debasing its standard and diluting its quality to the vanishing point? Is not every civilization bound to decay as soon as it begins to penetrate the masses?" Historians disagree on the lessons of history, often for the best of reasons. History *does* have lessons for the present, but historians will never be able to agree what they are. The greatest lesson that ancient Rome can teach us is that it disintegrated, declined, and fell. We may draw different conclusions from this fact, but we cannot ignore it. Gibbon's *Decline and Fall of the Roman Empire*—regardless of the conclusions we draw from it—remains for us, as it was for Gibbon's contemporaries, a great history, and a handbook for survival that cannot be ignored.

PETER P. WITONSKI

North Massapequa, N. Y.
February 1973

PART 1

The Empire in the Age of the Antonines *(Chapters I and II)*

Gibbon began his history with an account of the Empire of the Antonines, which he viewed as the high point in human history, the period during which the human race was happier and more prosperous than it has ever been, before or since. In the selections that follow, he deals with the extent and internal prosperity of the Empire, which, at this time, controlled the "civilized" world.

CHAPTER I

In the second century of the Christian era, the Empire of Rome comprehended the fairest part of the earth, and the most civilised portion of mankind. The frontiers of that extensive monarchy were guarded by ancient renown and disciplined valour. The gentle but powerful influence of laws and manners had gradually cemented the union of the provinces. Their peaceful inhabitants enjoyed and abused the advantages of wealth and luxury. The image of a free constitution was preserved with decent reverence: the Roman senate appeared to possess the sovereign authority, and devolved on the emperors all the executive powers of government. . . .

The principal conquests of the Romans were achieved under the republic; and the emperors, for the most part, were satisfied with preserving those dominions which had been acquired by the policy of the senate, the active emulation of the consuls, and the martial enthusiasm of the people. The seven first centuries were filled with a rapid succession of triumphs; but it was reserved for Augustus to relinquish the ambitious design of subduing the whole earth, and to introduce a spirit of moderation into the public councils. Inclined to peace by his temper and situation, it was easy for him to discover that Rome, in her present exalted situation, had much less to hope than to fear from the chance of arms; and that, in the prosecution of remote wars, the undertaking became every day more difficult, the event more doubtful, and the possession more precarious, and lest beneficial. The experience of Augustus added weight to these salutary reflections, and effectually convinced him that, by the prudent vigour of his counsels, it would be easy to secure every concession which the safety or the dignity of Rome might require from the most formidable Barbarians. Instead of exposing his person and his legions to the arrows of the Parthians, he obtained, by an honourable treaty, the restitution of the standards and prisoners which had been taken in the defeat of Crassus.

. . . On the death of that emperor, his testament was publicly read in the senate. He bequeathed, as a valuable legacy to his successors, the advice of confining the empire within those limits, which Nature seemed to have placed as its permanent bulwarks and boundaries; on the west the Atlantic ocean; the Rhine and Danube on the north; the Euphrates on the east; and towards the south, the sandy deserts of Arabia and Africa.*

Happily for the repose of mankind, the moderate system recommended by the wisdom of Augustus, was adopted by the fears and vices of his immediate successors. Engaged in the pursuit of pleasure, or in the exercise of tyranny, the first Cæsars seldom showed themselves to the armies, or to the provinces; nor were they disposed to suffer, that those triumphs which *their* indolence neglected should be usurped by the conduct and valour of their lieutenants. The military fame of a subject was considered as an insolent invasion of the Imperial prerogative; and it became the duty, as well as interest, of every Roman general, to guard the frontiers intrusted to his care, without aspiring to conquests which might have proved no less fatal to himself than to the vanquished barbarians.†

*Tacit. Annal. 1. ii., Dion Cassius, 1. lvi. p. 833, and the speech of Augustus himself, in Julian's Cæsars. It receives great light from the learned notes of his French translator M. Spanheim.

†Germanicus, Suetonius Paulinus, and Agricola, were checked and recalled in the course of their victories. Corbulo was put to death. Military merit, as it is admirably expressed by Tacitus, was, in the strictest sense of the word, *imperatoria virtus*.

The only accession which the Roman empire received, during the first century of the Christian era, was the province of Britain. In this single instance the successors of Cæsar and Augustus were persuaded to follow the example of the former, rather than the precept of the latter. The proximity of its situation to the coast of Gaul seemed to invite their arms; the pleasing, though doubtful intelligence, of a pearl fishery, attracted their avarice;* and as Britain was viewed in the light of a distinct and insulated world, the conquest scarcely formed any exception to the general system of continental measures. After a war of about forty years, undertaken by the most stupid, maintained by the most dissolute, and terminated by the most timid of all the emperors, the far greater part of the island submitted to the Roman yoke. . . .

Such was the state of the Roman frontiers, and such the maxims of Imperial policy, from the death of Augustus to the accession of Trajan. That virtuous and active prince had received the education of a soldier, and possessed the talents of a general. The peaceful system of his predecessors was interrupted by scenes of war and conquest; and the legions, after a long interval, beheld a military emperor at their head. The first exploits of Trajan were against the Dacians, the most warlike of men, who dwelt beyond the Danube, and who, during the reign of Domitian, had insulted with impunity the Majesty of Rome. To the strength and fierceness of barbarians, they added a contempt for life, which was derived from a warm persuasion of the immortality and transmigration of the soul. Decebalus, the Dacian king, approved himself a rival not unworthy of Trajan; nor did he despair of his own and the public fortune, till, by the confession of his enemies, he had exhausted every resource both of valour and policy. This memorable war, with a very short suspension of hostilities, lasted five years; and as the emperor could exert, without control, the whole force of the state, it was terminated by an absolute submission of the barbarians. The new province of Dacia, which formed a second exception to the precept of Augustus, was about 1300 miles in circumference. Its natural boundaries were the Dniester, the Teyss [Theiss modern form], or Tibiscus, the Lower Danube, and the Euxine Sea. . . .

Trajan was ambitious of fame; and as long as mankind shall continue

*Cæsar himself conceals that ignoble motive; but it is mentioned by Suetonius, c. 47. The British pearls proved, however, of little value, on account of their dark and livid colour. Tacitus observes, with reason (in Agricola, c. 12), that it was an inherent defect. "Ego facilius crediderim, naturam margaritis deesse quam nobis avaritiam."

to bestow more liberal applause on their destroyers than on their benefactors, the thirst of military glory will ever be the vice of the most exalted characters. The praises of Alexander, transmitted by a succession of poets and historians, had kindled a dangerous emulation in the mind of Trajan. Like him the Roman emperor undertook an expedition against the nations of the east, but he lamented with a sigh, that his advanced age scarcely left him any hopes of equalling the renown of the son of Philip. Yet the success of Trajan, however transient, was rapid and specious. The degenerate Parthians, broken by intestine discord, fled before his arms. He descended the river Tigris in triumph, from the mountains of Armenia to the Persian gulf. He enjoyed the honour of being the first, as he was the last, of the Roman generals, who ever navigated that remote sea. His fleets ravaged the coasts of Arabia; and Trajan vainly flattered himself that he was approaching towards the confines of India. Every day the astonished senate received the intelligence of new names and new nations, that acknowledged his sway. They were informed that the kings of Bosphorus, Colchos, Iberia, Albania, Osrhoene, and even the Parthian monarch himself, had accepted their diadems from the hands of the emperor; that the independent tribes of the Median and Carduchian hills had implored his protection; and that the rich countries of Armenia, Mesopotamia, and Assyria, were reduced into the state of provinces. But the death of Trajan soon clouded the splendid prospect; and it was justly to be dreaded, that so many distant nations would throw off the unaccustomed yoke, when they were no longer restrained by the powerful hand which had imposed it. . . .

The martial and ambitious spirit of Trajan formed a very singular contrast with the moderation of his successor. The restless activity of Hadrian was not less remarkable, when compared with the gentle repose of Antoninus Pius. The life of the former was almost a perpetual journey; and as he possessed the various talents of the soldier, the statesman, and the scholar, he gratified his curiosity in the discharge of his duty. Careless of the difference of seasons and of climates, he marched on foot, and bare-headed, over the snows of Caledonia, and the sultry plains of the Upper Egypt; nor was there a province of the empire which, in the course of his reign, was not honoured with the presence of the monarch. But the tranquil life of Antoninus Pius was spent in the bosom of Italy; and, during the twenty-three years that he directed the public administration, the longest journeys of that amiable prince extended no farther than from his palace in Rome to the retirement of his Lanuvian Villa.

Notwithstanding this difference in their personal conduct, the general system of Augustus was equally adopted and uniformly pursued by Hadrian and by the two Antonines. They persisted in the design of maintaining the dignity of the empire, without attempting to enlarge its limits. By every honourable expedient they invited the friendship of the barbarians; and endeavoured to convince mankind that the Roman power, raised above the temptation of conquest, was actuated only by the love of order and justice. During a long period of forty-three years their virtuous labours were crowned with success; and if we except a few slight hostilities that served to exercise the legions of the frontier, the reigns of Hadrian and Antoninus Pius offer the fair prospect of universal peace.* The Roman name was revered among the most remote nations of the earth. The fiercest barbarians frequently submitted their differences to the arbitration of the emperor; and we are informed by a contemporary historian, that he had seen ambassadors who were refused the honour which they came to solicit, of being admitted into the rank of subjects.

The terror of the Roman arms added weight and dignity to the moderation of the emperors. They preserved peace by a constant preparation for war; and while justice regulated their conduct, they announced to the nations on their confines that they were as little disposed to endure as to offer an injury. The military strength, which it had been sufficient for Hadrian and the elder Antoninus to display, was exerted against the Parthians and the Germans by the emperor Marcus. The hostilities of the barbarians provoked the resentment of that philosophic monarch, and, in the prosecution of a just defence, Marcus and his generals obtained many signal victories, both on the Euphrates and on the Danube. The military establishment of the Roman empire, which thus assured either its tranquillity or success, will now become the proper and important object of our attention.

*We must, however, remember, that, in the time of Hadrian, a rebellion of the Jews raged with religious fury, though only in a single province: Pausanias (l. viii. c. 43) mentions two necessary and successful wars, conducted by the generals of Pius. 1st, Against the wandering Moors, who were driven into the solitudes of Atlas. 2nd, Against the Brigantes of Britain, who had invaded the Roman province. Both these wars (with several other hostilities) are mentioned in the Augustan History, p. 19.

In the purer ages of the commonwealth, the use of arms was reserved for those ranks of citizens who had a country to love, a property to defend, and some share in enacting those laws, which it was their interest, as well as duty, to maintain. But in proportion as the public freedom was lost in extent of conquest, war was gradually improved into an art, and degraded into a trade.* The legions themselves, even at the time when they were recruited in the most distant provinces, were supposed to consist of Roman citizens. That distinction was generally considered either as a legal qualification or as a proper recompense for the soldier; but a more serious regard was paid to the essential merit of age, strength, and military stature.† In all levies, a just preference was given to the climates of the North over those of the South: the race of men born to the exercise of arms was sought for in the country rather than in cities; and it was very reasonably presumed, that the hardy occupations of smiths, carpenters, and huntsmen, would supply more vigour and resolution than the sedentary trades which are employed in the service of luxury. After every qualification of property had been laid aside, the armies of the Roman emperors were still commanded, for the most part, by officers of a liberal birth and education; but the common soldiers, like the mercenary troops of modern Europe, were drawn from the meanest, and very frequently from the most profligate, of mankind.

That public virtue which among the ancients was denominated patriotism, is derived from a strong sense of our own interest in the preservation and prosperity of the free government of which we are members. Such a sentiment, which had rendered the legions of the republic almost invincible, could make but a very feeble impression on the mercenary servants of a despotic prince; and it became necessary to supply that defect by other motives, of a different, but not less forcible nature; honour and religion. The peasant, or mechanic, imbibed the useful prejudice that he was advanced to the more dignified profession of arms, in which his rank and reputation would depend on his own valour; and that, although the prowess of a private soldier

*The poorest rank of soldiers possessed above forty pounds sterling (Dionys. Halicarn. iv. 17), a very high qualification, at a time when money was so scarce, that an ounce of silver was equivalent to seventy pound weight of brass. The populace, excluded by the ancient constitution, were indiscriminately admitted by Marius. Sallust. de Bell. Jugurth. c. 91.

†Cæsar formed his legion Alauda, of Gauls and strangers: but it was during the licence of civil war; and after the victory, he gave them the freedom of the city for their reward.

must often escape the notice of fame, his own behaviour might sometimes confer glory or disgrace on the company, the legion, or even the army, to whose honours he was associated. On his first entrance into the service, an oath was administered to him, with every circumstance of solemnity. He promised never to desert his standard, to submit his own will to the commands of his leaders, and to sacrifice his life for the safety of the emperor and the empire. The attachment of the Roman troops to their standards was inspired by the united influence of religion and of honour. The golden eagle, which glittered in the front of the legion, was the object of their fondest devotion; nor was it esteemed less impious than it was ignominious, to abandon that sacred ensign in the hour of danger. These motives, which derived their strength from the imagination, were enforced by fears and hopes of a more substantial kind. Regular pay, occasional donatives, and a stated recompense, after the appointed time of service, alleviated the hardships of the military life,* whilst, on the other hand, it was impossible for cowardice or disobedience to escape the severest punishment. The centurions were authorised to chastise with blows, the generals had a right to punish with death; and it was an inflexible maxim of Roman discipline, that a good soldier should dread his officers far more than the enemy. From such laudable arts did the valour of the Imperial troops receive a degree of firmness and docility, unattainable by the impetuous and irregular passions of barbarians. . . .

Spain, the western extremity of the empire, of Europe, and of the ancient world, has, in every age, invariably preserved the same natural limits; the Pyrenæan mountains, the Mediterranean, and the Atlantic Ocean. That great peninsula, at present so unequally divided between two sovereigns, was distributed by Augustus into three provinces, Lusitania, Bætica, and Tarraconensis. The kingdom of Portugal now fills the place of the warlike country of the Lusitanians; and the loss sustained by the former, on the side of the East, is compensated by an accession of territory towards the North. . . .

*Gronovius de Pecunia vetere, 1. iii. p. 120, etc. The emperor Domitian raised the annual stipend of the legionaries to twelve pieces of gold, which, in his time, was equivalent to about ten of our guineas. This pay, somewhat higher than our own, had been, and was afterwards, gradually increased, according to the progress of wealth and military government. After twenty years' service, the veteran received three thousand denarii (about one hundred pounds sterling), or a proportionable allowance of land. The pay and advantages of the guards were, in general, about double those of the legions.

Ancient Gaul, as it contained the whole country between the Pyrenees, the Alps, the Rhine, and the Ocean, was of greater extent than modern France. To the dominions of that powerful monarchy, with its recent acquisitions of Alsace and Lorraine, we must add the duchy of Savoy, the cantons of Switzerland, the four electorates of the Rhine, and the territories of Liege, Luxemburg, Hainault, Flanders, and Brabant. When Augustus gave laws to the conquests of his father, he introduced a division of Gaul equally adapted to the progress of the legions, to the course of the rivers, and to the principal national distinctions, which had comprehended above an hundred independent states.* The sea-coast of the Mediterranean, Languedoc, Provence, and Dauphiné, received their provincial appellation from the colony of Narbonne. The government of Aquitaine was extended from the Pyrenees to the Loire. The country between the Loire and the Seine was styled the Celtic Gaul, and soon borrowed a new denomination from the celebrated colony of Lugdunum, or Lyons. The Belgic lay beyond the Seine, and in more ancient times had been bounded only by the Rhine; but a little before the age of Cæsar the Germans, abusing their superiority of valour, had occupied a considerable portion of the Belgic territory. The Roman conquerors very eagerly embraced so flattering a circumstance, and the Gallic frontier of the Rhine, from Basil to Leyden, received the pompous names of the Upper and the Lower Germany. Such, under the reign of the Antonines, were the six provinces of Gaul; the Narbonnese, Aquitaine, the Celtic, or Lyonnese, the Belgic, and the two Germanies.

We have already had occasion to mention the conquest of Britain . . . It comprehended all England, Wales, and the Lowlands of Scotland, as far as Dumbarton and Edinburgh. Before Britain lost her freedom, the country was irregularly divided between thirty tribes of barbarians, of whom the most considerable were the Belgæ in the West, the Brigantes in the North, the Silures in South Wales, and the Iceni in Norfolk and Suffolk. As far as we can either trace or credit the resemblance of manners and language, Spain, Gaul, and Britain were peopled by the same hardy race of savages. Before they yielded to the Roman arms, they often disputed the field, and often renewed the

*One hundred and fifteen *cities* appear in the Notitia of Gaul; and it is well known that this appellation was applied not only to the capital town, but to the whole territory of each state. But Plutarch and Appian increase the number of tribes to three or four hundred.

contest. After their submission they constituted the western division of the European provinces, which extended from the columns of Hercules to the wall of Antoninus and from the mouth of the Tagus to the sources of the Rhine and Danube.

Before the Roman conquest, the country which is now called Lombardy was not considered as a part of Italy. It had been occupied by a powerful colony of Gauls, who settling themselves along the banks of the Po, from Piedmont to Romagna, carried their arms and diffused their name from the Alps to the Apennine. The Ligurians dwelt on the rocky coast, which now forms the republic of Genoa. Venice was yet unborn; but the territories of that state, which lie to the east of the Adige, were inhabited by the Venetians. The middle part of the peninsula that now composes the duchy of Tuscany and the ecclesiastical state, was the ancient seat of the Etruscans and Umbrians; to the former of whom Italy was indebted for the first rudiments of civilised life. The Tiber rolled at the foot of the seven hills of Rome, and the country of the Sabines, the Latins, and the Volsci, from that river to the frontiers of Naples, was the theatre of her infant victories. On that celebrated ground the first consuls deserved triumphs; their successors adorned villas, and *their* posterity have erected convents. Capua and Campania possessed the immediate territory of Naples; the rest of the kingdom was inhabited by many warlike nations, the Marsi, the Samnites, the Apulians, and the Lucanians; and the sea-coasts had been covered by the flourishing colonies of the Greeks. We may remark, that when Augustus divided Italy into eleven regions, the little province of Istria was annexed to that seat of Roman sovereignty.

The European provinces of Rome were protected by the course of the Rhine and the Danube. The latter of those mighty streams, which rises at the distance of only thirty miles from the former, flows above thirteen hundred miles, for the most part, to the south-east, collects the tribute of sixty navigable rivers, and is, at length, through six mouths, received into the Euxine, which appears scarcely equal to such an accession of waters. The provinces of the Danube soon acquired the general appellation of Illyricum, or the Illyrian frontier,* and were esteemed the most warlike of the empire; but they deserve to be more particularly considered under the names of Rhætia, Noricum,

*The name of Illyricum originally belonged to the sea-coast of the Adriatic, and was gradually extended by the Romans from the Alps to the Euxine Sea. Severini Pannonia, i. 1. c. 3.

Pannonia, Dalmatia, Dacia, Mæsia, Thrace, Macedonia, and Greece.

The province of Rhætia, which soon extinguished the name of the Vindelicians, extended from the summit of the Alps to the banks of the Danube; from its source, as far as its conflux with the Inn. The greatest part of the flat country is subject to the elector of Bavaria; the city of Augsburg is protected by the constitution of the German empire; the Grisons are safe in their mountains, and the country of Tyrol is ranked among the numerous provinces of the house of Austria.

The wide extent of territory, which is included between the Inn, the Danube, and the Save; Austria, Styria, Carinthia, Carniola, the Lower Hungary, and Sclavonia, was known to the ancients under the names of Noricum and Pannonia. In their original state of independence, their fierce inhabitants were intimately connected. Under the Roman government they were frequently united, and they still remain the patrimony of a single family. They now contain the residence of a German prince, who styles himself Emperor of the Romans, and form the centre, as well as strength, of the Austrian power. It may not be improper to observe, that if we except Bohemia, Moravia, the northern skirts of Austria, and a part of Hungary, between the Theiss and the Danube, all the other dominions of the House of Austria were comprised within the limits of the Roman empire.

Dalmatia, to which the name of Illyricum more properly belonged, was a long but narrow tract between the Save and the Adriatic. The best part of the sea-coast, which still retains its ancient appellation, is a province of the Venetian state, and the seat of the little republic of Ragusa.* The inland parts have assumed the Sclavonian names of Croatia and Bosnia; the former obeys an Austrian governor, the latter a Turkish pasha; but the whole country is still infested by tribes of barbarians, whose savage independence irregularly marks the doubtful limit of the Christian and Mahometan power. . . .

The appellation of Roumelia, which is still bestowed by the Turks on the extensive countries of Thrace, Macedonia, and Greece, preserves the memory of their ancient state under the Roman empire. In the time of the Antonines, the martial regions of Thrace, from the

*[Ragusa, after being Greek first, then Roman, then an independent republic, was later a dependent republic under the protection successively of Byzantium, Venice, Hungary, and the Porte. From 1808 to 1814 it was part of Illyria. In 1814 it was included in the Austrian empire, and is now in Jugoslavia.]

mountains of Hæmus and Rhodope, to the Bosphorus and the Hellespont, had assumed the form of a province. Notwithstanding the change of masters and of religion, the new city of Rome, founded by Constantine on the banks of the Bosphorus, has ever since remained the capital of a great monarchy. The kingdom of Macedonia, which, under the reign of Alexander, gave laws to Asia, derived more solid advantages from the policy of the two Philips; and with its dependencies of Epirus and Thessaly, extended from the Ægean to the Ionian Sea. When we reflect on the fame of Thebes and Argos, of Sparta and Athens, we can scarcely persuade ourselves that so many immortal republics of ancient Greece were lost in a single province of the Roman empire, which, from the superior influence of the Achæan league, was usually denominated the province of Achaia.

Such was the state of Europe under the Roman emperors. . . . The name of Asia Minor is attributed with some propriety to the peninsula, which, confined betwixt the Euxine and the Mediterranean, advances from the Euphrates towards Europe. The most extensive and flourishing district, westward of Mount Taurus and the river Halys, was dignified by the Romans with the exclusive title of Asia. The jurisdiction of that province extended over the ancient monarchies of Troy, Lydia, and Phrygia, the maritime countries of the Pamphylians, Lycians, and Carians, and the Grecian colonies of Ionia, which equalled in arts, though not in arms, the glory of their parent. The kingdoms of Bithynia and Pontus possessed the northern side of the peninsula from Constantinople to Trebizond. On the opposite side, the province of Cilicia was terminated by the mountains of Syria: the inland country, separated from the Roman Asia by the river Halys, and from Armenia by the Euphrates, had once formed the independent kingdom of Cappadocia. In this place we may observe that the northern shores of the Euxine, beyond Trebizond in Asia, and beyond the Danube in Europe, acknowledged the sovereignty of the emperors, and received at their hands either tributary princes or Roman garrisons. Budzak, Crim Tartary, Circassia, and Mingrelia, are the modern appellations of those savage countries.

Under the successors of Alexander, Syria was the seat of the Seleucidæ, who reigned over Upper Asia, till the successful revolt of the Parthians confined their dominions between the Euphrates and the Mediterranean. When Syria became subject to the Romans, it formed the eastern frontier of their empire; nor did that province, in its utmost latitude, know any other bounds than the mountains of Cappadocia to the north, and towards the south the confines of Egypt, and the Red Sea. Phœnicia and Palestine were sometimes annexed to, and sometimes separated from, the jurisdiction of Syria. The former of these was a narrow and rocky coast; the latter was a territory scarcely superior to Wales, either in fertility or extent. Yet Phœnicia and Palestine will for ever live in the memory of mankind . . . A sandy desert alike destitute of wood and water skirts along the doubtful confine of Syria, from the Euphrates to the Red Sea. The wandering life of the Arabs was inseparably connected with their independence; and wherever, on some spots less barren than the rest, they ventured to form any settled habitation, they soon became subjects to the Roman empire.

The geographers of antiquity have frequently hesitated to what portion of the globe they should ascribe Egypt.* By its situation that celebrated kingdom is included within the immense peninsula of Africa; but it is accessible only on the side of Asia, whose revolutions, in almost every period of history, Egypt has humbly obeyed. A Roman præfect was seated on the splendid throne of the Ptolemies; and the iron sceptre of the Mamalukes is now in the hands of a Turkish pasha. The Nile flows down the country, above five hundred miles from the tropic of Cancer to the Mediterranean, and marks, on either side, the extent of fertility by the measure of its inundations. Cyrene, situate towards the west, and along the sea-coast, was first a Greek colony, afterwards a province of Egypt, and is now lost in the desert of Barca.

From Cyrene to the ocean, the coast of Africa extends above fifteen hundred miles; yet so closely is it pressed between the Mediterranean and the Sahara, or sandy desert, that its breadth seldom exceeds fourscore or an hundred miles. The eastern division was considered by the Romans as the more peculiar and proper province of Africa. Till the arrival of the Phœnician colonies, that fertile country was inhabited by the Libyans, the most savage of mankind. Under the immediate jurisdiction of Carthage, it became the centre of commerce and empire; but the republic of Carthage is now degenerated into the

*Ptolemy and Strabo, with the modern geographers, fix the Isthmus of Suez as the boundary of Asia and Africa. Dionysius, Mela, Pliny, Sallust, Hirtius, and Solinus, have preferred for that purpose the western branch of the Nile, or even the great Catabathmus, or descent, which last would assign to Asia, not only Egypt, but part of Libya.

feeble and disorderly states of Tripoli and Tunis. The military government of Algiers oppresses the wide extent of Numidia, as it was once united under Massinissa and Jugurtha: but in the time of Augustus, the limits of Numidia were contracted; and, at least, two-thirds of the country acquiesced in the name of Mauritania, with the epithet of Cæsariensis. The genuine Mauritania, or country of the Moors, which, from the ancient city of Tingi, or Tangier, was distinguished by the appellation of Tingitana, is represented by the modern kingdom of Fez. Sallè, on the Ocean, long infamous for its piratical depredations, was noticed by the Romans, as the extreme object of their power, and almost of their geography. A city of their foundation may still be discovered near Mequinez, the residence of the barbarian whom we condescend to style the Emperor of Morocco; but it does not appear that his more southern dominions, Morocco itself, and Segelmessa, were ever comprehended within the Roman province. The western parts of Africa are intersected by the branches of Mount Atlas, a name so idly celebrated by the fancy of poets; but which is now diffused over the immense ocean that rolls between the ancient and the new continent. . . . The empire was above two thousand miles in breadth, from the wall of Antoninus and the northern limits of Dacia, to mount Atlas and the tropic of Cancer; . . . it extended, in length, more than three thousand miles from the Western Ocean to the Euphrates; . . . it was situated in the finest part of the Temperate Zone, between the twenty-fourth and fifty-sixth degrees of northern latitude; and . . . it was supposed to contain above sixteen hundred thousand square miles, for the most part of fertile and well-cultivated land.

CHAPTER II

It is not alone by the rapidity, or extent of conquest, that we should estimate the greatness of Rome. The sovereign of the Russian deserts commands a larger portion of the globe. In the seventh summer after his passage of the Hellespont, Alexander erected the Macedonian trophies on the banks of the Hyphasis.* Within less than a century, the irresistible Zingis, and the Mogul princes of his race, spread their cruel

*They were erected about midway between Lahor and Delhi. The conquests of Alexander in Hindostan were confined to the Punjab, a country watered by the five great streams of the Indus.

devastations and transient empire from the sea of China to the confines of Egypt and Germany. But the firm edifice of Roman power was raised and preserved by the wisdom of ages. The obedient provinces of Trajan and the Antonines were united by laws and adorned by arts. They might occasionally suffer from the partial abuse of delegated authority; but the general principle of government was wise, simple, and beneficent. They enjoyed the religion of their ancestors, whilst in civil honours and advantages they were exalted, by just degrees, to an equality with their conquerors. . . .

Rome, the capital of a great monarchy, was incessantly filled with subjects and strangers from every part of the world, who all introduced and enjoyed the favourite superstitions of their native country. Every city in the empire was justified in maintaining the purity of its ancient ceremonies; and the Roman senate, using the common privilege, sometimes interposed, to check this inundation of foreign rites. The Egyptian superstition, of all the most contemptible and abject, was frequently prohibited; the temples of Serapis and Isis demolished and their worshippers banished from Rome and Italy.* But the zeal of fanaticism prevailed over the cold and feeble efforts of policy. The exiles returned, the proselytes multiplied, the temples were restored with increasing splendour, and Isis and Serapis at length assumed their place among the Roman deities. Nor was this indulgence a departure from the old maxims of government. In the purest ages of the commonwealth, Cybele and Æsculapius had been invited by solemn embassies; and it was customary to tempt the protectors of besieged cities, by the promise of more distinguished honours than they possessed in their native country. Rome gradually became the common temple of her subjects; and the freedom of the city was bestowed on all the gods of mankind.

The narrow policy of preserving, without any foreign mixture, the pure blood of the ancient citizens, had checked the fortune, and hastened the ruin, of Athens and Sparta. The aspiring genius of Rome

*In the year of Rome 701, the temple of Isis and Serapis was demolished by the order of the Senate (Dion Cassius, 1. xl. p. 252), and even by the hands of the consul (Valerius Maximus, 1, 3). After the death of Cæsar, it was restored at the public expense (Dion, 1. xlvii. p. 501). When Augustus was in Egypt, he revered the majesty of Serapis (Dion, 1. ii. p. 647); but in the Pomærium of Rome, and a mile round it, he prohibited the worship of the Egyptian gods (Dion. 1. liii. p. 679, 1. liv. p. 735). They remained however, very fashionable under his reign (Ovid. de Art. Amand. 1. i.) and that of his successor, till the justice of Tiberius was provoked to some acts of severity (Tacit. Annal. ii. 85. Joseph. Antiquit. 1. xviii. c. 3).

sacrificed vanity to ambition, and deemed it more prudent, as well as honourable, to adopt virtue and merit for her own wheresoever they were found, among slaves or strangers, enemies or barbarians. During the most flourishing era of the Athenian commonwealth, the number of citizens gradually decreased from about thirty to twenty-one thousand. If, on the contrary, we study the growth of the Roman republic, we may discover, that, nowithstanding the incessant demands of wars and colonies, the citizens, who, in the first census of Servius Tullius, amounted to no more than eighty-three thousand, were multiplied, before the commencement of the social war, to the number of four hundred and sixty-three thousand men, able to bear arms in the service of their country. When the allies of Rome claimed an equal share of honours and privileges, the senate indeed preferred the chance of arms to an ignominious concession. The Samnites and the Lucanians paid the severe penalty of their rashness; but the rest of the Italian states, as they successively returned to their duty, were admitted into the bosom of the republic, and soon contributed to the ruin of public freedom. Under a democratical government, the citizens exercise the powers of sovereignty; and those powers will be first abused, and afterwards lost, if they are committed to an unwieldy multitude. But when the popular assemblies had been suppressed by the administration of the emperors, the conquerors were distinguished from the vanquished nations, only as the first and most honourable order of subjects; and their increase, however rapid, was no longer exposed to the same dangers. Yet the wisest princes, who adopted the maxims of Augustus, guarded with the strictest care the dignity of the Roman name, and diffused the freedom of the city with a prudent liberality.*

Till the privileges of Romans had been progressively extended to all the inhabitants of the empire, an important distinction was preserved between Italy and the provinces. The former was esteemed the centre of public unity, and the firm basis of the constitution. Italy claimed the birth, or at least the residence, of the emperors and the senate.† The estates of the Italians were exempt from taxes, their persons from the

*Mæcenas had advised him to declare by one edict, all his subjects, citizens. But we may justly suspect that the historian Dion was the author of a counsel, so much adapted to the practice of his own age, and so little to that of Augustus.

†The senators were obliged to have one-third of their own landed property in Italy. Plin. 1. vi. ep. 19. The qualification was reduced by Marcus to one-fourth. Since the reign of Trajan, Italy had sunk nearer to the level of the provinces.

arbitrary jurisdiction of governors. Their municipal corporations, formed after the perfect model of the capital, were intrusted, under the immediate eye of the supreme power, with the execution of the laws. From the foot of the Alps to the extremity of Calabria, all the natives of Italy were born citizens of Rome. Their partial distinctions were obliterated, and they insensibly coalesced into one great nation, united by language, manners, and civil institutions, and equal to the weight of a powerful empire. The republic gloried in her generous policy, and was frequently rewarded by the merit and services of her adopted sons. Had she always confined the distinction of Romans to the ancient families within the walls of the city, that immortal name would have been deprived of some of its noblest ornaments. Virgil was a native of Mantua; Horace was inclined to doubt whether he should call himself an Apulian or a Lucanian: it was in Padua that an historian was found worthy to record the majestic series of Roman victories. The patriot family of the Catos emerged from Tusculum; and the little town of Arpinum claimed the double honour of producing Marius and Cicero, the former of whom deserved, after Romulus and Camillus, to be styled the Third Founder of Rome; and the latter, after saving his country from the designs of Catiline, enabled her to contend with Athens for the palm of eloquence.

The provinces of the empire . . . were destitute of any public force; or constitutional freedom. In Etruria, in Greece, and in Gaul, it was the first care of the senate to dissolve those dangerous confederacies, which taught mankind, that as the Roman arts prevailed by division, they might be resisted by union. Those princes, whom the ostentation of gratitude or generosity permitted for a while to hold a precarious sceptre, were dismissed from their thrones as soon as they had performed their appointed task of fashioning to the yoke the vanquished nations. The free states and cities which had embraced the cause of Rome, were rewarded with a nominal alliance, and insensibly sunk into real servitude. The public authority was everywhere exercised by the ministers of the senate and of the emperors, and that authority was absolute, and without control. But the same salutary maxims of government, which had secured the peace and obedience of Italy, were extended to the most distant conquests. A nation of Romans was gradually formed in the provinces, by the double expedient of introducing colonies, and of admitting the most faithful and deserving of the provincials to the freedom of Rome.

"Wheresoever the Roman conquers, he inhabits," is a very just observation of Seneca, confirmed by history and experience. The natives of Italy, allured by pleasure or by interest, hastened to enjoy the advantages of victory; and we may remark, that about forty years after the reduction of Asia, eighty thousand Romans were massacred in one day, by the cruel orders of Mithridates. These voluntary exiles were engaged, for the most part, in the occupations of commerce, agriculture, and the farm of the revenue. But after the legions were rendered permanent by the emperors, the provinces were peopled by a race of soldiers; and the veterans, whether they received the reward of their service in land or in money, usually settled with their families in the country where they had honourably spent their youth. Throughout the empire, but more particularly in the western parts, the most fertile districts, and the most convenient situations, were reserved for the establishment of colonies; some of which were of a civil, and others of a military nature. In their manners and internal policy, the colonies formed a perfect representation of their great parent; and they were soon endeared to the natives by the ties of friendship and alliance, they effectually diffused a reverence for the Roman name, and a desire, which was seldom disappointed, of sharing, in due time, its honours and advantages. The municipal cities insensibly equalled the rank and splendour of the colonies; and in the reign of Hadrian, it was disputed which was the preferable condition, of those societies which had issued from, or those which had been received into the bosom of Rome. The right of Latium, as it was called, conferred on the cities to which it had been granted a more partial favour. The magistrates only, at the expiration of their office, assumed the quality of Roman citizens; but as those offices were annual, in a few years they circulated round the principal families. Those of the provincials who were permitted to bear arms in the legions; those who exercised any civil employment; all, in a word, who performed any public service, or displayed any personal talents, were rewarded with a present, whose value was continually diminished by the increasing liberality of the emperors. Yet even, in the age of the Antonines, when the freedom of the city had been bestowed on the greater number of their subjects, it was still accompanied with very solid advantages. The bulk of the people acquired, with that title, the benefit of the Roman laws, particularly in the interesting articles of marriage, testaments, and inheritances; and the road of fortune was open to those whose pretensions were seconded by favour or merit. The grandsons of the Gauls, who had besieged Julius Cæsar in Alesia, commanded legions, governed provinces, and were admitted into the senate of Rome. Their ambition, instead of disturbing the tranquillity of the state, was intimately connected with its safety and greatness.

So sensible were the Romans of the influence of language over national manners, that it was their most serious care to extend, with the progress of their arms, the use of the Latin tongue. The ancient dialects of Italy, the Sabine, the Etruscan, and the Venetian, sunk into oblivion; but in the provinces, the east was less docile than the west, to the voice of its victorious preceptors. This obvious difference marked the two portions of the empire with a distinction of colours, which, though it was in some degree concealed during the meridian splendour of prosperity, became gradually more visible as the shades of night descended upon the Roman world. The western countries were civilised by the same hands which subdued them. As soon as the barbarians were reconciled to obedience, their minds were opened to any new impressions of knowledge and politeness. The language of Virgil and Cicero, though with some inevitable mixture of corruption, was so universally adopted in Africa, Spain, Gaul, Britain, and Pannonia,* that the faint traces of the Punic or Celtic idioms were preserved only in the mountains, or among the peasants.† Education and study insensibly inspired the natives of those countries with the sentiments of Romans; and Italy gave fashions as well as laws to her Latin provincials. They solicited with more ardour, and obtained with more facility, the freedom and honours of the state; supported the national dignity in letters** and in arms; and, at length, in the person of Trajan, produced an emperor whom the Scipios would not have disowned for their countryman. . . .

It was by such institutions that the nations of the empire insensibly melted away into the Roman name and people. But there still remained, in the centre of every province and of every family, an un-

*Apuleius and Augustin will answer for Africa; Strabo for Spain and Gaul; Tacitus, in the Life of Agricola, for Britain; and Velleius Paterculus, for Pannonia. To them we may add the language of the Inscriptions.

†The Celtic was preserved in the mountains of Wales, Cornwall, and Armorica. We may observe that Apuleius reproaches an African youth, who lived among the populace, with the use of the Punic; whilst he had almost forgot Greek, and neither could nor would speak Latin (Apolog. p. 596). The greater part of St. Austin's congregations were strangers to the Punic.

**Spain alone produced Columella, the Senecas, Lucan, Martial, and Quintilian.

happy condition of men who endured the weight, without sharing the benefits, of society. In the free states of antiquity the domestic slaves were exposed to the wanton rigour of despotism. The perfect settlement of the Roman empire was preceded by ages of violence and rapine. The slaves consisted, for the most part, of barbarian captives, taken in thousands by the chance of war, purchased at a vile price, accustomed to a life of independence, and impatient to break and to revenge their fetters. Against such internal enemies, whose desperate insurrections had more than once reduced the republic to the brink of destruction, the most severe regulations, and the most cruel treatment, seemed almost justified by the great law of self-preservation. But when the principal nations of Europe, Asia, and Africa, were united under the laws of one sovereign, the source of foreign supplies flowed with much less abundance, and the Romans were reduced to the milder but more tedious method of propagation. In their numerous families, and particularly in their country estates, they encouraged the marriage of their slaves. The sentiments of nature, the habits of education, and the possession of a dependent species of property, contributed to alleviate the hardships of servitude. The existence of a slave became an object of greater value, and though his happiness still depended on the temper and circumstances of the master, the humanity of the latter, instead of being restrained by fear, was encouraged by the sense of his own interest. The progress of manners was accelerated by the virtue or policy of the emperors; and by the edicts of Hadrian and the Antonines, the protection of the laws was extended to the most abject part of mankind. The jurisdiction of life and death over the slaves, a power long exercised and often abused, was taken out of private hands, and reserved to the magistrates alone. The subterraneous prisons were abolished; and, upon a just complaint of intolerable treatment, the injured slave obtained either his deliverance, or a less cruel master.

Hope, the best comfort of our imperfect condition, was not denied to the Roman slave; and if he had any opportunity of rendering himself either useful or agreeable, he might very naturally expect that the diligence and fidelity of a few years would be rewarded with the inestimable gift of freedom. The benevolence of the master was so frequently prompted by the meaner suggestions of vanity and avarice, that the laws found it more necessary to restrain than to encourage a profuse and undistinguishing liberality, which might degenerate into a very dangerous abuse. It was a maxim of ancient jurisprudence, that a slave had not any country of his own, he acquired with his liberty an admission into the political society of which his patron was a member. The consequences of this maxim would have prostituted the privileges of the Roman city to a mean and promiscuous multitude. . . .

The number of subjects who acknowledged the laws of Rome, of citizens, of provincials, and of slaves, cannot now be fixed with such a degree of accuracy, as the importance of the object would deserve. We are informed that when the emperor Claudius exercised the office of censor, he took an account of six millions nine hundred and forty-five thousand Roman citizens, who, with the proportion of women and children, must have amounted to about twenty millions of souls. The multitude of subjects of an inferior rank was uncertain and fluctuating. . . .

Domestic peace and union were the natural consequences of the moderate and comprehensive policy embraced by the Romans. If we turn our eyes towards the monarchies of Asia, we shall behold despotism in the centre, and weakness in the extremities; the collection of the revenue, or the administration of justice, enforced by the presence of an army; hostile barbarians established in the heart of the country, hereditary satraps usurping the dominion of the provinces, and subjects inclined to rebellion, though incapable of freedom. But the obedience of the Roman world was uniform, voluntary, and permanent. The vanquished nations, blended into one great people, resigned the hope, nay even the wish, of resuming their independence, and scarcely considered their own existence as distinct from the existence of Rome. The established authority of the emperors pervaded without an effort the wide extent of their dominions, and was exercised with the same facility on the banks of the Thames, or of the Nile, as on those of the Tiber.

Whatever evils either reason or declamation have imputed to extensive empire, the power of Rome was attended with some beneficial consequences to mankind; and the same freedom of intercourse which extended the vices, diffused likewise the improvements of social life. In the more remote ages of antiquity, the world was unequally divided. The east was in the immemorial possession of arts and luxury;

whilst the west was inhabited by rude and warlike barbarians, who either disdained agriculture, or to whom it was totally unknown. Under the protection of an established government, the productions of happier climates, and the industry of more civilised nations, were gradually introduced into the western countries of Europe; and the natives were encouraged, by an open and profitable commerce, to multiply the former, as well as to improve the latter. . . .

Agriculture is the foundation of manufactures; since the productions of nature are the materials of art. Under the Roman empire, the labour of an industrious and ingenious people was variously, but incessantly employed, in the service of the rich. In their dress, their table, their houses and their furniture, the favourites of fortune united every refinement of conveniency, of elegance, and of splendour, whatever could soothe their pride or gratify their sensuality. Such refinements, under the odious name of luxury, have been severely arraigned by the moralists of every age; and it might perhaps be more conducive to the virtue, as well as happiness, of mankind, if all possessed the necessaries, and none the superfluities, of life. But in the present imperfect condition of society, luxury, though it may proceed from vice or folly, seems to be the only means that can correct the unequal distribution of property. The diligent mechanic, and the skilful artist, who have obtained no share of the division of the earth, receive a voluntary tax from the possessors of land; and the latter are prompted, by a sense of interest, to improve those estates, with whose produce they may purchase additional pleasures. This operation, the particular effects of which are felt in every society, acted with much more diffusive energy in the Roman world. The provinces would soon have been exhausted of their wealth, if the manufactures and commerce of luxury had not insensibly restored to the industrious subjects the sums which were exacted from them by the arms and authority of Rome. As long as the circulation was confined within the bounds of the empire, it impressed the political machine with a new degree of activity, and its consequences, sometimes beneficial, could never become pernicious.

But it is no easy task to confine luxury within the limits of an empire. The most remote countries of the ancient world were ransacked to supply the pomp and delicacy of Rome. The forests of Scythia afforded some valuable furs. Amber was brought over land from the shores of the Baltic to the Danube; and the barbarians were astonished at the price which they received in exchange for so useless a commodity.* There was a considerable demand for Babylonian carpets and other manufactures of the East; but the most important and unpopular branch of foreign trade was carried on with Arabia and India. Every year, about the time of the summer solstice, a fleet of an hundred and twenty vessels sailed from Myos-hormos, a port of Egypt, on the Red Sea. By the periodical assistance of the Monsoons, they traversed the ocean in about forty days. The coast of Malabar, or the island of Ceylon, was the usual term of their navigation, and it was in those markets that the merchants from the more remote countries of Asia expected their arrival. The return of the fleet of Egypt was fixed to the months of December or January; and as soon as their rich cargo had been transported on the backs of camels, from the Red Sea to the Nile, and had descended that river as far as Alexandria, it was poured, without delay, into the capital of the empire. The objects of oriental traffic were splendid and trifling: silk, a pound of which was esteemed not inferior in value to a pound of gold; precious stones, among which the pearl claimed the first rank after the diamond; and a variety of aromatics, that were consumed in religious worship and the pomp of funerals. . . .

Notwithstanding the propensity of mankind to exalt the past, and to depreciate the present, the tranquil and prosperous state of the empire was warmly felt, and honestly confessed, by the provincials as well as Romans. "They acknowledged that the true principles of social life, laws, agriculture, and science, which had been first invented by the wisdom of Athens, were now firmly established by the power of Rome, under whose auspicious influence the fiercest barbarians were united by an equal government and common language. They affirm, that with the improvement of arts, the human species was visibly multiplied. They celebrate the increasing splendour of the cities, the beautiful face of the country, cultivated and adorned like an immense garden; and the long festival of peace, which was enjoyed by so many nations, forgetful of their ancient animosities, and delivered from the apprehension of future danger." Whatever suspicions may be suggested by the air of rhetoric and declamation, which seems to prevail

*Tacit. Germania, c. 45. Plin. Hist. Nat. xxxviii. 11. The latter observed, with some humour, that even fashion had not yet found out the use of amber. Nero sent a Roman knight to purchase great quantities on the spot where it was produced, the coast of modern Prussia.

in these passages, the substance of them is perfectly agreeable to historic truth.

It was scarcely possible that the eyes of contemporaries should discover in the public felicity the latent causes of decay and corruption. This long peace, and the uniform government of the Romans, introduced a slow and secret poison into the vitals of the empire. The minds of men were gradually reduced to the same level, the fire of genius was extinguished, and even the military spirit evaporated. The natives of Europe were brave and robust, Spain, Gaul, Britain, and Illyricum supplied the legions with excellent soldiers, and constituted the real strength of the monarchy. Their personal valour remained, but they no longer possessed that public courage which is nourished by the love of independence, the sense of national honour, the presence of danger, and the habit of command. They received laws and governors from the will of their sovereign, and trusted for their defence to a mercenary army. The posterity of their boldest leaders was contented with the rank of citizens and subjects. The most aspiring spirits resorted to the court or standard of the emperors; and the deserted provinces, deprived of political strength or union, insensibly sunk into the languid indifference of private life.

The love of letters, almost inseparable from peace and refinement, was fashionable among the subjects of Hadrian and the Antonines, who were themselves men of learning and curiosity. It was diffused over the whole extent of their empire; the most northern tribes of Britons had acquired a taste for rhetoric; Homer as well as Virgil were transcribed and studied on the banks of the Rhine and Danube; and the most liberal rewards sought out the faintest glimmerings of literary merit. The sciences of physic and astronomy were successfully cultivated by the Greeks; the observations of Ptolemy and the writings of Galen are studied by those who have improved their discoveries and corrected their errors; but if we except the inimitable Lucian, this age of indolence passed away without having produced a single writer of original genius, or who excelled in the arts of elegant composition. The authority of Plato and Aristotle, of Zeno and Epicurus, still reigned in the schools; and their systems, transmitted with blind deference from one generation of disciples to another, precluded every generous attempt to exercise the powers, or enlarge the limits, of the human mind. The beauties of the poets and orators, instead of kindling a fire like their own, inspired only cold and servile imitations: or if any ventured to deviate from those models, they deviated at the same time from good sense and propriety. On the revival of letters, the youthful vigour of the imagination, after a long repose, national emulation, a new religion, new languages, and a new world, called forth the genius of Europe. But the provincials of Rome, trained by a uniform artificial foreign education, were engaged in a very unequal competition with those bold ancients, who, by expressing their genuine feelings in their native tongue, had already occupied every place of honour. The name of Poet was almost forgotten; that of Orator was usurped by the sophists. A cloud of critics, of compilers, of commentators, darkened the face of learning, and the decline of genius was soon followed by the corruption of taste.

The sublime Longinus, who in somewhat a later period, and in the court of a Syrian queen, preserved the spirit of ancient Athens, observes and laments this degeneracy of his contemporaries, which debased their sentiments, enervated their courage, and depressed their talents. "In the same manner," says he, "as some children always remain pigmies, whose infant limbs have been too closely confined; thus our tender minds, fettered by the prejudices and habits of a just servitude, are unable to expand themselves, or to attain that well-proportioned greatness which we admire in the ancients; who living under a popular government, wrote with the same freedom as they acted."* This diminutive stature of mankind, if we pursue the metaphor, was daily sinking below the old standard, and the Roman world was indeed peopled by a race of pygmies; when the fierce giants of the north broke in, and mended the puny breed. They restored a manly spirit of freedom; and after the revolution of ten centuries, freedom became the happy parent of taste and science.

*Longin. de Sublim. c. 43, p. 229, edit. Toll. Here too we may say of Longinus, "his own example strengthens all his laws." Instead of proposing his sentiments with a manly boldness, he insinuates them with the most guarded caution, puts them into the mouth of a friend; and, as far as we can collect from a corrupted text, makes a show of refuting them himself. [The author of the treatise *On the Sublime* is now recognised to have been an otherwise unknown rhetor of the 1st century A.D.]

PART 2

The Progress of Christianity *(Chapter XV)*

Gibbon's chapters on the rise of Christianity are the most disputed parts of his book. His anti-Christian views, which he later defended with great eloquence in his *Vindication,* have been a subject of great controversy among historians. Few modern scholars agree with Gibbon's analysis. In these selections he discusses the progress of Christianity before its acceptance as the religion of the Empire.

CHAPTER XV

A candid but rational inquiry into the progress and establishment of Christianity may be considered as a very essential part of the history of the Roman empire.* While that great body was invaded by open violence, or undermined by slow decay, a pure and humble religion gently insinuated itself into the minds of men, grew up in silence and obscurity, derived new vigour from opposition, and finally erected the triumphant banner of the Cross on the ruins of the Capitol. Nor was the influence of Christianity confined to the period or to the limits of the Roman empire. After a revolution of thirteen or fourteen centuries, that religion is still professed by the nations of Europe, the most distinguished portion of human kind in arts and learning as well as in arms. . . .

Our curiosity is naturally prompted to inquire by what means the

*Gibbon's language in this chapter is, it must be emphasized, the language of the Enlightenment. His views on Christianity are prejudiced in the extreme. (P.W.)

Christian faith obtained so remarkable a victory over the established religions of the earth. To this inquiry an obvious but satisfactory answer may be returned; that it was owing to the convincing evidence of the doctrine itself, and to the ruling providence of its great Author. But as truth and reason seldom find so favourable a reception in the world, and as the wisdom of Providence frequently condescends to use the passions of the human heart, and the general circumstances of mankind, as instruments to execute its purpose, we may still be permitted, though with becoming submission, to ask, not indeed what were the first, but what were the secondary causes of the rapid growth of the Christian church? It will, perhaps, appear that it was most effectually favoured and assisted by the five following causes:—I. The inflexible, and, if we may use the expression, the intolerant zeal of the Christians, derived, it is true, from the Jewish religion, but purified from the narrow and unsocial spirit which, instead of inviting, had deterred the Gentiles from embracing the law of Moses. II. The doctrine of a future life, improved by every additional circumstance which could give weight and efficacy to that important truth. III. The miraculous powers ascribed to the primitive church. IV. The pure and austere morals of the Christians. V. The union and discipline of the Christian republic, which gradually formed an independent and increasing state in the heart of the Roman empire.

I. We have already described the religious harmony of the ancient world, and the facility with which the most different and even hostile nations embraced, or at least respected, each other's superstitions. A single people refused to join in the common intercourse of mankind. The Jews, who, under the Assyrian and Persian monarchies, had languished for many ages the most despised portion of their slaves, emerged from obscurity under the successors of Alexander; and as they multiplied to a surprising degree in the East, and afterwards in the West, they soon excited the curiosity and wonder of other nations. The sullen obstinacy with which they maintained their peculiar rites and unsocial manners seemed to mark them out a distinct species of men, who boldly professed, or who faintly disguised, their implacable hatred to the rest of human-kind. Neither the violence of Antiochus, nor the arts of Herod, nor the example of the circumjacent nations, could ever persuade the Jews to associate with the institutions of Moses the elegant mythology of the Greeks. According to the maxims of universal toleration, the Romans protected a superstition which they despised. The polite Augustus condescended to give orders that sacrifices should be offered for his prosperity in the temple of Jerusalem; while the meanest of the posterity of Abraham, who should have paid the same homage to the Jupiter of the Capitol, would have been an object of abhorrence to himself and to his brethren. But the moderation of the conquerors was insufficient to appease the jealous prejudices of their subjects, who were alarmed and scandalised at the ensigns of paganism, which necessarily introduced themselves into a Roman province. . . .

The Jewish religion was admirably fitted for defence, but it was never designed for conquest; and it seems probable that the number of proselytes was never much superior to that of apostates. The divine promises were originally made, and the distinguishing rite of circumcision was enjoined, to a single family. When the posterity of Abraham had multiplied like the sands of the sea, the Deity, from whose mouth they received a system of laws and ceremonies, declared himself the proper and as it were the national God of Israel; and with the most jealous care separated his favourite people from the rest of mankind. The conquest of the land of Canaan was accompanied with so many wonderful and with so many bloody circumstances, that the victorious Jews were left in a state of irreconcilable hostility with all their neighbours. They had been commanded to extirpate some of the most idolatrous tribes, and the execution of the Divine will had seldom been retarded by the weakness of humanity. With the other nations they were forbidden to contract any marriages or alliances; and the prohibition of receiving them into the congregation, which in some cases was perpetual, almost always extended to the third, to the seventh, or even to the tenth generation. The obligation of preaching to the Gentiles the faith of Moses had never been inculcated as a precept of the law, nor were the Jews inclined to impose it on themselves as a voluntary duty.

In the admission of new citizens that unsocial people was actuated by the selfish vanity of the Greeks rather than by the generous policy of Rome. The descendants of Abraham were flattered by the opinion that they alone were the heirs of the covenant, and they were apprehensive of diminishing the value of their inheritance by sharing it too easily with the strangers of the earth. A larger acquaintance with mankind extended their knowledge without correcting their prejudices; and whenever the God of Israel acquired any new votaries, he was much more indebted to the inconstant humour of polytheism than to the active zeal of his own missionaries. The religion of Moses seems to be instituted for a particular country as well as for a single nation; and if a strict obedience had been paid to the order that every male, three times in the year, should present himself before the Lord Jehovah, it would have been impossible that the Jews could ever have spread themselves beyond the narrow limits of the promised land. That obstacle was indeed removed by the destruction of the temple of Jerusalem; but the most considerable part of the Jewish religion was involved in its destruction; and the Pagans, who had long wondered at the strange report of an empty sanctuary, were at a loss to discover what could be the object, or what could be the instruments, of a worship which was destitute of temples and of altars, of priests and of sacrifices. Yet even in their fallen state, the Jews, still asserting their lofty and exclusive privileges, shunned, instead of courting, the society of strangers. They still insisted with inflexible rigour on those parts of the law which it was in their power to practise. Their peculiar distinctions of days, of meats, and a variety of trivial though burdensome observances, were so many objects of disgust and aversion for the other nations, to whose habits and prejudices they were diametrically opposite. The painful and even dangerous rite of circumcision was alone capable of repelling a willing proselyte from the door of the synagogue.

Under these circumstances, Christianity offered itself to the world, armed with the strength of the Mosaic law, and delivered from the weight of its fetters. An exclusive zeal for the truth of religion and the unity of God was as carefully inculcated in the new as in the ancient system: and whatever was now revealed to mankind concerning the nature and designs of the Supreme Being was fitted to increase their reverence for that mysterious doctrine. The divine authority of Moses and the prophets was admitted, and even established, as the firmest basis of Christianity. From the beginning of the world an uninterrupted series of predictions had announced and prepared the long-expected coming of the Messiah, who, in compliance with the gross apprehensions of the Jews, had been more frequently represented under the character of a King and Conqueror, than under that of a Prophet, a Martyr, and the Son of God. By his expiatory sacrifice the imperfect sacrifices of the temple were at once consummated and abolished. The ceremonial law, which consisted only of types and figures, was succeeded by a pure and spiritual worship, equally adapted to all climates, as well as to every condition of mankind; and to the initiation of blood, was substituted a more harmless initiation of water. The promise of divine favour, instead of being partially confined to the posterity of Abraham, was universally proposed to the freeman and the slave, to the Greek and to the barbarian, to the Jew and to the Gentile. Every privilege that could raise the proselyte from earth to heaven, that could exalt his devotion, secure his happiness, or even gratify that secret pride which, under the semblance of devotion, insinuates itself into the human heart, was still reserved for the members of the Christian church; but at the same time all mankind was permitted, and even solicited, to accept the glorious distinction, which was not only proffered as a favour, but imposed as an obligation. It became the most sacred duty of a new convert to diffuse among his friends and relations the inestimable blessing which he had received, and to warn them against a refusal that would be severely punished as a criminal disobedience to the will of a benevolent but all-powerful Deity.

The enfranchisement of the church from the bonds of the synagogue was a work, however, of some time and of some difficulty. The Jewish converts, who acknowledged Jesus in the character of the Messiah foretold by their ancient oracles, respected him as a prophetic teacher of virtue and religion; but they obstinately adhered to the ceremonies of their ancestors, and were desirous of imposing them on the Gentiles, who continually augmented the number of believers. These Judaising Christians seem to have argued with some degree of plausibility from the Divine origin of the Mosaic law, and from the immutable perfections of its great Author. They affirmed, *that,* if the Being who is the same through all eternity had designed to abolish those sacred rites which had served to distinguish his chosen people, the repeal of them would have been no less clear and solemn than their first promulgation: *that,* instead of those frequent declarations which either suppose or assert the perpetuity of the Mosaic religion, it would have been represented as a provisionary scheme intended to last only till the coming of the Messiah, who should instruct mankind in a more perfect mode of faith and of worship: *that* the Messiah himself, and his disciples who conversed with him on earth, instead of authorising by their example the most minute observances of the Mosaic law, would have published to the world the abolition of those useless and obsolete ceremonies, without suffering Christianity to remain during so many years obscurely confounded among the sects of the Jewish church. Arguments like these appear to have been used in the defence of the expiring cause of the Mosaic law; but the industry of our learned divines has abundantly explained the ambiguous language of the Old Testament, and the ambiguous conduct of the apostolic teachers. It was proper gradually to unfold the system of the Gospel, and to pronounce with the utmost caution and tenderness a sentence of condemnation so repugnant to the inclination and prejudices of the believing Jews. . . .

While the orthodox church preserved a just medium between excessive veneration and improper contempt for the law of Moses, . . . various heretics deviated into equal but opposite extremes of error and extravagance. From the acknowledged truth of the Jewish religion, the Ebionites had concluded that it could never be abolished. From its supposed imperfections, the Gnostics as hastily inferred that it never was instituted by the wisdom of the Deity. There are some objections against the authority of Moses and the prophets which too readily present themselves to the sceptical mind; though they can only be derived from our ignorance of remote antiquity, and from our incapacity to form an adequate judgment of the Divine economy. These objections were eagerly embraced and as petulantly urged by the vain science of the Gnostics. As those heretics were, for the most part, averse to the pleasures of sense, they morosely arraigned the polygamy of the patriarchs, the gallantries of David, and the seraglio of Solomon. The conquest of the land of Canaan, and the extirpation of the unsuspecting natives, they were at a loss how to reconcile with the common notions of humanity and justice. But when they recollected the sanguinary list of murders, of executions, and of massacres, which stain almost every page of the Jewish annals, they acknowledged that the barbarians of Palestine had exercised as much compassion towards their idolatrous enemies as they had ever shown to their friends or countrymen. . . . The Mosaic account of the creation and fall of man was treated with profane derision by the Gnostics, who would not listen with patience to the repose of the Deity after six days' labour, to the rib of Adam, the garden of Eden, the trees of life and of knowledge, the speaking serpent, the forbidden fruit, and the condemnation pronounced against humankind for the venial offence of their first progenitors. The God of Israel was impiously represented by the Gnostics as a being liable to passion and to error, capricious in his favour, implacable in his resentment, meanly jealous of his superstitious worship, and confining his partial providence to a single people, and to this transitory life. In such a character they could discover none of the features of the wise and omnipotent Father of the universe. They allowed that the religion of the Jews was somewhat less criminal than the idolatry of the Gentiles: but it was their fundamental doctrine that the Christ whom they adored as the first and brightest emanation of the Deity appeared upon earth to rescue mankind from their various errors, and to reveal a *new* system of truth and perfection. The most learned of the fathers, by a very singular condescension, have imprudently admitted the sophistry of the Gnostics. Acknowledging that the literal sense is repugnant to every principle of faith as well as reason, they deem themselves secure and invulnerable behind the ample veil of allegory, which they carefully spread over every tender part of the Mosaic dispensation.

It has been remarked with more ingenuity than truth that the virgin purity of the church was never violated by schism or heresy before the reign of Trajan or Hadrian, about one hundred years after the death of Christ. We may observe with much more propriety that, during that period, the disciples of the Messiah were indulged in a freer latitude both of faith and practice than has ever been allowed in succeeding ages. As the terms of communion were insensibly narrowed, and the spiritual authority of the prevailing party was exercised with increasing severity, many of its most respectable adherents, who were called upon to renounce, were provoked to assert their private opinions, to pursue the consequences of their mistaken principles, and openly to erect the standard of rebellion against the unity of the church. The Gnostics were distinguished as the most polite, the most learned, and the most wealthy of the Christian name; and that general appellation, which expressed a superiority of knowledge, was either assumed by their own pride, or ironically bestowed by the envy of their adversaries. They were almost without exception of the race of the Gentiles, and their principal founders seem to have been natives of Syria or

Egypt, where the warmth of the climate disposes both the mind and the body to indolent and contemplative devotion. The Gnostics blended with the faith of Christ many sublime but obscure tenets, which they derived from oriental philosophy, and even from the religion of Zoroaster, concerning the eternity of matter, the existence of two principles, and the mysterious hierarchy of the invisible world. As soon as they launched out into that vast abyss, they delivered themselves to the guidance of a disordered imagination; and as the paths of error are various and infinite, the Gnostics were imperceptibly divided into more than fifty particular sects, of whom the most celebrated appear to have been the Basilidians, the Valentinians, the Marcionites, and, in a still later period, the Manichæans. Each of these sects could boast of its bishops and congregations, of its doctors and martyrs; and, instead of the Four Gospels adopted by the church, the heretics produced a multitude of histories, in which the actions and discourses of Christ and of his apostles were adapted to their respective tenets. The success of the Gnostics was rapid and extensive. They covered Asia and Egypt, established themselves in Rome, and sometimes penetrated into the provinces of the West. For the most part they arose in the second century, flourished during the third, and were suppressed in the fourth or fifth, by the prevalence of more fashionable controversies, and by the superior ascendant of the reigning power. Though they constantly disturbed the peace, and frequently disgraced the name of religion, they contributed to assist rather than to retard the progress of Christianity. The Gentile converts, whose strongest objections and prejudices were directed against the law of Moses, could find admission into many Christian societies, which required not from their untutored mind any belief of an antecedent revelation. Their faith was insensibly fortified and enlarged, and the church was ultimately benefited by the conquests of its most inveterate enemies.

But whatever difference of opinion might subsist between the Orthodox, the Ebionites, and the Gnostics, concerning the divinity or the obligation of the Mosaic law, they were all equally animated by the same exclusive zeal, and by the same abhorrence for idolatry, which had distinguished the Jews from the other nations of the ancient world. . . . The Christians, who, by the interposition of evil spirits, could so readily explain every præternatural appearance, were disposed and even desirous to admit the most extravagant fictions of the Pagan mythology. But the belief of the Christian was accompanied with horror. The most trifling mark of respect to the national worship he considered as a direct homage yielded to the dæmon, and as an act of rebellion against the majesty of God.

In consequence of this opinion, it was the first but arduous duty of a Christian to preserve himself pure and undefiled by the practice of idolatry. . . . The innumerable deities and rites of polytheism were closely interwoven with every circumstance of business or pleasure, of public or of private life; and it seemed impossible to escape the observance of them, without, at the same time, renouncing the commerce of mankind, and all the offices and amusements of society. . . . The Christian, who with pious horror avoided the abomination of the circus or the theatre, found himself encompassed with infernal snares in every convivial entertainment, as often as his friends, invoking the hospitable deities, poured out libations to each other's happiness. . . . Even the common language of Greece and Rome abounded with familiar but impious expressions, which the imprudent Christian might too carelessly utter, or too patiently hear. . . .

II. The writings of Cicero* represent in the most lively colours the ignorance, the errors, and the uncertainty of the ancient philosophers with regard to the immortality of the soul. When they are desirous of arming their disciples against the fear of death, they inculcate, as an obvious though melancholy position, that the fatal stroke of our dissolution releases us from the calamities of life; and that those can no longer suffer who no longer exist. Yet there were a few sages of Greece and Rome who had conceived a more exalted, and, in some respects, a juster idea of human nature, though it must be confessed that, in the sublime inquiry, their reason had been often guided by their imagination, and that their imagination had been prompted by their vanity. When they viewed with complacency the extent of their own mental powers, when they exercised the various faculties of memory, of fancy, and of judgment, in the most profound speculations or the most important labours, and when they reflected on the desire of fame, which transported them into future ages, far beyond the bounds of death and of the grave, they were unwilling to confound themselves

*In particular, the first book of the Tusculan Questions, and the treatise De Senectute, and the Somnium Scipionis, contain, in the most beautiful language, everything that Grecian philosophy or Roman good sense could possibly suggest on this dark but important object.

with the beasts of the field, or to suppose that a being, for whose dignity they entertained the most sincere admiration, could be limited to a spot of earth, and to a few years of duration. With this favourable prepossession they summoned to their aid the science, or rather the language, of Metaphysics. They soon discovered that, as none of the properties of matter will apply to the operations of the mind, the human soul must consequently be a substance distinct from the body, pure, simple, and spiritual, incapable of dissolution, and susceptible of a much higher degree of virtue and happiness after the release from its corporeal prison. From these specious and noble principles the philosophers who trod in the footsteps of Plato deduced a very unjustifiable conclusion, since they asserted, not only the future immortality, but the past eternity of the human soul, which they were too apt to consider as a portion of the infinite and self-existing spirit which pervades and sustains the universe. A doctrine thus removed beyond the senses and the experience of mankind might serve to amuse the leisure of a philosophic mind; or, in the silence of solitude, it might sometimes impart a ray of comfort to desponding virtue; but the faint impression which had been received in the schools was soon obliterated by the commerce and business of active life. . . .

. . . The most sublime efforts of philosophy can extend no farther than feebly to point out the desire, the hope, or, at most, the probability of a future state; there is nothing, except a divine revelation that can ascertain the existence and describe the condition of the invisible country which is destined to receive the souls of men after their separation from the body. But we may perceive several defects inherent to the popular religions of Greece and Rome which rendered them very unequal to so arduous a task. 1. The general system of their mythology was unsupported by any solid proofs; and the wisest among the Pagans had already disclaimed its usurped authority. 2. The description of the infernal regions had been abandoned to the fancy of painters and of poets, who peopled them with so many phantoms and monsters who dispensed their rewards and punishments with so little equity, that a solemn truth, the most congenial to the human heart, was oppressed and disgraced by the absurd mixture of the wildest fictions. 3. The doctrine of a future state was scarcely considered among the devout polytheists of Greece and Rome as a fundamental article of faith. The providence of the gods, as it related to public communities rather than to private individuals, was principally displayed on the visible theatre of the present world. The petitions which were offered on the altars of Jupiter or Apollo expressed the anxiety of their worshippers for temporal happiness, and their ignorance or indifference concerning a future life. The important truth of the immortality of the soul was inculcated with more diligence as well as success in India, in Assyria, in Egypt, and in Gaul; and since we cannot attribute such a difference to the superior knowledge of the barbarians, we must ascribe it to the influence of an established priesthood, which employed the motives of virtue as the instrument of ambition.

We might naturally expect that a principle so essential to religion would have been revealed in the clearest terms to the chosen people of Palestine, and that it might safely have been intrusted to the hereditary priesthood of Aaron. It is incumbent on us to adore the mysterious dispensations of Providence, when we discover that the doctrine of the immortality of the soul is omitted in the law of Moses; it is darkly insinuated by the prophets; and during the long period which elapsed between the Egyptian and the Babylonian servitudes, the hopes as well as fears of the Jews appear to have been confined within the narrow compass of the present life. After Cyrus had permitted the exiled Nation to return into the promised land, and after Ezra had restored the ancient records of their religion, two celebrated sects, the Sadducees and the Pharisees, insensibly arose at Jerusalem. The former, selected from the more opulent and distinguished ranks of society, were strictly attached to the literal sense of the Mosaic law, and they piously rejected the immortality of the soul as an opinion that received no countenance from the divine book, which they revered as the only rule of their faith. To the authority of Scripture the Pharisees added that of tradition, and they accepted, under the name of traditions, several speculative tenets from the philosophy or religion of the eastern nations. The doctrines of fate or predestination, of angels and spirits, and of a future state of rewards and punishments, were in the number of these new articles of belief; and as the Pharisees, by the austerity of their manners, had drawn into their party the body of the Jewish people, the immortality of the soul became the prevailing sentiment of the synagogue under the reign of the Asmonæan princes and pontiffs. The temper of the Jews was incapable of contenting itself with such a cold and languid assent as might satisfy the mind of a Polytheist; and as soon as they admitted the idea of a future state, they embraced it with the zeal which has always formed the characteristic of the nation. Their zeal, however, added nothing to its evidence, or even probability; and it was still necessary that the doctrine of life and immortality, which had been dictated by nature, approved by reason, and received by superstition, should obtain the sanction of divine truth from the authority and example of Christ.

When the promise of eternal happiness was proposed to mankind on condition of adopting the faith, and of observing the precepts, of the Gospel, it is no wonder that so advantageous an offer should have been accepted by great numbers of every religion, of every rank, and of every province in the Roman empire. The ancient Christians were animated by a contempt for their present existence, and by a just confidence of immortality, of which the doubtful and imperfect faith of modern ages cannot give us any adequate notion. In the primitive church the influence of truth was very powerfully strengthened by an opinion which, however it may deserve respect for its usefulness and antiquity, has not been found agreeable to experience. It was universally believed that the end of the world, and the kingdom of heaven, were at hand. The near approach of this wonderful event had been predicted by the apostles; the tradition of it was preserved by their earliest disciples, and those who understood in their literal sense the discourses of Christ himself were obliged to expect the second and glorious coming of the Son of Man in the clouds, before that generation was totally extinguished which had beheld his humble condition upon earth, and which might still be witness of the calamities of the Jews under Vespasian or Hadrian. The revolution of seventeen centuries has instructed us not to press too closely the mysterious language of prophecy and revelation; but as long as, for wise purposes, this error was permitted to subsist in the church, it was productive of the most salutary effects on the faith and practice of Christians, who lived in the awful expectation of that moment when the globe itself, and all the various race of mankind, should tremble at the appearance of their divine Judge.*

*This expectation was countenanced by the twenty-fourth chapter of St. Matthew, and by the first epistle of St. Paul to the Thessalonians. Erasmus removes the difficulty by the help of allegory and metaphor; and the learned Grotius ventures to insinuate, that, for wise purposes, the pious deception was permitted to take place.

The ancient and popular doctrine of the Millennium was intimately connected with the second coming of Christ. As the works of the creation had been finished in six days, their duration in their present state, according to a tradition which was attributed to the prophet Elijah, was fixed to six thousand years. By the same analogy it was inferred that this long period of labour and contention, which was now almost elapsed, would be succeeded by a joyful Sabbath of a thousand years; and that Christ, with the triumphant band of the saints and the elect who had escaped death, or who had been miraculously revived, would reign upon earth till the time appointed for the last and general resurrection. So pleasing was this hope to the mind of believers, that the *New Jerusalem,* the seat of this blissful kingdom, was quickly adorned with all the gayest colours of the imagination. . . . The assurance of such a Millennium was carefully inculcated by a succession of fathers from Justin Martyr and Irenæus, who conversed with the immediate disciples of the apostles, down to Lactantius, who was preceptor to the son of Constantine. Though it might not be universally received, it appears to have been the reigning sentiment of the orthodox believers; and it seems so well adapted to the desires and apprehensions of mankind, that it must have contributed in a very considerable degree to the progress of the Christian faith. But when the edifice of the church was almost completed, the temporary support was laid aside. The doctrine of Christ's reign upon earth was at first treated as a profound allegory, was considered by degrees as a doubtful and useless opinion, and was at length rejected as the absurd invention of heresy and fanaticism. A mysterious prophecy, which still forms a part of the sacred canon, but which was thought to favour the exploded sentiment, has very narrowly escaped the proscription of the church.*

Whilst the happiness and glory of a temporal reign were promised to the disciples of Christ, the most dreadful calamities were denounced

*In the council of Laodicea (about the year 360) the Apocalypse was tacitly excluded from the sacred canon by the same churches of Asia to which it is addressed; and we may learn from the complaint of Sulpicius Severus that their sentence had been ratified by the greater number of Christians of his time. From what causes then is the Apocalypse at present so generally received by the Greek, the Roman, and the Protestant churches? The following ones may be assigned:—1. The Greeks were subdued by the authority of an impostor, who, in the sixth century, assumed the character of Dionysius the Areopagite. 2. A just apprehension that the grammarians might become more important than the theologians engaged the council of Trent to fix the seal of their infallibility on all the books of Scripture contained in the Latin Vulgate, in the number of which the Apocalypse was fortunately included (Fr. Paolo, Istoria del Concilio Tridentino, 1. ii.). 3. The advantage of turning those mysterious prophecies against the See of Rome inspired the Protestants with uncommon veneration for so useful an ally. See the ingenious and elegant discourses of the present bishop of Lichfield on that unpromising subject. . . .

against an unbelieving world. The edification of the new Jerusalem was to advance by equal steps with the destruction of the mystic Babylon; and as long as the emperors who reigned before Constantine persisted in the profession of idolatry, the epithet of Babylon was applied to the city and to the empire of Rome. A regular series was prepared of all the moral and physical evils which can afflict a flourishing nation; intestine discord, and the invasion of the fiercest barbarians from the unknown regions of the North; pestilence and famine, comets and eclipses, earthquakes and inundations. All these were only so many preparatory and alarming signs of the great catastrophe of Rome, when the country of the Scipios and Cæsars should be consumed by a flame from Heaven, and the city of the seven hills, with her palaces, her temples, and her triumphal arches, should be buried in a vast lake of fire and brimstone. It might, however, afford some consolation to Roman vanity, that the period of their empire would be that of the world itself; which, as it had once perished by the element of water, was destined to experience a second and a speedy destruction from the element of fire. In the opinion of a general conflagration the faith of the Christian very happily coincided with the tradition of the East, the philosophy of the Stoics, and the analogy of Nature; and even the country which, from religious motives, had been chosen for the origin and principal scene of the conflagration, was the best adapted for that purpose by natural and physical causes—by its deep caverns, beds of sulphur, and numerous volcanoes, of which those of Ætna, of Vesuvius, and of Lipari exhibit a very imperfect representation. The calmest and most intrepid sceptic could not refuse to acknowledge that the destruction of the present system of the world by fire was in itself extremely probable. The Christian, who founded his belief much less on the fallacious arguments of reason than on the authority of tradition and the interpretation of Scripture, expected it with terror and confidence as a certain and approaching event; and as his mind was perpetually filled with the solemn idea, he considered every disaster that happened to the empire as an infallible symptom of an expiring world.

III. The supernatural gifts, which even in this life were ascribed to the Christians above the rest of mankind, must have conduced to their own comfort, and very frequently to the conviction of infidels. Besides the occasional prodigies, which might sometimes be effected by the immediate interposition of the Deity when he suspended the laws of Nature for the service of religion, the Christian church, from the time of the apostles and their first disciples,* has claimed an uninterrupted succession of miraculous powers, the gift of tongues, of vision, and of prophecy, the power of expelling dæmons, of healing the sick, and of raising the dead. The knowledge of foreign languages was frequently communicated to the contemporaries of Irenæus, though Irenæus himself was left to struggle with the difficulties of a barbarous dialect whilst he preached the Gospel to the natives of Gaul. The divine inspiration, whether it was conveyed in the form of a waking or of a sleeping vision, is described as a favour very liberally bestowed on all ranks of the faithful, on women as on elders, on boys as well as upon bishops. When their devout minds were sufficiently prepared by a course of prayer, of fasting, and of vigils, to receive the extraordinary impulse, they were transported out of their senses, and delivered in ecstasy what was inspired, being mere organs of the Holy Spirit, just as a pipe or flute is of him who blows into it. We may add that the design of these visions was, for the most part, either to disclose the future history, or to guide the present administration, of the church. . . .

. . . The most curious, or the most credulous, among the Pagans were often persuaded to enter into a society which asserted an actual claim of miraculous powers. The primitive Christians perpetually trod on mystic ground, and their minds were exercised by the habits of believing the most extraordinary events. They felt, or they fancied, that on every side they were incessantly assaulted by dæmons, comforted by visions, instructed by prophecy, and surprisingly delivered from danger, sickness, and from death itself, by the supplications of the church. The real or imaginary prodigies, of which they so frequently conceived themselves to be the objects, the instruments, or the spectators, very happily disposed them to adopt with the same ease, but with far greater justice, the authentic wonders of the evangelic history; and thus miracles that exceeded not the measure of their own experience inspired them with the most lively assurance of mysteries which were acknowledged to surpass the limits of their understanding. It is

*Notwithstanding the evasions of Dr. Middleton, it is impossible to overlook the clear traces of visions and inspiration which may be found in the apostolic fathers. (Gibbon's note) See Introduction. (P.W.)

this deep impression of supernatural truths which has been so much celebrated under the name of faith; a state of mind described as the surest pledge of the Divine favour and of future felicity, and recommended as the first or perhaps the only merit of a Christian. According to the more rigid doctors, the moral virtues, which may be equally practised by infidels, are destitute of any value or efficacy in the work of our justification.

IV. But the primitive Christian demonstrated his faith by his virtues; and it was very justly supposed that the Divine persuasion, which enlightened or subdued the understanding, must at the same time purify the heart and direct the actions of the believer. The first apologists of Christianity who justify the innocence of their brethren, and the writers of a later period who celebrate the sanctity of their ancestors, display, in the most lively colours, the reformation of manners which was introduced into the world by the preaching of the Gospel. As it is my intention to remark only such human causes as were permitted to second the influence of revelation, I shall slightly mention two motives which might naturally render the lives of the primitive Christians much purer and more austere than those of their Pagan contemporaries or their degenerate successors—repentance for their past sins, and the laudable desire of supporting the reputation of the society in which they were engaged. . . .

. . . . The friends of Christianity may acknowledge without a blush that many of the most eminent saints had been before their baptism the most abandoned sinners. Those persons who in the world had followed, though in an imperfect manner, the dictates of benevolence and propriety, derived such a calm satisfaction from the opinion of their own rectitude as rendered them much less susceptible of the sudden emotions of shame, of grief, and of terror, which have given birth to so many wonderful conversions. After the example of their Divine Master, the missionaries of the Gospel disdained not the society of men, and especially of women, oppressed by the consciousness, and very often by the effects, of their vices. As they emerged from sin and superstition to the glorious hope of immortality, they resolved to devote themselves to a life, not only of virtue, but of penitence. The desire of perfection became the ruling passion of their soul; and it is well known that, while reason embraces a cold mediocrity, our passions hurry us with rapid violence over the space which lies between the most opposite extremes.

When the new converts had been enrolled in the number of the faithful, and were admitted to the sacraments of the church, they found themselves restrained from relapsing into their past disorders by another consideration of a less spiritual but of a very innocent and respectable nature. Any particular society that has departed from the great body of the nation, or the religion to which it belonged, immediately becomes the object of universal as well as invidious observation. In proportion to the smallness of its numbers, the character of the society may be affected by the virtue and vices of the persons who compose it; and every member is engaged to watch with the most vigilant attention over his own behaviour, and over that of his brethren, since, as he must expect to incur a part of the common disgrace, he may hope to enjoy a share of the common reputation. When the Christians of Bithynia were brought before the tribunal of the younger Pliny, they assured the proconsul that, far from being engaged in any unlawful conspiracy, they were bound by a solemn obligation to abstain from the commission of those crimes which disturb the private or public peace of society, from theft, robbery, adultery, perjury, and fraud. Near a century afterwards, Tertullian with an honest pride could boast that very few Christians had suffered by the hand of the executioner, except on account of their religion.* Their serious and sequestered life, averse to the gay luxury of the age, inured them to chastity, temperance, economy, and all the sober and domestic virtues. As the greater number were of some trade or profession, it was incumbent on them, by the strictest integrity and the fairest dealing, to remove the suspicions which the profane are too apt to conceive against the appearances of sanctity. The contempt of the world exercised them in the habits of humility, meekness, and patience. The more they were persecuted, the more closely they adhered to each other. Their mutual charity and unsuspecting confidence has been remarked by infidels, and was too often abused by perfidious friends.

It is a very honourable circumstance for the morals of the primitive Christians, that even their faults, or rather errors, were derived from an excess of virtue. The bishops and doctors of the church, whose evidence attests, and whose authority might influence, the professions, the principles, and even the practice of their contemporaries, had studied the Scriptures with less skill than devotion; and they often

*. . . He adds, however, with some degree of hesitation, "Aut si [et] aliud, jam non Christianus."

received in the most literal sense those rigid precepts of Christ and the apostles to which the prudence of succeeding commentators has applied a looser and more figurative mode of interpretation. Ambitious to exalt the perfection of the Gospel above the wisdom of philosophy, the zealous fathers have carried the duties of self-mortification, of purity, and of patience, to a height which it is scarcely possible to attain, and much less to preserve, in our present state of weakness and corruption. A doctrine so extraordinary and so sublime must inevitably command the veneration of the people; but it was ill calculated to obtain the suffrage of those worldly philosophers who, in the conduct of this transitory life, consult only the feelings of nature and the interest of society. . . .

The acquisition of knowledge, the exercise of our reason or fancy, and the cheerful flow of unguarded conversation, may employ the leisure of a liberal mind. Such amusements, however, were rejected with abhorrence, or admitted with the utmost caution, by the severity of the fathers, who despised all knowledge that was not useful to salvation, and who considered all levity of discourse as a criminal abuse of the gift of speech. . . . Gay apparel, magnificent houses, and elegant furniture were supposed to unite the double guilt of pride and of sensuality: a simple and mortified appearance was more suitable to the Christian who was certain of his sins and doubtful of his salvation. In their censures of luxury the fathers are extremely minute and circumstantial . . . When Christianity was introduced among the rich and the polite, the observation of these singular laws was left, as it would be at present, to the few who were ambitious of superior sanctity. But it is always easy, as well as agreeable, for the inferior ranks of mankind to claim a merit from the contempt of that pomp and pleasure which fortune has placed beyond their reach. The virtue of the primitive Christians, like that of the first Romans, was very frequently guarded by poverty and ignorance. . . .

The Christians were not less averse to the business than to the pleasures of this world. The defence of our persons and property they knew not how to reconcile with the patient doctrine which enjoined an unlimited forgiveness of past injuries, and commanded them to invite the repetition of fresh insults. Their simplicity was offended by the use of oaths, by the pomp of magistracy, and by the active contention of public life; nor could their humane ignorance be convinced that it was lawful on any occasion to shed the blood of our fellow-creatures, either by the sword of justice or by that of war, even though their criminal or hostile attempts should threaten the peace and safety of the whole community. It was acknowledged that, under a less perfect law, the powers of the Jewish constitution had been exercised, with the approbation of Heaven, by inspired prophets and by anointed kings. The Christians felt and confessed that such institutions might be necessary for the present system of the world, and they cheerfully submitted to the authority of their Pagan governors. But while they inculcated the maxims of passive obedience, they refused to take any active part in the civil administration or the military defence of the empire. Some indulgence might perhaps be allowed to those persons who, before their conversion, were already engaged in such violent and sanguinary occupations; but it was impossible that the Christians, without renouncing a more sacred duty, could assume the character of soldiers, of magistrates, or of princes. This indolent, or even criminal disregard to the public welfare, exposed them to the contempt and reproaches of the Pagans, who very frequently asked, what must be the fate of the empire, attacked on every side by the barbarians, if all mankind should adopt the pusillanimous sentiments of the new sect? To this insulting question the Christian apologists returned obscure and ambiguous answers, as they were unwilling to reveal the secret cause of their security; the expectation that, before the conversion of mankind was accomplished, war, government, the Roman empire, and the world itself, would be no more. It may be observed that, in this instance likewise, the situation of the first Christians coincided very happily with their religious scruples, and that their aversion to an active life contributed rather to excuse them from the service than to exclude them from the honours of the state and army.

V. But the human character, however it may be exalted or depressed by a temporary enthusiasm, will return by degrees to its proper and natural level, and will resume those passions that seem the most adapted to its present condition. The primitive Christians were dead to the business and pleasures of the world; but their love of action, which could never be entirely extinguished, soon revived, and found a new occupation in the government of the church. A separate society, which attacked the established religion of the empire, was obliged to adopt some form of internal policy, and to appoint a sufficient number of ministers, intrusted not only with the spiritual functions, but even with the temporal direction of the Christian commonwealth. The safety of the society, its honour, its aggrandisement, were productive, even in the most pious minds, of a spirit of patriotism, such as the first of the Romans had felt for the republic, and sometimes of a similar indifference in the use of whatever means might probably conduce to so desirable an end. The ambition of raising themselves or their friends to the honours and offices of the church was disguised by the laudable intention of devoting to the public benefit the power and consideration which, for that purpose only, it became their duty to solicit. In the exercise of their functions they were frequently called upon to detect the errors of heresy or the arts of faction, to oppose the designs of perfidious brethren, to stigmatise their characters with deserved infamy, and to expel them from the bosom of a society whose peace and happiness they had attempted to disturb. The ecclesiastical governors of the Christians were taught to unite the wisdom of the serpent with the innocence of the dove; but as the former was refined, so the latter was insensibly corrupted, by the habits of government. In the church as well as in the world, the persons who were placed in any public station rendered themselves considerable by their eloquence and firmness, by their knowledge of mankind, and by their dexterity in business; and while they concealed from others, and perhaps from themselves, the secret motives of their conduct, they too frequently relapsed into all the turbulent passions of active life, which were tinctured with an additional degree of bitterness and obstinacy from the infusion of spiritual zeal.

The government of the church has often been the subject, as well as the prize, of religious contention. The hostile disputants of Rome, of Paris, of Oxford, and of Geneva, have alike struggled to reduce the primitive and apostolic model* to the respective standards of their own policy. The few who have pursued this inquiry with more candour and impartiality are of opinion that the apostles declined the office of legislation, and rather chose to endure some partial scandals and divisions, than to exclude the Christians of a future age from the liberty of varying their forms of ecclesiastical government according

*The aristocratical party in France, as well as in England, has strenuously maintained the divine origin of bishops. But the Calvinistical presbyters were impatient of a superior; and the Roman Pontiff refused to acknowledge an equal. . . .

to the changes of times and circumstances. The scheme of policy which, under their approbation, was adopted for the use of the first century, may be discovered from the practice of Jerusalem, of Ephesus, or of Corinth. The societies which were instituted in the cities of the Roman empire were united only by the ties of faith and charity. Independence and equality formed the basis of their internal constitution. The want of discipline and human learning was supplied by the occasional assistance of the *prophets,* who were called to that function without distinction of age, of sex, or of natural abilities, and who, as often as they felt the divine impulse, poured forth the effusions of the Spirit in the assembly of the faithful. But these extraordinary gifts were frequently abused or misapplied by the prophetic teachers. They displayed them at an improper season, presumptuously disturbed the service of the assembly, and by their pride or mistaken zeal they introduced, particularly into the apostolic church of Corinth, a long and melancholy train of disorders. As the institution of prophets became useless, and even pernicious, their powers were withdrawn, and their office abolished.

The public functions of religion were solely intrusted to the established ministers of the church, the *bishops* and the *presbyters;* two appellations which, in their first origin, appear to have distinguished the same office and the same order of persons. The name of Presbyter was expressive of their age, or rather of their gravity and wisdom. The title of Bishop denoted their inspection over the faith and manners of the Christians who were committed to their pastoral care. In proportion to the respective numbers of the faithful, a larger or smaller number of these *episcopal presbyters* guided each infant congregation with equal authority and with united counsels.

But the most perfect equality of freedom requires the directing hand of a superior magistrate: and the order of public deliberations soon introduces the office of a president, invested at least with the authority of collecting the sentiments, and of executing the resolutions, of the assembly. A regard for the public tranquillity, which would so frequently have been interrupted by annual or by occasional elections, induced the primitive Christians to constitute an honourable and perpetual magistracy, and to choose one of the wisest and most holy among their presbyters to execute, during his life, the duties of their ecclesiastical governor. It was under these circumstances that the lofty title of Bishop began to raise itself above the humble appellation of Presbyter; and while the latter remained the most natural distinction for the members of every Christian senate, the former was appropriated to the dignity of its new president. The advantages of this episcopal form of government, which appears to have been introduced before the end of the first century, were so obvious, and so important for the future greatness, as well as the present peace, of Christianity, that it was adopted without delay by all the societies which were already scattered over the empire, had acquired in a very early period the sanction of antiquity, and is still revered by the most powerful churches, both of the East and of the West, as a primitive and even as a divine establishment. . . .

Such was the . . . constitution by which the Christians were governed more than an hundred years after the death of the apostles. Every society formed within itself a separate and independent republic; and although the most distant of these little states maintained a mutual as well as friendly intercourse of letters and deputations, the Christian world was not yet connected by any supreme authority or legislative assembly. As the numbers of the faithful were gradually multiplied, they discovered the advantages that might result from a closer union of their interest and designs. Towards the end of the second century, the churches of Greece and Asia adopted the useful institutions of provincial synods, and they may justly be supposed to have borrowed the model of a representative council from the celebrated examples of their own country, the Amphictyons, the Achæan league, or the assemblies of the Ionian cities. It was soon established as a custom and as a law, that the bishops of the independent churches should meet in the capital of the province at the stated periods of spring and autumn. Their deliberations were assisted by the advice of a few distinguished presbysters, and moderated by the presence of a listening multitude. Their decrees, which were styled Canons, regulated every important controversy of faith and discipline; and it was natural to believe that a liberal effusion of the Holy Spirit would be poured on the united assembly of the delegates of the Christian people. The institution of synods was so well suited to private ambition and to public interest, that in the space of a few years it was received throughout the whole empire. A regular correspondence was established between the provincial councils, which mutually communicated and approved their respective proceedings; and the catholic church soon assumed the form, and acquired the strength, of a great fœderative republic.

As the legislative authority of the particular churches was insensibly superseded by the use of councils, the bishops obtained by their alliance a much larger share of executive and arbitrary power; and as soon as they were connected by a sense of their common interest, they were enabled to attack, with united vigour, the original rights of their clergy and people. The prelates of the third century imperceptibly changed the language of exhortation into that of command, scattered the seeds of future usurpations, and supplied, by Scripture allegories and declamatory rhetoric, their deficiency of force and of reason. They exalted the unity and power of the church, as it was represented in the EPISCOPAL OFFICE, of which every bishop enjoyed an equal and undivided portion. Princes and magistrates, it was often repeated, might boast an earthly claim to a transitory dominion: it was the episcopal authority alone which was derived from the Deity, and extended itself over this and over another world. The bishops were the vicegerents of Christ, the successors of the apostles, and the mystic substitutes of the high priest of the Mosaic law. Their exclusive privilege of conferring the sacerdotal character invaded the freedom both of clerical and of popular elections: and if, in the administration of the church, they still consulted the judgment of the presbyters or the inclination of the people, they most carefully inculcated the merit of such a voluntary condescension. The bishops acknowledged the supreme authority which resided in the assembly of their brethren; but in the government of his peculiar diocese each of them exacted from his *flock* the same implicit obedience as if that favourite metaphor had been literally just, and as if the shepherd had been of a more exalted nature than that of his sheep. . . .

The same causes which at first had destroyed the equality of the presbyters introduced among the bishops a pre-eminence of rank, and from thence a superiority of jurisdiction. As often as in the spring and autumn they met in provincial synod, the difference of personal merit and reputation was very sensibly felt among the members of the assembly, and the multitude was governed by the wisdom and eloquence of the few. But the order of public proceedings required a more regular and less invidious distinction; the office of perpetual presidents in the councils of each province was conferred on the bishops of the principal city; and these aspiring prelates, who soon acquired the lofty titles of Metropolitans and Primates, secretly prepared themselves to usurp over their episcopal brethren the same authority which the bishops had so lately assumed above the college of presbyters. Nor was it long before an emulation of pre-eminence and power prevailed among the Metropolitans themselves, each of them affecting to display, in the most pompous terms, the temporal honours and advantages of the city over which he presided; the numbers and opulence of the Christians who were subject to their pastoral care; the saints and martyrs who had arisen among them; and the purity with which they preserved the tradition of the faith as it had been transmitted through a series of orthodox bishops from the apostle or the apostolic disciple to whom the foundation of their church was ascribed. From every cause, either of a civil or of an ecclesiastical nature, it was easy to foresee that Rome must enjoy the respect, and would soon claim the obedience, of the provinces. The society of the faithful bore a just proportion to the capital of the empire; and the Roman church was the greatest, the most numerous, and, in regard to the West, the most ancient of all the Christian establishments, many of which had received their religion from the pious labours of her missionaries. Instead of *one* apostolic founder, the utmost boast of Antioch, of Ephesus, or of Corinth, the banks of the Tiber were supposed to have been honoured with the preaching and martyrdom of the *two* most eminent among the apostles; and the bishops of Rome very prudently claimed the inheritance of whatsoever prerogatives were attributed either to the person or to the office of St. Peter.* The bishops of Italy and of the provinces were disposed to allow them a primacy of order and association (such was their very accurate expression) in the Christian aristocracy. But the power of a monarch was rejected with abhorrence, and the aspiring genius of Rome experienced from the nations of Asia and Africa a more vigorous resistance to her spiritual than she had formerly done to her temporal dominion. The patriotic Cyprian, who ruled with the most absolute sway the church of Carthage and the provincial synods, opposed with

*It is in French only that the famous allusion to St. Peter's name is exact. Tu es *Pierre,* et sur cette *pierre.*—The same is imperfect in Greek, Latin, Italian, etc., and totally unintelligible in our Teutonic languages.

resolution and success the ambition of the Roman pontiff, artfully connected his own cause with that of the eastern bishops, and, like Hannibal, sought out new allies in the heart of Asia. If this Punic war was carried on without any effusion of blood, it was owing much less to the moderation than to the weakness of the contending prelates. Invectives and excommunications were *their* only weapons; and these, during the progress of the whole controversy, they hurled against each other with equal fury and devotion. The hard necessity of censuring either a pope or a saint and martyr distresses the modern Catholics whenever they are obliged to relate the particulars of a dispute in which the champions of religion indulged such passions as seem much more adapted to the senate or to the camp.

The progress of the ecclesiastical authority gave birth to the memorable distinction of the laity and of the clergy, which had been unknown to the Greeks and Romans. The former of these appellations comprehended the body of the Christian people; the latter, according to the signification of the word, was appropriated to the chosen portion that had been set apart for the service of religion; a celebrated order of men which has furnished the most important, though not always the most edifying, subjects for modern history. Their mutual hostilities sometimes disturbed the peace of the infant church, but their zeal and activity were united in the common cause, and the love of power, which (under the most artful disguises) could insinuate itself into the breasts of bishops and martyrs, animated them to increase the number of their subjects, and to enlarge the limits of the Christian empire. They were destitute of any temporal force, and they were for a long time discouraged and oppressed, rather than assisted, by the civil magistrate; but they had acquired, and they employed within their own society, the two most efficacious instruments of government, rewards and punishments; the former derived from the pious liberality, the latter from the devout apprehensions, of the faithful. . . .

The well-tempered mixture of liberality and rigour, the judicious dispensation of rewards and punishments, according to the maxims of policy as well as justice, constituted the *human* strength of the church.* The bishops, whose paternal care extended itself to the government of both worlds, were sensible of the importance of these prerogatives;

*This section is prefaced by a long elaboration of the Church's acquisition of great wealth, which, Gibbon emphasizes, was totally under the control of the bishops. (P.W.)

and, covering their ambition with the fair pretence of the love of order, they were jealous of any rival in the exercise of a discipline so necessary to prevent the desertion of those troops which had enlisted themselves under the banner of the Cross, and whose numbers every day became more considerable. From the imperious declamations of Cyprian we should naturally conclude that the doctrines of excommunication and penance formed the most essential part of religion; and that it was much less dangerous for the disciples of Christ to neglect the observance of the moral duties than to despise the censures and authority of their bishops. Sometimes we might imagine that we were listening to the voice of Moses, when he commanded the earth to open, and to swallow up, in consuming flames, the rebellious race which refused obedience to the priesthood of Aaron; and we should sometimes suppose that we heard a Roman consul asserting the majesty of the republic, and declaring his inflexible resolution to enforce the rigour of the laws. "If such irregularities are suffered with impunity" (it is thus that the bishop of Carthage chides the lenity of his colleague), "if such irregularities are suffered, there is an end of EPISCOPAL VIGOUR; an end of the sublime and divine power of governing the Church; an end of Christianity itself." Cyprian had renounced those temporal honours which it is probable he would never have obtained; but the acquisition of such absolute command over the consciences and understanding of a congregation, however obscure or despised by the world, is more truly grateful to the pride of the human heart than the possession of the most despotic power imposed by arms and conquest on a reluctant people. . . .

It has been observed, with truth as well as propriety, that the conquests of Rome prepared and facilitated those of Christianity. In the second chapter of this work we have attempted to explain in what manner the most civilised provinces of Europe, Asia, and Africa were united under the dominion of one sovereign, and gradually connected by the most intimate ties of laws, of manners, and of language. The Jews of Palestine, who had fondly expected a temporal deliverer, gave so cold a reception to the miracles of the divine prophet, that it was found unnecessary to publish, or at least to preserve, any Hebrew gospel. The authentic histories of the actions of Christ were composed in the Greek language, at a considerable distance from Jerusalem, and after the Gentile converts were grown extremely numerous. As soon as those histories were translated into the Latin tongue they were perfectly intelligible to all the subjects of Rome, excepting only to the peasants of Syria and Egypt, for whose benefit particular versions were afterwards made. The public highways, which had been constructed for the use of the legions, opened an easy passage for the Christian missionaries from Damascus to Corinth, and from Italy to the extremity of Spain or Britain; nor did those spiritual conquerors encounter any of the obstacles which usually retard or prevent the introduction of a foreign religion into a distant country. There is the strongest reason to believe that before the reigns of Diocletian and Constantine the faith of Christ had been preached in every province, and in all the great cities of the empire; but the foundation of the several congregations, the numbers of the faithful who composed them, and their proportion to the unbelieving multitude, are now buried in obscurity or disguised by fiction and declamation. Such imperfect circumstances, however, as have reached our knowledge concerning the increase of the Christian name in Asia and Greece, in Egypt, in Italy, and in the West, we shall now proceed to relate, without neglecting the real or imaginary acquisitions which lay beyond the frontiers of the Roman empire.

The rich provinces that extend from the Euphrates to the Ionian sea were the principal theatre on which the apostle of the Gentiles displayed his zeal and piety. The seeds of the Gospel, which he had scattered in a fertile soil, were diligently cultivated by his disciples; and it should seem that, during the two first centuries, the most considerable body of Christians was contained within those limits. Among the societies which were instituted in Syria, none were more ancient or more illustrious than those of Damascus, of Berœa or Aleppo, and of Antioch. The prophetic introduction of the Apocalypse has described and immortalised the seven churches of Asia—Ephesus, Smyrna, Pergamus, Thyatira, Sardes, Laodicea, and Philadelphia; and their colonies were soon diffused over that populous country. In a very early period, the islands of Cyprus and Crete, the provinces of Thrace and Macedonia, gave a favourable reception to the new religion; and Christian republics were soon founded in the cities of Corinth, of Sparta, and of Athens. The antiquity of the Greek and Asiatic churches allowed a sufficient space of time for their increase and multiplication; and even the swarms of Gnostics and other heretics serve to display the flourishing condition of the orthodox church, since the appellation of heretics has always been applied to the less numerous party. To these domestic testimonies we may add the confession, the complaints, and the apprehensions of the Gentiles themselves. From the writings of Lucian, a philosopher who had studied mankind, and who describes their manners in the most lively colours, we may learn that, under the reign of Commodus, his native country of Pontus was filled with Epicureans and *Christians.* Within fourscore years after the death of Christ, the humane Pliny laments the magnitude of the evil which he vainly attempted to eradicate. In his very curious epistle to the emperor Trajan he affirms that the temples were almost deserted, that the sacred victims scarcely found any purchasers, and that the superstition had not only infected the cities, but had even spread itself into the villages and the open country of Pontus and Bithynia.

Without descending into a minute scrutiny of the expressions or of the motives of those writers who either celebrate or lament the progress of Christianity in the East, it may in general be observed that none of them have left us any grounds from whence a just estimate might be formed of the real numbers of the faithful in those provinces. One circumstance, however, has been fortunately preserved, which seems to cast a more distinct light on this obscure but interesting subject. Under the reign of Theodosius, after Christianity had enjoyed, during more than sixty years, the sunshine of Imperial favour, the ancient and illustrious church of Antioch consisted of one hundred thousand persons, three thousand of whom were supported out of the public oblations. The splendour and dignity of the queen of the East, the acknowledged populousness of Cæsarea, Seleucia, and Alexandria, and the destruction of two hundred and fifty thousand souls in the earthquake which afflicted Antioch under the elder Justin, are so many convincing proofs that the whole number of its inhabitants was not less than half a million, and that the Christians, however multiplied by zeal and power, did not exceed a fifth part of that great city. How different a proportion must we adopt when we compare the persecuted with the triumphant church, the West with the East, remote villages with populous towns, and countries recently converted to the faith with the place where the believers first received the appellation of Christians! It must not, however, be dissembled that, in another passage, Chrysostom, to whom we are indebted for this useful information, computes the multitude of the faithful as even superior to that of the Jews and Pagans. But the solution of this apparent difficulty is easy and obvious. The eloquent preacher draws a parallel between the civil and the ecclesiastical constitution of Antioch; between the list of Christians who had acquired heaven by baptism, and the list of citizens who had a right to share the public liberality. Slaves, strangers, and infants were comprised in the former; they were excluded from the latter.

The extensive commerce of Alexandria, and its proximity to Palestine, gave an easy entrance to the new religion. It was at first embraced by great numbers of the Therapeutæ, or Essenians, of the lake Mareotis, a Jewish sect which had abated much of its reverence for the Mosaic ceremonies. The austere life of the Essenians, their fasts and excommunications, the community of goods, the love of celibacy, their zeal for martyrdom, and the warmth though not the purity of their faith, already offered a very lively image of the primitive discipline. It was in the school of Alexandria that the Christian theology appears to have assumed a regular and scientifical form; and when Hadrian visited Egypt, he found a church composed of Jews and of Greeks, sufficiently important to attract the notice of that inquisitive prince. But the progress of Christianity was for a long time confined within the limits of a single city, which was itself a foreign colony, and till the close of the second century the predecessors of Demetrius were the only prelates of the Egyptian church. Three bishops were consecrated by the hands of Demetrius, and the number was increased to twenty by his successor Heraclas. The body of the natives, a people distinguished by a sullen inflexibility of temper, entertained the new doctrine with coldness and reluctance; and even in the time of Origen it was rare to meet with an Egyptian who had surmounted his early prejudices in favour of the sacred animals of his country. As soon, indeed, as Christianity ascended the throne, the zeal of those barbarians obeyed the prevailing impulsion; the cities of Egypt were filled with bishops, and the deserts of Thebais swarmed with hermits.

A perpetual stream of strangers and provincials flowed into the capacious bosom of Rome. Whatever was strange or odious, whoever was guilty or suspected, might hope, in the obscurity of that immense capital, to elude the vigilance of the law. In such a various conflux of nations, every teacher, either of truth or of falsehood, every founder, whether of a virtuous or a criminal association, might easily multiply his disciples or accomplices. The Christians of Rome, at the time of the accidental persecution of Nero, are represented by Tacitus as already amounting to a very great multitude, and the language of that great historian is almost similar to the style employed by Livy, when he relates the introduction and the suppression of the rites of Bacchus. After the Bacchanals had awakened the severity of the senate, it was likewise apprehended that a very great multitude, as it were *another people,* had been initiated into those abhorred mysteries. A more careful inquiry soon demonstrated that the offenders did not exceed seven thousand; a number indeed sufficiently alarming when considered as the object of public justice. It is with the same candid allowance that we should interpret the vague expressions of Tacitus, and in a former instance of Pliny, when they exaggerate the crowds of deluded fanatics who had forsaken the established worship of the gods. The church of Rome was undoubtedly the first and most populous of the empire; and we are possessed of an authentic record which attests the state of religion in that city about the middle of the third century, and after a peace of thirty-eight years. The clergy, at that time, consisted of a bishop, forty-six presbyters, seven deacons, as many sub-deacons, forty-two acolythes, and fifty readers, exorcists, and porters. The number of widows, of the infirm, and of the poor, who were maintained by the oblations of the faithful, amounted to fifteen hundred. From reason, as well as from the analogy of Antioch, we may venture to estimate the Christians of Rome at about fifty thousand. The populousness of that great capital cannot perhaps be exactly ascertained; but the most modest calculation will not surely reduce it lower than a million of inhabitants, of whom the Christians might constitute at the most a twentieth part.

The western provincials appeared to have derived the knowledge of Christianity from the same source which had diffused among them the language, the sentiments, and the manners of Rome. In this more important circumstance, Africa, as well as Gaul, was gradually fashioned to the imitation of the capital. Yet notwithstanding the many favourable occasions which might invite the Roman missionaries to visit their Latin provinces, it was late before they passed either the sea or the Alps; nor can we discover in those great countries any assured traces either of faith or of persecution that ascend higher than the reign of the Antonines. The slow progress of the Gospel in the cold climate of Gaul was extremely different from the eagerness with which it seems to have been received on the burning sands of Africa. The African Christians soon formed one of the principal members of the primitive church. The practice introduced into that province of appointing bishops to the most inconsiderable towns, and very frequently to the most obscure villages, contributed to multiply the splendour and importance of their religious societies, which during the course of the third century were animated by the zeal of Tertullian, directed by the abilities of Cyprian, and adorned by the eloquence of Lactantius. But if, on the contrary, we turn our eyes toward Gaul, we must content ourselves with discovering, in the time of Marcus Antoninus, the feeble and united congregations of Lyons and Vienne; and even as late as the reign of Decius we are assured that in a few cities only—Arles, Narbonne, Toulouse, Limoges, Clermont, Tours, and Paris—some scattered churches were supported by the devotion of a small number of Christians. . . . From Gaul, which claimed a just pre-eminence of learning and authority over all the countries on this side of the Alps, the light of the Gospel was more faintly reflected on the remote provinces of Spain and Britain; and if we may credit the vehement assertions of Tertullian, they had already received the first rays of the faith when he addressed his Apology to the magistrates of the emperor Severus. . . .

The progress of Christianity was not confined to the Roman empire; and, according to the primitive fathers, who interpret facts by prophecy, the new religion, within a century after the death of its Divine Author, had already visited every part of the globe. "There exists not," says Justin Martyr, "a people, whether Greek or barbarian, or any other race of men, by whatsoever appellation or manners they may be distinguished, however ignorant of arts or agriculture, whether they dwell under tents, or wander about in covered waggons, among whom prayers are not offered up in the name of a crucified Jesus to the Father and Creator of all things." But this splendid exaggeration, which even at present it would be extremely difficult to reconcile with the real state of mankind, can be considered only as the rash sally of a devout but careless writer, the measure of whose belief was regulated by that of his wishes. But neither the belief nor the wishes of the fathers can alter the truth of history. It will still remain an undoubted fact that the barbarians of Scythia and Germany, who afterwards subverted the Roman monarchy, were involved in the darkness of paganism; and that even the conversion of Iberia, of Armenia, or of Æthiopia, was not attempted with any degree of success till the sceptre was in the hands of an orthodox emperor. Before that time the various accidents of war and commerce might indeed diffuse an imperfect knowledge of the Gospel among the tribes of Caledonia, and among the borderers of the Rhine, the Danube, and the Euphrates. Beyond the last-mentioned river, Edessa was distinguished by a firm and early adherence to the faith. From Edessa the principles of Christianity were easily introduced into the Greek and Syrian cities which obeyed the successors of Artaxerxes; but they do not appear to have made any deep impression on the minds of the Persians, whose religious system, by the labours of a well-disciplined order of priests, had been constructed with much more art and solidity than the uncertain mythology of Greece and Rome. . . .

. . . The Christian religion, which addressed itself to the whole human race, must consequently collect a far greater number of proselytes from the lower than from the superior ranks of life. This innocent and natural circumstance has been improved into a very odious imputation, which seems to be less strenuously denied by the apologists than it is urged by the adversaries of the faith; that the new sect of Christians was almost entirely composed of the dregs of the populace, of peasants and mechanics, of boys and women, of beggars and slaves, the last of whom might sometimes introduce the missionaries into the rich and noble families to which they belonged. These obscure teachers (such was the charge of malice and infidelity) are as mute in public as they are loquacious and dogmatical in private. Whilst they cautiously avoid the dangerous encounter of philosophers, they mingle with the rude and illiterate crowd, and insinuate themselves into those minds whom their age, their sex, or their education has the best disposed to receive the impression of superstitious terrors. . . .

. . . As the humble faith of Christ diffused itself through the world, it was embraced by several persons who derived some consequence from the advantages of nature or fortune. Aristides, who presented an eloquent apology to the emperor Hadrian, was an Athenian philosopher. Justin Martyr had sought divine knowledge in the schools of Zeno, of Aristotle, of Pythagoras, and of Plato, before he fortunately was accosted by the old man, or rather the angel, who turned his attention to the study of the Jewish prophets. Clemens of Alexandria had acquired much various reading in the Greek, and Tertullian in the Latin, language. Julius Africanus and Origen possessed a very considerable share of the learning of their times; and although the style of Cyprian is very different from that of Lactantius, we might almost discover that both those writers had been public teachers of rhetoric. Even the study of philosophy was at length introduced among the Christians, but it was not always productive of the most salutary effects . . .

. . . The names of Seneca, of the elder and the younger Pliny, of Tacitus, of Plutarch, of Galen, of the slave Epictetus, and of the emperor Marcus Antoninus, adorn the age in which they flourished, and exalt the dignity of human nature. They filled with glory their respective stations, either in active or contemplative life; their excellent understandings were improved by study; philosophy had purified their minds from the prejudices of the popular superstition; and their days were spent in the pursuit of truth and the practice of virtue. Yet all these sages (it is no less an object of surprise than of concern) overlooked or rejected the perfection of the Christian system. Their language or their silence equally discover their contempt for the growing sect which in their time had diffused itself over the Roman empire. Those among them who condescend to mention the Christians consider them only as obstinate and perverse enthusiasts, who exacted an implicit submission to their mysterious doctrines, without being able to produce a single argument that could engage the attention of men of sense and learning.

It is at least doubtful whether any of these philosophers perused the apologies which the primitive Christians repeatedly published in behalf of themselves and of their religion; but it is much to be lamented that such a cause was not defended by abler advocates. They expose with superfluous wit and eloquence the extravagance of Polytheism. They interest our compassion by displaying the innocence and sufferings of their injured brethren. But when they would demonstrate the divine origin of Christianity, they insist much more strongly on the predictions which announced, than on the miracles which accompanied, the appearance of the Messiah. Their favourite argument might serve to edify a Christian or to convert a Jew, since both the one and the other acknowledge the authority of those prophecies, and both are obliged, with devout reverence, to search for their sense and their accomplishment. But this mode of persuasion loses much of its weight and influence when it is addressed to those who neither understand nor respect the Mosaic dispensation and the prophetic style. In the unskilful hands of Justin and of the succeeding apologists, the sublime meaning of the Hebrew oracles evaporates in distant types, affected conceits, and cold allegories; and even their authenticity was rendered suspicious to an unenlightened Gentile, by the mixture of pious forgeries which, under the names of Orpheus, Hermes, and the Sibyls, were obtruded on him as of equal value with the genuine inspirations of Heaven. . . .

But how shall we excuse the supine inattention of the Pagan and philosophic world to those evidences which were presented by the hand of Omnipotence, not to their reason, but to their senses? During the age of Christ, of his apostles, and of their first disciples, the doctrine which they preached was confirmed by innumerable prodigies. The lame walked, the blind saw, the sick were healed, the dead were raised, dæmons were expelled, and the laws of Nature were frequently suspended for the benefit of the church. But the sages of Greece and Rome turned aside from the awful spectacle, and, pursuing the ordinary occupations of life and study, appeared unconscious of any alterations in the moral or physical government of the world. Under the reign of Tiberius, the whole earth, or at least a celebrated province of the Roman empire, was involved in a preternatural darkness of three hours. Even this miraculous event, which ought to have excited the wonder, the curiosity, and the devotion of mankind, passed without notice in an age of science and history. It happened during the lifetime of Seneca and the elder Pliny, who must have experienced the immediate effects, or received the earliest intelligence, of the prodigy. Each of these philosophers, in a laborious work, has recorded all the great phenomena of Nature, earthquakes, meteors, comets, and eclipses, which his indefatigable curiosity could collect. Both the one and the other have omitted to mention the greatest phenomenon to which the mortal eye has been witness since the creation of the globe. A distinct chapter of Pliny is designed for eclipses of an extraordinary nature and unusual duration; but he contents himself with describing the singular defect of light which followed the murder of Cæsar, when, during the greatest part of a year, the orb of the sun appeared pale and without splendour. This season of obscurity, which cannot surely be compared with the preternatural darkness of the Passion, had been already celebrated by most of the poets and historians of that memorable age.

PART 3

Church and State in the Empire *(Chapter XVI)*

In dealing with the Roman government's conduct towards the Christians during the period from Nero to Constantine, Gibbon devotes much space to emphasizing its basically tolerant attitude, although he elaborates in equal detail on the persecution of the early Christians. It was during the reign of Diocletian, who reformed the imperial system, that the Church came into direct conflict with the Roman state. Those Romans who supported Diocletian's government, viewed the state religion as a crucial factor in the revitalization of the Empire. In 303, under great pressure from anti-Christian elements, the aging Diocletian outlawed Christian churches, assemblies, and books. This was followed by edicts ordering the imprisonment of Christian leaders, who were commanded to offer sacrifices to the Roman gods under the threat of death. But Christianity could not be stopped, and under Diocletian's heir, Constantine the Great, it was to become the religion of the Empire.

CHAPTER XVI

. . . The religious policy of the ancient world seems to have assumed a more stern and intolerant character to oppose the progress of Christianity. About fourscore years after the death of Christ, his innocent disciples were punished with death by the sentence of a proconsul of the most amiable and philosophic character, and according to the laws of an emperor distinguished by the wisdom and justice of his general administration. The apologies which were repeatedly addressed to the successors of Trajan are filled with the most pathetic complaints that the Christians, who obeyed the dictates and solicited the liberty of conscience, were alone, among all the subjects of the Roman empire, excluded from the common benefits of their auspicious government. The deaths of a few eminent martyrs have been recorded with care; and from the time that Christianity was invested with the supreme power, the governors of the church have been no less diligently employed in displaying the cruelty, than in imitating the conduct, of their Pagan adversaries. To separate (if it be possible) a few authentic as well as interesting facts from an undigested mass of fiction and error, and to relate, in a clear and rational manner, the causes, the extent, the duration, and the most important circumstances of the persecutions to which the first Christians were exposed, is the design of the present chapter. . . .

Since the Jews, who rejected with abhorrence the deities adored by their sovereign and by their fellow-subjects, enjoyed, however, the free exercise of their unsocial religion, there must have existed some other cause which exposed the disciples of Christ to those severities from which the posterity of Abraham was exempt. The difference between them is simple and obvious, but, according to the sentiments of antiquity, it was of the highest importance. The Jews were a *nation,* the Christians were a *sect:* and if it was natural for every community to respect the sacred institutions of their neighbours, it was incumbent on them to persevere in those of their ancestors. The voice of oracles, the precepts of philosophers, and the authority of the laws, unanimously enforced this national obligation. By their lofty claim of superior sanctity the Jews might provoke the Polytheists to consider them as an odious and impure race. By disdaining the intercourse of other nations they might deserve their contempt. The laws of Moses might be for the most part frivolous or absurd; yet, since they had been received during many ages by a large society, his followers were justified by the example of mankind, and it was universally acknowledged that they had a right to practise what it would have been criminal in them to neglect. But this principle, which protected the Jewish synagogue, afforded not any favour or security to the primitive church. By embracing the faith of the Gospel the Christians incurred the supposed guilt of an unnatural and unpardonable offence. They dissolved the sacred ties of custom and education, violated the religious institutions of their country, and presumptuously despised whatever their fathers had believed as true or had reverenced as sacred. Nor was this apostasy (if we may use the expression) merely of a partial or local kind; since the pious deserter who withdrew himself from the temples of Egypt or Syria would equally disdain to seek an asylum in those of Athens or Carthage. Every Christian rejected with contempt the superstitions of his family, his city, and his province. The whole body of Christians unanimously refused to hold any communion with the gods of Rome, of the empire, and of mankind. It was in vain that the oppressed believer asserted the inalienable rights of conscience and private judgment. Though his situation might excite the pity, his arguments could never reach the understanding, either of the philosophic or of the believing part of the Pagan world. To their apprehensions it was no less a matter of surprise that any individuals should entertain scruples against complying with the established mode of worship than if they had conceived a sudden abhorrence to the manners, the dress, or the language of their native country. . . .

The precautions with which the disciples of Christ performed the offices of religion were at first dictated by fear and necessity; but they were continued from choice. By imitating the awful secrecy which reigned in the Eleusinian mysteries, the Christians had flattered themselves that they should render their sacred institutions more respectable in the eyes of the Pagan world. But the event, as it often happens to the operations of subtile policy, deceived their wishes and their expectations. It was concluded that they only concealed what they would have blushed to disclose. Their mistaken prudence afforded an opportunity for malice to invent, and for suspicious credulity to believe, the horrid tales which described the Christians as the most wicked of human kind, who practised in their dark recesses every abomination that a depraved fancy could suggest, and who solicited the favour of their unknown God by the sacrifice of every moral virtue. There were many who pretended to confess or to relate the ceremonies of this abhorred society. It was asserted, "that a new-born infant, entirely covered over with flour, was presented, like some mystic symbol of initiation, to the knife of the proselyte, who unknowingly inflicted many a secret and mortal wound on the innocent victim of his error; that as soon as the cruel deed was perpetrated, the sectaries drank up the blood, greedily tore asunder the quivering members, and pledged themselves to eternal secrecy, by a mutual consciousness of guilt. It was as confidently affirmed that this inhuman sacrifice was succeeded by a suitable entertainment, in which intemperance served as a provocative to brutal lust; till, at the appointed moment, the lights were suddenly extinguished, shame was banished, nature was forgotten; and, as accident might direct, the darkness of the night was polluted by the incestuous commerce of sisters and brothers, of sons and of mothers." . . .

Amidst the frequent revolutions of the empire the Christians . . . flourished in peace and prosperity, and *notwithstanding a celebrated era of martyrs** has been deduced from the accession of Diocletian, the new system of policy, introduced and maintained by the wisdom of that prince, continued, during more than eighteen years, to breathe the mildest and most liberal spirit of religious toleration. The mind of Diocletian himself was less adapted indeed to speculative inquiries than to the active labours of war and government. His prudence rendered him averse to any great innovation, and, though his temper was not very susceptible of zeal or enthusiasm, he always maintained an habitual regard for the ancient deities of the empire. But the leisure of the two empresses, of his wife Prisca, and of Valeria his daughter, permitted them to listen with more attention and respect to the truths of Christianity, which in every age has acknowledged its important obligations to female devotion. The principal eunuchs, Lucian and Dorotheus, Gorgonius and Andrew, who attended the person, possessed the favour, and governed the household of Diocletian, protected by their powerful influence the faith which they had embraced. Their example was imitated by many of the most considerable officers of the palace, who, in their respective stations, had the care of the Imperial ornaments, of the robes, of the furniture, of the jewels, and even of the private treasury; and, though it might sometimes be incumbent on them to accompany the emperor when he sacrificed in the temple, they enjoyed, with their wives, their children, and their slaves, the free exercise of the Christian religion. Diocletian and his colleagues frequently conferred the most important offices on those persons who

*Emphasis added. (P.W.)

avowed their abhorrence for the worship of the gods, but who had displayed abilities proper for the service of the state. The bishops held an honourable rank in their respective provinces, and were treated with distinction and respect, not only by the people, but by the magistrates themselves. Almost in every city the ancient churches were found insufficient to contain the increasing multitude of proselytes; and in their place more stately and capacious edifices were erected for the public worship of the faithful. The corruption of manners and principles, so forcibly lamented by Eusebius, may be considered, not only as a consequence, but as a proof, of the liberty which the Christians enjoyed and abused under the reign of Diocletian. Prosperity had relaxed the nerves of discipline. Fraud, envy, and malice prevailed in every congregation. The presbyters aspired to the episcopal office, which every day became an object more worthy of their ambition. The bishops, who contended with each other for ecclesiastical preeminence, appeared by their conduct to claim a secular and tyrannical power in the church; and the lively faith which still distinguished the Christians from the Gentiles was shown much less in their lives than in their controversial writings.

Notwithstanding this seeming security, an attentive observer might discern some symptoms that threatened the church with a more violent persecution than any which she had yet endured. The zeal and rapid progress of the Christians awakened the Polytheists from their supine indifference in the cause of those deities whom custom and education had taught them to revere. The mutual provocations of a religious war, which had already continued above two hundred years, exasperated the animosity of the contending parties. The Pagans were incensed at the rashness of a recent and obscure sect, which presumed to accuse their countrymen of error, and to devote their ancestors to eternal misery. . . .

Although the policy of Diocletian and the humanity of Constantius inclined them to preserve inviolate the maxims of toleration, it was soon discovered that their two associates, Maximian and Galerius, entertained the most implacable aversion for the name and religion of the Christians. The minds of those princes had never been enlightened by science; education had never softened their temper. They owed their greatness to their swords, and in their most elevated fortune they still retained their superstitious prejudices of soldiers and peasants. In the general administration of the provinces they obeyed the laws which their benefactor had established; but they frequently found occasions of exercising within their camp and palaces a secret persecution, for which the imprudent zeal of the Christians sometimes offered the most specious pretences. A sentence of death was executed upon Maximilianus, an African youth, who had been produced by his own father before the magistrate as a sufficient and legal recruit, but who obstinately persisted in declaring that his conscience would not permit him to embrace the profession of a soldier. It could scarcely be expected that any government should suffer the action of Marcellus the centurion to pass with impunity. On the day of a public festival, that officer threw away his belt, his arms, and the ensigns of his office, and exclaimed with a loud voice that he would obey none but Jesus Christ the eternal King, and that he renounced for ever the use of carnal weapons, and the service of an idolatrous master. The soldiers, as soon as they recovered from their astonishment, secured the person of Marcellus. He was examined in the city of Tingi by the president of that part of Mauritania; and as he was convicted by his own confession, he was condemned and beheaded for the crime of desertion. Examples of such a nature savour much less of religious persecution than of martial or even civil law: but they served to alienate the mind of the emperors, to justify the severity of Galerius, who dismissed a great number of Christian officers from their employments; and to authorise the opinion that a sect of enthusiasts, which avowed principles so repugnant to the public safety, must either remain useless, or would soon become dangerous subjects of the empire.

After the success of the Persian war had raised the hopes and the reputation of Galerius, he passed a winter with Diocletian in the palace of Nicomedia; and the fate of Christianity became the object of their secret consultations. The experienced emperor was still inclined to pursue measures of lenity; and though he readily consented to exclude the Christians from holding any employments in the household or the army, he urged in the strongest terms the danger as well as cruelty of shedding the blood of those deluded fanatics. Galerius at length extorted from him the permission of summoning a council, composed of a few persons the most distinguished in the civil and military departments of the state. The important question was agitated in their presence, and those ambitious courtiers easily discerned that it was incumbent on them to second, by their eloquence, the importunate violence of the Cæsar. It may be presumed that they insisted on every topic which might interest the pride, the piety, or the fears, of their sovereign in the destruction of Christianity. Perhaps they represented that the glorious work of the deliverance of the empire was left imperfect, as long as an independent people was permitted to subsist and multiply in the heart of the provinces. The Christians (it might speciously be alleged), renouncing the gods and the institutions of Rome, had constituted a distinct republic, which might yet be suppressed before it had acquired any military force; but which was already governed by its own laws and magistrates, was possessed of a public treasure, and was intimately connected in all its parts by the frequent assemblies of the bishops, to whose decrees their numerous and opulent congregations yielded an implicit obedience. Arguments like these may seem to have determined the reluctant mind of Diocletian to embrace a new system of persecution: but though we may suspect, it is not in our power to relate, the secret intrigues of the palace, the private views and resentments, the jealousy of women or eunuchs, and all those trifling but decisive causes which so often influence the fate of empires and the councils of the wisest monarchs.*

The pleasure of the emperors was at length signified to the Christians, who, during the course of this melancholy winter, had expected, with anxiety, the result of so many secret consultations. The twenty-third of February, which coincided with the Roman festival of the Terminalia, was appointed (whether from accident or design) to set bounds to the progress of Christianity. At the earliest dawn of day the Prætorian præfect, accompanied by several generals, tribunes, and officers of the revenue, repaired to the principal church of Nicomedia, which was situated on an eminence in the most populous and beautiful part of the city. The doors were instantly broke open; they rushed into the sanctuary; and as they searched in vain for some visible object of worship, they were obliged to content themselves with committing to the flames the volumes of Holy Scripture. The ministers of Diocletian were followed by a numerous body of guards and pioneers, who

*The only circumstance which we can discover is the devotion and jealousy of the mother of Galerius. She is described by Lactantius as Deorum montium cultrix; mulier admodum superstitiosa. She had a great influence over her son, and was offended by the disregard of some of her Christian servants.

marched in order of battle, and were provided with all the instruments used in the destruction of fortified cities. By their incessant labour, a sacred edifice, which towered above the Imperial palace, and had long excited the indignation and envy of the Gentiles, was in a few hours levelled with the ground.

The next day the general edict of persecution was published; and though Diocletian, still averse to the effusion of blood, had moderated the fury of Galerius, who proposed that every one refusing to offer sacrifice should immediately be burnt alive, the penalties inflicted on the obstinacy of the Christians might be deemed sufficiently rigorous and effectual. It was enacted that their churches, in all the provinces of the empire, should be demolished to their foundations; and the punishment of death was denounced against all who should presume to hold any secret assemblies for the purpose of religious worship. The philosophers, who now assumed the unworthy office of directing the blind zeal of persecution, had diligently studied the nature and genius of the Christian religion; and as they were not ignorant that the speculative doctrines of the faith were supposed to be contained in the writings of the prophets, of the evangelists, and of the apostles, they most probably suggested the order that the bishops and presbyters should deliver all their sacred books into the hands of the magistrates; who were commanded, under the severest penalties, to burn them in a public and solemn manner. By the same edict, the property of the church was at once confiscated; and the several parts of which it might consist were either sold to the highest bidder, united to the Imperial domain, bestowed on the cities and corporations, or granted to the solicitations of rapacious courtiers. After taking such effectual measures to abolish the worship and to dissolve the government of the Christians, it was thought necessary to subject to the most intolerable hardships the condition of those perverse individuals who should still reject the religion of nature, of Rome, and of their ancestors. Persons of a liberal birth were declared incapable of holding any honours or employments; slaves were for ever deprived of the hopes of freedom; and the whole body of the people were put out of the protection of the law. The judges were authorised to hear and to determine every action that was brought against a Christian. But the Christians were not permitted to complain of any injury which they themselves had suffered; and thus those unfortunate sectaries were exposed to the severity, while they were excluded from the benefits, of public justice. This new species of martyrdom, so painful and lingering, so obscure and ignominious, was, perhaps, the most proper to weary the constancy of the faithful: nor can it be doubted that the passions and interest of mankind were disposed on this occasion to second the designs of the emperors. But the policy of a well-ordered government must sometimes have interposed in behalf of the oppressed Christians; nor was it possible for the Roman princes entirely to remove the apprehension of punishment, or to connive at every act of fraud and violence, without exposing their own authority and the rest of their subjects to the most alarming dangers.

This edict was scarcely exhibited to the public view, in the most conspicuous place of Nicomedia, before it was torn down by the hands of a Christian, who expressed at the same time, by the bitterest invectives, his contempt as well as abhorrence for such impious and tyrannical governors. His offence, according to the mildest laws, amounted to treason, and deserved death. And if it be true that he was a person of rank and education, those circumstances could serve only to aggravate his guilt. He was burnt, or rather roasted, by a slow fire; and his executioners, zealous to revenge the personal insult which had been offered to the emperors, exhausted every refinement of cruelty, without being able to subdue his patience, or to alter the steady and insulting smile which, in his dying agonies, he still preserved in his countenance. The Christians, though they confessed that his conduct had not been strictly conformable to the laws of prudence, admired the divine fervour of his zeal; and the excessive commendations which they lavished on the memory of their hero and martyr contributed to fix a deep impression of terror and hatred in the mind of Diocletian.

His fears were soon alarmed by the view of a danger from which he very narrowly escaped. Within fifteen days the palace of Nicomedia, and even the bedchamber of Diocletian, were twice in flames; and though both times they were extinguished without any material damage, the singular repetition of the fire was justly considered as an evident proof that it had not been the effect of chance or negligence. The suspicion naturally fell on the Christians; and it was suggested, with some degree of probability, that those desperate fanatics, provoked by their present sufferings, and apprehensive of impending calamities, had entered into a conspiracy with their faithful brethren, the eunuchs of the palace, against the lives of two emperors whom they detested as the irreconcilable enemies of the church of God. Jealousy and resentment prevailed in every breast, but especially in that of Diocletian. A great number of persons, distinguished either by the offices which they had filled or by the favour which they had enjoyed, were thrown into prison. Every mode of torture was put in practice, and the court, as well as city, was polluted with many bloody executions. But as it was found impossible to extort any discovery of this mysterious transaction, it seems incumbent on us either to presume the innocence, or to admire the resolution, of the sufferers. A few days afterwards Galerius hastily withdrew himself from Nicomedia, declaring that, if he delayed his departure from that devoted palace, he should fall a sacrifice to the rage of the Christians. The ecclesiastical historians, from whom alone we derive a partial and imperfect knowledge of this persecution, are at a loss how to account for the fears and danger of the emperors. Two of these writers, a prince and a rhetorician, were eye-witnesses of the fire of Nicomedia. The one ascribes it to lightning and the divine wrath, the other affirms that it was kindled by the malice of Galerius himself.

As the edict against the Christians was designed for a general law of the whole empire, and as Diocletian and Galerius, though they might not wait for the consent, were assured of the concurrence, of the Western princes, it would appear more consonant to our ideas of policy that the governors of all the provinces should have received secret instructions to publish, on one and the same day, this declaration of war within their respective departments. It was at least to be expected that the convenience of the public highways and established posts would have enabled the emperors to transmit their orders with the utmost despatch from the palace of Nicomedia to the extremities of the Roman world; and that they would not have suffered fifty days to elapse before the edict was published in Syria, and near four months before it was signified to the cities of Africa. This delay may perhaps be imputed to the cautious temper of Diocletian, who had yielded a reluctant consent to the measures of persecution, and who was desirous of trying the experiment under his more immediate eye before he gave way to the disorders and discontent which it must inevitably occasion in the distant provinces. At first, indeed, the magistrates were restrained from the effusion of blood; but the use of every other severity was permitted, and even recommended to their zeal; nor could the Christians, though they cheerfully resigned the ornaments of their churches, resolve to interrupt their religious assemblies, or to deliver their sacred books to the flames. The pious obstinacy of Felix, an African bishop, appears to have embarrassed the subordinate ministers of the government. The curator of his city sent him in chains to the proconsul. The proconsul transmitted him to the Prætorian præfect of Italy; and Felix, who disdained even to give an evasive answer, was a length beheaded at Venusia, in Lucania, a place on which the birth of Horace has conferred fame. This precedent, and perhaps some Imperial rescript, which was issued in consequence of it, appeared to authorise the governors of provinces in punishing with death the refusal of the Christians to deliver up their sacred books. There were undoubtedly many persons who embraced this opportunity of obtaining the crown of martyrdom; but there were likewise too many who purchased an ignominious life by discovering and betraying the Holy Scripture into the hands of infidels. A great number even of bishops and presbyters acquired, by this criminal compliance, the opprobrious epithet of *Traditors;* and their offence was productive of much present scandal and of much future discord in the African church.

The copies as well as the versions of Scripture were already so multiplied in the empire, that the most severe inquisition could no longer be attended with any fatal consequences; and even the sacrifice of those volumes which, in every congregation, were preserved for public use, required the consent of some treacherous and unworthy Christians. But the ruin of the churches was easily effected by the authority of the government and by the labour of the Pagans. In some provinces, however, the magistrates contented themselves with shutting up the places of religious worship. In others they more literally complied with the terms of the edict; and, after taking away the doors, the benches, and the pulpit, which they burnt as it were in a funeral pile, they completely demolished the remainder of the edifice.* It is perhaps to this melancholy occasion that we should apply a very remarkable story, which is related with so many circumstances of

*The ancient monuments, published at the end of Optatus, p. 261, etc., describe, in a very circumstantial manner, the proceedings of the governors in the destruction of churches. They made a minute inventory of the plate, etc., which they found in them. That of the church of Cirta, in Numidia, is still extant. It consisted of two chalices of gold and six of silver; six urns, one kettle, seven lamps, all likewise of silver; besides a large quantity of brass utensils and wearing apparel.

variety and improbability that it serves rather to excite than to satisfy our curiosity. In a small town in Phrygia, of whose name as well as situation we are left ignorant, it should seem that the magistrates and the body of the people had embraced the Christian faith; and as some resistance might be apprehended to the execution of the edict, the governor of the province was supported by a numerous detachment of legionaries. On their approach the citizens threw themselves into the church, with the resolution either of defending by arms that sacred edifice or of perishing in its ruins. They indignantly rejected the notice and permission which was given them to retire, till the soldiers, provoked by their obstinate refusal, set fire to the building on all sides, and consumed, by this extraordinary kind of martyrdom, a great number of Phrygians, with their wives and children.

Some slight disturbances, though they were suppressed almost as soon as excited, in Syria and the frontiers of Armenia, afforded the enemies of the church a very plausible occasion to insinuate that those troubles had been secretly fomented by the intrigues of the bishops, who had already forgotten their ostentatious professions of passive and unlimited obedience.* The resentment, or the fears, of Diocletian at length transported him beyond the bounds of moderation which he had hitherto preserved, and he declared, in a series of cruel edicts, his intention of abolishing the Christian name. By the first of these edicts the governors of the provinces were directed to apprehend all persons of the ecclesiastical order; and the prisons destined for the vilest criminals were soon filled with a multitude of bishops, presbyters, deacons, readers, and exorcists. By a second edict the magistrates were commanded to employ every method of severity which might reclaim them from their odious superstition, and oblige them to return to the established worship of the gods. This rigorous order was extended, by a subsequent edict, to the whole body of Christians, who were exposed to a violent and general persecution. Instead of those salutary restraints which had required the direct and solemn testimony of an accuser, it became the duty as well as the interest of the Imperial officers to discover, to pursue, and to torment the most obnoxious among the faithful. Heavy penalties were denounced against all who

*Eusebius . . . thinks that he has discovered the Syrian rebellion in an oration of Libanius; and that it was a rash attempt of the tribune Eugenius, who with only five hundred men seized Antioch, and might perhaps allure the Christians by the promise of religious toleration. . . .

should presume to save a proscribed sectary from the just indignation of the gods and of the emperors. Yet, notwithstanding the severity of this law, the virtuous courage of many of the Pagans, in concealing their friends or relations, affords an honourable proof that the rage of superstition had not extinguished in their minds the sentiments of nature and humanity.

Diocletian had no sooner published his edicts against the Christians than, as if he had been desirous of committing to other hands the work of persecution, he divested himself of the Imperial purple. The character and situation of his colleagues and successors sometimes urged them to enforce, and sometimes inclined them to suspend, the execution of these rigorous laws; nor can we acquire a just and distinct idea of this important period of ecclesiastical history unless we separately consider the state of Christianity, in the different parts of the empire, during the space of ten years which elapsed between the first edicts of Diocletian and the final peace of the church.

The mild and humane temper of Constantius was averse to the oppression of any part of his subjects. The principal offices of his palace were exercised by Christians. He loved their persons, esteemed their fidelity, and entertained not any dislike to their religious principles. But as long as Constantius remained in the subordinate station of Cæsar, it was not in his power openly to reject the edicts of Diocletian, or to disobey the commands of Maximian. His authority contributed, however, to alleviate the sufferings which he pitied and abhorred. He consented with reluctance to the ruin of the churches, but he ventured to protect the Christians themselves from the fury of the populace and from the rigour of the laws. The provinces of Gaul (under which we may probably include those of Britain) were indebted for the singular tranquillity which they enjoyed to the gentle interposition of their sovereign. But Datianus, the president or governor of Spain, actuated either by zeal or policy, chose rather to execute the public edicts of the emperors than to understand the secret intentions of Constantius; and it can scarcely be doubted that his provincial administration was stained with the blood of a few martyrs. The elevation of Constantius to the supreme and independent dignity of Augustus gave a free scope to the exercise of his virtues, and the shortness of his reign did not prevent him from establishing a system of toleration of which he left the precept and the example to his son Constantine. His fortunate son, from the first moment of his accession declaring himself the protector of the church, at length deserved the appellation of the first emperor who publicly professed and established the Christian religion. The motives of his conversion, as they may variously be deduced from benevolence, from policy, from conviction, or from remorse, and the progress of the revolution, which, under his powerful influence and that of his sons, rendered Christianity the reigning religion of the Roman empire, will form a very interesting and important chapter in the second volume of this history. At present it may be sufficient to observe that every victory of Constantine was productive of some relief or benefit to the church.

The provinces of Italy and Africa experienced a short but violent persecution. The rigorous edicts of Diocletian were strictly and cheerfully executed by his associate Maximian, who had long hated the Christians, and who delighted in acts of blood and violence. In the autumn of the first year of the persecution the two emperors met at Rome to celebrate their triumph: several oppressive laws appear to have issued from their secret consultations, and the diligence of the magistrates was animated by the presence of their sovereigns. After Diocletian had divested himself of the purple, Italy and Africa were administered under the name of Severus, and were exposed, without defence, to the implacable resentment of his master Galerius. Among the martyrs of Rome, Adauctus deserves the notice of posterity. He was of a noble family in Italy, and had raised himself, through the successive honours of the palace, to the important office of treasurer of the private demesnes. Adauctus is the more remarkable for being the only person of rank and distinction who appears to have suffered death during the whole course of this general persecution.

The revolt of Maxentius immediately restored peace to the churches of Italy and Africa, and the same tyrant who oppressed every other class of his subjects showed himself just, humane, and even partial, towards the afflicted Christians. He depended on their gratitude and affection, and very naturally presumed that the injuries which they had suffered, and the dangers which they still apprehended, from his most inveterate enemy, would secure the fidelity of a party already considerable by their numbers and opulence. Even the conduct of Maxentius towards the bishops of Rome and Carthage may be considered as the proof of his toleration, since it is probable that the most orthodox princes would adopt the same measures with regard to their established clergy. Marcellus, the former of those prelates, had thrown the capital into confusion by the severe penance which he imposed on a great number of Christians who, during the late persecution, had renounced or dissembled their religion. The rage of faction broke out in frequent and violent seditions; the blood of the faithful was shed by each other's hands; and the exile of Marcellus, whose prudence seems to have been less eminent than his zeal, was found to be the only measure capable of restoring peace to the distracted church of Rome. The behaviour of Mensurius, bishop of Carthage, appears to have been still more reprehensible. A deacon of that city had published a libel against the emperor. The offender took refuge in the episcopal palace, and, though it was somewhat early to advance any claims of ecclesiastical immunities, the bishop refused to deliver him up to the officers of justice. For this treasonable resistance Mensurius was summoned to court, and, instead of receiving a legal sentence of death or banishment, he was permitted, after a short examination, to return to his diocese. Such was the happy condition of the Christian subjects of Maxentius, that, whenever they were desirous of procuring for their own use any bodies of martyrs, they were obliged to purchase them from the most distant provinces of the East. A story is related of Aglae, a Roman lady, descended from a consular family, and possessed of so ample an estate that it required the management of seventy-three stewards. Among these Boniface was the favourite of his mistress, and, as Aglae mixed love with devotion, it is reported that he was admitted to share her bed. Her fortune enabled her to gratify the pious desire of obtaining some sacred relics from the East. She intrusted Boniface with a considerable sum of gold and a large quantity of aromatics, and her lover, attended by twelve horsemen and three covered chariots, undertook a remote pilgrimage as far as Tarsus in Cilicia.

The sanguinary temper of Galerius, the first and principal author of the persecution, was formidable to those Christians whom their misfortunes had placed within the limits of his dominions; and it may fairly be presumed that many persons of a middle rank, who were not confined by the chains either of wealth or of poverty, very frequently deserted their native country, and sought a refuge in the milder climate of the West. As long as he commanded only the armies and provinces of Illyricum, he could with difficulty either find or make a considerable number of martyrs in a warlike country which had entertained the missionaries of the Gospel with more coldness and reluctance than any other part of the empire.* But when Galerius had obtained the supreme power and the government of the East, he indulged in their fullest extent his zeal and cruelty, not only in the provinces of Thrace and Asia, which acknowledged his immediate jurisdiction, but in those of Syria, Palestine, and Egypt, where Maximin gratified his own inclination by yielding a rigorous obedience to the stern commands of his benefactor.

The frequent disappointments of his ambitious views, the experience of six years of persecution, and the salutary reflections which a lingering and painful distemper suggested to the mind of Galerius, at length convinced him that the most violent efforts of despotism are insufficient to extirpate a whole people, or to subdue their religious prejudices. Desirous of repairing the mischief that he had occasioned, he published in his own name, and in those of Licinius and Constantine, a general edict, which, after a pompous recital of the Imperial titles, proceeded in the following manner:

"Among the important cares which have occupied our mind for the utility and preservation of the empire, it was our intention to correct and re-establish all things according to the ancient laws and public discipline of the Romans. We were particularly desirous of reclaiming into the way of reason and nature the deluded Christians who had renounced the religion and ceremonies instituted by their fathers, and, presumptuously despising the practice of antiquity, had invented extravagant laws and opinions according to the dictates of their fancy, and had collected a various society from the different provinces of our empire. The edicts which we have published to enforce the worship of the gods having exposed many of the Christians to danger and distress, many having suffered death, and many more, who still persist in their impious folly, being left destitute of *any* public exercise of religion, we are disposed to extend to those unhappy men the effects of our wonted clemency. We permit them, therefore, freely to profess their private opinions, and to assemble in their conventicles without fear or molestation, provided always that they preserve a due respect

*During the four first centuries there exist few traces of either bishops or bishoprics in the western Illyricum. It has been thought probable that the primate of Milan extended his jurisdiction over Sirmium, the capital of that great province. . . .

to the established laws and government. By another rescript we shall signify our intentions to the judges and magistrates, and we hope that our indulgence will engage the Christians to offer up their prayers to the Deity whom they adore for our safety and prosperity, for their own, and for that of the republic." It is not usually in the language of edicts and manifestos that we should search for the real character of the secret motives of princes; but as these were the words of a dying emperor, his situation, perhaps, may be admitted as a pledge of his sincerity.

When Galerius subscribed this edict of toleration, he was well assured that Licinius would readily comply with the inclinations of his friend and benefactor, and that any measures in favour of the Christians would obtain the approbation of Constantine. But the emperor would not venture to insert in the preamble the name of Maximin, whose consent was of the greatest importance, and who succeeded a few days afterwards to the provinces of Asia. In the first six months, however, of his new reign, Maximin affected to adopt the prudent counsels of his predecessor; and though he never condescended to secure the tranquillity of the church by a public edict, Sabinus, his Prætorian præfect, addressed a circular letter to all the governors and magistrates of the provinces, expatiating on the Imperial clemency, acknowledging the invincible obstinacy of the Christians, and directing the officers of justice to cease their ineffectual prosecutions, and to connive at the secret assemblies of those enthusiasts. In consequence of these orders, great numbers of Christians were released from prison, or delivered from the mines. The confessors, singing hymns of triumph, returned into their own countries, and those who had yielded to the violence of the tempest, solicited with tears of repentance their re-admission into the bosom of the church.

But this treacherous calm was of short duration; nor could the Christians of the East place any confidence in the character of their sovereign. Cruelty and superstition were the ruling passions of the soul of Maximin. The former suggested the means, the latter pointed out the objects, of persecution. The emperor was devoted to the worship of the gods, to the study of magic, and to the belief of oracles. The prophets or philosophers, whom he revered as the favourites of Heaven, were frequently raised to the government of provinces, and admitted into his most secret councils. They easily convinced him that the Christians had been indebted for their victories to their regular discipline, and that the weakness of polytheism had principally flowed from a want of union and subordination among the ministers of religion. A system of government was therefore instituted, which was evidently copied from the policy of the church. In all the great cities of the empire, the temples were repaired and beautified by the order of Maximin, and the officiating priests of the various deities were subjected to the authority of a superior pontiff destined to oppose the bishop, and to promote the cause of paganism. These pontiffs acknowledged, in their turn, the supreme jurisdiction of the metropolitans or high priests of the province, who acted as the immediate vicegerents of the emperor himself. A white robe was the ensign of their dignity; and these new prelates were carefully selected from the most noble and opulent families. By the influence of the magistrates, and of the sacerdotal order, a great number of dutiful addresses were obtained, particularly from the cities of Nicomedia, Antioch, and Tyre, which artfully represented the well-known intentions of the court as the general sense of the people; solicited the emperor to consult the laws of justice rather than the dictates of his clemency; expressed their abhorrence of the Christians, and humbly prayed that those impious sectaries might at least be excluded from the limits of their respective territories. The answer of Maximin to the address which he obtained from the citizens of Tyre is still extant. He praises their zeal and devotion in terms of the highest satisfaction, descants on the obstinate impiety of the Christians, and betrays, by the readiness with which he consents to their banishment, that he considered himself as receiving, rather than as conferring, an obligation. The priests as well as the magistrates were empowered to enforce the execution of his edicts, which were engraved on tables of brass; and though it was recommended to them to avoid the effusion of blood, the most cruel and ignominious punishments were inflicted on the refractory Christians.

The Asiatic Christians had everything to dread from the severity of a bigoted monarch who prepared his measures of violence with such deliberate policy. But a few months had scarcely elapsed before the edicts published by the two Western emperors obliged Maximin to suspend the prosecution of his designs: the civil war which he so rashly undertook against Licinius employed all his attention; and the defeat and death of Maximin soon delivered the church from the last and most implacable of her enemies.

In this general view of the persecution which was first authorised by the edicts of Diocletian, I have purposely refrained from describing the particular sufferings and deaths of the Christian martyrs. It would have been an easy task, from the history of Eusebius, from the declamations of Lactantius, and from the most ancient acts, to collect a long series of horrid and disgusting pictures, and to fill many pages with racks and scourges, with iron hooks and red-hot beds, and with all the variety of tortures which fire and steel, savage beasts, and more savage executioners, could inflict on the human body. These melancholy scenes might be enlivened by a crowd of visions and miracles destined either to delay the death, to celebrate the triumph, or to discover the relics of those canonised saints who suffered for the name of Christ. But I cannot determine what I ought to transcribe, till I am satisfied how much I ought to believe. The gravest of the ecclesiastical historians, Eusebius himself, indirectly confesses that he has related whatever might redound to the glory, and that he has suppressed all that could tend to the disgrace, of religion. Such an acknowledgment will naturally excite a suspicion that a writer who has so openly violated one of the fundamental laws of history has not paid a very strict regard to the observance of the other; and the suspicion will derive additional credit from the character of Eusebius, which was less tinctured with credulity, and more practised in the arts of courts, than that of almost any of his contemporaries. On some particular occasions, when the magistrates were exasperated by some personal motives of interest or resentment, when the zeal of the martyrs urged them to forget the rules of prudence, and perhaps of decency, to overturn the altars, to pour out imprecations against the emperors, or to strike the judge as he sat on his tribunal, it may be presumed that every mode of torture which cruelty could invent, or constancy could endure, was exhausted on those devoted victims. Two circumstances, however, have been unwarily mentioned, which insinuate that the general treatment of the Christians who had been apprehended by the officers of justice was less intolerable than it is usually imagined to have been. 1. The confessors who were condemned to work in the mines were permitted by the humanity or the negligence of their keepers to build chapels, and freely to profess their religion in the midst of those dreary habitations. 2. The bishops were obliged to check and to censure the forward zeal of the Christians, who voluntarily threw themselves into the hands of the magistrates. Some of these were persons oppressed by poverty and debts, who blindly sought to terminate a miserable existence by a glorious death. Others were allured by the hope that a short confinement would expiate the sins of a whole life; and others again were actuated by the less honourable motive of deriving a plentiful subsistence, and perhaps a considerable profit, from the alms which the charity of the faithful bestowed on the prisoners. After the church had triumphed over all her enemies, the interest as well as vanity of the captives prompted them to magnify the merit of their respective suffering. A convenient distance of time or place gave an ample scope to the progress of fiction; and the frequent instances which might be alleged of holy martyrs whose wounds had been instantly healed, whose strength had been renewed, and whose lost members had miraculously been restored, were extremely convenient for the purpose of removing every difficulty, and of silencing every objection. The most extravagant legends, as they conduced to the honour of the church, were applauded by the credulous multitude, countenanced by the power of the clergy, and attested by the suspicious evidence of ecclesiastical history.

The vague descriptions of exile and imprisonment, of pain and torture, are so easily exaggerated or softened by the pencil of an artful orator, that we are naturally induced to inquire into a fact of a more distinct and stubborn kind; the number of persons who suffered death in consequence of the edicts published by Diocletian, his associates, and his successors. The recent legendaries record whole armies and cities which were at once swept away by the undistinguishing rage of persecution. The more ancient writers content themselves with pouring out a liberal effusion of loose and tragical invectives, without condescending to ascertain the precise number of those persons who were permitted to seal with their blood their belief of the Gospel. From the history of Eusebius it may however be collected that only nine bishops were punished with death; and we are assured, by his particular enumeration of the martyrs of Palestine, that no more than ninety-two Christians were entitled to that honourable appellation. As we are unacquainted with the degree of episcopal zeal and courage which prevailed at that time, it is not in our power to draw any useful inferences from the former of these facts: but the latter may serve to justify a very important and probable conclusion. According to the distribution of Roman provinces, Palestine may be considered as the sixteenth part of the Eastern empire:* and since there were some governors who, from a real or affected clemency, had preserved their hands unstained with the blood of the faithful, it is reasonable to believe that the country which had given birth to Christianity produced at least the sixteenth part of the martyrs who suffered death within the dominions of Galerius and Maximin; the whole might consequently amount to about fifteen hundred, a number which, if it is equally divided between the ten years of the persecution, will allow an annual consumption of one hundred and fifty martyrs. Allotting the same proportion to the provinces of Italy, Africa, and perhaps Spain, where, at the end of two or three years, the rigour of the penal laws was either suspended or abolished, the multitude of Christians in the Roman empire, on whom a capital punishment was inflicted by a judicial sentence, will be reduced to somewhat less than two thousand persons. Since it cannot be doubted that the Christians were more numerous, and their enemies more exasperated, in the time of Diocletian than they had ever been in any former persecution, this probable and moderate computation may teach us to estimate the number of primitive saints and martyrs who sacrificed their lives for the important purpose of introducing Christianity into the world.

We shall conclude this chapter by a melancholy truth which obtrudes itself on the reluctant mind; that, even admitting, without hesitation or inquiry, all that history has recorded, or devotion has feigned, on the subject of martyrdoms, it must still be acknowledged that the Christians, in the course of their intestine dissensions, have inflicted far greater severities on each other than they had experienced from the zeal of infidels. During the ages of ignorance which followed the subversion of the Roman empire in the West, the bishops of the Imperial city extended their dominion over the laity as well as clergy of the Latin church. The fabric of superstition which they had erected, and which might long have defied the feeble efforts of reason, was at length assaulted by a crowd of daring fanatics, who, from the twelfth to the sixteenth century, assumed the popular character of reformers. The church of Rome defended by violence the empire which she had acquired by fraud; a system of peace and benevolence was soon

*When Palestine was divided into three, the præfecture of the East contained forty-eight provinces. As the ancient distinctions of nations were long since abolished, the Romans distributed the provinces according to a general proportion of their extent and opulence.

disgraced by the proscriptions, wars, massacres, and the institution of the holy office. And as the reformers were animated by the love of civil as well as of religious freedom, the Catholic princes connected their own interest with that of the clergy, and enforced by fire and the sword the terrors of spiritual censures. In the Netherlands alone more than one hundred thousand of the subjects of Charles V. are said to have suffered by the hand of the executioner; and this extraordinary number is attested by Grotius, a man of genius and learning, who preserved his moderation amidst the fury of contending sects, and who composed the annals of his own age and country at a time when the invention of printing had facilitated the means of intelligence and increased the danger of detection. If we are obliged to submit our belief to the authority of Grotius, it must be allowed that the number of Protestants who were executed in a single province and a single reign far exceeded that of the primitive martyrs in the space of three centuries and of the Roman empire. But if the improbability of the fact itself should prevail over the weight of evidence; if Grotius should be convicted of exaggerating the merit and sufferings of the reformers; we shall be naturally led to inquire what confidence can be placed in the doubtful and imperfect monuments of ancient credulity; what degree of credit can be assigned to a courtly bishop and a passionate declaimer, who, under the protection of Constantine, enjoyed the exclusive privilege of recording the persecutions inflicted on the Christians by the vanquished rivals or disregarded predecessors of their gracious sovereign.

PART 4

Constantine and the Foundation of Constantinople *(Chapters XVII and XVIII)*

Inspired by visions during his campaign against Maxentius, Constantine became convinced that the God of the Christians was a militant deity, greater and stronger than the Unconquered Sun, which he had worshipped during most of his life until then. At the battle of the Milvian Bridge in 312, he ordered that the shields of his troops be marked with the Christian insignia. Like his father, Constantius, he had always been tolerant of Christianity, but his victory under the sign of the cross convinced him that the Christian God was all-powerful. He raised his sons as Christians, but put off his own baptism as a Christian until his deathbed, so that he could appear before his pagan subjects as their Pontifex Maximus. Constantine's greatest political achievement was the construction, between 324 and 330, of a new Rome on the shores of the Bosphorus, on the site of ancient Byzantium. The city, which he called Constantinople, was easily defended, possessed a splendid harbor, and was an ideal location for governing the Empire. He adorned Constantinople with treasures from the rest of the Empire, making it the heart of the Roman world. Constantine was a brilliant administrator, but his shortsighted emphasis on the East led to the abandonment of the West. The Republican ideals of the Western Empire were superseded by the vanity and ostentation of the East. Gibbon respected Constantine for improving upon Diocletian's reforms, but he remained highly critical of the decadent aspects of his rule.

CHAPTER XVII

The unfortunate Licinius was the last rival who opposed the greatness, and the last captive who adorned the triumph, of Constantine. After a tranquil and prosperous reign the conqueror bequeathed to his family the inheritance of the Roman empire; a new capital, a new policy, and a new religion; and the innovations which he established have been embraced and consecrated by succeeding generations. The age of the great Constantine and his sons is filled with important events; but the historian must be oppressed by their number and variety, unless he diligently separates from each other the scenes which are connected only by the order of time. He will describe the political institutions that gave strength and stability to the empire before he proceeds to relate the wars and revolutions which hastened its decline. He will adopt the division unknown to the ancients of civil and ecclesiastical affairs: the victory of the Christians, and their intestine discord, will supply copious and distinct materials both for edification and for scandal.

After the defeat and abdication of Licinius his victorious rival proceeded to lay the foundations of a city destined to reign in future times the mistress of the East, and to survive the empire and religion of Constantine. The motives, whether of pride or of policy, which first induced Diocletian to withdraw himself from the ancient seat of government, had acquired additional weight by the example of his successors and the habits of forty years. Rome was insensibly confounded with the dependent kingdoms which had once acknowledged her supremacy; and the country of the Cæsars was viewed with cold indifference by a martial prince, born in the neighbourhood of the Danube, educated in the courts and armies of Asia, and invested with the purple by the legions of Britain. The Italians, who had received Constantine as their deliverer, submissively obeyed the edicts which he sometimes condescended to address to the senate and people of Rome, but they were seldom honoured with the presence of their new sovereign. During the vigour of his age Constantine, according to the various exigencies of peace and war, moved with slow dignity or with active diligence along the frontiers of his extensive dominions; and was always prepared to take the field either against a foreign or a domestic enemy. But as he gradually reached the summit of prosperity and the decline of life, he began to meditate the design of fixing in a more permanent station the strength as well as majesty of the throne. In the choice of an advantageous situation he preferred the confines of Europe and Asia; to curb with a powerful arm the barbarians who dwelt between the Danube and the Tanais; to watch with an eye of jealousy the conduct of the Persian monarch, who indignantly supported the yoke of an ignominious treaty. With these views Diocletian had selected and embellished the residence of Nicomedia: but the memory of Diocletian was justly abhorred by the protector of the church; and Constantine was not insensible to the ambition of founding a city which might perpetuate the glory of his own name. During the late operations of the war against Licinius he had sufficient opportunity to contemplate, both as a soldier and as a statesman, the incomparable position of Byzantium; and to observe how strongly it was guarded by nature against an hostile attack, whilst it was accessible on every side to the benefits of commercial intercourse. Many ages before Constantine, one of the most judicious historians of antiquity* had described the advantages of a situation from whence a feeble colony of Greeks derived the command of the sea, and the honours of a flourishing and independent republic.†

If we survey Byzantium in the extent which it acquired with the august name of Constantinople, the figure of the Imperial city may be represented under that of an unequal triangle. The obtuse point, which advances towards the east and the shores of Asia, meets and repels the waves of the Thracian Bosphorus. The northern side of the city is bounded by the harbour, and the southern is washed by the Propontis or Sea of Marmora. The basis of the triangle is opposed to the west and terminates the continent of Europe. But the admirable form and division of the circumjacent land and water cannot, without a more ample explanation, be clearly or sufficiently understood.

The winding channel through which the waters of the Euxine flow with a rapid and incessant course towards the Mediterranean received the appellation of Bosphorus, a name not less celebrated in the history than in the fables of antiquity. A crowd of temples and of votive altars,

*Polybius . . . observes that the peace of the Byzantines was frequently disturbed and the extent of their territory contracted, by the inroads of the wild Thracians.

†The navigator Byzas, who was styled the son of Neptune, founded the city 656 . . . years before the Christian era. His followers were drawn from Argos and Megara. Byzantium was afterwards rebuilt and fortified by the Spartan general Pausanias. . . .

profusely scattered along its steep and woody banks, attested the unskilfulness, the terrors, and the devotion of the Grecian navigators who, after the example of the Argonauts, explored the dangers of the inhospitable Euxine. On these banks tradition long preserved the memory of the palace of Phineus, infested by the obscene harpies; and of the sylvan reign of Amycus, who defied the son of Leda to the combat of the Cestus. The straits of the Bosphorus are terminated by the Cyanean rocks, which, according to the description of the poets, had once floated on the face of the waters, and were destined by the gods to protect the entrance of the Euxine against the eye of profane curiosity. From the Cyanean rocks to the point and harbour of Byzantium the winding length of the Bosphorus extends about sixteen miles,* and its most ordinary breadth may be computed at about one mile and a half. The *new* castles of Europe and Asia are constructed, on either continent, upon the foundations of two celebrated temples, of Serapis and of Jupiter Urius. The *old* castles, a work of the Greek emperors, command the narrowest part of the channel, in a place where the opposite banks advance within five hundred paces of each other. These fortresses were restored and strengthened by Mahomet the Second when he meditated the siege of Constantinople: but the Turkish conqueror was most probably ignorant that, near two thousand years before his reign, Darius had chosen the same situation to connect the two continents by a bridge of boats.† At a small distance from the old castles we discover the little town of Chrysopolis, or Scutari, which may almost be considered as the Asiatic suburb of Constantinople. The Bosphorus, as it begins to open into the Propontis, passes between Byzantium and Chalcedon. The latter of those cities was built by the Greeks a few years before the former; and the blindness of its founders, who overlooked the superior advantages of the opposite coast, has been stigmatised by a proverbial expression of contempt.

The harbour of Constantinople, which may be considered as an arm of the Bosphorus, obtained, in a very remote period, the denomination of the *Golden Horn.* The curve which it describes might be compared

*The ancients computed one hundred and twenty stadia, or fifteen Roman miles. They measured only from the new castles, but they carried the straits as far as the town of Chalcedon.

†Darius engraved in Greek and Assyrian letters, on two marble columns, the names of his subject nations, and the amazing numbers of his land and sea forces. The Byzantines afterwards transported these columns into the city, and used them for the altars of their tutelar deities. . . .

to the horn of a stag, or as it should seem, with more propriety, to that of an ox. The epithet of *golden* was expressive of the riches which every wind wafted from the most distant countries into the secure and capacious port of Constantinople. The river Lycus, formed by the conflux of two little streams, pours into the harbour a perpetual supply of fresh water, which serves to cleanse the bottom and to invite the periodical shoals of fish to seek their retreat in that convenient recess. As the vicissitudes of tides are scarcely felt in those seas, the constant depth of the harbour allows goods to be landed on the quays without the assistance of boats; and it has been observed that, in many places, the largest vessels may rest their prows against the houses while their sterns are floating in the water. From the mouth of the Lycus to that of the harbour this arm of the Bosphorus is more than seven miles in length. The entrance is about five hundred yards broad, and a strong chain could be occasionally drawn across it to guard the port and city from the attack of an hostile navy.

Between the Bosphorus and the Hellespont, the shores of Europe and Asia receding on either side inclose the Sea of Marmora, which was known to the ancients by the denomination of Propontis. The navigation from the issue of the Bosphorus to the entrance of the Hellespont is about one hundred and twenty miles. Those who steer their westward course through the middle of the Propontis may at once descry the high lands of Thrace and Bithynia, and never lose sight of the lofty summit of Mount Olympus, covered with eternal snows. They leave on the left a deep gulf, at the bottom of which Nicomedia was seated, the imperial residence of Diocletian; and they pass the small islands of Cyzicus and Proconnesus before they cast anchor at Gallipoli, where the sea, which separates Asia from Europe, is again contracted into a narrow channel.

The geographers who, with the most skilful accuracy, have surveyed the form and extent of the Hellespont, assign about sixty miles for the winding course, and about three miles for the ordinary breadth, of those celebrated straits. But the narrowest part of the channel is found to the northward of the old Turkish castles, between the cities of Sestus and Abydus. It was here that the adventurous Leander braved the passage of the flood for the possession of his mistress. It was here likewise, in a place where the distance between the opposite banks cannot exceed five hundred paces, that Xerxes imposed a stupendous bridge of boats, for the purpose of transporting into Europe a hundred and seventy myriads of barbarians.* A sea contracted within such narrow limits may seem but ill to deserve the singular epithet of *broad,* which Homer, as well as Orpheus, has frequently bestowed on the Hellespont. But our ideas of greatness are of a relative nature: the traveller, and especially the poet, who sailed along the Hellespont, who pursued the windings of the stream, and contemplated the rural scenery, which appeared on every side to terminate the prospect, insensibly lost the remembrance of the sea; and his fancy painted those celebrated straits with all the attributes of a mighty river, flowing with a swift current, in the midst of a woody and inland country, and at length, through a wide mouth, discharging itself into the Ægean or Archipelago. Ancient Troy, seated on an eminence at the foot of Mount Ida, overlooked the mouth of the Hellespont, which scarcely received an accession of waters from the tribute of those immortal rivulets the Simois and Scamander. The Grecian camp had stretched twelve miles along the shore, from the Sigean to the Rhœtean promontory; and the flanks of the army were guarded by the bravest chiefs who fought under the banners of Agamemnon. The first of those promontories was occupied by Achilles with his invincible myrmidons, and the dauntless Ajax pitched his tents on the other. After Ajax had fallen a sacrifice to his disappointed pride and to the ingratitude of the Greeks, his sepulchre was erected on the ground where he had defended the navy against the rage of Jove and of Hector; and the citizens of the rising town of Rhœteum celebrated his memory with divine honours. Before Constantine gave a just preference to the situation of Byzantium, he had conceived the design of erecting the seat of empire on this celebrated spot, from whence the Romans derived their fabulous origin. The extensive plain which lies below ancient Troy, towards the Rhœtean promontory and the tomb of Ajax, was first chosen for his new capital; and, though the undertaking was soon relinquished, the stately remains of unfinished walls and towers attracted the notice of all who sailed through the straits of the Hellespont.

*See the seventh book of Herodotus, who has erected an elegant trophy to his own fame and to that of his country. The review appears to have been made with tolerable accuracy; but the vanity, first of the Persians, and afterwards of the Greeks, was interested to magnify the armament and the victory. I should much doubt whether the *invaders* have ever outnumbered the *men* of any country which they attacked.

We are at present qualified to view the advantageous position of Constantinople, which appears to have been formed by nature for the centre and capital of a great monarchy. Situated in the forty-first degree of latitude, the Imperial city commanded, from her seven hills, the opposite shores of Europe and Asia; the climate was healthy and temperate, the soil fertile, the harbour secure and capacious, and the approach on the side of the continent was of small extent and easy defence. The Bosphorus and the Hellespont may be considered as the two gates of Constantinople, and the prince who possessed those important passages could always shut them against a naval enemy and open them to the fleets of commerce. The preservation of the eastern provinces may, in some degree, be ascribed to the policy of Constantine, as the barbarians of the Euxine, who in the preceding age had poured their armaments into the heart of the Mediterranean, soon desisted from the exercise of piracy, and despaired of forcing this insurmountable barrier. When the gates of the Hellespont and Bosphorus were shut, the capital still enjoyed within their spacious enclosure every production which could supply the wants or gratify the luxury of its numerous inhabitants. The sea-coasts of Thrace and Bithynia, which languish under the weight of Turkish oppression, still exhibit a rich prospect of vineyards, of gardens, and of plentiful harvests; and the Propontis has ever been renowned for an inexhaustible store of the most exquisite fish, that are taken in their stated seasons, without skill, and almost without labour. But when the passages of the straits were thrown open for trade, they alternately admitted the natural and artificial riches of the north and south, of the Euxine and of the Mediterranean. Whatever rude commodities were collected in the forests of Germany and Scythia, as far as the sources of the Tanais and the Borysthenes; whatsoever was manufactured by the skill of Europe or Asia; the corn of Egypt, and the gems and spices of the farthest India, were brought by the varying winds into the port of Constantinople, which, for many ages, attracted the commerce of the ancient world.

The prospect of beauty, of safety, and of wealth, united in a single spot, was sufficient to justify the choice of Constantine. But as some decent mixture of prodigy and fable has, in every age, been supposed to reflect a becoming majesty on the origin of great cities, the emperor was desirous of ascribing his resolution not so much to the uncertain counsels of human policy as to the infallible and eternal decrees of divine wisdom. In one of his laws he has been careful to instruct posterity that, in obedience to the commands of God, he laid the everlasting foundations of Constantinople; and though he has not condescended to relate in what manner the celestial inspiration was communicated to his mind, the defect of his modest silence has been liberally supplied by the ingenuity of succeeding writers, who describe the nocturnal vision which appeared to the fancy of Constantine as he slept within the walls of Byzantium. The tutelar genius of the city, a venerable matron sinking under the weight of years and infirmities, was suddenly transformed into a blooming maid, whom his own hands adorned with all the symbols of Imperial greatness. The monarch awoke, interpreted the auspicious omen, and obeyed, without hesitation, the will of Heaven. The day which gave birth to a city or colony was celebrated by the Romans with such ceremonies as had been ordained by a generous superstition; and though Constantine might omit some rites which savoured too strongly of their Pagan origin, yet he was anxious to leave a deep impression of hope and respect on the minds of the spectators. On foot, with a lance in his hand, the emperor himself led the solemn procession, and directed the line which was traced as the boundary of the destined capital, till the growing circumference was observed with astonishment by the assistants, who, at length, ventured to observe that he had already exceeded the most ample measure of a great city. "I shall still advance," replied Constantine, "till HE, the invisible guide who marches before me, thinks proper to stop." Without presuming to investigate the nature or motives of this extraordinary conductor, we shall content ourselves with the more humble task of describing the extent and limits of Constantinople.

In the actual state of the city, the palace and gardens of the Seraglio occupy the eastern promontory, the first of the seven hills, and cover about one hundred and fifty acres of our own measure. The seat of Turkish jealousy and despotism is erected on the foundations of a Grecian republic; but it may be supposed that the Byzantines were tempted by the conveniency of the harbour to extend their habitations on that side beyond the modern limits of the Seraglio. The new walls of Constantine stretched from the port to the Propontis across the enlarged breadth of the triangle, at the distance of fifteen stadia from the ancient fortification, and with the city of Byzantium they enclosed five of the seven hills which, to the eyes of those who approach Constantinople, appear to rise above each other in beautiful order. About a century after the death of the founder, the new buildings, extending on one side up the harbour, and on the other along the Propontis, already covered the narrow ridge of the sixth and the broad summit of the seventh hill. The necessity of protecting those suburbs from the incessant inroads of the barbarians engaged the younger Theodosius to surround his capital with an adequate and permanent enclosure of walls.* From the eastern promontory to the golden gate, the extreme length of Constantinople was about three Roman miles, the circumference measured between ten and eleven, and the surface might be computed as equal to about two thousand English acres. It is impossible to justify the vain and credulous exaggerations of modern travellers, who have sometimes stretched the limits of Constantinople over the adjacent villages of the European and even of the Asiatic coast. But the suburbs of Pera and Galata, though situate beyond the harbour, may deserve to be considered as a part of the city;† and this addition may perhaps authorise the measure of a Byzantine historian, who assigns sixteen Greek (about fourteen Roman) miles for the circumference of his native city. Such an extent may seem not unworthy of an Imperial residence. Yet Constantinople must yield to Babylon and Thebes, to ancient Rome, to London, and even to Paris.

The master of the Roman world, who aspired to erect an eternal monument of the glories of his reign, could employ in the prosecution of that great work the wealth, the labour, and all that yet remained of the genius, of obedient millions. Some estimate may be formed of the expense bestowed with Imperial liberality on the foundation of Constantinople by the allowance of about two millions five hundred thousand pounds for the construction of the walls, the porticoes, and the aqueducts. The forests that overshadowed the shores of the Euxine, and the celebrated quarries of white marble in the little island of Proconnesus, supplied an inexhaustible stock of materials, ready to be conveyed, by the convenience of a short water-carriage, to the har-

* The new wall of Theodosius was constructed in the year 413. In 447 it was thrown down by an earthquake, and rebuilt in three months by the diligence of the præfect Cyrus. The suburb of the Blachernæ was first taken into the city in the reign of Heraclius. . . .

†The sycæ, or fig-trees, formed the thirteenth region, and were very much embellished by Justinian. It has since borne the names of Pera and Galata. The etymology of the former is obvious; that of the latter is unknown. . . .

bour of Byzantium. A multitude of labourers and artificers urged the conclusion of the work with incessant toil; but the impatience of Constantine soon discovered that, in the decline of the arts, the skill as well as numbers of his architects bore a very unequal proportion to the greatness of his designs. The magistrates of the most distant provinces were therefore directed to institute schools, to appoint professors, and, by the hopes of rewards and privileges, to engage in the study and practice of architecture a sufficient number of ingenious youths who had received a liberal education. The buildings of the new city were executed by such artificers as the reign of Constantine could afford; but they were decorated by the hands of the most celebrated masters of the age of Pericles and Alexander. To revive the genius of Phidias and Lysippus surpassed indeed the power of a Roman emperor; but the immortal productions which they had bequeathed to posterity were exposed without defence to the rapacious vanity of a despot. By his commands the cities of Greece and Asia were despoiled of their most valuable ornaments. The trophies of memorable wars, the objects of religious veneration, the most finished statues of the gods and heroes, of the sages and poets of ancient times, contributed to the splendid triumph of Constantinople; and gave occasion to the remark of the historian Cedrenus, who observes, with some enthusiasm, that nothing seemed wanting except the souls of the illustrious men whom these admirable monuments were intended to represent. But it is not in the city of Constantine, nor in the declining period of an empire, when the human mind was depressed by civil and religious slavery, that we should seek for the souls of Homer and of Demosthenes.

During the siege of Byzantium the conqueror had pitched his tent on the commanding eminence of the second hill. To perpetuate the memory of his success, he chose the same advantageous position for the principal Forum, which appears to have been of a circular or rather elliptical form. The two opposite entrances formed triumphal arches; the porticoes, which enclosed it on every side, were filled with statues, and the centre of the Forum was occupied by a lofty column, of which a mutilated fragment is now degraded by the appellation of the *burnt pillar*. This column was erected on a pedestal of white marble twenty feet high, and was composed of ten pieces of porphyry, each of which measured about ten feet in height, and about thirty-three in circumference. On the summit of the pillar, above one hundred and twenty feet from the ground, stood the colossal statue of Apollo. It was of bronze, had been transported either from Athens or from a town of Phrygia, and was supposed to be the work of Phidias. The artist had represented the god of day, or, as it was afterwards interpreted, the emperor Constantine himself, with a sceptre in his right hand, the globe of the world in his left, and a crown of rays glittering on his head. The Circus, or Hippodrome, was a stately building about four hundred paces in length, and one hundred in breadth. The space between the two *metæ* or goals was filled with statues and obelisks; and we may still remark a very singular fragment of antiquity, the bodies of three serpents twisted into one pillar of brass. Their triple heads had once supported the golden tripod which, after the defeat of Xerxes, was consecrated in the temple of Delphi by the victorious Greeks. The beauty of the Hippodrome has been long since defaced by the rude hands of the Turkish conquerors, but, under the similar appellation of Atmeidan, it still serves as a place of exercise for their horses. From the throne, whence the emperor viewed the Circensian games, a winding staircase descended to the palace; a magnificent edifice, which scarcely yielded to the residence of Rome itself, and which, together with the dependent courts, gardens, and porticoes, covered a considerable extent of ground upon the banks of the Propontis, between the Hippodrome and the church of St. Sophia.* We might likewise celebrate the baths, which still retained the name of Zeuxippus, after they had been enriched by the munificence of Constantine, with lofty columns, various marbles, and above threescore statues of bronze. But we should deviate from the design of this history if we attempted minutely to describe the different buildings or quarters of the city. It may be sufficient to observe that whatever could adorn the dignity of a great capital, or contribute to the benefit or pleasure of its numerous inhabitants, was contained within the walls of Constantinople. A particular description, composed about a century after its foundation, enumerates a capitol or school of learning, a circus, two theatres, eight public and one hundred and fifty-three private baths, fifty-two porticoes, five

*There are three topographical points which indicate the situation of the palace. 1. The staircase which connected it with the Hippodrome or Atmeidan. 2. A small artificial port on the Propontis, from whence there was an easy ascent, by a flight of marble steps, to the gardens of the palace. 3. The Augusteum was a spacious court, one side of which was occupied by the front of the palace, and another by the church of St. Sophia.

granaries, eight aqueducts or reservoirs of water, four spacious halls for the meetings of the senate or courts of justice, fourteen churches, fourteen palaces, and four thousand three hundred and eighty-eight houses which, for their size or beauty, deserved to be distinguished from the multitude of plebeian habitations.

The populousness of his favoured city was the next and most serious object of the attention of its founder. In the dark ages which succeeded the translation of the empire, the remote and the immediate consequences of that memorable event were strangely confounded by the vanity of the Greeks and the credulity of the Latins. It was asserted and believed that all the noble families of Rome, the senate, and the equestrian order, with their innumerable attendants, had followed their emperor to the banks of the Propontis; that a spurious race of strangers and plebeians was left to possess the solitude of the ancient capital; and that the lands of Italy, long since converted into gardens, were at once deprived of cultivation and inhabitants. In the course of this history such exaggerations will be reduced to their just value; yet, since the growth of Constantinople cannot be ascribed to the general increase of mankind and of industry, it must be admitted that this artificial colony was raised at the expense of the ancient cities of the empire. Many opulent senators of Rome and of the eastern provinces were probably invited by Constantine to adopt for their country the fortunate spot which he had chosen for his own residence. The invitations of a master are scarcely to be distinguished from commands, and the liberality of the emperor obtained a ready and cheerful obedience. He bestowed on his favourites the palaces which he had built in the several quarters of the city, assigned them lands and pensions for the support of their dignity, and alienated the demesnes of Pontus and Asia to grant hereditary estates by the easy tenure of maintaining a house in the capital. But these encouragements and obligations soon became superfluous, and were gradually abolished. Wherever the seat of government is fixed, a considerable part of the public revenue will be expended by the prince himself, by his ministers, by the officers of justice, and by the domestics of the palace. The most wealthy of the provincials will be attracted by the powerful motives of interest and duty, of amusement and curiosity. A third and more numerous class of inhabitants will insensibly be formed, of servants, of artificers, and of merchants, who derive their subsistence from their own labour, and from the wants or luxury of the superior ranks. In less than a century Constantinople disputed with Rome itself the pre-eminence of riches and numbers. New piles of buildings, crowded together with too little regard to health or convenience, scarcely allowed the intervals of narrow streets for the perpetual throng of men, of horses, and of carriages. The allotted space of ground was insufficient to contain the increasing people, and the additional foundations, which on either side were advanced into the sea, might alone have composed a very considerable city.

The frequent and regular distributions of wine and oil, of corn or bread, of money or provisions, had almost exempted the poorer citizens of Rome from the necessity of labour. The magnificence of the first Cæsars was in some measure imitated by the founder of Constantinople: but his liberality, however it might excite the applause of the people, has incurred the censure of posterity. A nation of legislators and conquerors might assert their claim to the harvests of Africa, which had been purchased with their blood; and it was artfully contrived by Augustus, that, in the enjoyment of plenty, the Romans should lose the memory of freedom. But the prodigality of Constantine could not be excused by any consideration either of public or private interest; and the annual tribute of corn imposed upon Egypt for the benefit of his new capital was applied to feed a lazy and insolent populace, at the expense of the husbandmen of an industrious province. Some other regulations of this emperor are less liable to blame, but they are less deserving of notice. He divided Constantinople into fourteen regions or quarters, dignified the public council with the appellation of senate, communicated to the citizens the privileges of Italy, and bestowed on the rising city the title of Colony, the first and most favoured daughter of ancient Rome. The venerable parent still maintained the legal and acknowledged supremacy, which was due to her age, to her dignity, and to the remembrance of her former greatness.

As Constantine urged the progress of the work with the impatience of a lover, the walls, the porticoes, and the principal edifices were completed in a few years, or, according to another account, in a few months: but this extraordinary diligence should excite the less admiration, since many of the buildings were finished in so hasty and imperfect a manner, that, under the succeeding reign, they were preserved with difficulty from impending ruin. But while they displayed the vigour and freshness of youth, the founder prepared to celebrate the dedication of his city. The games and largesses which crowned the pomp of this memorable festival may easily be supposed; but there is one circumstance of a more singular and permanent nature, which ought not entirely to be overlooked. As often as the birthday of the city returned, the statue of Constantine, framed by his order, of gilt wood, and bearing in its right hand a small image of the genius of the place, was erected on a triumphal car. The guards, carrying white tapers, and clothed in their richest apparel, accompanied the solemn procession as it moved through the Hippodrome. When it was opposite to the throne of the reigning emperor, he rose from his seat, and with grateful reverence adored the memory of his predecessor. At the festival of the dedication, an edict, engraved on a column of marble, bestowed the title of SECOND or NEW ROME on the city of Constantine. But the name of Constantinople has prevailed over that honourable epithet, and after the revolution of fourteen centuries still perpetuates the fame of its author.

The foundation of a new capital is naturally connected with the establishment of a new form of civil and military administration. The distinct view of the complicated system of policy introduced by Diocletian, improved by Constantine, and completed by his immediate successors, may not only amuse the fancy by the singular picture of a great empire, but will tend to illustrate the secret and internal causes of its rapid decay. In the pursuit of any remarkable institution, we may be frequently led into the more early or the more recent times of the Roman history; but the proper limits of this inquiry will be included within a period of about one hundred and thirty years, from the accession of Constantine to the publication of the Theodosian code; from which, as well as from the *Notitia* of the East and West, we derive the most copious and authentic information of the state of the empire. This variety of objects will suspend, for some time, the course of the narrative; but the interruption will be censured only by those readers who are insensible to the importance of laws and manners, while they peruse, with eager curiosity, the transient intrigues of a court, or the accidental event of a battle.

The manly pride of the Romans, content with substantial power, had left to the vanity of the East the forms and ceremonies of ostentatious greatness. But when they lost even the semblance of those virtues which were derived from their ancient freedom, the simplicity of Roman manners was insensibly corrupted by the stately affectation of the courts of Asia. The distinctions of personal merit and influence, so conspicuous in a republic, so feeble and obscure under a monarchy, were abolished by the despotism of the emperors; who substituted in their room a severe subordination of rank and office, from the titled slaves who were seated on the steps of the throne, to the meanest instruments of arbitrary power. This multitude of abject dependents was interested in the support of the actual government, from the dread of a revolution which might at once confound their hopes and intercept the reward of their services. In this divine hierarchy (for such it is frequently styled) every rank was marked with the most scrupulous exactness, and its dignity was displayed in a variety of trifling and solemn ceremonies, which it was a study to learn, and a sacrilege to neglect. The purity of the Latin language was debased, by adopting, in the intercourse of pride and flattery, a profusion of epithets which Tully would scarcely have understood, and which Augustus would have rejected with indignation. The principal officers of the empire were saluted, even by the sovereign himself, with the deceitful titles of your *Sincerity,* your *Gravity,* your *Excellency,* your *Eminence,* your *sublime and wonderful Magnitude,* your *illustrious and magnificent Highness.* The codicils or patents of their office were curiously emblazoned with such emblems as were best adapted to explain its nature and high dignity—the image or portrait of the reigning emperors; a triumphal car; the book of mandates placed on a table, covered with a rich carpet, and illuminated by four tapers; the allegorical figures of the provinces which they governed; or the appellations and standards of the troops whom they commanded. Some of these official ensigns were really exhibited in their hall of audience; others preceded their pompous march whenever they appeared in public; and every circumstance of their demeanour, their dress, their ornaments, and their train, was calculated to inspire a deep reverence for the representatives of supreme majesty. By a philosophic observer the system of the Roman government might have been mistaken for a splendid theatre, filled with players of every character and degree, who repeated the language, and imitated the passions, of their original model. . . .

A people elated by pride, or soured by discontent, is seldom qualified to form a just estimate of their actual situation. The subjects of Constantine were incapable of discerning the decline of genius and manly virtue, which so far degraded them below the dignity of their ancestors; but they could feel and lament the rage of tyranny, the relaxation of discipline, and the increase of taxes. The impartial historian, who acknowledges the justice of their complaints, will observe some favourable circumstances which tended to alleviate the misery of their condition. The threatening tempest of barbarians, which so soon subverted the foundations of Roman greatness, was still repelled, or suspended, on the frontiers. The arts of luxury and literature were cultivated, and the elegant pleasures of society were enjoyed, by the inhabitants of a considerable portion of the globe. The forms, the pomp, and the expense of the civil administration contributed to restrain the irregular licence of the soldiers; and although the laws were violated by power, or perverted by subtlety, the sage principles of the Roman jurisprudence preserved a sense of order and equity unknown to the despotic governments of the East. The rights of mankind might derive some protection from religion and philosophy; and the name of freedom, which could no longer alarm, might sometimes admonish, the successors of Augustus, that they did not reign over a nation of Slaves or Barbarians.

CHAPTER XVIII

The character of the prince who removed the seat of empire, and introduced such important changes into the civil and religious constitution of his country, has fixed the attention, and divided the opinions, of mankind. By the grateful zeal of the Christians the deliverer of the church has been decorated with every attribute of a hero, and even of a saint; while the discontent of the vanquished party has compared Constantine to the most abhorred of those tyrants who, by their vice and weakness, dishonoured the Imperial purple. . . .

The person, as well as the mind, of Constantine had been enriched by nature with her choicest endowments. His stature was lofty, his countenance majestic, his deportment graceful; his strength and activity were displayed in every manly exercise, and, from his earliest youth to a very advanced season of life, he preserved the vigour of his constitution by a strict adherence to the domestic virtues of chastity and temperance. He delighted in the social intercourse of familiar conversation; and though he might sometimes indulge his disposition to raillery with less reserve than was required by the severe dignity of his station, the courtesy and liberality of his manners gained the hearts of all who approached him. The sincerity of his friendship has been suspected; yet he showed, on some occasions, that he was not incapable of a warm and lasting attachment. The disadvantage of an illiterate education had not prevented him from forming a just estimate of the value of learning; and the arts and sciences derived some encouragement from the munificent protection of Constantine. In the despatch of business his diligence was indefatigable; and the active powers of his mind were almost continually exercised in reading, writing, or meditating, in giving audience to ambassadors, and in examining the complaints of his subjects. Even those who censured the propriety of his measures were compelled to acknowledge that he possessed magnanimity to conceive, and patience to execute, the most arduous designs, without being checked either by the prejudices of education or by the clamours of the multitude. In the field he infused his own intrepid spirit into the troops, whom he conducted with the talents of a consummate general; and to his abilities, rather than to his fortune, we may ascribe the signal victories which he obtained over the foreign and domestic foes of the republic. He loved glory as the reward, perhaps as the motive, of his labours. The boundless ambition which, from the moment of his accepting the purple at York, appears as the ruling passion of his soul, may be justified by the dangers of his own situation, by the character of his rivals, by the consciousness of superior merit, and by the prospect that his success would enable him to restore peace and order to the distracted empire. In his civil wars against Maxentius and Licinius he had engaged on his side the inclinations of the people, who compared the undissembled vices of those tyrants with the spirit of wisdom and justice which seemed to direct the general tenor of the administration of Constantine.*

Had Constantine fallen on the banks of the Tiber, or even in the

*The virtues of Constantine are collected for the most part from Eutropius and the younger Victor, two sincere pagans, who wrote after the extinction of his family. Even Zosimus and the *Emperor* Julian acknowledge his personal courage and military achievements.

plains of Hadrianople, such is the character which, with a few exceptions, he might have transmitted to posterity. But the conclusion of his reign (according to the moderate and indeed tender sentence of a writer of the same age) degraded him from the rank which he had acquired among the most deserving of the Roman princes. In the life of Augustus we behold the tyrant of the republic converted almost by imperceptible degrees into the father of his country and of human kind. In that of Constantine we may contemplate a hero, who had so long inspired his subjects with love and his enemies with terror, degenerating into a cruel and dissolute monarch, corrupted by his fortune, or raised by conquest above the necessity of dissimulation. The general peace which he maintained during the last fourteen years of his reign was a period of apparent splendour rather than of real prosperity; and the old age of Constantine was disgraced by the opposite yet reconcilable vices of rapaciousness and prodigality. The accumulated treasures found in the palaces of Maxentius and Licinius were lavishly consumed; the various innovations introduced by the conqueror were attended with an increasing expense; the cost of his buildings, his court, and his festivals required an immediate and plentiful supply; and the oppression of the people was the only fund which could support the magnificence of the sovereign. His unworthy favourites, enriched by the boundless liberality of their master, usurped with impunity the privilege of rapine and corruption. A secret but universal decay was felt in every part of the public administration, and the emperor himself, though he still retained the obedience, gradually lost the esteem, of his subjects. The dress and manners which, towards the decline of life, he chose to effect, served only to degrade him in the eyes of mankind. The Asiatic pomp which had been adopted by the pride of Diocletian assumed an air of softness and effeminacy in the person of Constantine. He is represented with false hair of various colours, laboriously arranged by the skilful artists of the times; a diadem of a new and more expensive fashion; a profusion of gems and pearls, of collars and bracelets; and a variegated flowing robe of silk, most curiously embroidered with flowers of gold. In such apparel, scarcely to be excused by the youth and folly of Elagabalus, we are at a loss to discover the wisdom of an aged monarch and the simplicity of a Roman veteran. A mind thus relaxed by prosperity and indulgence was incapable of rising to that magnanimity which disdains suspicion and dares to forgive. The deaths of Maximian and Licinius may perhaps be justified by the maxims of policy as they are taught in the schools of tyrants; but an impartial narrative of the executions, or rather murders, which sullied the declining age of Constantine, will suggest to our most candid thoughts the idea of a prince who could sacrifice, without reluctance, the laws of justice and the feelings of nature to the dictates either of his passions or of his interest.

The same fortune which so invariably followed the standard of Constantine seemed to secure the hopes and comforts of his domestic life. Those among his predecessors who had enjoyed the longest and most prosperous reigns, Augustus, Trajan, and Diocletian, had been disappointed of posterity; and the frequent revolutions had never allowed sufficient time for any Imperial family to grow up and multiply under the shade of the purple. But the royalty of the Flavian line, which had been first ennobled by the Gothic Claudius, descended through several generations; and Constantine himself derived from his royal father the hereditary honours which he transmitted to his children. The emperor had been twice married. Minervina, the obscure but lawful object of his youthful attachment, had left him only one son, who was called Crispus. By Fausta, the daughter of Maximian, he had three daughters, and three sons known by the kindred names of Constantine, Constantius, and Constans. The unambitious brothers of the great Constantine, Julius Constantius, Dalmatius, and Hannibalianus, were permitted to enjoy the most honourable rank and the most affluent fortune that could be consistent with a private station. The youngest of the three lived without a name and died without posterity. His two elder brothers obtained in marriage the daughters of wealthy senators, and propagated new branches of the Imperial race. Gallus and Julian afterwards became the most illustrious of the children of Julius Constantius, the *Patrician.* The two sons of Dalmatius, who had been decorated with the vain title of *Censor,* were named Dalmatius and Hannibalianus. The two sisters of the great Constantine, Anastasia and Eutropia, were bestowed on Optatus and Nepotianus, two senators of noble birth and of consular dignity. His third sister, Constantia, was distinguished by her pre-eminence of greatness and of misery. She remained the widow of the vanquished Licinius; and it was by her entreaties that an innocent boy, the offspring of their marriage, preserved, for some time, his life, the title of Cæsar, and a precarious hope of the succession. Besides the females and the allies of the Flavian house, ten or twelve males, to whom the language of modern courts would apply the title of princes of the blood, seemed, according to the order of their birth, to be destined either to inherit or to support the throne of Constantine. But in less than thirty years this numerous and increasing family was reduced to the persons of Constantius and Julian, who alone had survived a series of crimes and calamities such as the tragic poets have deplored in the devoted lines of Pelops and of Cadmus.

Crispus, the eldest son of Constantine, and the presumptive heir of the empire, is represented by impartial historians as an amiable and accomplished youth. The care of his education, or at least of his studies, was intrusted to Lactantius, the most eloquent of the Christians; a preceptor admirably qualified to form the taste and to excite the virtues of his illustrious disciple. At the age of seventeen Crispus was invested with the title of Cæsar, and the administration of the Gallic provinces, where the inroads of the Germans gave him an early occasion of signalising his military prowess. In the civil war which broke out soon afterwards, the father and son divided their powers; and this history has already celebrated the valour as well as conduct displayed by the latter in forcing the straits of the Hellespont, so obstinately defended by the superior fleet of Licinius. This naval victory contributed to determine the event of the war, and the names of Constantine and of Crispus were united in the joyful acclamations of their eastern subjects, who loudly proclaimed that the world had been subdued, and was now governed, by an emperor endowed with every virtue, and by his illustrious son, a prince beloved of Heaven, and the lively image of his father's perfections. The public favour, which seldom accompanies old age, diffused its lustre over the youth of Crispus. He deserved the esteem and he engaged the affections of the court, the army, and the people. The experienced merit of a reigning monarch is acknowledged by his subjects with reluctance, and frequently denied with partial and discontented murmurs; while, from the opening virtues of his successor, they fondly conceive the most unbounded hopes of private as well as public felicity.

This dangerous popularity soon excited the attention of Constantine, who, both as a father and as a king, was impatient of an equal. Instead of attempting to secure the allegiance of his son by the generous ties of confidence and gratitude, he resolved to prevent the mischiefs which might be apprehended from dissatisfied ambition. Crispus soon had reason to complain that, while his infant brother Constantius was sent with the title of Cæsar to reign over his peculiar department of the Gallic provinces, *he,* a prince of mature years, who had performed such recent and signal services, instead of being raised to the superior rank of Augustus, was confined almost a prisoner to his father's court, and exposed, without power or defence, to every calumny which the malice of his enemies could suggest. Under such painful circumstances the royal youth might not always be able to compose his behaviour or suppress his discontent; and we may be assured that he was encompassed by a train of indiscreet or perfidious followers, who assiduously studied to inflame, and who were perhaps instructed to betray, the unguarded warmth of his resentment. An edict of Constantine, published about this time, manifestly indicates his real or affected suspicions that a secret conspiracy had been formed against his person and government. By all the allurements of honours and rewards he invites informers of every degree to accuse, without exception, his magistrates or ministers, his friends or his most intimate favourites, protesting, with a solemn asseveration, that he himself will listen to the charge, that he himself will revenge his injuries; and concluding with a prayer, which discovers some apprehension of danger, that the providence of the Supreme Being may still continue to protect the safety of the emperor and of the empire.

The informers who complied with so liberal an invitation were sufficiently versed in the arts of courts to select the friends and adherents of Crispus as the guilty persons; nor is there any reason to distrust the veracity of the emperor, who had promised an ample measure of revenge and punishment. The policy of Constantine maintained, however, the same appearances of regard and confidence towards a son whom he began to consider as his most irreconcilable enemy. Medals were struck with the customary vows for the long and auspicious reign of the young Cæsar; and as the people, who was not admitted into the secrets of the palace, still loved his virtues and respected his dignity, a poet, who solicits his recall from exile, adores with equal devotion the majesty of the father and that of the son. The time was now arrived for celebrating the august ceremony of the twentieth year of the reign of Constantine, and the emperor, for that purpose, removed his court from Nicomedia to Rome, where the most splendid preparations had been made for his reception. Every eye and every tongue affected to express their sense of the general happiness, and the veil of ceremony and dissimulation was drawn for a while over the darkest designs of revenge and murder. In the midst of the festival the unfortunate Crispus was apprehended by order of the emperor, who laid aside the tenderness of a father without assuming the equity of a judge. The examination was short and private; and as it was thought decent to conceal the fate of the young prince from the eyes of the Roman people, he was sent under a strong guard to Pola, in Istria, where, soon afterwards, he was put to death, either by the hand of the executioner or by the more gentle operation of poison. The Cæsar Licinius, a youth of amiable manners, was involved in the ruin of Crispus, and the stern jealousy of Constantine was unmoved by the prayers and tears of his favourite sister, pleading for the life of a son whose rank was his only crime, and whose loss she did not long survive. . . .

Part 5

Julian the Apostate *(Chapter XXII)*

Constantine's heirs fought as much amongst themselves as they did to preserve his Christianized Empire. When his son Constantius finally gained imperial control, he found himself to be the master of a divided, poorly administered world. He elevated his cousin Julian to the rank of Caesar, giving him his daughter Helena in marriage at the same time. Julian was sent to Gaul to combat the Franks and Alamanni, and in 360 his victorious troops proclaimed him Augustus. After Constantius' death in 361, Julian became Emperor. Historians have dubbed Julian the "Apostate" because of his pagan religious views. He had been educated in the old philosophy and never truly accepted Christianity. Associating the old paganism with Rome's greatness, he hoped to establish a new paganism based on Neoplatonism. While many of his subjects embraced this new paganism, Julian never managed to obliterate the influence of Christianity, and it is doubtful whether he would have succeeded in attaining his goal even if he had lived to rule the Empire for more than three years.

CHAPTER XXII

. . . Philosophy had instructed Julian to compare the advantages of action and retirement; but the elevation of his birth and the accidents of his life never allowed him the freedom of choice. He might perhaps sincerely have preferred the groves of the Academy and the society of Athens; but he was constrained, at first by the will, and afterwards by the injustice of Constantius, to expose his person and fame to the dangers of Imperial greatness; and to make himself accountable to the world and to posterity for the happiness of millions. Julian recollected with terror the observation of his master Plato, that the government of our flocks and herds is always committed to beings of a superior species; and that the conduct of nations requires and deserves the celestial powers of the Gods or of the Genii. From this principle he justly concluded that the man who presumes to reign should aspire to the perfection of the divine nature; that he should purify his soul from her mortal and terrestrial part; that he should extinguish his appetites, enlighten his understanding, regulate his passions, and subdue the wild beast which, according to the lively metaphor of Aristotle, seldom fails to ascend the throne of a despot. The throne of Julian, which the death of Constantius fixed on an independent basis, was the seat of reason, of virtue, and perhaps of vanity. He despised the honours, renounced the pleasures, and discharged with incessant diligence the duties of his exalted station: and there were few among his subjects who would have consented to relieve him from the weight of the diadem, had they been obliged to submit their time and their actions to the rigorous laws which their philosophic emperor imposed on himself. One of his most intimate friends, who had often shared the frugal simplicity of his table, has remarked that his light and sparing diet (which was usually of the vegetable kind) left his mind and body always free and active for the various and important business of an author, a pontiff, a magistrate, a general, and a prince. In one and the same day he gave audience to several ambassadors, and wrote or dictated a great number of letters to his generals, his civil magistrates, his private friends, and the different cities of his dominions. He listened to the memorials which had been received, considered the subject of the petitions, and signified his intentions more rapidly than they could be taken in shorthand by the diligence of his secretaries. He possessed such flexibility of thought, and such firmness of attention, that he could employ his hand to write, his ear to listen, and his voice to dictate; and pursue at once three several trains of ideas without hesitation, and without error. While his ministers reposed, the prince flew with agility from one labour to another; and, after a hasty dinner, retired into his library till the public business which he had appointed for the evening summoned him to interrupt the prosecution of his studies. The supper of the emperor was still less substantial than the former meal; his sleep was never clouded by the fumes of indigestion; and, except in the short interval of a marriage which was the effect of policy rather than love, the chaste Julian never shared his bed with a female companion. He was soon awakened by the entrance of fresh secretaries, who had slept the preceding day; and his servants were obliged to wait alternately, while their indefatigable master allowed himself scarcely any other refreshment than the change of occupations. The predecessors of Julian, his uncle, his brother, and his cousin, indulged their puerile taste for the games of the Circus, under the specious pretence of complying with the inclinations of the people; and they frequently remained the greatest part of the day as idle spectators, and as a part of the splendid spectacle, till the ordinary round of twenty-four races was completely finished. On solemn festivals, Julian, who felt and professed an unfashionable dislike to these frivolous amusements, condescended to appear in the Circus; and, after bestowing a careless glance on five or six of the races, he hastily withdrew with the impatience of a philosopher, who considered every moment as lost that was not devoted to the advantage of the public or the improvement of his own mind. By this avarice of time he seemed to protract the short duration of his reign; and, if the dates were less securely ascertained, we should refuse to believe that only sixteen months elapsed between the death of Constantius and the departure of his successor for the Persian war. The actions of Julian can only be preserved by the care of the historian; but the portion of his voluminous writings which is still extant remains as a monument of the application, as well as of the genius, of the emperor. The Misopogon, the Cæsars, several of his orations, and his elaborate work against the Christian religion, were composed in the long nights of the two winters, the former of which he passed at Constantinople, and the latter at Antioch.

The reformation of the Imperial court was one of the first and most necessary acts of the government of Julian. Soon after his entrance into the palace of Constantinople he had occasion for the service of a barber. An officer, magnificently dressed, immediately presented himself. "It is a barber," exclaimed the prince, with affected surprise, "that I want, and not a receiver-general of the finances." He questioned the man concerning the profits of his employment, and was informed that, besides a large salary and some valuable perquisites, he enjoyed a daily allowance for twenty servants and as many horses. A thousand barbers, a thousand cupbearers, a thousand cooks, were distributed in the several offices of luxury; and the number of eunuchs could be compared only with the insects of a summer's day. The monarch who resigned to his subjects the superiority of merit and virtue was distinguished by the oppressive magnificence of his dress, his table, his buildings, and his train. The stately palaces erected by Constantine and his sons were decorated with many-coloured marbles and ornaments of massy gold. The most exquisite dainties were procured to gratify their pride rather than their taste; birds of the most distant climates, fish from the most remote seas, fruits out of their natural season, winter roses, and summer snows. The domestic crowd of the palace surpassed the expense of the legions; yet the smallest part of this costly multitude was subservient to the use, or even to the splendour, of the throne. The monarch was disgraced, and the people was injured, by the creation and sale of an infinite number of obscure and even titular employments; and the most worthless of mankind might purchase the privilege of being maintained, without the necessity of labour, from the public revenue. The waste of an enormous household, the increase of fees and perquisites, which were soon claimed as a lawful debt, and the bribes which they extorted from those who feared their enmity or solicited their favour, suddenly enriched these haughty menials. They abused their fortune, without considering their past or their future condition; and their rapine and venality could be equalled only by the extravagance of their dissipations. Their silken robes were embroidered with gold, their tables were served with delicacy and profusion; the houses which they built for their own use would have covered the farm of an ancient consul; and the most honourable citizens were obliged to dismount from their horses and respectfully to salute an eunuch whom they met on the public highway. The luxury of the palace excited the contempt and indignation of Julian, who usually slept on the ground, who yielded with reluctance to the indispensable calls of nature, and who placed his vanity not in emulating, but in despising the pomp of royalty.

By the total extirpation of a mischief which was magnified even beyond its real extent, he was impatient to relieve the distress and to appease the murmurs of the people, who support with less uneasiness the weight of taxes if they are convinced that the fruits of their industry are appropriated to the service of the state. But in the execution of this salutary work Julian is accused of proceeding with too much haste and inconsiderable severity. By a single edict he reduced the palace of Constantinople to an immense desert, and dismissed with ignominy the whole train of slaves and dependents,* without providing any just, or at least benevolent, exceptions for the age, the services, or the poverty of the faithful domestics of the Imperial family. Such indeed was the temper of Julian, who seldom recollected the fundamental maxim of Aristotle, that true virtue is placed at an equal distance between the opposite vices. The splendid and effeminate dress of the Asiatics, the curls and paint, the collars and bracelets, which had appeared so ridiculous in the person of Constantine, were consistently rejected by his philosophic successor. But, with the fopperies, Julian affected to renounce the decencies of dress; and seemed to value himself for his neglect of the laws of cleanliness. In a satirical performance, which was designed for the public eye, the emperor descants with pleasure, and even with pride, on the length of his nails and the inky blackness of his hands; protests that, although the greatest part of his body was covered with hair, the use of the razor was confined to his head alone; and celebrates with visible complacency the shaggy and *populous* beard which he fondly cherished, after the example of the philosophers of Greece. Had Julian consulted the simple dictates of reason, the first magistrate of the Romans would have scorned the affectation of Diogenes, as well as that of Darius.

But the work of public reformation would have remained imperfect if Julian had only corrected the abuses, without punishing the crimes, of his predecessor's reign. "We are now delivered," says he, in a familiar letter to one of his intimate friends, "we are now surprisingly delivered from the voracious jaws of the Hydra. I do not mean to apply that epithet to my brother Constantius. He is no more; may the earth lie light on his head! But his artful and cruel favourites studied to deceive and exasperate a prince whose natural mildness cannot be praised without some efforts of adulation. It is not, however, my intention that even those men should be oppressed: they are accused,

*Yet Julian himself was accused of bestowing whole towns on the eunuchs . . . Libanius contents himself with a cold but positive denial of the fact, which seems indeed to belong more properly to Constantius. This charge, however, may allude to some unknown circumstance.

and they shall enjoy the benefit of a fair and impartial trial." To conduct this inquiry, Julian named six judges of the highest rank in the state and army, and, as he wished to escape the reproach of condemning his personal enemies, he fixed this extraordinary tribunal at Chalcedon, on the Asiatic side of the Bosphorus, and transferred to the commissioners an absolute power to pronounce and execute their final sentence, without delay and without appeal. The office of president was exercised by the venerable præfect of the East, a *second* Sallust,* whose virtues conciliated the esteem of Greek sophists and of Christian bishops. He was assisted by the eloquent Mamertinus, one of the consuls elect, whose merit is loudly celebrated by the doubtful evidence of his own applause. But the civil wisdom of two magistrates was overbalanced by the ferocious violence of four generals, Nevitta, Agilo, Jovinus, and Arbetio. Arbetio, whom the public would have seen with less surprise at the bar than on the bench, was supposed to possess the secret of the commission; the armed and angry leaders of the Jovian and Herculian bands encompassed the tribunal, and the judges were alternately swayed by the laws of justice and by the clamours of faction.

The chamberlain Eusebius, who had so long abused the favour of Constantius, expiated, by an ignominious death, the insolence, the corruption, and cruelty of his servile reign. The executions of Paul and Apodemius (the former of whom was burnt alive) were accepted as an inadequate atonement by the widows and orphans of so many hundred Romans whom those legal tyrants had betrayed and murdered. But Justice herself (if we may use the pathetic expression of Ammianus) appeared to weep over the fate of Ursulus, the treasurer of the empire, and his blood accused the ingratitude of Julian, whose distress had been seasonably relieved by the intrepid liberality of that honest minister. The rage of the soldiers, whom he had provoked by his indiscretion, was the cause and the excuse of his death; and the emperor, deeply wounded by his own reproaches and those of the public, offered some consolation to the family of Ursulus by the restitution of his confiscated fortunes. Before the end of the year in which

*The two Sallusts, the præfect of Gaul and the præfect of the East, must be carefully distinguished . . . I have used the surname of *Secundus* as a convenient epithet. The second Sallust extorted the esteem of the Christians themselves; and Gregory Nazianzen, who condemned his religion, has celebrated his virtues . . .

they had been adorned with the ensigns of the prefecture and consulship, Taurus and Florentius were reduced to implore the clemency of the inexorable tribunal of Chalcedon. The former was banished to Vercellæ in Italy, and a sentence of death was pronounced against the latter. A wise prince should have rewarded the crime of Taurus: the faithful minister, when he was no longer able to oppose the progress of a rebel, had taken refuge in the court of his benefactor and his lawful sovereign. But the guilt of Florentius justified the severity of the judges, and his escape served to display the magnanimity of Julian, who nobly checked the interested diligence of an informer, and refused to learn what place concealed the wretched fugitive from his just resentment. Some months after the tribunal of Chalcedon had been dissolved, the prætorian vicegerent of Africa, the notary Gaudentius, and Artemius,* duke of Egypt, were executed at Antioch. Artemius had reigned the cruel and corrupt tyrant of a great province; Gaudentius had long practised the arts of calumny against the innocent, the virtuous, and even the person of Julian himself. Yet the circumstances of their trial and condemnation were so unskilfully managed that these wicked men obtained, in the public opinion, the glory of suffering for the obstinate loyalty with which they had supported the cause of Constantius. The rest of his servants were protected by a general act of oblivion, and they were left to enjoy with impunity the bribes which they had accepted either to defend the oppressed or to oppress the friendless. This measure, which, on the soundest principles of policy, may deserve our approbation, was executed in a manner which seemed to degrade the majesty of the throne. Julian was tormented by the importunities of a multitude, particularly of Egyptians, who loudly redemanded the gifts which they had imprudently or illegally bestowed; he foresaw the endless prosecution of vexatious suits, and he engaged a promise, which ought always to have been sacred, that if they would repair to Chalcedon, he would meet them in person, to hear and determine their complaints. But as soon as they were landed, he issued an absolute order, which prohibited the watermen from transporting any Egyptian to Constantinople, and thus detained his disappointed

*. . . The merit of Artemius, who demolished temples, and was put to death by an apostate, has tempted the Greek and Latin churches to honour him as a martyr. But as ecclesiastical history attests that he was not only a tyrant, but an Arian, it is not altogether easy to justify this indiscreet promotion. . . .

clients on the Asiatic shore, till, their patience and money being utterly exhausted, they were obliged to return with indignant murmurs to their native country.

The numerous army of spies, of agents, and informers enlisted by Constantius to secure the repose of one man, and to interrupt that of millions, was immediately disbanded by his generous successor. Julian was slow in his suspicions, and gentle in his punishments; and his contempt of treason was the result of judgment, of vanity, and of courage. Conscious of superior merit, he was persuaded that few among his subjects would dare to meet him in the field, to attempt his life, or even to seat themselves on his vacant throne. The philosopher could excuse the hasty sallies of discontent, and the hero could despise the ambitious projects which surpassed the fortune or the abilities of the rash conspirators. A citizen of Ancyra had prepared for his own use a purple garment, and this indiscreet action, which, under the reign of Constantius, would have been considered as a capital offence, was reported to Julian by the officious importunity of a private enemy. The monarch, after making some inquiry into the rank and character of his rival, despatched the informer with a present of a pair of purple slippers, to complete the magnificence of his Imperial habit. A more dangerous conspiracy was formed by ten of the domestic guards, who had resolved to assassinate Julian in the field of exercise near Antioch. Their intemperance revealed their guilt, and they were conducted in chains to the presence of their injured sovereign, who, after a lively representation of the wickedness and folly of their enterprise, instead of a death of torture, which they deserved and expected, pronounced a sentence of exile against the two principal offenders. The only instance in which Julian seemed to depart from his accustomed clemency was the execution of a rash youth, who, with a feeble hand, had aspired to seize the reins of empire. But that youth was the son of Marcellus, the general of cavalry, who, in the first campaign of the Gallic war, had deserted the standard of the Cæsar and the republic. Without appearing to indulge his personal resentment, Julian might easily confound the crime of the son and of the father; but he was reconciled by the distress of Marcellus, and the liberality of the emperor endeavoured to heal the wound which had been inflicted by the hand of justice.

Julian was not insensible of the advantages of freedom. From his studies he had imbibed the spirit of ancient sages and heroes; his life and fortunes had depended on the caprice of a tyrant; and, when he ascended the throne, his pride was sometimes mortified by the reflection that the slaves who would not dare to censure his defects were not worthy to applaud his virtues. He sincerely abhorred the system of oriental despotism which Diocletian, Constantine, and the patient habits of four score years, had established in the empire. A motive of superstition prevented the execution of the design which Julian had frequently meditated, of relieving his head from the weight of a costly diadem; but he absolutely refused the title of *Dominus* or *Lord,* a word which was grown so familiar to the ears of the Romans, that they no longer remembered its servile and humiliating origin. The office, or rather the name, of consul was cherished by a prince who contemplated with reverence the ruins of the republic; and the same behaviour which had been assumed by the prudence of Augustus was adopted by Julian from choice and inclination. On the calends of January, at break of day, the new consuls, Mamertinus and Nevitta, hastened to the palace to salute the emperor. As soon as he was informed of their approach, he leaped from his throne, eagerly advanced to meet them, and compelled the blushing magistrates to receive the demonstrations of his affected humility. From the palace they proceeded to the senate. The emperor, on foot, marched before their litters, and the gazing multitude admired the image of ancient times, or secretly blamed a conduct which, in their eyes, degraded the majesty of the purple. But the behaviour of Julian was uniformly supported. During the games of the Circus, he had, imprudently or designedly, performed the manumission of a slave in the presence of the consul. The moment he was reminded that he had trespassed on the jurisdiction of *another* magistrate, he condemned himself to pay a fine of ten pounds of gold, and embraced this public occasion of declaring to the world that he was subject, like the rest of his fellow-citizens, to the laws, and even to the forms, of the republic. The spirit of his administration, and his regard for the place of his nativity, induced Julian to confer on the senate of Constantinople the same honours, privileges, and authority which were still enjoyed by the senate of ancient Rome. A legal fiction was introduced and gradually established, that one half of the national council had migrated into the East, and the despotic successors of Julian, accepting the title of Senators, acknowledged themselves the members of a respectable body which was permitted to represent the majesty of the Roman name. From Constantinople the attention of the monarch was extended to the municipal senates of the provinces. He abolished, by repeated edicts, the unjust and pernicious exemptions which had withdrawn so many idle citizens from the service of their country; and by imposing an equal distribution of public duties, he restored the strength, the splendour, or, according to the glowing expression of Libanius, the soul of the expiring cities of his empire. The venerable age of Greece excited the most tender compassion in the mind of Julian, which kindled into rapture when he recollected the gods, the heroes, and the men superior to heroes and to gods, who had bequeathed to the latest posterity the monuments of their genius or the example of their virtues. He relieved the distress and restored the beauty of the cities of Epirus and Peloponnesus. Athens acknowledged him for her benefactor, Argos for her deliverer. The pride of Corinth, again rising from her ruins with the honours of a Roman colony, exacted a tribute from the adjacent republics for the purpose of defraying the games of the Isthmus, which were celebrated in the amphitheatre with the hunting of bears and panthers. From this tribute the cities of Elis, of Delphi, and of Argos, which had inherited from their remote ancestors the sacred office of perpetuating the Olympic, the Pythian, and the Nemean games, claimed a just exemption. The immunity of Elis and Delphi was respected by the Corinthians, but the poverty of Argos tempted the insolence of oppression, and the feeble complaints of its deputies were silenced by the decree of a provincial magistrate, who seems to have consulted only the interest of the capital in which he resided. Seven years after this sentence Julian allowed the cause to be referred to a superior tribunal, and his eloquence was interposed, most probably with success, in the defence of a city which had been the royal seat of Agamemnon, and had given to Macedonia a race of kings and conquerors.

The laborious administration of military and civil affairs, which were multiplied in proportion to the extent of the empire, exercised the abilities of Julian; but he frequently assumed the two characters of Orator and of Judge, which are almost unknown to the modern sovereigns of Europe. The arts of persuasion, so diligently cultivated by the first Cæsars, were neglected by the military ignorance and Asiatic pride of their successors, and, if they condescended to harangue the soldiers, whom they feared, they treated with silent disdain the senators, whom they despised. The assemblies of the senate, which Constantius had avoided, were considered by Julian as the place where he could exhibit with the most propriety the maxims of a republican and the talents of a rhetorician. He alternately practised, as in a school of declamation, the several modes of praise, of censure, of exhortation; and his friend Libanius has remarked that the study of Homer taught him to imitate the simple, concise style of Menelaus, the copiousness of Nestor, whose words descended like the flakes of a winter's snow, or the pathetic and forcible eloquence of Ulysses. The functions of a judge, which are sometimes incompatible with those of a prince, were exercised by Julian not only as a duty, but as an amusement; and although he might have trusted the integrity and discernment of his Prætorian præfects, he often placed himself by their side on the seat of judgment. The acute penetration of his mind was agreeably occupied in detecting and defeating the chicanery of the advocates, who laboured to disguise the truth of facts and to pervert the sense of the laws. He sometimes forgot the gravity of his station, asked indiscreet or unseasonable questions, and betrayed, by the loudness of his voice and the agitation of his body, the earnest vehemence with which he maintained his opinion against the judges, the advocates, and their clients. But his knowledge of his own temper prompted him to encourage, and even to solicit, the reproof of his friends and ministers: and whenever they ventured to oppose the irregular sallies of his passions, the spectators could observe the shame as well as the gratitude of their monarch. The decrees of Julian were almost always founded on the principles of justice, and he had the firmness to resist the two most dangerous temptations which assault the tribunal of a sovereign under the specious forms of compassion and equity. He decided the merits of the cause without weighing the circumstances of the parties; and the poor, whom he wished to relieve, were condemned to satisfy the just demands of a noble and wealthy adversary. He carefully distinguished the judge from the legislator; and though he meditated a necessary reformation of the Roman jurisprudence, he pronounced sentence according to the strict and literal interpretation of those laws which the magistrates were bound to execute and the subjects to obey.

The generality of princes, if they were stripped of their purple and cast naked into the world, would immediately sink to the lowest rank of society, without a hope of emerging from their obscurity. But the personal merit of Julian was, in some measure, independent of his fortune. Whatever had been his choice of life, by the force of intrepid courage, lively wit, and intense application, he would have obtained, or at least he would have deserved, the highest honours of his profession, and Julian might have raised himself to the rank of minister or general of the state in which he was born a private citizen. If the jealous caprice of power had disappointed his expectations; if he had prudently declined the paths of greatness, the employment of the same talents in studious solitude would have placed beyond the reach of kings his present happiness and his immortal fame. When we inspect with minute, or perhaps malevolent, attention the portrait of Julian, something seems wanting to the grace and perfection of the whole figure. His genius was less powerful and sublime than that of Cæsar, nor did he possess the consummate prudence of Augustus. The virtues of Trajan appear more steady and natural, and the philosophy of Marcus is more simple and consistent. Yet Julian sustained adversity with firmness, and prosperity with moderation. After an interval of one hundred and twenty years from the death of Alexander Severus, the Romans beheld an emperor who made no distinction between his duties and his pleasures, who laboured to relieve the distress and to revive the spirit of his subjects, and who endeavoured always to connect authority with merit, and happiness with virtue. Even faction, and religious faction, was constrained to acknowledge the superiority of his genius in peace as well as in war, and to confess, with a sigh, that the apostate Julian was a lover of his country, and that he deserved the empire of the world.*

*. . . Ductor fortissimus armis,
Conditor et legum celeberrimus, ore manuque
Consultor patriæ, sed non consultor habendæ
Religionis, amans tercentûm millia Divûm.
Perfidus ille Deo, quamvis non perfidus orbi.
Prudent. Apotheosis, 450, etc.

The consciousness of a generous sentiment seems to have raised the Christian poet above his usual mediocrity.

Part 6

The Ruin of Paganism *(Chapter XXVIII)*

With the death of Julian, the house of Constantine was extinguished, along with the influence of renascent paganism. Julian was succeeded by Jovian (363–64), who concluded an unfavorable settlement with the Persians and returned to Christianity. He died while still in Asia Minor, and was succeeded by Valentinian I (364–75), who, with his brother Valens (364–78), devoted his energies to defending the Rhenish and Danubian frontiers against the onslaught of the barbarians. After his death, and the death of his brother at the battle of Adrianople in 378, his son, Gratian (375–383), appointed Theodosius I (379–95), the son of Valentinian's most brilliant general, Theodosius the Elder, to act as junior Augustus in the East. Theodosius achieved a peace with the Goths in the Balkans, and, after the death of Gratian and his brother Valentinian II, reunited the Empire for a short period. Theodosius was the first Emperor to be baptized "in the true faith of the Trinity," as opposed to the Arianism and Athanasianism that prevailed before his emergence as a power. The combination of his military genius and his theological zeal (which was inspired by his mentor, St. Ambrose, the Bishop of Milan) enabled him to triumph over the pagans and the heretics, and to prolong—albeit briefly—the life of the Empire.

CHAPTER XXVIII

... The ruin of Paganism, in the age of Theodosius, is perhaps the only example of the total extirpation of any ancient and popular superstition, and may therefore deserve to be considered as a singular event in the history of the human mind. The Christians, more especially the clergy, had impatiently supported the prudent delays of Constantine and the equal toleration of the elder Valentinian; nor could they deem their conquest perfect or secure as long as their adversaries were permitted to exist. The influence which Ambrose and his brethren had acquired over the youth of Gratian and the piety of Theodosius was employed to infuse the maxims of persecution into the breasts of their Imperial proselytes. Two specious principles of religious jurisprudence were established, from whence they deduced a direct and rigorous conclusion against the subjects of the empire who still adhered to the ceremonies of their ancestors: *that* the magistrate is, in some measure, guilty of the crimes which he neglects to prohibit or to punish; and *that* the idolatrous worship of fabulous deities and real dæmons is the most abominable crime against the supreme majesty of the Creator. The laws of Moses and the examples of Jewish history were hastily, perhaps erroneously, applied by the clergy to the mild and universal reign of Christianity. The zeal of the emperors was excited to vindicate their own honour and that of the Deity; and the temples of the Roman world were subverted about sixty years after the conversion of Constantine.

From the age of Numa to the reign of Gratian, the Romans preserved the regular succession of the several colleges of the sacerdotal order. Fifteen PONTIFFS exercised their supreme jurisdiction over all things and persons that were consecrated to the service of the gods; and the various questions which perpetually arose in a loose and traditionary system were submitted to the judgment of their holy tribunal. Fifteen grave and learned AUGURS observed the face of the heavens, and prescribed the actions of heroes according to the flight of birds. Fifteen keepers of the Sibylline books (their name of QUINDECEMVIRS was derived from their number) occasionally consulted the history of future, and, as it should seem, of contingent events. Six VESTALS devoted their virginity to the guard of the sacred fire and of the unknown pledges of the duration of Rome, which no mortal had been suffered to behold with impunity. Seven EPULOS prepared the table of the gods, conducted the solemn procession, and regulated the ceremonies of the annual festival. The three FLAMENS of Jupiter, of Mars, and of Quirinus, were considered as the peculiar ministers of the three most powerful deities, who watched over the fate of Rome and of the universe. The KING of the SACRIFICES represented the person of Numa and of his successors in the religious functions, which could be performed only by royal hands. The confraternities of the SALIANS, the LUPERCALS, etc., practised such rites as might extort a smile of contempt from every reasonable man, with a lively confidence of recommending themselves to the favour of the immortal gods. The authority which the Roman priests had formerly obtained in the counsels of the republic was gradually abolished by the establishment of monarchy and the removal of the seat of empire. But the dignity of their sacred character was still protected by the laws and manners of their country; and they still continued, more especially the college of pontiffs, to exercise in the capital, and sometimes in the provinces, the rights of their ecclesiastical and civil jurisdiction. Their robes of purple, chariots of state, and sumptuous entertainments attracted the admiration of the people; and they received, from the consecrated lands and the public revenue, an ample stipend, which liberally supported the splendour of the priesthood and all the expenses of the religious worship of the state. As the service of the altar was not incompatible with the command of armies, the Romans, after their consulships and triumphs, aspired to the place of pontiff or of augur; the seats of Cicero and Pompey were filled, in the fourth century, by the most illustrious members of the senate; and the dignity of their birth reflected additional splendour on their sacerdotal character. The fifteen priests who composed the college of pontiffs enjoyed a more distinguished rank as the companions of their sovereign; and the Christian emperors condescended to accept the robe and ensigns which were appropriated to the office of supreme pontiff. But when Gratian ascended the throne, more scrupulous or more enlightened, he sternly rejected those profane symbols; applied to the service of the state or of the church the revenues of the priests and vestals; abolished their honours and immunities; and dissolved the ancient fabric of Roman superstition, which was supported by the opinions and habits of eleven hundred years. Paganism was still the constitutional religion of the senate.

The hall or temple in which they assembled was adorned by the statue and altar of Victory: a majestic female standing on a globe, with flowing garments, expanded wings, and a crown of laurel in her outstretched hand. The senators were sworn on the altar of the goddess to observe the laws of the emperor and of the empire; and a solemn offering of wine and incense was the ordinary prelude of their public deliberations. The removal of this ancient monument was the only injury which Constantius had offered to the superstition of the Romans. The altar of Victory was again restored by Julian, tolerated by Valentinian, and once more banished from the senate by the zeal of Gratian. But the emperor yet spared the statues of the gods which were exposed to the public veneration: four hundred and twenty-four temples, or chapels, still remained to satisfy the devotion of the people, and in every quarter of Rome the delicacy of the Christians was offended by the fumes of idolatrous sacrifice.

But the Christians formed the least numerous party in the senate of Rome; and it was only by their absence that they could express their dissent from the legal, though profane, acts of a Pagan majority. In that assembly the dying embers of freedom were, for a moment, revived and inflamed by the breath of fanaticism. Four respectable deputations were successively voted to the Imperial court, to represent the grievances of the priesthood and the senate, and to solicit the restoration of the altar of Victory. The conduct of this important business was intrusted to the eloquent Symmachus, a wealthy and noble senator, who united the sacred characters of pontiff and augur with the civil dignities of proconsul of Africa and præfect of the city. The breast of Symmachus was animated by the warmest zeal for the cause of expiring Paganism; and his religious antagonists lamented the abuse of his genius and the inefficacy of his moral virtues. The orator, whose petition is extant to the emperor Valentinian, was conscious of the difficulty and danger of the office which he had assumed. He cautiously avoids every topic which might appear to reflect on the religion of his sovereign; humbly declares that prayers and entreaties are his only arms; and artfully draws his arguments from the schools of rhetoric rather than from those of philosophy. Symmachus endeavours to seduce the imagination of a young prince, by displaying the attributes of the goddess of Victory; he insinuates that the confiscation of the revenues which were consecrated to the service of the gods was a measure unworthy of his liberal and disinterested character; and he maintains that the Roman sacrifices would be deprived of their force and energy, if they were no longer celebrated at the expense as well as in the name of the republic. Even scepticism is made to supply an apology for superstition. The great and incomprehensible *secret* of the universe eludes the inquiry of man. Where reason cannot instruct, custom may be permitted to guide; and every nation seems to consult the dictates of prudence, by a faithful attachment to those rites and opinions which have received the sanction of ages. If those ages have been crowned with glory and prosperity—if the devout people has frequently obtained the blessings which they have solicited at the altars of the gods—it must appear still more advisable to persist in the same salutary practice, and not to risk the unknown perils that may attend any rash innovations. The test of antiquity and success was applied with singular advantage to the religion of Numa; and ROME herself, the celestial genius that presided over the fates of the city, is introduced by the orator to plead her own cause before the tribunal of the emperors. "Most excellent princes," says the venerable matron, "fathers of your country! pity and respect my age, which has hitherto flowed in an uninterrupted course of piety. Since I do not repent, permit me to continue in the practice of my ancient rites. Since I am born free, allow me to enjoy my domestic institutions. This religion has reduced the world under my laws. These rites have repelled Hannibal from the city, and the Gauls from the Capitol. Were my grey hairs reserved for such intolerable disgrace? I am ignorant of the new system that I am required to adopt; but I am well assured that the correction of old age is always an ungrateful and ignominious office." The fears of the people supplied what the discretion of the orator had suppressed; and the calamities which afflicted or threatened the declining empire were unanimously imputed by the Pagans to the new religion of Christ and of Constantine.

But the hopes of Symmachus were repeatedly baffled by the firm and dextrous opposition of the archbishop of Milan, who fortified the emperors against the fallacious eloquence of the advocate of Rome. In this controversy Ambrose condescends to speak the language of a philosopher, and to ask, with some contempt, why it should be thought necessary to introduce an imaginary and invisible power as the cause of those victories, which were sufficiently explained by the valour and discipline of the legions. He justly derides the absurd reverence for antiquity, which could only tend to discourage the improvements of art and to replunge the human race into their original barbarism. From thence gradually rising to a more lofty and theological tone, he pronounces that Christianity alone is the doctrine of truth and salvation, and that every mode of Polytheism conducts its deluded votaries through the paths of error to the abyss of eternal perdition. Arguments like these, when they were suggested by a favourite bishop, had power to prevent the restoration of the altar of Victory; but the same arguments fell with much more energy and effect from the mouth of a conqueror, and the gods of antiquity were dragged in triumph at the chariot-wheels of Theodosius. In a full meeting of the senate the emperor proposed, according to the forms of the republic, the important question, whether the worship of Jupiter or that of Christ should be the religion of the Romans? The liberty of suffrages, which he affected to allow, was destroyed by the hopes and fears that his presence inspired; and the arbitrary exile of Symmachus was a recent admonition that it might be dangerous to oppose the wishes of the monarch. On a regular division of the senate, Jupiter was condemned and degraded by the sense of a very large majority; and it is rather surprising that any members should be found bold enough to declare, by their speeches and votes, that they were still attached to the interest of an abdicated deity. The hasty conversion of the senate must be attributed either to supernatural or to sordid motives; and many of these reluctant proselytes betrayed, on every favourable occasion, their secret disposition to throw aside the mask of odious dissimulation. But they were gradually fixed in the new religion, as the cause of the ancient became more hopeless; they yielded to the authority of the emperor, to the fashion of the times, and to the entreaties of their wives and children, who were instigated and governed by the clergy of Rome and the monks of the East. The edifying example of the Anician family was soon imitated by the rest of the nobility: the Bassi, the Paullini, the Gracchi, embraced the Christian religion; and "the luminaries of the world, the venerable assembly of Catos (such are the high-flown expressions of Prudentius), were impatient to strip themselves of their pontifical garment—to cast the skin of the old serpent—to assume the snowy robes of baptismal innocence—and to humble the pride of the consular fasces before the tombs of the martyrs." The citizens, who subsisted by their own industry, and the populace, who were supported by the public liberality, filled the churches of the Lateran and Vatican with an incessant throng of devout proselytes. The decrees of the senate, which proscribed the worship of idols, were ratified by the general consent of the Romans; the splendour of the Capitol was defaced, and the solitary temples were abandoned to ruin and contempt. Rome submitted to the yoke of the Gospel; and the vanquished provinces had not yet lost their reverence for the name and authority of Rome.

The filial piety of the emperors themselves engaged them to proceed with some caution and tenderness in the reformation of the eternal city. Those absolute monarchs acted with less regard to the prejudices of the provincials. The pious labour, which had been suspended near twenty years since the death of Constantius, was vigorously resumed, and finally accomplished, by the zeal of Theodosius. Whilst that warlike prince yet struggled with the Goths, not for the glory, but for the safety of the republic, he ventured to offend a considerable party of his subjects, by some acts which might perhaps secure the protection of Heaven, but which must seem rash and unseasonable in the eye of human prudence. The success of his first experiments against the Pagans encouraged the pious emperor to reiterate and enforce his edicts of proscription: the same laws which had been originally published in the provinces of the East, were applied, after the defeat of Maximus, to the whole extent of the Western empire; and every victory of the orthodox Theodosius contributed to the triumph of the Christian and catholic faith. He attacked superstition in her most vital part, by prohibiting the use of sacrifices, which he declared to be criminal as well as infamous; and if the terms of his edicts more strictly condemned the impious curiosity which examined the entrails of the victims, every subsequent explanation tended to involve in the same guilt the general practice of *immolation*, which essentially constituted the religion of the Pagans. As the temples had been erected for the purpose of sacrifice, it was the duty of a benevolent prince to remove from his subjects the dangerous temptation of offending against the laws which he had enacted. A special commission was granted to Cynegius, the Prætorian præfect of the East, and afterwards to the counts Jovius and Gaudentius, two officers of distinguished rank in the West, by which they were directed to shut the temples, to seize or destroy the instruments of idolatry, to abolish the privileges of the priests, and to confiscate the consecrated property for the benefit of the emperor, of the church, or of the army. Here the desolation might have stopped: and the naked edifices, which were no longer employed in the service of idolatry, might have been protected from the destructive rage of fanaticism. Many of those temples were the most splendid and beautiful monuments of Grecian architecture: and the emperor himself was interested not to deface the splendour of his own cities, or to diminish the value of his own possessions. Those stately edifices might be suffered to remain, as so many lasting trophies of the victory of Christ. In the decline of the arts, they might be usefully converted into magazines, manufactures, or places of public assembly: and perhaps, when the walls of the temple had been sufficiently purified by holy rites, the worship of the true Deity might be allowed to expiate the ancient guilt of idolatry. But as long as they subsisted, the Pagans fondly cherished the secret hope that an auspicious revolution, a second Julian, might again restore the altars of the gods: and the earnestness with which they addressed their unavailing prayers to the throne increased the zeal of the Christian reformers to extirpate, without mercy, the root of superstition. The laws of the emperors exhibit some symptoms of a milder disposition: but their cold and languid efforts were insufficient to stem the torrent of enthusiasm and rapine, which was conducted, or rather impelled, by the spiritual rulers of the church. In Gaul, the holy Martin, bishop of Tours, marched at the head of his faithful monks to destroy the idols, the temples, and the consecrated trees of his extensive diocese; and, in the execution of this arduous task, the prudent reader will judge whether Martin was supported by the aid of miraculous powers or of carnal weapons. In Syria, the divine and excellent Marcellus, as he is styled by Theodoret, a bishop animated with apostolic fervour, resolved to level with the ground the stately temples within the diocese of Apamea. His attack was resisted by the skill and solidity with which the temple of Jupiter had been constructed. The building was seated on an eminence: on each of the four sides the lofty roof was supported by fifteen massy columns, sixteen feet in circumference; and the large stones of which they were composed were firmly cemented with lead and iron. The force of the strongest and sharpest tools had been tried without effect. It was found necessary to undermine the foundations of the columns, which fell down as soon as the temporary wooden props had been consumed with fire; and the difficulties of the enterprise are described under the allegory of a black dæmon, who retarded, though he could not defeat, the operations of the Christian engineers. Elated with victory, Marcellus took the field in person against the powers of darkness; a numerous troop of soldiers and gladiators marched under the episcopal banner, and he successively attacked the villages and country temples of the diocese of Apamea. Whenever any resistance or danger was apprehended, the champion of the faith, whose lameness would not allow him either to fight or fly, placed himself at a convenient distance, beyond the reach of darts. But this prudence was the occasion of his death; he was surprised and slain by a body of exasperated rustics; and the synod of the province pronounced, without hesitation, that the holy Marcellus had sacrificed his life in the cause of God. In the support of this cause, the monks, who rushed with tumultuous fury from the desert, distinguished themselves by their zeal and diligence. They deserved the enmity of the Pagans; and some of them might deserve the reproaches of avarice and intemperance—of avarice, which they gratified with holy plunder; and of intemperance, which they indulged at the expense of the people, who foolishly admired their tattered garments, loud psalmody, and artificial paleness. A small number of temples was protected by the fears, the venality, the taste, or the prudence of the civil and ecclesiastical governors. The temple of the Celestial Venus at Carthage, whose sacred precincts formed a circumference of two miles, was judiciously converted into a Christian church; and a similar consecration has preserved inviolate the majestic dome of the Pantheon at Rome. But in almost every province of the Roman world, an army of fanatics, without authority and without discipline, invaded the peaceful inhabitants; and the ruin of the fairest structures of antiquity still displays the ravages of *those* barbarians who alone had time and inclination to execute such laborious destruction.

In this wide and various prospect of devastation, the spectator may distinguish the ruins of the temple of Serapis, at Alexandria. Serapis does not appear to have been one of the native gods, or monsters, who sprung from the fruitful soil of superstitious Egypt. The first of the Ptolemies had been commanded, by a dream, to import the mysterious stranger from the coast of Pontus, where he had been long adored by the inhabitants of Sinope; but his attributes and his reign were so imperfectly understood, that it became a subject of dispute whether he represented the bright orb of day, or the gloomy monarch of the subterraneous regions. The Egyptians, who were obstinately devoted to the religion of their fathers, refused to admit this foreign deity within the walls of their cities. But the obsequious priests, who were seduced by the liberality of the Ptolemies, submitted, without resistance, to the power of the god of Pontus: an honourable and domestic genealogy was provided; and this fortunate usurper was introduced into the throne and bed of Osiris, the husband of Isis, and the celestial monarch of Egypt. Alexandria, which claimed his peculiar protection, gloried in the name of the city of Serapis. His temple, which rivalled the pride and magnificence of the Capitol, was erected on the spacious summit of an artificial mount, raised one hundred steps above the level of the adjacent parts of the city; and the interior cavity was strongly supported by arches, and distributed into vaults and subterraneous apartments. The consecrated buildings were surrounded by a quadrangular portico; the stately halls and exquisite statues displayed the triumph of the arts; and the treasures of ancient learning were preserved in the famous Alexandrian library, which had arisen with new splendour from its ashes. After the edicts of Theodosius had severely prohibited the sacrifices of the Pagans, they were still tolerated in the city and temple of Serapis; and this singular indulgence was imprudently ascribed to the superstitious terrors of the Christians themselves: as if they had feared to abolish those ancient rites which could alone secure the inundations of the Nile, the harvests of Egypt, and the subsistence of Constantinople.

At that time the archiepiscopal throne of Alexandria was filled by Theophilus, the perpetual enemy of peace and virtue; a bold, bad man, whose hands were alternately polluted with gold and with blood. His pious indignation was excited by the honours of Serapis; and the insults which he offered to an ancient chapel of Bacchus convinced the Pagans that he meditated a more important and dangerous enterprise. In the tumultuous capital of Egypt, the slightest provocation was sufficient to inflame a civil war. The votaries of Serapis, whose strength and numbers were much inferior to those of their antagonists, rose in arms at the instigation of the philosopher Olympius, who exhorted them to die in the defence of the altars of the gods. These Pagan fanatics fortified themselves in the temple, or rather fortress, of Serapis; repelled the besiegers by daring sallies and a resolute defence; and, by the inhuman cruelties which they exercised on their Christian prisoners, obtained the last consolation of despair. The efforts of the prudent magistrate were usefully exerted for the establishment of a truce till the answer of Theodosius should determine the fate of Serapis. The two parties assembled, without arms, in the principal square; and the Imperial rescript was publicly read. But when a sentence of destruction against the idols of Alexandria was pronounced, the Christians sent up a shout of joy and exultation, whilst the unfortunate Pagans, whose fury had given way to consternation, retired with hasty and silent steps, and eluded, by their flight or obscurity, the resentment of their enemies. Theophilus proceeded to demolish the temple of Serapis, without any other difficulties than those which he found in the weight and solidity of the materials; but these obstacles proved so insuperable that he was obliged to leave the foundations, and to content himself with reducing the edifice itself to a heap of rubbish, a part of which was soon afterwards cleared away, to make room for a church erected in honour of the Christian martyrs. The valuable library of Alexandria was pillaged or destroyed; and near twenty years afterwards, the appearance of the empty shelves excited the regret and indignation of every spectator whose mind was not totally darkened by religious prejudice. The compositions of ancient genius, so many of which have irretrievably perished, might surely have been excepted from the wreck of idolatry, for the amusement and instruction of succeeding ages; and either the zeal or the avarice of the archbishop might have been satiated with the rich spoils which were the reward of his victory. While the images and vases of gold and silver were carefully melted, and those of a less valuable metal were contemptuously broken and cast into the streets, Theophilus laboured to expose the frauds and vices of the ministers of the idols: their dexterity in the management of the loadstone; their secret methods of introducing an human actor into a hollow statue; and their scandalous abuse of the confidence of devout husbands and unsuspecting females. Charges like these may seem to deserve some degree of credit, as they are not repugnant to the crafty and interested spirit of superstition. But the same spirit is equally prone to the base practice of insulting and calumniating a fallen enemy; and our belief is naturally checked by the reflection that it is much less difficult to invent a fictitious story than to support a practical fraud. The colossal statue of Serapis was involved in the ruin of his temple and religion. A great number of plates of different metals, artificially joined together, composed the majestic figure of the deity, who touched on either side the walls of the sanctuary. The aspect of Serapis, his sitting posture, and the sceptre which he bore in his left hand, were extremely similar to the ordinary representations of Jupiter. He was distinguished from Jupiter by the basket, or bushel, which was placed on his head; and by the emblematic monster which he held in his right hand; the head and body of a serpent branching into three tails, which were again terminated by the triple heads of a dog, a lion, and a wolf. It was confidently affirmed that, if any impious hand should dare to violate the majesty of the god, the heavens and the earth would instantly return to their original chaos. An intrepid soldier, animated by zeal, and armed with a weighty battle-axe, ascended the ladder; and even the Christian multitude expected with some anxiety the event of the combat. He aimed a vigorous stroke against the cheek of Serapis; the cheek fell to the ground; the thunder was still silent, and both the heavens and the earth continued to preserve their accustomed order and tranquillity. The victorious soldier repeated his blows: the huge idol was overthrown and broken in pieces; and the limbs of Serapis were ignominiously dragged through the streets of Alexandria. His mangled carcase was burnt in the amphitheatre, amidst the shouts of the populace; and many persons attributed their conversion to this discovery of the impotence of their tutelar deity. The popular modes of religion, that propose any visible and material objects of worship, have the advantage of adapting and familiarising themselves to the senses of mankind; but this advantage is counterbalanced by the various and inevitable accidents to which the faith of the idolater is exposed. It is scarcely possible that, in every disposition of mind, he should preserve his implicit reverence for the idols, or the relics, which the naked eye and the profane hand are unable to distinguish from the most common productions of art or nature; and if, in the hour of danger, their secret and miraculous virtue does not operate for their own preservation, he scorns the vain apologies of his priests, and justly derides the object and the folly of his superstitious attachment. After the fall of Serapis, some hopes were still entertained by the Pagans that the Nile would refuse his annual supply to the impious masters of Egypt; and the extraordinary delay of the inundation seemed to announce the displeasure of the river-god. But this delay was soon compensated by the rapid swell of the waters. They suddenly rose to such an unusual height as to comfort the discontented party with the pleasing expectation of a deluge; till the peaceful river again subsided to the well-known and fertilising level of sixteen cubits, or about thirty English feet.

The temples of the Roman empire were deserted or destroyed; but the ingenious superstition of the Pagans still attempted to elude the laws of Theodosius, by which all sacrifices had been severely prohibited. The inhabitants of the country, whose conduct was less exposed to the eye of malicious curiosity, disguised their *religious* under the appearance of *convivial* meetings. On the days of solemn festivals they assembled in great numbers under the spreading shade of some consecrated trees; sheep and oxen were slaughtered and roasted; and this rural entertainment was sanctified by the use of incense and by the hymns which were sung in honour of the gods. But it was alleged that, as no part of the animal was made a burnt-offering, as no altar was provided to receive the blood, and as the previous oblation of salt cakes and the concluding ceremony of libations were carefully omitted, these festal meetings did not involve the guests in the guilt or penalty of an illegal sacrifice. Whatever might be the truth of the facts or the merit of the distinction, these vain pretences were swept away by the last edict of Theodosius, which inflicted a deadly wound on the superstition of the Pagans. This prohibitory law is expressed in the most absolute and comprehensive terms. "It is our will and pleasure," says the emperor, "that none of our subjects, whether magistrates or private citizens, however exalted or however humble may be their rank and condition, shall presume in any city or in any place to worship an inanimate idol by the sacrifice of a guiltless victim." The act of sacrificing and the practice of divination by the entrails of the victim are declared (without any regard to the object of the inquiry) a crime of high treason against the state, which can be expiated only by the death of the guilty. The rites of Pagan superstition which might seem less bloody and atrocious are abolished as highly injurious to the truth and honour of religion; luminaries, garlands, frankincense, and libations of wine are specially enumerated and condemned; and the harmless claims of the domestic genius, of the household gods, are included in this rigorous proscription. The use of any of these profane and illegal ceremonies subjects the offender to the forfeiture of the house or estate where they have been performed; and if he has artfully chosen the property of another for the scene of his impiety, he is compelled to discharge, without delay, a heavy fine of twenty-five pounds of gold, or more than one thousand pounds sterling. A fine not less considerable is imposed on the connivance of the secret enemies of religion who shall neglect the duty of their respective stations, either to reveal or to punish the guilt of idolatry. Such was the persecuting spirit of the laws of Theodosius, which were repeatedly enforced by his sons and grandsons, with the loud and unanimous applause of the Christian world. . . .

The ruin of the Pagan religion is described by the sophists as a dreadful and amazing prodigy, which covered the earth with darkness and restored the ancient dominion of chaos and of night. They relate in solemn and pathetic strains that the temples were converted into sepulchres, and that the holy places, which had been adorned by the statues of the gods, were basely polluted by the relics of Christian martyrs. "The monks" (a race of filthy animals, to whom Eunapius is tempted to refuse the name of men) "are the authors of the new worship, which, in the place of those deities who are conceived by the understanding, has substituted the meanest and most contemptible slaves. The heads, salted and pickled, of those infamous malefactors, who for the multitude of their crimes have suffered a just and ignominious death; their bodies, still marked by the impression of the lash and the scars of those tortures which were inflicted by the sentence of the magistrate; such" (continues Eunapius) "are the gods which the earth produces in our days; such are the martyrs, the supreme arbitrators of our prayers and petitions to the Deity, whose tombs are now consecrated as the objects of the veneration of the people." Without approving the malice, it is natural enough to share the surprise of the sophist, the spectator of a revolution which raised those obscure victims of the laws of Rome to the rank of celestial and invisible protectors of the Roman empire. The grateful respect of the Christians for the martyrs of the faith was exalted, by time and victory, into religious adoration; and the most illustrious of the saints and prophets were deservedly associated to the honours of the martyrs. One hundred and fifty years after the glorious deaths of St. Peter and St. Paul, the Vatican and the Ostian road were distinguished by the tombs, or rather by the trophies, of those spiritual heroes. In the age which followed the conversion of Constantine, the emperors, the consuls, and the generals of armies devoutly visited the sepulchres of a tentmaker and a fisherman; and their venerable bones were deposited under the altars of Christ, on which the bishops of the royal city continually offered the unbloody sacrifice. The new capital of the Eastern world, unable to produce any ancient and domestic trophies, was enriched by the spoils of dependent provinces. The bodies of St. Andrew, St. Luke, and St. Timothy had reposed near three hundred years in the obscure graves from whence they were transported, in solemn pomp, to the church of the apostles, which the magnificence of Constantine had founded on the banks of the Thracian Bosphorus. About fifty years afterwards the same banks were honoured by the presence of Samuel, the judge and prophet of the people of Israel. His ashes, deposited in a golden vase, and covered with a silken veil, were delivered by the bishops into each other's hands. The relics of Samuel were received by the people with the same joy and reverence which they would have shown to the living prophet; the highways, from Palestine to the gates of Constantinople, were filled with an uninterrupted procession; and the emperor Arcadius himself, at the head of the most illustrious members of the clergy and senate, advanced to meet his extraordinary guest, who had always deserved and claimed the homage of kings. The example of Rome and Constantinople confirmed the faith and discipline of the catholic world. The honours of the saints and martyrs, after a feeble and ineffectual murmur of profane reason,* were universally established; and in the age of Ambrose and Jerom something was still deemed wanting to the sanctity of a Christian church, till it had been consecrated by some portion of holy relics, which fixed and inflamed the devotion of the faithful.

In the long period of twelve hundred years, which elapsed between the reign of Constantine and the reformation of Luther, the worship of saints and relics corrupted the pure and perfect simplicity of the Christian model; and some symptoms of degeneracy may be observed even

*The presbyter Vigilantius, the protestant of his age, firmly, though ineffectually, withstood the superstition of monks, relics, saints, fasts, etc., for which Jerom compares him to the Hydra, Cerberus, the Centaurs, etc., and considers him only as the organ of the Dæmon. Whoever will peruse the controversy of St. Jerom and Vigilantius, and St. Augustin's account of the miracles of St. Stephen, may speedily gain some idea of the spirit of the Fathers.

in the first generations which adopted and cherished this pernicious innovation.

I. The satisfactory experience that the relics of saints were more valuable than gold or precious stones stimulated the clergy to multiply the treasures of the church. Without much regard for truth or probability, they invented names for skeletons, and actions for names. The fame of the apostles, and of the holy men who had imitated their virtues, was darkened by religious fiction. To the invincible band of genuine and primitive martyrs they added myriads of imaginary heroes, who had never existed, except in the fancy of crafty or credulous legendaries; and there is reason to suspect that Tours might not be the only diocese in which the bones of a malefactor were adored instead of those of a saint. A superstitious practice, which tended to increase the temptations of fraud and credulity, insensibly extinguished the light of history and of reason in the Christian world.

II. But the progress of superstition would have been much less rapid and victorious if the faith of the people had not been assisted by the seasonable aid of visions and miracles to ascertain the authenticity and virtue of the most suspicious relics. In the reign of the younger Theodosius, Lucian, a presbyter of Jerusalem, and the ecclesiastical minister of the village of Caphargamala, about twenty miles from the city, related a very singular dream, which, to remove his doubts, had been repeated on three successive Saturdays. A venerable figure stood before him, in the silence of the night, with a long beard, a white robe, and a gold rod; announced himself by the name of Gamaliel; and revealed to the astonished presbyter, that his own corpse, with the bodies of his son Abibas, his friend Nicodemus, and the illustrious Stephen, the first martyr of the Christian faith, were secretly buried in the adjacent field. He added, with some impatience, that it was time to release himself and his companions from their obscure prison; that their appearance would be salutary to a distressed world; and that they had made choice of Lucian to inform the bishop of Jerusalem of their situation and their wishes. The doubts and difficulties which still retarded this important discovery were successively removed by new visions; and the ground was opened by the bishop, in the presence of an innumerable multitude. The coffins of Gamaliel, of his son, and of his friend, were found in regular order; but when the fourth coffin, which contained the remains of Stephen, was shown to the light, the earth trembled, and an odour such as that of Paradise was smelt, which instantly cured the various diseases of seventy-three of the assistants. The companions of Stephen were left in their peaceful residence of Caphargamala; but the relics of the first martyr were transported, in solemn procession, to a church constructed in their honour on Mount Sion; and the minute particles of those relics, a drop of blood, or the scrapings of a bone, were acknowledged, in almost every province of the Roman world, to possess a divine and miraculous virtue. The grave and learned Augustin, whose understanding scarcely admits the excuse of credulity, has attested the innumerable prodigies which were performed in Africa by the relics of St. Stephen; and this marvellous narrative is inserted in the elaborate work of the City of God, which the bishop of Hippo designed as a solid and immortal proof of the truth of Christianity. Augustin solemnly declares that he has selected those miracles only which were publicly certified by the persons who were either the objects, or the spectators, of the power of the martyr. Many prodigies were omitted or forgotten; and Hippo had been less favourably treated than the other cities of the province. And yet the bishop enumerates above seventy miracles, of which three were resurrections from the dead, in the space of two years, and within the limits of his own diocese. If we enlarge our view to all the dioceses, and all the saints, of the Christian world, it will not be easy to calculate the fables, and the errors, which issued from this inexhaustible source. But we may surely be allowed to observe that a miracle, in that age of superstition and credulity, lost its name and its merit, since it could scarcely be considered as a deviation from the ordinary and established laws of nature.

III. The innumerable miracles, of which the tombs of the martyrs were the perpetual theatre, revealed to the pious believer the actual state and constitution of the invisible world; and his religious speculations appeared to be founded on the firm basis of fact and experience. Whatever might be the condition of vulgar souls in the long interval between the dissolution and the resurrection of their bodies, it was evident that the superior spirits of the saints and martyrs did not consume that portion of their existence in silent and inglorious sleep. It was evident (without presuming to determine the place of their habitation, or the nature of their felicity) that they enjoyed the lively and active consciousness of their happiness, their virtue, and their powers; and that they had already secured the possession of their eternal reward. The enlargement of their intellectual faculties surpassed the measure of the human imagination; since it was proved by *experience* that they were capable of hearing and understanding the various petitions of their numerous votaries, who, in the same moment of time, but in the most distant parts of the world, invoked the name and assistance of Stephen or of Martin. The confidence of their petitioners was founded on the persuasion that the saints, who reigned with Christ, cast an eye of pity upon earth; that they were warmly interested in the prosperity of the catholic church; and that the individuals who imitated the example of their faith and piety were the peculiar and favourite objects of their most tender regard. Sometimes, indeed, their friendship might be influenced by considerations of a less exalted kind: they viewed with partial affection the places which had been consecrated by their birth, their residence, their death, their burial, or the possession of their relics. The meaner passions of pride, avarice, and revenge, may be deemed unworthy of a celestial breast; yet the saints themselves condescended to testify their grateful approbation of the liberality of their votaries; and the sharpest bolts of punishment were hurled against those impious wretches who violated their magnificent shrines, or disbelieved their supernatural power. Atrocious, indeed, must have been the guilt, and strange would have been the scepticism, of those men, if they had obstinately resisted the proofs of a divine agency, which the elements, the whole range of the animal creation, and even the subtle and invisible operations of the human mind, were compelled to obey* The immediate, and almost instantaneous, effects, that were supposed to follow the prayer, or the offence, satisfied the Christians of the ample measure of favour and authority which the saints enjoyed in the presence of the Supreme God; and it seemed almost superfluous to inquire whether they were continually obliged to intercede before the throne of grace, or whether they might not be permitted to exercise, according to the dictates of their benevolence and justice, the delegated powers of their subordinate ministry. The imagination, which had been raised by a painful effort to the contemplation and worship of the Universal Cause, ea-

*At Minorca, the relics of St. Stephen converted in eight days 540 Jews; with the help, indeed, of some wholesome severities, such as burning the synagogue, driving the obstinate infidels to starve among the rocks, etc.

gerly embraced such inferior objects of adoration as were more proportioned to its gross conceptions and imperfect faculties. The sublime and simple theology of the primitive Christians was gradually corrupted: and the MONARCHY of heaven, already clouded by metaphysical subtleties, was degraded by the introduction of a popular mythology which tended to restore the reign of polytheism.

IV. As the objects of religion were gradually reduced to the standard of the imagination, the rites and ceremonies were introduced that seemed most powerfully to affect the senses of the vulgar. If, in the beginning of the fifth century, Tertullian, or Lactantius, had been suddenly raised from the dead, to assist at the festival of some popular saint or martyr, they would have gazed with astonishment and indignation on the profane spectacle which had succeeded to the pure and spiritual worship of a Christian congregation. As soon as the doors of the church were thrown open, they must have been offended by the smoke of incense, the perfume of flowers, and the glare of lamps and tapers, which diffused, at noon-day, a gaudy, superfluous, and, in their opinion, a sacrilegious light. If they approached the balustrade of the altar, they made their way through the prostrate crowd, consisting, for the most part, of strangers and pilgrims, who resorted to the city on the vigil of the feast; and who already felt the strong intoxication of fanaticism, and, perhaps, of wine. Their devout kisses were imprinted on the walls and pavement of the sacred edifice; and their fervent prayers were directed, whatever might be the language of their church, to the bones, the blood, or the ashes of the saint, which were usually concealed, by a linen or silken veil, from the eyes of the vulgar. The Christians frequented the tombs of the martyrs, in the hope of obtaining, from their powerful intercession, every sort of spiritual, but more especially of temporal, blessings. They implored the preservation of their health, or the cure of their infirmities; the fruitfulness of their barren wives, or the safety and happiness of their children. Whenever they undertook any distant or dangerous journey, they requested that the holy martyrs would be their guides and protectors on the road; and if they returned without having experienced any misfortune, they again hastened to the tombs of the martyrs, to celebrate, with grateful thanksgivings, their obligations to the memory and relics of those heavenly patrons. The walls were hung round with symbols of the favours which they had received; eyes, and hands, and feet, of gold and silver: and edifying pictures, which could not long escape the abuse of indiscreet or idolatrous devotion, represented the image, the attributes, and the miracles of the tutelar saint. The same uniform original spirit of superstition might suggest, in the most distant ages and countries, the same methods of deceiving the credulity, and of affecting the senses of mankind: but it must ingenuously be confessed that the ministers of the Catholic Church thereby imitated the profane model which they were impatient to destroy. The most respectable bishops had persuaded themselves that the ignorant rustics would more cheerfully renounce the superstitions of Paganism, if they found some resemblance, some compensation, in the bosom of Christianity. The religion of Constantine achieved, in less than a century, the final conquest of the Roman empire: but the victors themselves were insensibly subdued by the arts of their vanquished rivals.

Part 7

Justinian *(Chapter XL)*

Under Justinian I (527–65) and his brilliant Empress, Theodora, Roman law reached its apotheosis. At the very moment when the Gothic kingdom in Italy was fading into oblivion, Justinian provided the Byzantines with a period of constructive and successful administration. He built fortresses throughout the Empire, rebuilt numerous ancient monuments, and supervised the construction of the most famous example of Byzantine architecture, the church of Hagia Sophia in Constantinople. Justinian also hoped to revive the Empire. His general, Belisarius, conquered the Vandals (533–34) and Berbers (546–48), returning North Africa to imperial control. Belisarius and other generals subsequently defeated the Ostrogoths in Italy, partially restoring the old imperial unity, and in 554 the Byzantines defeated the Visigoths in Iberia, recovering the southern part of the peninsula. Unfortunately, Justinian devoted too great an effort to the Western Empire, neglecting the East—much to the regret of future generations.

CHAPTER XL

The emperor Justinian was born near the ruins of Sardica (the modern Sophia), of an obscure race* of barbarians, the inhabitants of a wild

*The names of these Dardanian peasants are Gothic, and almost English: *Justinian* is a translation of *uprauda (upright);* his father *Sabatius* (in Græco-barbarous language *stipes*) was styled in his village *Istock (Stock);* his mother Bigleniza was softened into Vigilantia.

and desolate country, to which the names of Dardania, of Dacia, and of Bulgaria have been successively applied. . . .

From his elevation to his death, Justinian governed the Roman empire thirty-eight years, seven months, and thirteen days. The events of his reign, which excite our curious attention by their number, variety, and importance, are diligently related by the secretary of Belisarius, a rhetorician, whom eloquence had promoted to the rank of senator and præfect of Constantinople. According to the vicissitudes of courage or servitude, of favour or disgrace, Procopius successively composed the *history,* the *panegyric,* and the *satire* of his own times. The eight books of the Persian, Vandalic, and Gothic wars, which are continued in the five books of Agathias, deserve our esteem as a laborious and successful imitation of the Attic, or at least of the Asiatic, writers of ancient Greece. His facts are collected from the personal experience and free conversation of a soldier, a statesman, and a traveller; his style continually aspires, and often attains, to the merit of strength and elegance; his reflections, more especially in the speeches, which he too frequently inserts, contain a rich fund of political knowledge; and the historian, excited by the generous ambition of pleasing and instructing posterity, appears to disdain the prejudices of the people and the flattery of courts. The writings of Procopius were read and applauded by his contemporaries: but, although he respectfully laid them at the foot of the throne, the pride of Justinian must have been wounded by the praise of a hero who perpetually eclipses the glory of his inactive sovereign. The conscious dignity of independence was subdued by the hopes and fears of a slave; and the secretary of Belisarius laboured for pardon and reward in the six books of the Imperial *edifices.* He had dexterously chosen a subject of apparent splendour, in which he could loudly celebrate the genius, the magnificence, and the piety of a prince who, both as a conqueror and legislator, had surpassed the puerile virtues of Themistocles and Cyrus. Disappointment might urge the flatterer to secret revenge; and the first glance of favour might again tempt him to suspend and suppress a libel in which the Roman Cyrus is degraded into an odious and contemptible tyrant, in which both the emperor and his consort Theodora are seriously represented as two dæmons who had assumed a human form for the destruction of mankind. Such base inconsistency must doubtless sully the reputation, and detract from the credit, of

Procopius: yet, after the venom of his malignity has been suffered to exhale, the residue of the *anecdotes,* even the most disgraceful facts, some of which had been tenderly hinted in his public history, are established by their internal evidence, or the authentic monuments of the times. From these various materials I shall now proceed to describe the reign of Justinian, which will deserve and occupy an ample space. The present chapter will explain the elevation and character of Theodora, the factions of the circus, and the peaceful administration of the sovereign of the East. In the three succeeding chapters I shall relate the wars of Justinian, which achieved the conquest of Africa and Italy; and I shall follow the victories of Belisarius and Narses, without disguising the vanity of their triumphs, or the hostile virtue of the Persian and Gothic heroes. The series of this volume will embrace the jurisprudence and theology of the emperor; the controversies and sects which still divide the Oriental church; the reformation of the Roman law which is obeyed or respected by the nations of modern Europe.

In the exercise of supreme power, the first act of Justinian was to divide it with the woman whom he loved, the famous Theodora, whose strange elevation cannot be applauded as the triumph of female virtue. Under the reign of Anastasius, the care of the wild beasts maintained by the green faction at Constantinople was intrusted to Acacius, a native of the isle of Cyprus, who, from his employment, was surnamed the master of the bears. This honourable office was given after his death to another candidate, notwithstanding the diligence of his widow, who had already provided a husband and a successor. Acacius had left three daughters, Comito,* THEODORA, and Anastasia, the eldest of whom did not then exceed the age of seven years. On a solemn festival, these helpless orphans were sent by their distressed and indignant mother, in the garb of suppliants, into the midst of the theatre: the green faction received them with contempt, the blues with compassion; and this difference, which sunk deep into the mind of Theodora, was felt long afterwards in the administration of the empire. As they improved in age and beauty, the three sisters were successively devoted to the public and private pleasures of the Byzantine

*Comito was afterwards married to Sittas duke of Armenia, the father, perhaps, at least she might be the mother, of the empress Sophia. Two nephews of Theodora may be the sons of Anastasia (Aleman. p. 30, 31).

people; and Theodora, after following Comito on the stage, in the dress of a slave, with a stool on her head, was at length permitted to exercise her independent talents. She neither danced, nor sung, nor played on the flute; her skill was confined to the pantomime arts; she excelled in buffoon characters; and as often as the comedian swelled her cheeks, and complained with a ridiculous tone and gesture of the blows that were inflicted, the whole theatre of Constantinople resounded with laughter and applause. The beauty of Theodora was the subject of more flattering praise, and the source of more exquisite delight. Her features were delicate and regular; her complexion, though somewhat pale, was tinged with a natural colour; every sensation was instantly expressed by the vivacity of her eyes; her easy motions displayed the graces of a small but elegant figure; and either love or adulation might proclaim that painting and poetry were incapable of delineating the matchless excellence of her form. But this form was degraded by the facility with which it was exposed to the public eye, and prostituted to licentious desire. Her venal charms were abandoned to a promiscuous crowd of citizens and strangers, of every rank and of every profession: the fortunate lover who had been promised a night of enjoyment was often driven from her bed by a stronger or more wealthy favourite; and when she passed through the streets, her presence was avoided by all who wished to escape either the scandal or the temptation. The satirical historian has not blushed to describe the naked scenes which Theodora was not ashamed to exhibit in the theatre. After exhausting the arts of sensual pleasure, she most ungratefully murmured against the parsimony of Nature; but her murmurs, her pleasures, and her arts, must be veiled in the obscurity of a learned language. After reigning for some time the delight and contempt of the capital, she condescended to accompany Ecebolus, a native of Tyre, who had obtained the government of the African Pentapolis. But this union was frail and transient: Ecebolus soon rejected an expensive or faithless concubine; she was reduced at Alexandria to extreme distress; and in her laborious return to Constantinople, every city of the East admired and enjoyed the fair Cyprian, whose merit appeared to justify her descent from the peculiar island of Venus. The vague commerce of Theodora, and the most detestable precautions, preserved her from the danger which she feared; yet once, and once only, she became a mother. The infant was saved and educated in Arabia by his father, who imparted to him on his death-bed that he was the son of an empress. Filled with ambitious hopes, the unsuspecting youth immediately hastened to the palace of Constantinople, and was admitted to the presence of his mother. As he was never more seen, even after the decease of Theodora, she deserves the foul imputation of extinguishing with his life a secret so offensive to her imperial virtue.

In the most abject state of her fortune and reputation, some vision, either of sleep or of fancy, had whispered to Theodora the pleasing assurance that she was destined to become the spouse of a potent monarch. Conscious of her approaching greatness, she returned from Paphlagonia to Constantinople; assumed, like a skilful actress, a more decent character; relieved her poverty by the laudable industry of spinning wool; and affected a life of chastity and solitude in a small house, which she afterwards changed into a magnificent temple. Her beauty, assisted by art or accident, soon attracted, captivated, and fixed, the patrician Justinian, who already reigned with absolute sway under the name of his uncle. Perhaps she contrived to enhance the value of a gift which she had so often lavished on the meanest of mankind; perhaps she inflamed, at first by modest delays, and at last by sensual allurements, the desires of a lover who, from nature or devotion, was addicted to long vigils and abstemious diet. When his first transports had subsided, she still maintained the same ascendant over his mind by the more solid merit of temper and understanding. Justinian delighted to ennoble and enrich the object of his affection: the treasures of the East were poured at her feet, and the nephew of Justin was determined, perhaps by religious scruples, to bestow on his concubine the sacred and legal character of a wife. But the laws of Rome expressly prohibited the marriage of a senator with any female who had been dishonoured by a servile origin or theatrical profession: the empress Lupicina or Euphemia, a barbarian of rustic manners, but of irreproachable virtue, refused to accept a prostitute for her niece; and even Vigilantia, the superstitious mother of Justinian, though she acknowledged the wit and beauty of Theodora, was seriously apprehensive lest the levity and arrogance of that artful paramour might corrupt the piety and happiness of her son. These obstacles were removed by the inflexible constancy of Justinian. He patiently expected the death of the empress; he despised the tears of his mother, who soon sunk under the weight of her affliction; and a law was promulgated, in the name of the emperor Justin, which abolished the rigid jurisprudence of antiquity. A glorious repentance (the words of the edict) was left open for the unhappy females who had prostituted their persons on the theatre, and they were permitted to contract a legal union with the most illustrious of the Romans. This indulgence was speedily followed by the solemn nuptials of Justinian and Theodora; her dignity was gradually exalted with that of her lover; and, as soon as Justin had invested his nephew with the purple, the patriarch of Constantinople placed the diadem on the heads of the emperor and empress of the East. But the usual honours which the severity of Roman manners had allowed to the wives of princes could not satisfy either the ambition of Theodora or the fondness of Justinian. He seated her on the throne as an equal and independent colleague in the sovereignty of the empire, and an oath of allegiance was imposed on the governors of the provinces in the joint names of Justinian and Theodora. The Eastern world fell prostrate before the genius and fortune of the daughter of Acacius. The prostitute who, in the presence of innumerable spectators, had polluted the theatre of Constantinople, was adored as a queen in the same city, by grave magistrates, orthodox bishops, victorious generals, and captive monarchs.

Those who believe that the female mind is totally depraved by the loss of chastity will eagerly listen to all the invectives of private envy or popular resentment, which have dissembled the virtues of Theodora, exaggerated her vices, and condemned with rigour the venal or voluntary sins of the youthful harlot. From a motive of shame or contempt, she often declined the servile homage of the multitude, escaped from the odious light of the capital, and passed the greatest part of the year in the palaces and gardens which were pleasantly seated on the seacoast of the Propontis and the Bosphorus. Her private hours were devoted to the prudent as well as grateful care of her beauty, the luxury of the bath and table, and the long slumber of the evening and the morning. Her secret apartments were occupied by the favourite women and eunuchs, whose interests and passions she indulged at the expense of justice: the most illustrious personages of the state were crowded into a dark and sultry antechamber; and when at last, after tedious attendance, they were admitted to kiss the feet of Theodora, they experienced, as her humour might suggest, the silent arrogance of an empress or the capricious levity of a comedian. Her rapacious avarice to accumulate an immense treasure may be excused by the apprehension of her husband's death, which could leave no alternative between ruin and the throne; and fear as well as ambition might exasperate Theodora against two generals who, during a malady of the emperor, had rashly declared that they were not disposed to acquiesce in the choice of the capital. But the reproach of cruelty, so repugnant even to her softer vices, has left an indelible stain on the memory of Theodora. Her numerous spies observed and zealously reported every action, or word, or look, injurious to their royal mistress. Whomsoever they accused were cast into her peculiar prisons,* inaccessible to the inquiries of justice; and it was rumoured that the torture of the rack or scourge had been inflicted in the presence of a female tyrant, insensible to the voice of prayer or of pity. Some of these unhappy victims perished in deep unwholesome dungeons, while others were permitted, after the loss of their limbs, their reason, or their fortune, to appear in the world, the living monuments of her vengeance, which was commonly extended to the children of those whom she had suspected or injured. The senator or bishop whose death or exile Theodora had pronounced, was delivered to a trusty messenger, and his diligence was quickened by a menace from her own mouth. "If you fail in the execution of my commands, I swear by him who liveth for ever that your skin shall be flayed from your body."

If the creed of Theodora had not been tainted with heresy, her exemplary devotion might have atoned, in the opinion of her contemporaries, for pride, avarice, and cruelty; but if she employed her influence to assuage the intolerant fury of the emperor, the present age will allow some merit to her religion, and much indulgence to her speculative errors. The name of Theodora was introduced, with equal honour, in all the pious and charitable foundations of Justinian; and the most benevolent institution of his reign may be ascribed to the sympathy of the empress for her less fortunate sisters, who had been seduced or compelled to embrace the trade of prostitution. A palace, on the Asiatic side of the Bosphorus, was converted into a stately and spacious monastery, and a liberal maintenance was assigned to five hun-

*Her prisons, a labyrinth, a Tartarus . . . were under the palace. Darkness is propitious to cruelty, but it is likewise favourable to calumny and fiction.

dred women who had been collected from the streets and brothels of Constantinople. In this safe and holy retreat they were devoted to perpetual confinement; and the despair of some, who threw themselves headlong into the sea, was lost in the gratitude of the penitents who had been delivered from sin and misery by their generous benefactress. The prudence of Theodora is celebrated by Justinian himself; and his laws are attributed to the sage counsels of his most reverend wife, whom he had received as the gift of the Deity. Her courage was displayed amidst the tumult of the people and the terrors of the court. Her chastity, from the moment of her union with Justinian, is founded on the silence of her implacable enemies; and although the daughter of Acacius might be satiated with love, yet some applause is due to the firmness of a mind which could sacrifice pleasure and habit to the stronger sense either of duty or interest. The wishes and prayers of Theodora could never obtain the blessing of a lawful son, and she buried an infant daughter, the sole offspring of her marriage. Notwithstanding this disappointment, her dominion was permanent and absolute; she preserved, by art or merit, the affections of Justinian; and their seeming dissensions were always fatal to the courtiers who believed them to be sincere. Perhaps her health had been impaired by the licentiousness of her youth; but it was always delicate, and she was directed by her physicians to use the Pythian warm-baths. In this journey the empress was followed by the Prætorian præfect, the great treasurer, several counts and patricians, and a splendid train of four thousand attendants: the highways were repaired at her approach; a palace was erected for her reception; and as she passed through Bithynia she distributed liberal alms to the churches, the monasteries, and the hospitals, that they might implore Heaven for the restoration of her health. At length, in the twenty-fourth year of her marriage, and the twenty-second of her reign, she was consumed by a cancer; and the irreparable loss was deplored by her husband, who, in the room of a theatrical prostitute, might have selected the purest and most noble virgin of the East.

A material difference may be observed in the games of antiquity: the most eminent of the Greeks were actors, the Romans were merely spectators. The Olympic stadium was open to wealth, merit, and ambition; and if the candidates could depend on their personal skill and activity, they might pursue the footsteps of Diomede and Menelaus, and conduct their own horses in the rapid career. Ten, twenty, forty chariots, were allowed to start at the same instant; a crown of leaves was the reward of the victor, and his fame, with that of his family and country, was chanted in lyric strains more durable than monuments of brass and marble. But a senator, or even a citizen, conscious of his dignity, would have blushed to expose his person or his horses in the circus of Rome. The games were exhibited at the expense of the republic, the magistrates, or the emperors; but the reins were abandoned to servile hands; and if the profits of a favourite charioteer sometimes exceeded those of an advocate, they must be considered as the effects of popular extravagance, and the high wages of a disgraceful profession. The race, in its first institution, was a simple contest of two chariots, whose drivers were distinguished by *white* and *red* liveries: two additional colours, a light *green* and a cærulean *blue,* were afterwards introduced; and, as the races were repeated twenty-five times, one hundred chariots contributed in the same day to the pomp of the circus. The four *factions* soon acquired a legal establishment and a mysterious origin, and their fanciful colours were derived from the various appearances of nature in the four seasons of the year; the red dog-star of summer, the snows of winter, the deep shades of autumn, and the cheerful verdure of the spring. Another interpretation preferred the elements to the seasons, and the struggle of the green and blue was supposed to represent the conflict of the earth and sea. Their respective victories announced either a plentiful harvest or a prosperous navigation, and the hostility of the husbandmen and mariners was somewhat less absurd than the blind ardour of the Roman people, who devoted their lives and fortunes to the colour which they had espoused. Such folly was disdained and indulged by the wisest princes; but the names of Caligula, Nero, Vitellius, Verus, Commodus, Caracalla, and Elagabalus, were enrolled in the blue or green factions of the circus: they frequented their stables, applauded their favourites, chastised their antagonists, and deserved the esteem of the populace by the natural or affected imitation of their manners. The bloody and tumultuous contest continued to disturb the public festivity till the last age of the spectacles of Rome; and Theodoric, from a motive of justice or affection, interposed his authority to protect the greens against the violence of a consul and a patrician who were passionately addicted to the blue faction of the circus.

Constantinople adopted the follies, though not the virtues, of ancient Rome; and the same factions which had agitated the circus raged with redoubled fury in the hippodrome. Under the reign of Anastasius, this popular frenzy was inflamed by religious zeal; and the greens, who had treacherously concealed stones and daggers under baskets of fruit, massacred at a solemn festival three thousand of their blue adversaries. From the capital this pestilence was diffused into the provinces and cities of the East, and the sportive distinction of two colours produced two strong and irreconcilable factions, which shook the foundations of a feeble government. The popular dissensions, founded on the most serious interest or holy pretence, have scarcely equalled the obstinacy of this wanton discord, which invaded the peace of families, divided friends and brothers, and tempted the female sex, though seldom seen in the circus, to espouse the inclinations of their lovers, or to contradict the wishes of their husbands. Every law, either human or divine, was trampled under foot; and as long as the party was successful, its deluded followers appeared careless of private distress or public calamity. The licence, without the freedom, of democracy, was revived at Antioch and Constantinople, and the support of a faction became necessary to every candidate for civil or ecclesiastical honours. A secret attachment to the family or sect of Anastasius was imputed to the greens; the blues were zealously devoted to the cause of orthodoxy and Justinian, and their grateful patron protected, above five years, the disorders of a faction whose seasonable tumults overawed the palace, the senate, and the capitals of the East. Insolent with royal favour, the blues affected to strike terror by a peculiar and barbaric dress—the long hair of the Huns, their close sleeves and ample garments, a lofty step, and a sonorous voice. In the day they concealed their two-edged poniards, but in the night they boldly assembled in arms and in numerous bands, prepared for every act of violence and rapine. Their adversaries of the green faction, or even inoffensive citizens, were stripped and often murdered by these nocturnal robbers, and it became dangerous to wear any gold buttons or girdles, or to appear at a late hour in the streets of a peaceful capital. A daring spirit, rising with impunity, proceeded to violate the safeguard of private houses; and fire was employed to facilitate the attack, or to conceal the crimes, of these factious rioters. No place was safe or sacred from their depredations; to gratify either avarice or revenge they profusely spilt the blood of the innocent; churches and altars were polluted by atrocious murders, and it was the boast of the assassins that their dexterity could always inflict a mortal wound with a single stroke of their dagger. The dissolute youth of Constantinople adopted the blue livery of disorder; the laws were silent, and the bonds of society were relaxed; creditors were compelled to resign their obligations; judges to reverse their sentence; masters to enfranchise their slaves; fathers to supply the extravagance of their children; noble matrons were prostituted to the lust of their servants; beautiful boys were torn from the arms of their parents; and wives, unless they preferred a voluntary death, were ravished in the presence of their husbands. The despair of the greens, who were persecuted by their enemies and deserted by the magistrate, assumed the privilege of defence, perhaps of retaliation; but those who survived the combat were dragged to execution, and the unhappy fugitives, escaping to woods and caverns, preyed without mercy on the society from whence they were expelled. Those ministers of justice who had courage to punish the crimes and to brave the resentment of the blues became the victims of their indiscreet zeal: a præfect of Constantinople fled for refuge to the holy sepulchre, a count of the East was ignominiously whipped, and a governor of Cilicia was hanged, by the order of Theodora, on the tomb of two assassins whom he had condemned for the murder of his groom, and a daring attack upon his own life. An aspiring candidate may be tempted to build his greatness on the public confusion, but it is the interest as well as duty of a sovereign to maintain the authority of the laws. The first edict of Justinian, which was often repeated and sometimes executed, announced his firm resolution to support the innocent, and to chastise the guilty, of every denomination and *colour.* Yet the balance of justice was still inclined in favour of the blue faction, by the secret affection, the habits, and the fears of the emperor; his equity, after an apparent struggle, submitted without reluctance to the implacable passions of Theodora, and the empress never forgot or forgave the injuries of the comedian. At the accession of the younger Justin, the proclamation of equal and rigorous justice indirectly condemned the partiality of the former reign. "Ye blues, Justinian is no more! ye greens, he is still alive!"

A sedition, which almost laid Constantinople in ashes, was excited by the mutual hatred and momentary reconciliation of the two factions. In the fifth year of his reign Justinian celebrated the festival of the ides of January: the games were incessantly disturbed by the clamorous discontent of the greens; till the twenty-second race the emperor maintained his silent gravity; at length, yielding to his impatience, he condescended to hold, in abrupt sentences, and by the voice of a crier, the most singular dialogue that ever passed between a prince and his subjects. Their first complaints were respectful and modest; they accused the subordinate ministers of oppression, and proclaimed their wishes for the long life and victory of the emperor. "Be patient and attentive, ye insolent railers!" exclaimed Justinian; "be mute, ye Jews, Samaritans, and Manichæans!" The greens still attempted to awaken his compassion. "We are poor, we are innocent, we are injured, we dare not pass through the streets: a general persecution is exercised against our name and colour. Let us die, O emperor! but let us die by your command, and for your service!" But the repetition of partial and passionate invectives degraded, in their eyes, the majesty of the purple; they renounced allegiance to the prince who refused justice to his people, lamented that the father of Justinian had been born, and branded his son with the opprobrious names of a homicide, an ass, and a perjured tyrant. "Do you despise your lives?" cried the indignant monarch. The blues rose with fury from their seats, their hostile clamours thundered in the hippodrome, and their adversaries, deserting the unequal contest, spread terror and despair through the streets of Constantinople. At this dangerous moment, seven notorious assassins of both factions, who had been condemned by the præfect, were carried round the city, and afterwards transported to the place of execution in the suburb of Pera. Four were immediately beheaded; a fifth was hanged; but, when the same punishment was inflicted on the remaining two, the rope broke, they fell alive to the ground, the populace applauded their escape, and the monks of St. Conon, issuing from the neighbouring convent, conveyed them in a boat to the sanctuary of the church. As one of these criminals was of the blue, and the other of the green, livery, the two factions were equally provoked by the cruelty of their oppressor or the ingratitude of their patron, and a short truce was concluded till they had delivered their prisoners and satisfied their revenge. The palace of the præfect, who withstood the seditious torrent, was instantly burnt, his officers and guards were massacred, the prisons were forced open, and freedom was restored to those who could only use it for the public destruction. A military force which had been despatched to the aid of the civil magistrate was fiercely encountered by an armed multitude, whose numbers and boldness continually increased: and the Heruli, the wildest barbarians in the service of the empire, overturned the priests and their relics, which, from a pious motive, had been rashly interposed to separate the bloody conflict. The tumult was exasperated by this sacrilege; the people fought with enthusiasm in the cause of God; the women, from the roofs and windows, showered stones on the heads of the soldiers, who darted firebrands against the houses; and the various flames, which had been kindled by the hands of citizens and strangers, spread without control over the face of the city. The conflagration involved the cathedral of St. Sophia, the baths of Zeuxippus, a part of the palace from the first entrance to the altar of Mars, and the long portico from the palace to the forum of Constantine: a large hospital, with the sick patients, was consumed; many churches and stately edifices were destroyed; and an immense treasure of gold and silver was either melted or lost. From such scenes of horror and distress the wise and wealthy citizens escaped over the Bosphorus to the Asiatic side, and during five days Constantinople was abandoned to the factions, whose watchword, NIKA, *vanquish!* has given a name to this memorable sedition.

As long as the factions were divided, the triumphant blues and desponding greens appeared to behold with the same indifference the disorders of the state. They agreed to censure the corrupt management of justice and the finance; and the two responsible ministers, the artful Tribonian and the rapacious John of Cappadocia, were loudly arraigned as the authors of the public misery. The peaceful murmurs of the people would have been disregarded: they were heard with respect when the city was in flames; the quæstor and the præfect were instantly removed, and their offices were filled by two senators of blameless integrity. After this popular concession Justinian proceeded to the hippodrome to confess his own errors, and to accept the repentance of his grateful subjects; but they distrusted his assurances, though solemnly pronounced in the presence of the holy gospels; and the emperor, alarmed by their distrust, retreated with precipitation to the strong fortress of the palace. The obstinacy of the tumult was now imputed to a secret and ambitious conspiracy, and a suspicion was entertained that the insurgents, more especially the green faction, had been supplied with arms and money by Hypatius and Pompey, two patricians who could neither forget with honour, nor remember with safety, that they were the nephews of the emperor Anastasius. Capriciously trusted, disgraced, and pardoned by the jealous levity of the monarch, they had appeared as loyal servants before the throne, and, during five days of the tumult, they were detained as important hostages; till at length, the fears of Justinian prevailing over his prudence, he viewed the two brothers in the light of spies, perhaps of assassins, and sternly commanded them to depart from the palace. After a fruitless representation that obedience might lead to involuntary treason, they retired to their houses, and in the morning of the sixth day Hypatius was surrounded and seized by the people, who, regardless of his virtuous resistance and the tears of his wife, transported their favourite to the forum of Constantine, and, instead of a diadem, placed a rich collar on his head. If the usurper, who afterwards pleaded the merit of his delay, had complied with the advice of his senate, and urged the fury of the multitude, their first irresistible effort might have oppressed or expelled his trembling competitor. The Byzantine palace enjoyed a free communication with the sea, vessels lay ready at the garden-stairs, and a secret resolution was already formed to convey the emperor with his family and treasures to a safe retreat at some distance from the capital.

Justinian was lost, if the prostitute whom he raised from the theatre had not renounced the timidity as well as the virtues of her sex. In the midst of a council where Belisarius was present, Theodora alone displayed the spirit of a hero, and she alone, without apprehending his future hatred, could save the emperor from the imminent danger and his unworthy fears. "If flight," said the consort of Justinian, "were the only means of safety, yet I should disdain to fly. Death is the condition of our birth, but they who have reigned should never survive the loss of dignity and dominion. I implore Heaven that I may never be seen, not a day, without my diadem and purple; that I may no longer behold the light when I cease to be saluted with the name of queen. If you resolve, O Cæsar! to fly, you have treasures; behold the sea, you have ships; but tremble lest the desire of life should expose you to wretched exile and ignominious death. For my own part, I adhere to the maxim of antiquity, that the throne is a glorious sepulchre." The firmness of a woman restored the courage to deliberate and act, and courage soon discovers the resources of the most desperate situation. It was an easy and a decisive measure to revive the animosity of the factions; the blues were astonished at their own guilt and folly, that a trifling injury should provoke them to conspire with their implacable enemies against a gracious and liberal benefactor; they again proclaimed the majesty of Justinian; and the greens, with their upstart emperor, were left alone in the hippodrome. The fidelity of the guards was doubtful; but the military force of Justinian consisted in three thousand veterans, who had been trained to valour and discipline in the Persian and Illyrian wars. Under the command of Belisarius and Mundus, they silently marched in two divisions from the palace, forced their obscure way through narrow passages, expiring flames, and falling edifices, and burst open at the same moment the two opposite gates of the hippodrome. In this narrow space the disorderly and affrighted crowd was incapable of resisting on either side a firm and regular attack; the blues signalised the fury of their repentance, and it is computed that above thirty thousand persons were slain in the merciless and promiscuous carnage of the day. Hypatius was dragged from his throne, and conducted with his brother Pompey to the feet of the emperor; they implored his clemency, but their crime was manifest, their innocence uncertain, and Justinian had been too much terrified to forgive. The next morning the two nephews of Anastasius, with eighteen *illustrious* accomplices, of patrician or consular rank, were privately executed by the soldiers, their bodies were thrown into the sea, their palaces razed, and their fortunes confiscated. The hippodrome itself was condemned, during several years, to a mournful silence; with the restoration of the games the same disorders revived, and the blue and green factions continued to afflict the reign of Justinian, and to disturb the tranquillity of the Eastern empire.

That empire, after Rome was barbarous, still embraced the nations whom she had conquered beyond the Hadriatic, and as far as the frontiers of Ethiopia and Persia. Justinian reigned over sixty-four provinces and nine hundred and thirty-five cities; his dominions were blessed by nature with the advantages of soil, situation, and climate, and the improvements of human art had been perpetually diffused along the coast of the Mediterranean and the banks of the Nile from ancient Troy to the Egyptian Thebes. Abraham had been relieved by the well-known plenty of Egypt; the same country, a small and populous tract, was still capable of exporting each year two hundred and sixty thousand quarters of wheat for the use of Constantinople; and the capital of Justinian was supplied with the manufactures of Sidon fifteen centuries after they had been celebrated in the poems of Homer. The annual powers of vegetation, instead of being exhausted by two thousand harvests, were renewed and invigorated by skilful husbandry, rich manure, and seasonable repose. The breed of domestic animals was infinitely multiplied. Plantations, buildings, and the instruments of labour and luxury, which are more durable than the term of human life, were accumulated by the care of successive generations. Tradition preserved, and experience simplified, the humble practice of the arts; society was enriched by the division of labour and the facility of exchange; and every Roman was lodged, clothed, and subsisted by the industry of a thousand hands. The invention of the loom and distaff has been piously ascribed to the gods. In every age a variety of animal and vegetable productions, hair, skins, wool, flax, cotton, and at length *silk,* have been skilfully manufactured to hide or adorn the human body; they were stained with an infusion of permanent colours, and the pencil was successfully employed to improve the labours of the loom. In the choice of those colours which imitate the beauties of nature, the freedom of taste and fashion was indulged; but the deep purple which the Phœnicians extracted from a shell-fish was restrained to the sacred person and palace of the emperor, and the penalties of treason were denounced against the ambitious subjects who dared to usurp the prerogative of the throne.

I need not explain that *silk* is originally spun from the bowels of a caterpillar, and that it composes the golden tomb from whence a worm emerges in the form of a butterfly. Till the reign of Justinian, the silkworms who feed on the leaves of the white mulberry-tree were confined to China; those of the pine, the oak, and the ash were common in the forests both of Asia and Europe; but as their education is more difficult, and their produce more uncertain, they were generally neglected, except in the little island of Ceos, near the coast of Attica. A thin gauze was procured from their webs, and this Cean manufacture, the invention of a woman, for female use, was long admired both in the East and at Rome. Whatever suspicions may be raised by the garments of the Medes and Assyrians, Virgil is the most ancient writer who expressly mentions the soft wool which was combed from the trees of the Seres or Chinese; and this natural error, less marvellous than the truth, was slowly corrected by the knowledge of a valuable insect, the first artificer of the luxury of nations. That rare and elegant luxury was censured, in the reign of Tiberius, by the gravest of the Romans; and Pliny, in affected though forcible language, has condemned the thirst of gain, which explored the last confines of the earth for the pernicious purpose of exposing to the public eye naked draperies and transparent matrons. A dress which showed the turn of the limbs and colour of the skin might gratify vanity or provoke desire; the silks which had been closely woven in China were sometimes unravelled by the Phœnician women, and the precious materials were multiplied by a looser texture, and the intermixture of linen threads. Two hundred years after the age of Pliny the use of pure or even of mixed silks was confined to the female sex, till the opulent citizens of Rome and the provinces were insensibly familiarised with the example of Elagabalus, the first who, by this effeminate habit, had sullied the dignity of an emperor and a man. Aurelian complained that a pound of silk was sold at Rome for twelve ounces of gold; but the supply increased with the demand, and the price diminished with the supply. If accident or monopoly sometimes raised the value even above the standard of Aurelian, the manufacturers of Tyre and Berytus were sometimes compelled, by the operation of the same causes, to content themselves with a ninth part of that extravagant rate. A law was thought necessary to discriminate the dress of comedians from that of senators, and of the silk exported from its native country the far greater part was consumed by the subjects of Justinian. They were still more intimately acquainted with a shell-fish of the Mediterranean, surnamed the silkworm of the sea: the fine wool or hair by which the mother-of-pearl affixes itself to the rock is now manufactured for curiosity rather than use; and a robe obtained from the same singular materials was the gift of the Roman emperor to the satraps of Armenia.

A valuable merchandise of small bulk is capable of defraying the expense of land-carriage, and the caravans traversed the whole latitude of Asia in two hundred and forty-three days from the Chinese ocean to the sea-coast of Syria. Silk was immediately delivered to the Romans by the Persian merchants, who frequented the fairs of Armenia and Nisibis; but this trade, which in the intervals of truce was oppressed by avarice and jealousy, was totally interrupted by the long wars of the rival monarchies. The Great King might proudly number Sogdiana, and even *Serica,* among the provinces of his empire, but his real dominion was bounded by the Oxus, and his useful intercourse with the Sogdoites, beyond the river, depended on the pleasure of their conquerors, the white Huns and the Turks, who successively reigned over that industrious people. Yet the most savage dominion has not extirpated the seeds of agriculture and commerce in a region which is celebrated as one of the four gardens of Asia; the cities of Samarcand and Bochara are advantageously seated for the exchange of its various productions, and their merchants purchased from the Chinese the raw or manufactured silk which they transported into Persia for the use of the Roman empire. In the vain capital of China the Sogdian caravans were entertained as the suppliant embassies of tributary kingdoms, and, if they returned in safety, the bold adventure was rewarded with exorbitant gain. But the difficult and perilous march from Samarcand to the first town of Shensi could not be performed in less than sixty, eighty, or one hundred days; as soon as they had passed the Jaxartes they entered the desert, and the wandering hordes, unless they are restrained by armies and garrisons, have always considered the citizen and the traveller as the objects of lawful rapine. To escape the Tartar robbers and the tyrants of Persia, the silk-caravans explored a more southern road: they traversed the mountains of Thibet, descended the streams of the Ganges or the Indus, and patiently expected, in the ports of Guzerat and Malabar, the annual fleets of the West. But the dangers of the desert were found less intolerable than toil, hunger, and the loss of time; the attempt was seldom renewed, and the only European who has passed that unfrequented way applauds his own diligence that, in nine months after his departure from Pekin, he reached the mouth of the Indus. The ocean, however, was open to the free communication of mankind. From the great river to the tropic of Cancer the provinces of China were subdued and civilised by the emperors of the North; they were filled about the time of the Christian era with cities and men, mulberry-trees and their precious inhabitants; and if the Chinese, with the knowledge of the compass, had possessed the genius of the Greeks or Phœnicians, they might have spread their discoveries over the southern hemisphere. I am not qualified to examine, and I am not disposed to believe, their distant voyages to the Persian Gulf or the Cape of Good Hope; but their ancestors might equal the labours and success of the present race, and the sphere of their navigation might extend from the isles of Japan to the straits of Malacca, the Pillars, if we may apply that name, of an Oriental Hercules. Without losing sight of land, they might sail along the coast to the extreme promontory of Achin, which is annually visited by ten or twelve ships laden with the productions, the manufactures, and even the artificers of China; the island of Sumatra and the opposite peninsula are faintly delineated as the regions of gold and silver, and the trading cities named in the geography of Ptolemy may indicate that this wealth was not solely derived from the mines. The direct interval between Sumatra and Ceylon is about three hundred leagues; the Chinese and Indian navigators were conducted by the flight of birds and periodical winds, and the ocean might be securely traversed in square-built ships, which, instead of iron, were sewed together with the strong thread of the cocoanut. Ceylon, Serendib, or Taprobana was divided between two hostile princes, one of whom possessed the mountains, the elephants, and the luminous carbuncle, and the other enjoyed the more solid riches of domestic industry, foreign trade, and the capacious harbour of Trinquemale, which received and dismissed the fleets of the East and West. In this hospitable isle, at an equal distance (as it was computed) from their respective countries, the silk-merchants of China, who had collected in their voyages aloes, cloves, nutmeg, and sandal-wood, maintained a free and beneficial commerce with the inhabitants of the Persian Gulf. The subjects of the Great King exalted, without a rival, his power and magnificence; and the Roman, who confounded their vanity by comparing his paltry coin with a gold medal of the emperor Anastasius, had sailed to Ceylon, in an Æthiopian ship, as a simple passenger.

As silk became of indispensable use, the emperor Justinian saw with concern that the Persians had occupied by land and sea the monopoly of this important supply, and that the wealth of his subjects was continually drained by a nation of enemies and idolators. An active government would have restored the trade of Egypt and the navigation of the Red Sea, which had decayed with the prosperity of the empire; and the Roman vessels might have sailed for the purchase of silk to the ports of Ceylon, of Malacca, or even of China. Justinian embraced a more humble expedient, and solicited the aid of his Christian allies, the Æthiopians of Abyssinia, who had recently acquired the arts of navigation, the spirit of trade, and the seaport of Adulis, still decorated with the trophies of a Grecian conqueror. Along the African coast they penetrated to the equator in search of gold, emeralds, and aromatics; but they wisely declined an unequal competition, in which they must be always prevented by the vicinity of the Persians to the markets of India: and the emperor submitted to the disappointment till his wishes were gratified by an unexpected event. The Gospel had been preached to the Indians: a bishop already governed the Christians of St. Thomas on the pepper-coast of Malabar; a church was planted in Ceylon, and the missionaries pursued the footsteps of commerce to the extremities of Asia. Two Persian monks had long resided in China, perhaps in the royal city of Nankin, the seat of a monarch addicted to foreign superstitions, and who actually received an embassy from the isle of Ceylon. Amidst their pious occupations they viewed with a curious eye the common dress of the Chinese, the manufactures of silk, and the myriads of silkworms, whose education (either on trees or in houses) had once been considered as the labour of queens. They soon discovered that it was impracticable to transport the short-lived insect, but that in the eggs a numerous progeny might be preserved and multiplied in a distant climate. Religion or interest had more power over the Persian monks than the love of their country: after a long journey they arrived at Constantinople, imparted their project to the emperor, and were liberally encouraged by the gifts and promises of Justinian. To the historians of that prince a campaign at the foot of Mount Caucasus has seemed more deserving of a minute relation than the labours of these missionaries of commerce, who again entered China, deceived a jealous people by concealing the eggs of the silk-worm in a hollow cane, and returned in triumph with the spoils of the East. Under their direction the eggs were hatched at the proper season by the artificial heat of dung; the worms were fed with mulberry-leaves; they lived and laboured in a foreign climate; a sufficient number of butterflies was saved to propagate the race, and trees were planted to supply the nourishment of the rising generations. Experience and reflection corrected the errors of a new attempt, and the Sogdoite ambassadors acknowledged in the succeeding reign that the Romans were not inferior to the natives of China in the education of the insects and the manufactures of silk, in which both China and Constantinople have been surpassed by the industry of modern Europe. I am not insensible of the benefits of elegant luxury; yet I reflect with some pain that if the importers of silk had introduced the art of printing, already practised by the Chinese, the comedies of Menander and the entire decads of Livy would have been perpetuated in the editions of the sixth century. A larger view of the globe might at least have promoted the improvement of speculative science; but the Christian geography was forcibly extracted from texts of Scripture, and the study of nature was the surest symptom of an unbelieving mind. The orthodox faith confined the habitable world to *one* temperate zone, and represented the earth as an oblong surface, four hundred days' journey in length, two hundred in breadth, encompassed by the ocean and covered by the solid crystal of the firmament.

The subjects of Justinian were dissatisfied with the times and with the government. Europe was overrun by the barbarians and Asia by the monks: the poverty of the West discouraged the trade and manufactures of the East: the produce of labour was consumed by the unprofitable servants of the church, the state, and the army; and a rapid decrease was felt in the fixed and circulating capitals which constitute the national wealth. The public distress had been alleviated by the economy of Anastasius, and that prudent emperor accumulated an immense treasure while he delivered his people from the most odious or oppressive taxes. Their gratitude universally applauded the abolition of the *gold of affliction,* a personal tribute on the industry of the poor, but more intolerable, as it should seem, in the form than in the substance, since the flourishing city of Edessa paid only one hundred and forty pounds of gold, which was collected in four years from ten thousand artificers. Yet such was the parsimony which supported this liberal disposition, that, in a reign of twenty-seven years, Anastasius saved from his annual revenue the enormous sum of thirteen millions sterling, or three hundred and twenty thousand pounds of gold. His example was neglected, and his treasure was abused, by the nephew of Justin. The riches of Justinian were speedily exhausted by alms and buildings, by ambitious wars and ignominious treaties. His revenues were found inadequate to his expenses. Every art was tried to extort from the people the gold and silver which he scattered with a lavish hand from Persia to France: his reign was marked by the vicissitudes, or rather by the combat, of rapaciousness and avarice, of splendour and poverty; he lived with the reputation of hidden treasures, and bequeathed to his successor the payment of his debts. Such a character has been justly accused by the voice of the people and of posterity: but public discontent is credulous . . .

The fortifications of Europe and Asia were multiplied by Justinian; but the repetition of those timid and fruitless precautions exposes, to a philosophic eye, the debility of the empire. From Belgrade to the Euxine, from the conflux of the Save to the mouth of the Danube, a chain of above fourscore fortified places was extended along the banks of the great river. Single watch-towers were changed into spacious citadels; vacant walls, which the engineers contracted or enlarged according to the nature of the ground, were filled with colonies or garrisons; a strong fortress defended the ruins of Trajan's bridge; and several military stations affected to spread beyond the Danube the pride of the Roman name. But that name was divested of its terrors; the barbarians, in their annual inroads, passed and contemptuously repassed before these useless bulwarks; and the inhabitants of the frontier, instead of reposing under the shadow of the general defence, were compelled to guard with incessant vigilance their separate habitations. The solitude of ancient cities was replenished; the new foundations of Justinian acquired, perhaps too hastily, the epithets of impregnable and populous; and the auspicious place of his own nativity attracted the grateful reverence of the vainest of princes. Under the name of *Justiniana prima,* the obscure village of Tauresium became the seat of an archbishop and a præfect, whose jurisdiction extended over seven warlike provinces of Illyricum; and the corrupt appellation of *Giustendil* still indicates, about twenty miles to the south of Sophia, the residence of a Turkish sanjak. For the use of the emperor's countrymen, a cathedral, a palace, and an aqueduct were speedily constructed; the public and private edifices were adapted to the greatness of a royal city; and the strength of the walls resisted, during the lifetime of Justinian, the unskilful assaults of the Huns and Sclavonians. Their progress was sometimes retarded, and their hopes of rapine were disappointed, by the innumerable castles which, in the provinces of Dacia, Epirus, Thessaly, Macedonia, and Thrace, appeared to cover the whole face of the country. Six hundred of these forts were built or repaired by the emperor; but it seems reasonable to believe that the far greater part consisted only of a stone or brick tower in the midst of a square or circular area, which was surrounded by a wall and ditch, and afforded in a moment of danger some protection to the peasants and cattle of the neighbouring villages. Yet these military works, which exhausted the public treasure, could not remove the just apprehensions of Justinian and his European subjects. The warmbaths of Anchialus, in Thrace, were rendered as safe as they were salutary; but the rich pastures of Thessalonica were foraged by the Scythian cavalry; the delicious vale of Tempe, three hundred miles from the Danube, was continually alarmed by the sound of war; and no unfortified spot, however distant or solitary, could securely enjoy the blessings of peace. The straits of Thermopylæ, which seemed to protect, but which had so often betrayed, the safety of Greece, were diligently strengthened by the labours of Justinian. From the edge of the sea-shore, through the forests and valleys, and as far as the summit of the Thessalian mountains, a strong wall was continued which occupied every practicable entrance. Instead of a hasty crowd of peasants, a garrison of two thousand soldiers was stationed along the rampart, granaries of corn and reservoirs of water were provided for their use, and, by a precaution that inspired the cowardice which it foresaw, convenient fortresses were erected for their retreat. The walls of Corinth, overthrown by an earthquake, and the mouldering bulwarks of Athens and Platæa, were carefully restored; the barbarians were discouraged by the prospect of successive and painful seiges, and the naked cities of Peloponnesus were covered by the fortifications of the isthmus of Corinth. At the extremity of Europe, another peninsula, the Thracian Chersonesus, runs three days' journey into the sea, to form, with the adjacent shores of Asia, the straits of the Hellespont. The intervals between eleven populous towns were filled by lofty woods, fair pastures, and arable lands; and the isthmus, of thirty-seven stadia or furlongs, had been fortified by a Spartan general nine hundred years before the reign of Justinian. In an age of freedom and valour the slightest rampart may prevent a surprise; and Procopius appears insensible of the superiority of ancient times, while he praises the solid construction and double parapet of a wall whose long arms stretched on either side into the sea, but whose strength was deemed insufficient to guard the Chersonesus, if each city, and particularly Gallipoli and Sestus, had not been secured by their peculiar fortifications. The *long* wall, as it was emphatically styled, was a work as disgraceful in the object as it was respectable in the execution. The riches of a capital diffuse themselves over the neighbouring country, and the territory of Constantinople, a paradise of nature, was adorned with the luxurious gardens and villas of the senators and opulent citizens. But their wealth served only to attract the bold and rapacious barbarians; the noblest of the Romans, in the bosom of peaceful indolence, were led away into Scythian captivity; and their sovereign might view from his palace the hostile flames which were insolently spread to the gates of the Imperial city. At the distance only of forty miles, Anastasius was constrained to establish a last frontier; his long wall of sixty miles, from the Propontis to the Euxine, proclaimed the impotence of his arms; and as the danger became more imminent, new fortifications were added by the indefatigable prudence of Justinian. . . .

Justinian suppressed the schools of Athens and the consulship of Rome, which had given so many sages and heroes to mankind.* Both these institutions had long since degenerated from their primitive glory, yet some reproach may be justly inflicted on the avarice and jealousy of a prince by whose hand such venerable ruins were destroyed.

Athens, after her Persian triumphs, adopted the philosophy of Ionia and the rhetoric of Sicily; and these studies became the patrimony of a city whose inhabitants, about thirty thousand males, condensed, within the period of a single life, the genius of ages and millions. Our sense of the dignity of human nature is exalted by the simple recollection that Isocrates was the companion of Plato and Xenophon; that he assisted, perhaps with the historian Thucydides, at the first representations of the Œdipus of Sophocles and the Iphigenia of Euripides; and that his pupils Æschines and Demosthenes contended for the crown of patriotism in the presence of Aristotle, the master of Theophrastus, who taught at Athens with the founders of the Stoic and Epicurean sects. The ingenuous youth of Attica enjoyed the benefits of their domestic education, which was communicated without envy to the rival cities. Two thousand disciples heard the lessons of Theophrastus; the schools of rhetoric must have been still more populous than those of philosophy; and a rapid succession of students diffused the fame of

*This action was profoundly to influence the Middle Ages. Greek thought was not revived again until the twelfth century, and then in poor Latin translations derived from Arabic. (P.W.)

their teachers as far as the utmost limits of the Grecian language and name. Those limits were enlarged by the victories of Alexander; the arts of Athens survived her freedom and dominion; and the Greek colonies which the Macedonians planted in Egypt, and scattered over Asia, undertook long and frequent pilgrimages to worship the Muses in their favourite temple on the banks of the Ilissus. The Latin conquerors respectfully listened to the instructions of their subjects and captives; the names of Cicero and Horace were enrolled in the schools of Athens; and after the perfect settlement of the Roman empire, the natives of Italy, of Africa, and of Britain, conversed in the groves of the Academy with their fellow-students of the East. The studies of philosophy and eloquence are congenial to a popular state, which encourages the freedom of inquiry, and submits only to the force of persuasion. In the republics of Greece and Rome the art of speaking was the powerful engine of patriotism or ambition; and the schools of rhetoric poured forth a colony of statesmen and legislators. When the liberty of public debate was suppressed, the orator, in the honourable profession of an advocate, might plead the cause of innocence and justice; he might abuse his talents in the more profitable trade of panegyric; and the same precepts continued to dictate the fanciful declamations of the sophist, and the chaster beauties of historical composition. The systems which professed to unfold the nature of God, of man, and of the universe, entertained the curiosity of the philosophic student; and according to the temper of his mind, he might doubt with the Sceptics, or decide with the Stoics, sublimely speculate with Plato, or severely argue with Aristotle. The pride of the adverse sects had fixed an unattainable term of moral happiness and perfection: but the race was glorious and salutary; the disciples of Zeno, and even those of Epicurus, were taught both to act and to suffer; and the death of Petronius was not less effectual than that of Seneca to humble a tyrant by the discovery of his impotence. The light of science could not indeed be confined within the walls of Athens. Her incomparable writers address themselves to the human race; the living masters emigrated to Italy and Asia; Berytus, in later times, was devoted to the study of the law; astronomy and physic were cultivated in the museum of Alexandria; but the Attic schools of rhetoric and philosophy maintained their superior reputation from the Peloponnesian war to the reign of Justinian. Athens, though situate in a barren soil, possessed a pure air, a free navigation, and the monuments of ancient art. That sacred retirement was seldom disturbed by the business of trade or government; and the last of the Athenians were distinguished by their lively wit, the purity of their taste and language, their social manners, and some traces, at least in discourse, of the magnanimity of their fathers. In the suburbs of the city, the *Academy* of the Platonists, the *Lyceum* of the Peripatetics, the *Portico* of the Stoics, and the *Garden* of the Epicureans, were planted with trees and decorated with statues; and the philosophers, instead of being immured in a cloister, delivered their instructions in spacious and pleasant walks, which at different hours were consecrated to the exercises of the mind and body. The genius of the founders still lived in those venerable seats; the ambition of succeeding to the masters of human reason excited a generous emulation; and the merit of the candidates was determined, on each vacancy, by the free voices of an enlightened people. The Athenian professors were paid by their disciples: according to their mutual wants and abilities, the price appears to have varied from a mina to a talent; and Isocrates himself, who derides the avarice of the sophists, required, in his school of rhetoric, about thirty pounds from each of his hundred pupils. The wages of industry are just and honourable, yet the same Isocrates shed tears at the first receipt of a stipend: the Stoic might blush when he was hired to preach the contempt of money; and I should be sorry to discover that Aristotle or Plato so far degenerated from the example of Socrates as to exchange knowledge for gold. But some property of lands and houses was settled, by the permission of the laws, and the legacies of deceased friends, on the philosophic chairs of Athens. Epicurus bequeathed to his disciples the gardens which he had purchased for eighty minæ or two hundred and fifty pounds, with a fund sufficient for their frugal subsistence and monthly festivals; and the patrimony of Plato afforded an annual rent, which, in eight centuries, was gradually increased from three to one thousand pieces of gold. The schools of Athens were protected by the wisest and most virtuous of the Roman princes. The library, which Hadrian founded, was placed in a portico adorned with pictures, statues, and a roof of alabaster, and supported by one hundred columns of Phrygian marble. The public salaries were assigned by the generous spirit of the Antonines; and each professor, of politics, of rhetoric, of the Platonic, the Peripatetic, the Stoic, and the Epicurean philosophy, received an annual stipend of ten thousand drachmæ, or more than three hundred pounds sterling. After the death of Marcus, these liberal donations, and the privileges attached to the *thrones* of science, were abolished and revived, diminished and enlarged; but some vestige of royal bounty may be found under the successors of Constantine; and their arbitrary choice of an unworthy candidate might tempt the philosophers of Athens to regret the days of independence and poverty. It is remarkable that the impartial favour of the Antonines was bestowed on the four adverse sects of philosophy, which they considered as equally useful, or at least as equally innocent. Socrates had formerly been the glory and the reproach of his country; and the first lessons of Epicurus so strangely scandalised the pious ears of the Athenians, that by his exile, and that of his antagonists, they silenced all vain disputes concerning the nature of the gods. But in the ensuing year they recalled the hasty decree, restored the liberty of the schools, and were convinced by the experience of ages that the moral character of philosophers is not affected by the diversity of their theological speculations.

The Gothic arms were less fatal to the schools of Athens than the establishment of a new religion, whose ministers superseded the exercise of reason, resolved every question by an article of faith, and condemned the infidel or sceptic to eternal flames. In many a volume of laborious controversy they exposed the weakness of the understanding and the corruption of the heart, insulted human nature in the sages of antiquity, and proscribed the spirit of philosophical inquiry, so repugnant to the doctrine, or at least to the temper, of a humble believer. The surviving sect of the Platonists, whom Plato would have blushed to acknowledge, extravagantly mingled a sublime theory with the practice of superstition and magic; and as they remained alone in the midst of a Christian world, they indulged a secret rancour against the government of the church and state, whose severity was still suspended over their heads. About a century after the reign of Julian, Proclus was permitted to teach in the philosophic chair of the Academy; and such was his industry, that he frequently, in the same day, pronounced five lessons, and composed seven hundred lines. His sagacious mind explored the deepest questions of morals and metaphysics, and he ventured to urge eighteen arguments against the Christian doctrine of the creation of the world. But in the intervals of study he *personally* conversed with Pan, Æsculapius, and Minerva, in whose mysteries he was secretly initiated, and whose prostrate statues he adored; in the devout persuasion that the philosopher, who is a citizen of the universe, should be the priest of its various deities. An eclipse of the sun announced his approaching end; and his Life, with that of his scholar Isidore, compiled by two of their most learned disciples, exhibits a deplorable picture of the second childhood of human reason. Yet the golden chain, as it was fondly styled, of the Platonic succession, continued forty-four years from the death of Proclus to the edict of Justinian, which imposed a perpetual silence on the schools of Athens, and excited the grief and indignation of the few remaining votaries of Grecian science and superstition. Seven friends and philosophers, Diogenes and Hermias, Eulalius and Priscian, Damascius, Isidore, and Simplicius, who dissented from the religion of their sovereign, embraced the resolution of seeking in a foreign land the freedom which was denied in their native country. They had heard, and they credulously believed, that the republic of Plato was realised in the despotic government of Persia, and that a patriot king reigned over the happiest and most virtuous of nations. They were soon astonished by the natural discovery that Persia resembled the other countries of the globe; that Chosroes, who affected the name of a philosopher, was vain, cruel, and ambitious; that bigotry, and a spirit of intolerance, prevailed among the Magi; that the nobles were haughty, the courtiers servile, and the magistrates unjust; that the guilty sometimes escaped, and that the innocent were often oppressed. The disappointment of the philosophers provoked them to overlook the real virtues of the Persians; and they were scandalised, more deeply perhaps than became their profession, with the plurality of wives and concubines, the incestuous marriages, and the custom of exposing dead bodies to the dogs and vultures, instead of hiding them in the earth, or consuming them with fire. Their repentance was expressed by a precipitate return, and they loudly declared that they had rather die on the borders of the empire than enjoy the wealth and favour of the barbarian. From this journey, however, they derived a benefit which reflects the purest lustre on the character of Chosroes. He required that the seven sages who had visited the court of Persia should be exempted from the penal laws which Justinian enacted against his Pagan subjects; and this privilege, expressly stipulated in a treaty of peace, was guarded by the vigilance of a powerful mediator. Simplicius and his companions ended their lives in peace and obscurity; and as they left no disciples, they terminate the long list of Grecian philosophers, who may be justly praised, notwithstanding their defects, as the wisest and most virtuous of their contemporaries. The writings of Simplicius are now extant. His physical and metaphysical commentaries on Aristotle have passed away with the fashion of the times; but his moral interpretation of Epictetus is preserved in the library of nations, as a classic book, most excellently adapted to direct the will, to purify the heart, and to confirm the understanding, by a just confidence in the nature both of God and man.

About the same time that Pythagoras first invented the appellation of philosopher, liberty and the consulship were founded at Rome by the elder Brutus. The revolutions of the consular office, which may be viewed in the successive lights of a substance, a shadow, and a name, have been occasionally mentioned in the present history. The first magistrates of the republic had been chosen by the people, to exercise, in the senate and in the camp, the powers of peace and war, which were afterwards translated to the emperors. But the tradition of ancient dignity was long revered by the Romans and barbarians. A Gothic historian applauds the consulship of Theodoric as the height of all temporal glory and greatness; the king of Italy himself congratulates those annual favourites of fortune who, without the cares, enjoyed the splendour of the throne; and at the end of a thousand years two consuls were created by the sovereigns of Rome and Constantinople for the sole purpose of giving a date to the year and a festival to the people. But the expenses of this festival, in which the wealthy and the vain aspired to surpass their predecessors, insensibly arose to the enormous sum of fourscore thousand pounds; the wisest senators declined a useless honour which involved the certain ruin of their families, and to this reluctance I should impute the frequent chasms in the last age of the consular *Fasti.* The predecessors of Justinian had assisted from the public treasures the dignity of the less opulent candidates; the avarice of that prince preferred the cheaper and more convenient method of advice and regulation. Seven *processions* or spectacles were the number to which his edict confined the horse and chariot races, the athletic sports, the music and pantomimes of the theatre, and the hunting of wild beasts; and small pieces of silver were discreetly substituted to the gold medals, which had always excited tumult and drunkenness when they were scattered with a profuse hand among the populace. Notwithstanding these precautions and his own example, the succession of consuls finally ceased in the thirteenth year of Justinian, whose despotic temper might be gratified by the silent extinction of a title which admonished the Romans of their ancient freedom. Yet the annual consulship still lived in the minds of the people; they fondly expected its speedy restoration; they applauded the gracious condescension of successive princes, by whom it was assumed in the first year of their reign; and three centuries elapsed, after the death of Justinian, before that obsolete dignity, which had been suppressed by custom, could be abolished by law. The imperfect mode of distinguishing each year by the name of a magistrate was usefully supplied by the date of a permanent era: the creation of the world, according to the Septuagint version, was adopted by the Greeks; and the Latins, since the age of Charlemagne, have computed their time from the birth of Christ.

PART 8

The Byzantine Empire *(Chapters XLVIII and LIII)*

Most contemporary historians of Byzantium view the reign of Heraclius as the end of the Empire. Although he defeated Persia and recovered Syria and Egypt, his victories coincided with the rise of the Arabs, who attacked Constantinople in 678. With the ruin of the Persian Empire, the incursions of the Bulgars, and the advance of Islam, the Eastern Empire was destined to collapse, and this is what most fascinated Gibbon about moribund Byzantium. His account of the collapse of the Eastern Empire is sketchy and dated, but his brilliant insights render his analysis more than worthy of contemporary attention.

CHAPTER XLVIII

I have now deduced from Trajan to Constantine, from Constantine to Heraclius, the regular series of the Roman emperors; and faithfully exposed the prosperous and adverse fortunes of their reigns. Five centuries of the decline and fall of the empire have already elapsed; but a period of more than eight hundred years still separates me from the term of my labours, the taking of Constantinople by the Turks. Should I persevere in the same course, should I observe the same measure, a prolix and slender thread would be spun through many a volume, nor would the patient reader find an adequate reward of instruction or amusement. At every step, as we sink deeper in the decline and fall of the Eastern empire, the annals of each succeeding reign would impose a more ungrateful and melancholy task. These annals must continue to repeat a tedious and uniform tale of weakness and misery; the natural connection of causes and events would be broken by frequent and hasty transitions, and a minute accumulation of circumstances must destroy the light and effect of those general pictures which compose the use and ornament of a remote history. From the time of Heraclius the Byzantine theatre is contracted and darkened: the line of empire, which had been defined by the laws of Justinian and the arms of Belisarius, recedes on all sides from our view; the Roman name, the proper subject of our inquiries, is reduced to a narrow corner of Europe, to the lonely suburbs of Constantinople; and the fate of the Greek empire has been compared to that of the Rhine, which loses itself in the sands before its waters can mingle with the ocean. The scale of dominion is diminished to our view by the distance of time and place; nor is the loss of external splendour compensated by the nobler gifts of virtue and genius. In the last moments of her decay Constantinople was doubtless more opulent and populous than Athens at her most flourishing era, when a scanty sum of six thousand talents, or twelve hundred thousand pounds sterling, was possessed by twenty-one thousand male citizens of an adult age. But each of these citizens was a freeman who dared to assert the liberty of his thoughts, words, and actions; whose person and property were guarded by equal law; and who exercised his independent vote in the government of the republic. Their numbers seem to be multiplied by the strong and various discriminations of character; under the shield of freedom, on the wings of emulation and vanity, each Athenian aspired to the level of the national dignity; from this commanding eminence some chosen spirits soared beyond the reach of a vulgar eye; and the chances of superior merit in a great and populous kingdom, as they are proved by experience, would excuse the computation of imaginary millions. The territories of Athens, Sparta, and their allies, do not exceed a moderate province of France or England; but after the trophies of Salamis and Platæa, they expand in our fancy to the gigantic size of Asia, which had been trampled under the feet of the victorious Greeks. But the subjects of the Byzantine empire, who assume and dishonour the names both of Greeks and Romans, present a dead uniformity of abject vices, which are neither softened by the weakness of humanity nor animated by the vigour of memorable crimes. The freemen of antiquity might repeat with generous enthusiasm the sentence of Homer, "that on the first day of his servitude the captive is deprived of one half of his manly virtue." But the poet had only seen the effects of civil or domestic slavery, nor could he foretell that the second moiety of manhood must be annihilated by the spiritual despotism, which shackles not only the actions but even the thoughts of the prostrate votary. By this double yoke the Greeks were oppressed under the successors of Heraclius; the tyrant, a law of eternal justice, was degraded by the vices of his subjects; and on the throne, in the camp, in the schools, we search, perhaps with fruitless diligence, the names and characters that may deserve to be rescued from oblivion. Nor are the defects of the subject compensated by the skill and variety of the painters. Of a space of eight hundred years, the four first centuries are overspread with a cloud interrupted by some faint and broken rays of historic light: in the lives of the emperors, from Maurice to Alexius, Basil the Macedonian has alone been the theme of a separate work; and the absence, or loss, or imperfection of contemporary evidence, must be poorly supplied by the doubtful authority of more recent compilers. The four last centuries are exempt from the reproach of penury: and with the Comnenian family the historic muse of Constantinople again revives, but her apparel is gaudy, her motions are without elegance or grace. A succession of priests, or courtiers, treads in each other's footsteps in the same path of servitude and superstition: their views are narrow, their judgment is feeble or corrupt: and we close the volume of copious barrenness, still ignorant of the causes of events, the characters of the actors, and the manners of the times, which they celebrate or deplore. The observation which has been applied to a man may be extended to a whole people, that the energy of the sword is communicated to the pen; and it will be found by experience that the tone of history will rise or fall with the spirit of the age.

From these considerations I should have abandoned without regret the Greek slaves and their servile historians, had I not reflected that the fate of the Byzantine monarchy is *passively* connected with the most splendid and important revolutions which have changed the state of the world. The space of the lost provinces was immediately replenished with new colonies and rising kingdoms: the active virtues of peace and war deserted from the vanquished to the victorious nations; and it is in their origin and conquests, in their religion and government, that we must explore the causes and effects of the decline and fall of the Eastern empire. Nor will this scope of narrative, the riches and variety of these materials, be incompatible with the unity of design and composition. As, in his daily prayers, the Musulman of Fez or Delhi still turns his face towards the temple of Mecca, the historian's eye shall be always fixed on the city of Constantinople. The excursive line may embrace the wilds of Arabia and Tartary, but the circle will be ultimately reduced to the decreasing limit of the Roman monarchy.

On this principle I shall now establish the plan of the last two volumes of the present work. The first chapter will contain, in a regular series, the emperors who reigned at Constantinople during a period of six hundred years, from the days of Heraclius to the Latin conquest: a rapid abstract, which may be supported by a *general* appeal to the order and text of the original historians. In this introduction I shall confine myself to the revolutions of the throne, the succession of families, the personal characters of the Greek princes, the mode of their life and death, the maxims and influence of their domestic government, and the tendency of their reign to accelerate or suspend the downfall of the Eastern empire. Such a chronological review will serve to illustrate the various argument of the subsequent chapters; and each circumstance of the eventful story of the barbarians will adapt itself in a proper place to the Byzantine annals. The internal state of the empire, and the dangerous heresy of the Paulicians, which shook the East and enlightened the West, will be the subject of two separate chapters; but these inquiries must be postponed till our farther progress shall have opened the view of the world in the ninth and tenth centuries of the Christian era. After this foundation of Byzantine history, the following nations will pass before our eyes, and each will occupy the space to which it may be entitled by greatness or merit, or the degree of connection with the Roman world and the present age. I. The FRANKS; a general appellation which includes all the barbarians of France, Italy, and Germany, who were united by the sword and sceptre of Charlemagne. The persecution of images and their votaries separated Rome and Italy from the Byzantine throne, and prepared the restoration of the Roman empire in the West. II. The ARABS or SARACENS. Three ample chapters will be devoted to this curious and interesting object. In the first, after a picture of the country and its inhabitants, I shall investigate the character of Mohammed; the character, religion, and success of the prophet. In the second I shall lead the Arabs to the conquest of Syria, Egypt, and Africa, the provinces of the Roman empire; nor can I check their victorious career till they have overthrown the monarchies of Persia and Spain. In the third I shall inquire how Constantinople and Europe were saved by the luxury and arts, the division and decay, of the empire of the caliphs. A single chapter will include, III. The BULGARIANS, IV. HUNGARIANS, and V. RUSSIANS, who assaulted by sea or by land the provinces and the capital; but the last of these, so important in their present greatness, will excite some curiosity in their origin and infancy. VI. The NORMANS; or rather the private adventurers of that warlike people, who founded a powerful kingdom in Apulia and Sicily, shook the throne of Constantinople, displayed the trophies of chivalry, and almost realised the wonders of romance. VII. The LATINS; the subjects of the pope, the nations of the West, who enlisted under the banner of the cross for the recovery or relief of the holy sepulchre. The Greek emperors were terrified and preserved by the myriads of pilgrims who marched to Jerusalem with Godfrey of Bouillon and the peers of Christendom. The second and third crusades trod in the footsteps of the first: Asia and Europe were mingled in a sacred war of two hundred years; and the Christian powers were bravely resisted and finally expelled by Saladin and the Mamalukes of Egypt. In these memorable crusades a fleet and army of French and Venetians were diverted from Syria to the Thracian Bosphorus: they assaulted the capital, they subverted the Greek monarchy: and a dynasty of Latin princes was seated near threescore years on the throne of Constantine. VIII. The GREEKS themselves, during this period of captivity and exile, must be considered as a foreign nation; the enemies, and again the sovereigns of Constantinople. Misfortune had rekindled a spark of national virtue; and the Imperial series may be continued with some dignity from their restoration to the Turkish conquest. IX. The MOGULS and TARTARS. By the arms of Zingis and his descendants the globe was shaken from China to Poland and Greece: the sultans were overthrown: the caliphs fell, and the Cæsars trembled on their throne. The victories of Timour suspended above fifty years the final ruin of the Byzantine empire. X. I have already noticed the first appearance of the TURKS; and the names of the fathers, of *Seljuk* and *Othman,* discriminate the two successive dynasties of the nation which emerged in the eleventh century from the Scythian wilderness. The former established a potent and splendid kingdom from the banks of the Oxus to Antioch and Nice; and the first crusade was provoked by the violation of Jerusalem and the danger of Constantinople. From a humble origin the *Ottomans* arose the scourge and terror of Christendom. Constantinople was besieged and taken by Mohammed II., and his triumph annihilates the remnant, the image, the title, of the Roman empire in the East. The schism of the Greeks will be connected with their last calamities and the restoration of learning in the Western world. I shall return from the captivity of the new to the ruins of ancient ROME; and the venerable name, the interesting theme, will shed a ray of glory on the conclusion of my labours. . . .

. . . If we compute the number and duration of the reigns, it will be found that a period of six hundred years is filled by sixty emperors, including in the Augustan list some female sovereigns, and deducting some usurpers who were never acknowledged in the capital, and some princes who did not live to possess their inheritance. The average proportion will allow ten years for each emperor—far below the chronological rule of Sir Isaac Newton, who, from the experience of more recent and regular monarchies, has defined about eighteen or twenty years as the term of an ordinary reign. The Byzantine empire was most tranquil and prosperous when it could acquiesce in hereditary succession: five dynasties, the Heraclian, Isaurian, Amorian, Basilian, and Comnenian families, enjoyed and transmitted the royal patrimony during their respective series of five, four, three, six, and four generations; several princes number the years of their reign with those of their infancy; and Constantine the Seventh and his two grandsons occupy the space of an entire century. But in the intervals of the Byzantine dynasties the succession is rapid and broken, and the name of a successful candidate is speedily erased by a more fortunate competitor. Many were the paths that led to the summit of royalty: the fabric of rebellion was overthrown by the stroke of conspiracy, or undermined by the silent arts of intrigue: the favourites of the soldiers or people, of the senate or clergy, of the women and eunuchs, were alternately clothed with the purple: the means of their elevation were base, and their end was often contemptible or tragic. A being of the nature of man, endowed with the same faculties, but with a longer measure of existence, would cast down a smile of pity and contempt on the crimes and follies of human ambition, so eager, in a narrow span, to grasp at a precarious and short-lived enjoyment. It is thus that the experience of history exalts and enlarges the horizon of our intellectual view. In a composition of some days, in a perusal of some hours, six hundred years have rolled away, and the duration of a life or reign is contracted to a fleeting moment: the grave is ever beside the throne; the success of a criminal is almost instantly followed by the loss of his prize; and our immortal reason survives and disdains the sixty phantoms of kings who have passed before our eyes, and faintly dwell on our remembrance. The observation, that in every age and climate ambition has prevailed with the same commanding energy, may abate the surprise of a philosopher; but while he condemns the vanity, he may search the motive of this universal desire to obtain and hold the sceptre of dominion. To the greater part of the Byzantine series we cannot reasonably ascribe the love of fame and of mankind. The virtue alone of John Comnenus was beneficent and pure: the most illustrious of the princes who precede or follow that respectable name have trod with some dexterity and vigour the crooked and bloody paths of a selfish policy: in scrutinising the imperfect characters of Leo the Isaurian, Basil the First, and Alexius Comnenus, of Theophilus, the second Basil, and Manuel Comnenus, our esteem and censure are almost equally balanced; and the remainder of the Imperial crowd could only desire and expect to be forgotten by posterity. Was personal happiness the aim and object of their ambition? I shall not descant on the vulgar topics of the misery of kings; but I may surely observe that their condition, of all others, is the most pregnant with fear, and the least susceptible of hope. For these opposite passions a larger scope was allowed in the revolutions of antiquity than in the smooth and solid temper of the modern world, which cannot easily repeat either the triumph of Alexander or the fall of Darius. But the peculiar infelicity of the Byzantine princes exposed them to domestic perils, without affording any lively promise of foreign conquest. From the pinnacle of greatness Andronicus was precipitated by a death more cruel and shameful than that of the vilest malefactor; but the most glorious of his predecessors had much more to dread from their subjects than to hope from their enemies. The army was licentious without spirit, the nation turbulent without freedom: the barbarians of the East and West pressed on the monarchy, and the loss of the provinces was terminated by the final servitude of the capital.

The entire series of Roman emperors, from the first of the Cæsars to the last of the Constantines, extends above fifteen hundred years: and the term of dominion, unbroken by foreign conquest, surpasses the measure of the ancient monarchies—the Assyrians or Medes, the successors of Cyrus, or those of Alexander.

CHAPTER LIII

A ray of historic light seems to beam from the darkness of the tenth century. We open with curiosity and respect the royal volumes of Constantine Porphyrogenitus, which he composed at a mature age for the instruction of his son, and which promise to unfold the state of the Eastern empire, both in peace and war, both at home and abroad. In the first of these works he minutely describes the pompous ceremonies of the church and palace of Constantinople, according to his own practice and that of his predecessors. In the second he attempts an accurate survey of the provinces, the *themes,* as they were then denominated, both of Europe and Asia. The system of Roman tactics, the discipline and order of the troops, and the military operations by land and sea, are explained in the third of these didactic collections, which may be ascribed to Constantine or his father Leo. In the fourth, of the administration of the empire, he reveals the secrets of the Byzantine policy, in friendly or hostile intercourse with the nations of the earth. The literary labours of the age, the practical systems of law, agriculture, and history, might redound to the benefit of the subject, and the honour of the Macedonian princes. The sixty books of the *Basilics,* the code and pandects of civil jurisprudence, were gradually framed in the three first reigns of that prosperous dynasty. The art of agriculture had amused the leisure, and exercised the pens, of the best and wisest of the ancients; and their chosen precepts are comprised in the twenty books of the *Geoponics* of Constantine. At his command the historical examples of vice and virtue were methodised in fifty-three books, and every citizen might apply to his contemporaries or himself the lesson or the warning of past times. From the august character of a legislator, the sovereign of the East descends to the more humble office of a teacher and a scribe; and if his successors and subjects were regardless of his paternal cares, *we* may inherit and enjoy the everlasting legacy.

A closer survey will indeed reduce the value of the gift and the gratitude of posterity: in the possession of these Imperial treasures we may still deplore our poverty and ignorance; and the fading glories of their authors will be obliterated by indifference or contempt. The Basilics will sink to a broken copy, a partial and mutilated version in the Greek language, of the laws of Justinian; but the sense of the old civilians is often superseded by the influence of bigotry: and the absolute prohibition of divorce, concubinage, and interest for money, enslaves the freedom of trade and the happiness of private life. In the historical book a subject of Constantine might admire the inimitable virtues of Greece and Rome: he might learn to what a pitch of energy and elevation the human character had formerly aspired. But a contrary effect must have been produced by a new edition of the lives of the saints, which the great logothete, or chancellor of the empire, was directed to prepare; and the dark fund of superstition was enriched by the fabulous and florid legends of Simon the *Metaphrast.* The merits and miracles of the whole calendar are of less account in the eyes of a sage than the toil of a single husbandman, who multiplies the gifts of the Creator and supplies the food of his brethren. Yet the royal authors of the *Geoponics* were more seriously employed in expounding the precepts of the destroying art, which has been taught since the days of Xenophon as the art of heroes and kings. But the *Tactics* of Leo and Constantine are mingled with the baser alloy of the age in which they lived. It was destitute of original genius; they implicitly transcribe the rules and maxims which had been confirmed by victories. It was unskilled in the propriety of style and method; they blindly confound the most distant and discordant institutions, the phalanx of Sparta and that of Macedon, the legions of Cato and Trajan, of Augustus and Theodosius. Even the use, or at least the importance, of these military rudiments may be fairly questioned: their general theory is dictated by reason; but the merit, as well as difficulty, consists in the application. The discipline of a soldier is formed by exercise rather than by study: the talents of a commander are appropriated to those calm, though rapid, minds, which nature produces to decide the fate of armies and nations: the former is the habit of a life, the latter the glance of a moment; and the battles won by lessons of tactics may be numbered with the epic poems created from the rules of criticism. The book of ceremonies is a recital, tedious yet imperfect, of the despicable pageantry which had infected the church and state since the gradual decay of the purity of the one and the power of the other. A review of the themes or provinces might promise such authentic and useful information as the curiosity of government only can obtain, instead of traditionary fables on the origin of the cities, and malicious epigrams on the vices of their inhabitants. Such information the historian would have been pleased to record; nor should his silence be condemned if the most interesting objects, the population of the capital and provinces, the amount of the taxes and revenues, the numbers of subjects and strangers who served under the Imperial standard, have been unnoticed by Leo the Philosopher and his son Constantine. His treatise of the public administration is stained with the same blemishes; yet it is discriminated by peculiar merit: the antiquities of the nations may be doubtful or fabulous; but the geography and manners of the barbaric world are delineated with curious accuracy. Of these nations the Franks alone were qualified to observe in their turn, and to describe, the metropolis of the East. The ambassador of the great Otho, a bishop of Cremona, has painted the state of Constantinople about the middle of the tenth century: his style is glowing, his narrative lively, his observation keen; and even the prejudices and passions of Liutprand are stamped with an original character of freedom and genius. From this scanty fund of foreign and domestic materials I shall investigate the form and substance of the Byzantine empire; the provinces and wealth, the civil government and military force, the character and literature, of the Greeks in a period of six hundred years, from the reign of Heraclius to the successful invasion of the Franks or Latins.

After the final division between the sons of Theodosius, the swarms of barbarians from Scythia and Germany overspread the provinces and extinguished the empire of ancient Rome. The weakness of Constantinople was concealed by extent of dominion; her limits were inviolate, or at least entire; and the kingdom of Justinian was enlarged by the splendid acquisition of Africa and Italy. But the possession of these new conquests was transient and precarious, and almost a moiety of the Eastern empire was torn away by the arms of the Saracens. Syria and Egypt were oppressed by the Arabian caliphs, and, after the reduction of Africa, their lieutenants invaded and subdued the Roman province which had been changed into the Gothic monarchy of Spain. The islands of the Mediterranean were not inaccessible to their naval powers; and it was from their extreme stations, the harbours of Crete and the fortresses of Cilicia, that the faithful or rebel emirs insulted the majesty of the throne and capital. The remaining provinces, under the obedience of the emperors, were cast into a new mould; and the jurisdiction of the presidents, the consulars, and the counts was superseded by the institution of the *themes,* or military governments, which prevailed under the successors of Heraclius, and are described by the pen of the royal author. Of the twenty-nine themes, twelve in Europe and seventeen in Asia, the origin is obscure, the etymology doubtful or capricious, the limits were arbitrary and fluctuating; but some particular names that sound the most strangely to our ear were derived from the character and attributes of the troops that were maintained at the expense and for the guard of the respective divisions. The vanity of the Greek princes most eagerly grasped the shadow of conquest and the memory of lost dominion. A new Mesopotamia was created on the western side of the Euphrates; the appellation and prætor of Sicily were transferred to a narrow slip of Calabria; and a fragment of the duchy of Beneventum was promoted to the style and title of the theme of Lombardy. In the decline of the Arabian empire the successors of Constantine might indulge their pride in more solid advantages. The victories of Nicephorus, John Zimisces, and Basil the Second, revived the fame, and enlarged the boundaries, of the Roman name; the province of Cilicia, the metropolis of Antioch, the islands of Crete and Cyprus were restored to the allegiance of Christ and Cæsar; one-third of Italy was annexed to the throne of Constantinople, the kingdom of Bulgaria was destroyed, and the last sovereigns of the Macedonian dynasty extended their sway from the sources of the Tigris to the neighbourhood of Rome. In the eleventh century the prospect was again clouded by new enemies and new misfortunes; the relics of Italy were swept away by the Norman adventurers, and almost all the Asiatic branches were dissevered from the Roman trunk by the Turkish conquerors. After these losses the emperors of the Comnenian family continued to reign from the Danube to

Peloponnesus, and from Belgrade to Nice, Trebizond, and the winding stream of the Meander. The spacious provinces of Thrace, Macedonia, and Greece were obedient to their sceptre; the possession of Cyprus, Rhodes, and Crete was accompanied by the fifty islands of the Ægean or Holy Sea, and the remnant of their empire transcends the measure of the largest of the European kingdoms.

The same princes might assert, with dignity and truth, that of all the monarchs of Christendom they possessed the greatest city, the most ample revenue, the most flourishing and populous state. With the decline and fall of the empire the cities of the West had decayed and fallen; nor could the ruins of Rome, or the mud walls, wooden hovels, and narrow precincts of Paris and London, prepare the Latin stranger to contemplate the situation and extent of Constantinople, her stately palaces and churches, and the arts and luxury of an innumerable people. Her treasures might attract, but her virgin strength had repelled, and still promised to repel, the audacious invasion of the Persian and Bulgarian, the Arab and the Russian. The provinces were less fortunate and impregnable, and few districts, few cities, could be discovered which had not been violated by some fierce barbarian, impatient to despoil, because he was hopeless to possess. From the age of Justinian the Eastern empire was sinking below its former level; the powers of destruction were more active than those of improvement; and the calamities of war were embittered by the more permanent evils of civil and ecclesiastical tyranny. The captive who had escaped from the barbarians was often stripped and imprisoned by the ministers of his sovereign; the Greek superstition relaxed the mind by prayer, and emaciated the body by fasting; and the multitude of convents and festivals diverted many hands and many days from the temporal service of mankind. Yet the subjects of the Byzantine empire were still the most dexterous and diligent of nations; their country was blessed by nature with every advantage of soil, climate, and situation; and, in the support and restoration of the arts, their patient and peaceful temper was more useful than the warlike spirit and feudal anarchy of Europe. The provinces that still adhered to the empire were repeopled and enriched by the misfortunes of those which were irrecoverably lost. From the yoke of the caliphs, the Catholics of Syria, Egypt, and Africa retired to the allegiance of their prince, to the society of their brethren; the movable wealth, which eludes the search of oppression, accompanied and alleviated their exile, and Constantinople received into her bosom the fugitive trade of Alexandria and Tyre. The chiefs of Armenia and Scythia, who fled from hostile or religious persecution, were hospitably entertained; their followers were encouraged to build new cities and to cultivate waste lands; and many spots, both in Europe and Asia, preserved the name, the manners, or at least the memory, of these national colonies. Even the tribes of barbarians who had seated themselves in arms on the territory of the empire were gradually reclaimed to the laws of the church and state, and, as long as they were separated from the Greeks their posterity supplied a race of faithful and obedient soldiers. Did we possess sufficient materials to survey the twenty-nine themes of the Byzantine monarchy, our curiosity might be satisfied with a chosen example: it is fortunate enough that the clearest light should be thrown on the most interesting province, and the name of PELOPONNESUS will awaken the attention of the classic reader.

As early as the eighth century, in the troubled reign of the Iconoclasts, Greece, and even Peloponnesus, were overrun by some Sclavonian bands who outstripped the royal standard of Bulgaria. The strangers of old, Cadmus, and Danaus, and Pelops, had planted in that fruitful soil the seeds of policy and learning; but the savages of the north eradicated what yet remained of their sickly and withered roots. In this irruption the country and the inhabitants were transformed; the Grecian blood was contaminated; and the proudest nobles of Peloponnesus were branded with the names of foreigners and *slaves.* By the diligence of succeeding princes, the land was in some measure purified from the barbarians; and the humble remnant was bound by an oath of obedience, tribute, and military service, which they often renewed and often violated. The siege of Patras was formed by a singular concurrence of the Sclavonians of Peloponnesus and the Saracens of Africa. In their last distress a pious fiction of the approach of the prætor of Corinth revived the courage of the citizens. Their sally was bold and successful; the strangers embarked, the rebels submitted, and the glory of the day was ascribed to a phantom or a stranger, who fought in the foremost ranks under the character of St. Andrew the Apostle. The shrine which contained his relics was decorated with the trophies of victory, and the captive race was for ever devoted to the service and vassalage of the metropolitan church of Patras. By the revolt of two Sclavonian tribes in the neighbourhood of Helos and

Lacedæmon, the peace of the peninsula was often disturbed. They sometimes insulted the weakness, and sometimes resisted the oppression, of the Byzantine government, till at length the approach of their hostile brethren extorted a golden bull to define the rights and obligations of the Ezzerites and Milengi, whose annual tribute was defined at twelve hundred pieces of gold. From these strangers the Imperial geographer has accurately distinguished a domestic and perhaps original race, who, in some degree, might derive their blood from the much-injured Helots. The liberality of the Romans, and especially of Augustus, had enfranchised the maritime cities from the dominion of Sparta; and the continuance of the same benefit ennobled them with the title of *Eleuthero,* or Free-Laconians. In the time of Constantine Porphyrogenitus they had acquired the name of *Mainotes,* under which they dishonour the claim of liberty by the inhuman pillage of all that is shipwrecked on their rocky shores. Their territory, barren of corn but fruitful of olives, extended to the Cape of Malea: they accepted a chief or prince from the Byzantine prætor; and a light tribute of four hundred pieces of gold was the badge of their immunity rather than of their dependence. The freemen of Laconia assumed the character of Romans, and long adhered to the religion of the Greeks. By the zeal of the emperor Basil, they were baptised in the faith of Christ: but the altars of Venus and Neptune had been crowned by these rustic votaries five hundred years after they were proscribed in the Roman world. In the theme of Peloponnesus forty cities were still numbered, and the declining state of Sparta, Argos, and Corinth may be suspended in the tenth century, at an equal distance, perhaps, between their antique splendour and their present desolation. The duty of military service, either in person or by substitute, was imposed on the lands or benefices of the province; a sum of five pieces of gold was assessed on each of the substantial tenants; and the same capitation was shared among several heads of inferior value. On the proclamation of an Italian war, the Peloponnesians excused themselves by a voluntary oblation of one hundred pounds of gold (four thousand pounds sterling), and a thousand horses with their arms and trappings. The churches and monasteries furnished their contingent; a sacrilegious profit was extorted from the sale of ecclesiastical honours; and the indigent bishop of Leucadia was made responsible for a pension of one hundred pieces of gold.

But the wealth of the province, and the trust of the revenue, were founded on the fair and plentiful produce of trade and manufactures; and some symptoms of liberal policy may be traced in a law which exempts from all personal taxes the mariners of Peloponnesus, and the workmen in parchment and purple. This denomination may be fairly applied or extended to the manufactures of linen, woollen, and more especially of silk: the two former of which had flourished in Greece since the days of Homer; and the last was introduced perhaps as early as the reign of Justinian. These arts, which were exercised at Corinth, Thebes, and Argos, afforded food and occupation to a numerous people: the men, women, and children were distributed according to their age and strength; and if many of these were domestic slaves, their masters, who directed the work and enjoyed the profit, were of a free and honourable condition. The gifts which a rich and generous matron of Peloponnesus presented to the emperor Basil, her adopted son, were doubtless fabricated in the Grecian looms. Danielis bestowed a carpet of fine wool, of a pattern which imitated the spots of a peacock's tail, of a magnitude to overspread the floor of a new church, erected in the triple name of Christ, of Michael the archangel, and of the prophet Elijah. She gave six hundred pieces of silk and linen, of various use and denomination: the silk was painted with the Tyrian dye, and adorned by the labours of the needle; and the linen was so exquisitely fine, that an entire piece might be rolled in the hollow of a cane. In his description of the Greek manufactures, an historian of Sicily discriminates their price, according to the weight and quality of the silk, the closeness of the texture, the beauty of the colours, and the taste and materials of the embroidery. A single, or even a double or treble thread was thought sufficient for ordinary sale; but the union of six threads composed a piece of stronger and more costly workmanship. Among the colours, he celebrates, with affectation of eloquence, the fiery blaze of the scarlet, and the softer lustre of the green. The embroidery was raised either in silk or gold: the more simple ornament of stripes or circles was surpassed by the nicer imitation of flowers: the vestments that were fabricated for the palace or the altar often glittered with precious stones; and the figures were delineated in strings of Oriental pearls. Till the twelfth century, Greece alone, of all the countries of Christendom, was possessed of the insect who is taught by nature, and of the workmen who are instructed by art, to prepare this elegant luxury. But the secret had been stolen by the dexterity and diligence of the Arabs: the caliphs of the East and West scorned to borrow from the unbelievers their furniture and apparel; and two cities of Spain, Almeria and Lisbon, were famous for the manufacture, the use, and perhaps the exportation of silk. It was first introduced into Sicily by the Normans; and this emigration of trade distinguishes the victory of Roger from the uniform and fruitless hostilities of every age. After the sack of Corinth, Athens, and Thebes, his lieutenant embarked with a captive train of weavers and artificers of both sexes, a trophy glorious to their master and disgraceful to the Greek emperor. The king of Sicily was not insensible of the value of the present; and, in the restitution of the prisoners, he excepted only the male and female manufacturers of Thebes and Corinth, who labour, says the Byzantine historian, under a barbarous lord, like the old Eretrians in the service of Darius. A stately edifice, in the palace of Palermo, was erected for the use of this industrious colony; and the art was propagated by their children and disciples to satisfy the increasing demand of the western world. The decay of the looms of Sicily may be ascribed to the troubles of the island and the competition of the Italian cities. In the year thirteen hundred and fourteen, Lucca alone, among her sister republics, enjoyed the lucrative monopoly. A domestic revolution dispersed the manufacturers to Florence, Bologna, Venice, Milan, and even the countries beyond the Alps; and thirteen years after this event, the statutes of Modena enjoin the planting of mulberry-trees and regulate the duties on raw silk. The northern climates are less propitious to the education of the silkworm; but the industry of France and England is supplied and enriched by the productions of Italy and China.

. . . In every monarchy the substantial powers of government must be divided and exercised by the ministers of the palace and treasury, the fleet and army. The titles alone can differ; and in the revolution of ages, the counts and præfects, the prætor and quæstor, insensibly descended, while their servants rose above their heads to the first honours of the state. 1. In a monarchy, which refers every object to the person of the prince, the care and ceremonies of the palace form the most respectable department. The *Curopalata,* so illustrious in the age of Justinian, was supplanted by the *Protovestiare,* whose primitive functions were limited to the custody of the wardrobe. From thence his jurisdiction was extended over the numerous menials of pomp and luxury; and he presided with his silver wand at the public and private audience. 2. In the ancient system of Constantine, the name of *Logothete,* or accountant, was applied to the receivers of the finances: the principal officers were distinguished as the Logothetes of the domain, of the posts, the army, the private and public treasure; and the *great Logothete,* the supreme guardian of the laws and revenues, is compared with the chancellor of the Latin monarchies. His discerning eye pervaded the civil administration; and he was assisted, in due subordination, by the eparch or præfect of the city, the first secretary, and the keepers of the privy seal, the archives, and the red and purple ink which was reserved for the sacred signature of the emperor alone. The introductor and interpreter of foreign ambassadors were the great *Chiauss* and the *Dragoman,* two names of Turkish origin, and which are still familiar to the Sublime Porte. 3. From the humble style and service of guards, the *Domestics* insensibly rose to the station of generals; the military themes of the East and West, the legions of Europe and Asia, were often divided, till the *great Domestic* was finally invested with the universal and absolute command of the land forces. The *Protostrator,* in his original functions, was the assistant of the emperor when he mounted on horseback: he gradually became the lieutenant of the great Domestic in the field; and his jurisdiction extended over the stables, the cavalry, and the royal train of hunting and hawking. The *Stratopedarch* was the great judge of the camp: the *Protospathaire* commanded the guards; the *Constable,* the *great Æteriarch,* and the *Acolyth,* were the separate chiefs of the Franks, the barbarians, and the Varangi, or English, the mercenary strangers, who, in the decay of the national spirit, formed the nerve of the Byzantine armies. 4. The naval powers were under the command of the *great Duke;* in his absence they obeyed the *great Drungaire* of the fleet; and, in *his* place, the *Emir,* or *Admiral,* a name of Saracen extraction, but which has been naturalised in all the modern languages of Europe. Of these officers, and of many more whom it would be useless to enumerate, the civil and military hierarchy was framed. Their honours and emoluments, their dress and titles, their mutual salutations and respective pre-eminence, were balanced with more exquisite labour than would have fixed the constitution of a free people; and the code was almost perfect when this baseless fabric, the monument of pride and servitude, was for ever buried in the ruins of the empire.

In the Byzantine palace the emperor was the first slave of the ceremonies which he imposed, of the rigid forms which regulated each word and gesture, besieged him in the palace, and violated the leisure of his rural solitude. But the lives and fortunes of millions hung on his arbitrary will; and the firmest minds, superior to the allurements of pomp and luxury, may be seduced by the more active pleasure of commanding their equals. The legislative and executive powers were centred in the person of the monarch, and the last remains of the authority of the senate were finally eradicated by Leo the Philosopher. A lethargy of servitude had benumbed the minds of the Greeks: in the wildest tumults of rebellion they never aspired to the idea of a free constitution; and the private character of the prince was the only source and measure of their public happiness. Superstition riveted their chains; in the church of St. Sophia he was solemnly crowned by the patriarch; at the foot of the altar they pledged their passive and unconditional obedience to his government and family. On his side he engaged to abstain as much as possible from the capital punishments of death and mutilation; his orthodox creed was subscribed with his own hand, and he promised to obey the decrees of the seven synods and the canons of the holy church. But the assurance of mercy was loose and indefinite: he swore, not to his people, but to an invisible judge; and except in the inexpiable guilt of heresy, the ministers of heaven were always prepared to preach the indefeasible right, and to absolve the venial transgressions, of their sovereign. The Greek ecclesiastics were themselves the subjects of the civil magistrate: at the nod of a tyrant the bishops were created, or transferred, or deposed, or punished with an ignominious death; whatever might be their wealth or influence, they could never succeed like the Latin clergy in the establishment of an independent republic; and the patriarch of Constantinople condemned, what he secretly envied, the temporal greatness of his Roman brother. Yet the exercise of boundless despotism is happily checked by the laws of nature and necessity. In proportion to his wisdom and virtue, the master of an empire is confined to the path of his sacred and laborious duty. In proportion to his vice and folly, he drops the sceptre too weighty for his hands; and the motions of the royal image are ruled by the imperceptible thread of some minister or favourite, who undertakes for his private interest to exercise the task of the public oppression. In some fatal moment the most absolute monarch may dread the reason or the caprice of a nation of slaves; and experience has proved that whatever is gained in the extent is lost in the safety and solidity of regal power.

Whatever titles a despot may assume, whatever claims he may assert, it is on the sword that he must ultimately depend to guard him against his foreign and domestic enemies. From the age of Charlemagne to that of the Crusades the world (for I overlook the remote monarchy of China) was occupied and disputed by the three great empires or nations of the Greeks, the Saracens, and the Franks. Their military strength may be ascertained by a comparison of their courage, their arts and riches, and their obedience to a supreme head, who might call into action all the energies of the state. The Greeks, far inferior to their rivals in the first, were superior to the Franks, and at least equal to the Saracens, in the second and third of these warlike qualifications.

The wealth of the Greeks enabled them to purchase the service of the poorer nations, and to maintain a naval power for the protection of their coasts and the annoyance of their enemies. A commerce of mutual benefit exchanged the gold of Constantinople for the blood of the Sclavonians and Turks, the Bulgarians and Russians: their valour contributed to the victories of Nicephorus and Zimisces; and if a hostile people pressed too closely on the frontier, they were recalled to the defence of their country, and the desire of peace, by the well-managed attack of a more distant tribe. The command of the Mediterranean, from the mouth of the Tanais to the Columns of Hercules, was always claimed, and often possessed, by the successors of Constantine. Their capital was filled with naval stores and dexterous artificers: the situation of Greece and Asia, the long coasts, deep gulfs, and numerous islands, accustomed their subjects to the exercise of navigation; and the trade of Venice and Amalfi supplied a nursery of seamen to the Imperial fleet. . . .

The invention of the Greek fire did not, like that of gunpowder, produce a total revolution in the art of war. To these liquid combustibles the city and empire of Constantine owed their deliverance; and they were employed in sieges and sea-fights with terrible effect. But they were either less improved, or less susceptible of improvement: the engines of antiquity, the catapultæ, balistæ, and battering-rams, were still of most frequent and powerful use in the attack and defence of fortifications; nor was the decision of battles reduced to the quick and heavy *fire* of a line of infantry, whom it were fruitless to protect with armour against a similar fire of their enemies. Steel and iron were still the common instruments of destruction and safety; and the helmets, cuirasses, and shields of the tenth century did not, either in form or substance, essentially differ from those which had covered the companions of Alexander or Achilles. But instead of accustoming the modern Greeks, like the legionaries of old, to the constant and easy use of this salutary weight, their armour was laid aside in light chariots, which followed the march, till, on the approach of an enemy, they resumed with haste and reluctance the unusual encumbrance. Their offensive weapons consisted of swords, battle-axes, and spears; but the Macedonian pike was shortened a fourth of its length, and reduced to the more convenient measure of twelve cubits or feet. The sharpness of the Scythian and Arabian arrows had been severely felt; and the emperors lament the decay of archery as a cause of the public misfortunes, and recommend, as an advice and a command, that the military youth, till the age of forty, should assiduously practise the exercise of the bow. The *bands,* or regiments, were usually three hundred strong; and, as a medium between the extremes of four and sixteen, the foot-soldiers of Leo and Constantine were formed eight deep; but the cavalry charged in four ranks, from the reasonable consideration that the weight of the front could not be increased by any pressure of the hindmost horses. If the ranks of the infantry or cavalry were sometimes doubled, this cautious array betrayed a secret distrust of the courage of the troops, whose numbers might swell the appearance of the line, but of whom only a chosen band would dare to encounter the spears and swords of the barbarians. The order of battle must have varied according to the ground, the object, and the adversary; but their ordinary disposition, in two lines and a reserve, presented a succession of hopes and resources most agreeable to the temper as well as the judgment of the Greeks. In case of a repulse, the first line fell back into the intervals of the second; and the reserve, breaking into two divisions, wheeled round the flanks to improve the victory or cover the retreat. Whatever authority could enact was accomplished, at least in theory, by the camps and marches, the exercises and evolutions, the edicts and books, of the Byzantine monarch. Whatever art could produce from the forge, the loom, or the laboratory, was abundantly supplied by the riches of the prince and the industry of his numerous workmen. But neither authority nor art could frame the most important machine, the soldier himself; and if the *ceremonies* of Constantine always suppose the safe and triumphal return of the emperor, his *tactics* seldom soar above the means of escaping a defeat and procrastinating the war. Notwithstanding some transient success, the Greeks were sunk in their own esteem and that of their neighbours. A cold hand and a loquacious tongue was the vulgar description of the nation; the author of the Tactics was besieged in his capital; and the last of the barbarians, who trembled at the name of the Saracens or Franks, could proudly exhibit the medals of gold and silver which they had extorted from the feeble sovereign of Constantinople. What spirit their government and character denied might have been inspired, in some degree, by the influence of religion; but the religion of the Greeks could only teach them to suffer and to yield. The emperor Nicephorus, who restored for a moment the discipline and glory of the Roman name, was desirous of bestowing the honours of martyrdom on the Christians who lost their lives in a holy war against the infidels. But this political law was defeated by the opposition of the patriarch, the bishops, and the principal senators; and they strenuously urged the canons of St. Basil, that all who were polluted by the bloody trade of a soldier should be separated, during three years, from the communion of the faithful.

These scruples of the Greeks have been compared with the tears of the primitive Moslems when they were held back from battle; and this contrast of base superstition and high-spirited enthusiasm unfolds to a philosophic eye the history of the rival nations. The subjects of the last caliphs had undoubtedly degenerated from the zeal and faith of the companions of the prophet. Yet their martial creed represented the Deity as the author of war; the vital though latent spark of fanaticism still glowed in the heart of their religion, and among the Saracens who dwelt on the Christian borders it was frequently rekindled to a lively and active flame. Their regular force was formed of the valiant slaves who had been educated to guard the person and accompany the standard of their lord; but the Musulman people of Syria and Cilicia, of Africa and Spain, was awakened by the trumpet which proclaimed a holy war against the infidels. The rich were ambitious of death or victory in the cause of God; the poor were allured by the hopes of plunder; and the old, the infirm, and the women assumed their share of meritorious service by sending their substitutes, with arms and horses, into the field. These offensive and defensive arms were similar in strength and temper to those of the Romans, whom they far excelled in the management of the horse and the bow; the massy silver of their belts, their bridles, and their swords displayed the magnificence of a prosperous nation; and, except some black archers of the South, the Arabs disdained the naked bravery of their ancestors. Instead of waggons they were attended by a long train of camels, mules, and asses; the multitude of these animals, whom they bedecked with flags and streamers, appeared to swell the pomp and magnitude of their host, and the horses of the enemy were often disordered by the uncouth figure and odious smell of the camels of the East. Invincible by their patience of thirst and heat, their spirits were frozen by a winter's cold, and the consciousness of their propensity to sleep exacted the most rigorous precautions against the surprises of the night. Their order of battle was a long square of two deep and solid lines; the first of archers, the second of cavalry. In their engagements by sea and land they sustained with patient firmness the fury of the attack, and seldom advanced to the charge till they could discern and oppress the lassitude of their foes. But if they were repulsed and broken, they knew not how to rally or renew the combat, and their dismay was heightened by the superstitious prejudice that God had declared himself on the side of their enemies. The decline and fall of the caliphs countenanced this fearful opinion, nor were there wanting, among the Mohammedans and Christians, some obscure prophecies which prognosticated their alternate defeats. The unity of the Arabian empire was dissolved, but the independent fragments were equal to populous and powerful kingdoms, and in their naval and military armaments an emir of Aleppo or Tunis might command no despicable fund of skill, and industry, and treasure. In their transactions of peace and war with the Saracens, the princes of Constantinople too often felt that these barbarians had nothing barbarous in their discipline, and that, if they were destitute of original genius, they had been endowed with a quick spirit of curiosity and imitation. The model was indeed more perfect than the copy; their ships, and engines, and fortifications were of a less skilful construction; and they confess, without shame, that the same God who has given a tongue to the Arabians had more nicely fashioned the hands of the Chinese and the heads of the Greeks.

A name of some German tribes between the Rhine and the Weser had spread its victorious influence over the greatest part of Gaul, Germany, and Italy; and the common appellation of FRANKS was applied by the Greeks and Arabians to the Christians of the Latin church, the nations of the West, who stretched beyond *their* knowledge to the shores of the Atlantic Ocean. The vast body had been inspired and united by the soul of Charlemagne; but the division and degeneracy of his race soon annihilated the Imperial power, which would have rivalled the Cæsars of Byzantium, and revenged the indignities of the Christian name. The enemies no longer feared, nor could the subjects any longer trust, the application of a public revenue, the labours of trade and manufactures in the military service, the mutual aid of provinces and armies, and the naval squadrons which were regularly stationed from the mouth of the Elbe to that of the Tiber. In the beginning of the tenth century the family of Charlemagne had almost disappeared; his monarchy was broken into many hostile and independent states; the regal title was assumed by the most ambitious chiefs; their revolt was imitated in a long subordination of anarchy and discord; and the nobles of every province disobeyed their sovereign, oppressed their vassals, and exercised perpetual hostilities against their equals and neighbours. Their private wars, which overturned the fabric of government, fomented the martial spirit of the nation. In the system of modern Europe the power of the sword is possessed, at least in fact, by five or six mightly potentates; their operations are conducted on a distant frontier by an order of men who devote their lives to the study and practice of the military art: the rest of the country and community enjoys in the midst of war the tranquillity of peace, and is only made sensible of the change by the aggravation or decrease of the public taxes. In the disorders of the tenth and eleventh centuries every peasant was a soldier, and every village a fortification; each wood or valley was a scene of murder and rapine; and the lords of each castle were compelled to assume the character of princes and warriors. To their own courage and policy they boldly trusted for the safety of their family, the protection of their lands, and the revenge of their injuries; and, like the conquerors of a larger size, they were too apt to transgress the privilege of defensive war. The powers of the mind and body were hardened by the presence of danger and necessity of resolution: the same spirit refused to desert a friend and to forgive an enemy; and, instead of sleeping under the guardian care of the magistrate, they proudly disdained the authority of the laws. In the days of feudal anarchy the instruments of agriculture and art were converted into the weapons of bloodshed; the peaceful occupations of civil and ecclesiastical society were abolished or corrupted; and the bishop who exchanged his mitre for a helmet was more forcibly urged by the manners of the times than by the obligation of his tenure.

The love of freedom and of arms was felt with conscious pride by the Franks themselves, and is observed by the Greeks with some degree of amazement and terror. "The Franks," says the emperor Constantine, "are bold and valiant to the verge of temerity; and their dauntless spirit is supported by the contempt of danger and death. In the field, and in close onset, they press to the front and rush headlong against the enemy, without deigning to compute either his numbers or their own. Their ranks are formed by the firm connections of consanguinity and friendship; and their martial deeds are prompted by the desire of saving or revenging their dearest companions. In their eyes a retreat is a shameful flight, and flight is indelible infamy." A nation endowed with such high and intrepid spirit must have been secure of victory if these advantages had not been counterbalanced by many weighty defects. The decay of their naval power left the Greeks and Saracens in possession of the sea for every purpose of annoyance and supply. In the age which preceded the institution of knighthood the Franks were rude and unskilful in the service of cavalry; and in all perilous emergencies their warriors were so conscious of their ignorance, that they chose to dismount from their horses and fight on foot. Unpractised in the use of pikes or of missile weapons, they were encumbered by the length of their swords, the weight of their armour, the magnitude of their shields, and, if I may repeat the satire of the meagre Greeks, by their unwieldy intemperance. Their independent spirit disdained the yoke of subordination, and abandoned the standard of their chief if he attempted to keep the field beyond the term of their stipulation or service. On all sides they were open to the snares of an enemy less brave but more artful than themselves. They might be bribed, for the barbarians were venal; or surprised in the night, for they neglected the precautions of a close encampment or vigilant sentinels. The fatigues of a summer's campaign exhausted their strength and patience, and they sunk in despair if their voracious appetite was disappointed of a plentiful supply of wine and of food.

This general character of the Franks was marked with some national and local shades, which I should ascribe to accident rather than to climate, but which were visible both to natives and to foreigners. An ambassador of the great Otho declared, in the palace of Constantinople, that the Saxons could dispute with swords better than with pens, and that they preferred inevitable death to the dishonour of turning their backs to an enemy. It was the glory of the nobles of France that, in their humble dwellings, war and rapine were the only pleasure, the sole occupation, of their lives. They affected to deride the palaces, the banquets, the polished manners of the Italians, who in the estimate of the Greeks themselves had degenerated from the liberty and valour of the ancient Lombards.

By the well-known edict of Caracalla, his subjects, from Britain to Egypt, were entitled to the name and privileges of Romans, and their national sovereign might fix his occasional or permanent residence in any province of their common country. In the division of the East and West an ideal unity was scrupulously preserved, and in their titles, laws, and statutes the successors of Arcadius and Honorius announced themselves as the inseparable colleagues of the same office, as the joint sovereigns of the Roman world and city, which were bounded by the same limits. After the fall of the Western monarchy the majesty of the purple resided solely in the princes of Constantinople, and of these Justinian was the first who, after a divorce of sixty years, regained the dominion of ancient Rome, and asserted, by the right of conquest, the august title of Emperor of the Romans. A motive of vanity or discontent solicited one of his successors, Constans the Second, to abandon the Thracian Bosphorus and to restore the pristine honours of the Tiber: an extravagant project (exclaims the malicious Byzantine), as if he had despoiled a beautiful and blooming virgin, to enrich, or rather to expose, the deformity of a wrinkled and decrepit matron. But the sword of the Lombards opposed his settlement in Italy; he entered Rome not as a conqueror, but as a fugitive, and, after a visit of twelve days, he pillaged and for ever deserted the ancient capital of the world. The final revolt and separation of Italy was accomplished about two centuries after the conquests of Justinian, and from his reign we may date the gradual oblivion of the Latin tongue. That legislator had composed his Institutes, his Code, and his Pandects in a language which he celebrates as the proper and public style of the Roman government, the consecrated idiom of the palace and senate of Constantinople, of the camps and tribunals of the East. But this foreign dialect was unknown to the people and soldiers of the Asiatic provinces, it was imperfectly understood by the greater part of the interpreters of the laws and the ministers of the state. After a short conflict, nature and habit prevailed over the obsolete institutions of human power: for the general benefit of his subjects Justinian promulgated his novels in the two languages, the several parts of his voluminous jurisprudence were successively translated, the original was forgotten, the version was studied, and the Greek, whose intrinsic merit deserved indeed the preference, obtained a legal as well as popular establishment in the Byzantine monarchy. The birth and residence of succeeding princes estranged them from the Roman idiom; Tiberius by the Arabs, and Maurice by the Italians, are distinguished as the first of the Greek Cæsars, as the founders of a new dynasty and empire; the silent revolution was accomplished before the death of Heraclius, and the ruins of the Latin speech were darkly preserved in the terms of jurisprudence and the acclamations of the palace. After the restoration of the Western empire by Charlemagne and the Othos, the names of Franks and Latins acquired an equal signification and extent, and these haughty barbarians asserted, with some justice, their superior claim to the language and dominion of Rome. They insulted the aliens of the East who had renounced the dress and idiom of Romans, and their reasonable practice will justify the frequent appellation of Greeks. But this contemptuous appellation was indignantly rejected by the prince and people to whom it is applied. Whatsoever changes had been introduced by the lapse of ages, they alleged a lineal and unbroken succession from Augustus and Constantine; and, in the lowest period of degeneracy and decay, the name of ROMANS adhered to the last fragments of the empire of Constantinople.

While the government of the East was transacted in Latin, the Greek was the language of literature and philosophy, nor could the masters of this rich and perfect idiom be tempted to envy the borrowed learning and imitative taste of their Roman disciples. After the fall of Paganism, the loss of Syria and Egypt, and the extinction of the schools of Alexandria and Athens, the studies of the Greeks insensibly retired to some regular monasteries, and, above all, to the royal college of Constantinople, which was burnt in the reign of Leo the Isaurian. In the pompous style of the age, the president of that foundation was named the Sun of Science; his twelve associates, the professors in the different arts and faculties, were the twelve signs of the zodiac; a library of thirty-six thousand five hundred volumes was open to their inquiries; and they could show an ancient manuscript of Homer, on a roll of parchment one hundred and twenty feet in length, the intestines, as it was fabled, of a prodigious serpent. But the seventh and eighth centuries were a period of discord and darkness; the library was burnt, the college was abolished, the Iconoclasts are represented as the foes of antiquity, and a savage ignorance and contempt of letters has disgraced the princes of the Heraclean and Isaurian dynasties.

In the ninth century we trace the first dawnings of the restoration of science. After the fanaticism of the Arabs had subsided, the caliphs aspired to conquer the arts, rather than the provinces, of the empire: their liberal curiosity rekindled the emulation of the Greeks, brushed away the dust from their ancient libraries, and taught them to know and reward the philosophers, whose labours had been hitherto repaid by the pleasure of study and the pursuit of truth. The Cæsar Bardas, the uncle of Michael the Third, was the generous protector of letters, a title which alone has preserved his memory and excused his ambition. A particle of the treasures of his nephew was sometimes diverted from the indulgence of vice and folly; a school was opened in the palace of Magnaura, and the presence of Bardas excited the emulation of the masters and students. At their head was the philosopher Leo, archbishop of Thessalonica; his profound skill in astronomy and the mathematics was admired by the strangers of the East, and this occult science was magnified by vulgar credulity, which modestly supposes that all knowledge superior to its own must be the effect of inspiration or magic. At the pressing entreaty of the Cæsar, his friend, the celebrated Photius, renounced the freedom of a secular and studious life, ascended the patriarchal throne, and was alternately excommunicated and absolved by the synods of the East and West. By the confession even of priestly hatred, no art or science, except poetry, was foreign to this universal scholar, who was deep in thought, indefatigable in reading, and eloquent in diction. Whilst he exercised the office of protospathaire, or captain of the guards, Photius was sent ambassador to the caliph of Bagdad. The tedious hours of exile, perhaps of confinement, were beguiled by the hasty composition of his *Library,* a living monument of erudition and criticism. Two hundred and fourscore writers, historians, orators, philosophers, theologians, are reviewed without any regular method; he abridges their narrative or doctrine, apreciates their style and character, and judges even the fathers of the church with a discreet freedom which often breaks through the superstition of the times. The emperor Basil, who lamented the defects of his own education, intrusted to the care of Photius his son and successor Leo the Philosopher, and the reign of that prince and of his son Constantine Porphyrogenitus forms one of the most prosperous eras of the Byzantine literature. By their munificence the treasures of antiquity were deposited in the Imperial library; by their pens, or those of their associates, they were imparted in such extracts and abridgments as might amuse the curiosity, without oppressing the indolence, of the public. Besides the *Basilics,* or code of laws, the arts of husbandry and war, of feeding or destroying the human species, were propagated with equal diligence; and the history of Greece and Rome was digested into fifty-three heads or titles, of which two only (of embassies, and of virtues and vices) have escaped the injuries of time. In every station the reader might contemplate the image of the past world, apply the lesson or warning of each page, and learn to admire, perhaps to imitate, the examples of a brighter period. I shall not expatiate on the works of the Byzantine Greeks, who, by the assiduous study of the ancients, have deserved, in some measure, the remembrance and gratitude of the moderns. The scholars of the present age may still enjoy the benefit of the philosophical commonplace-book of Stobæus, the grammatical and historic lexicon of Suidas, the Chiliads of Tzetzes, which comprise six hundred narratives in twelve thousand verses, and the commentaries on Homer of Eustathius archbishop of Thessalonica, who, from his horn of plenty, has poured the names and authorities of four hundred writers. From these originals, and from the numerous tribe of scholiasts and critics, some estimate may be formed of the literary wealth of the twelfth century. Constantinople was enlightened by the genius of Homer and Demosthenes, of Aristotle and Plato; and in the enjoyment or neglect of our present riches we must envy the generation that could still peruse the history of Theopompus, the orations of Hyperides, the comedies of Menander, and the odes of Alcæus and Sappho. The frequent labour of illustration attests not only the existence but the popularity of the Grecian classics; the general knowledge of the age may be deduced from the example of two learned females, the empress Eudocia and the princess Anna Comnena, who cultivated, in the purple, the arts of rhetoric and philosophy. The vulgar dialect of the city was gross and barbarous: a more correct and elaborate style distinguished the discourse, or at least the compositions, of the church and palace, which sometimes affected to copy the purity of the Attic models.

In our modern education, the painful though necessary attainment of two languages which are no longer living may consume the time and damp the ardour of the youthful student. The poets and orators were long imprisoned in the barbarous dialects of our Western ancestors, devoid of harmony or grace; and their genius, without precept or example, was abandoned to the rude and native powers of their judgment and fancy. But the Greeks of Constantinople, after purging away the impurities of their vulgar speech, acquired the free use of their ancient language, the most happy composition of human art, and a familiar knowledge of the sublime masters who had pleased or instructed the first of nations. But these advantages only tend to aggravate the reproach and shame of a degenerate people. They held in their lifeless hands the riches of their fathers, without inheriting the spirit which had created and improved that sacred patrimony: they read, they praised, they compiled, but their languid souls seemed alike incapable of thought and action. In the revolution of ten centuries, not a single discovery was made to exalt the dignity or promote the happiness of mankind. Not a single idea has been added to the speculative systems of antiquity, and a succession of patient disciples became in their turn the dogmatic teachers of the next servile generation. Not a single composition of history, philosophy, or literature, has been saved from oblivion by the intrinsic beauties of style or sentiment, of original fancy, or even of successful imitation. In prose, the least offensive of the Byzantine writers are absolved from censure by their naked and unpresuming simplicity: but the orators, most eloquent in their own conceit, are the farthest removed from the models whom they affect to emulate. In every page our taste and reason are wounded by the choice of gigantic and obsolete words, a stiff and intricate phraseology, the discord of images, the childish play of false or unseasonable ornament, and the painful attempt to elevate themselves, to astonish the reader, and to involve a trivial meaning in the smoke of obscurity and exaggeration. Their prose is soaring to the vicious affectation of poetry: their poetry is sinking below the flatness and insipidity of prose. The tragic, epic, and lyric muses were silent and inglorious: the bards of Constantinople seldom rose above a riddle or epigram, a panegyric or tale; they forgot even the rules of prosody; and with the melody of Homer yet sounding in their ears, they confound all measure of feet and syllables in the impotent strains which have received the name of *political* or city verses. The minds of the Greeks were bound in the fetters of a base and imperious superstition, which extends her dominion round the circle of profane science. Their understandings were bewildered in metaphysical controversy: in the belief of visions and miracles they had lost all principles of moral evidence, and their taste was vitiated by the homilies of the monks, an absurd medley of declamation and Scripture. Even these contemptible studies were no longer dignified by the abuse of superior talents: the leaders of the Greek church were humbly content to admire and copy the oracles of antiquity, nor did the schools or pulpit produce any rivals of the fame of Athanasius and Chrysostom.

In all the pursuits of active and speculative life, the emulation of states and individuals is the most powerful spring of the efforts and improvements of mankind. The cities of ancient Greece were cast in the happy mixture of union and independence, which is repeated on a larger scale, but in a looser form, by the nations of modern Europe: the union of language, religion, and manners, which renders them the spectators and judges of each other's merit: the independence of government and interest, which asserts their separate freedom, and excites them to strive for pre-eminence in the career of glory. The situation of the Romans was less favourable; yet in the early ages of the republic, which fixed the national character, a similar emulation was kindled among the states of Latium and Italy; and in the arts and sciences they aspired to equal or surpass their Grecian masters. The empire of the Cæsars undoubtedly checked the activity and progress of the human mind: its magnitude might indeed allow some scope for domestic competition; but when it was gradually reduced, at first to the East, and at last to Greece and Constantinople, the Byzantine subjects were degraded to an abject and languid temper, the natural effect of their solitary and insulated state. From the North they were oppressed by nameless tribes of barbarians, to whom they scarcely imparted the appellation of men. The language and religion of the more polished Arabs were an insurmountable bar to all social intercourse. The conquerors of Europe were their brethren in the Christian faith; but the speech of the Franks or Latins was unknown, their manners were rude, and they were rarely connected, in peace or war, with the successors of Heraclius. Alone in the universe, the self-satisfied pride of the Greeks was not disturbed by the comparison of foreign merit; and it is no wonder if they fainted in the race, since they had neither competitors to urge their speed, nor judges to crown their victory. The nations of Europe and Asia were mingled by the expeditions to the Holy Land; and it is under the Comnenian dynasty that a faint emulation of knowledge and military virtue was rekindled in the Byzantine empire.

PART 9

The Crusades *(Chapter LVIII)*

With the rise of the Seljuk Turks, the Byzantine Emperor turned to Western Europe for help, and to his great surprise he discovered that the "barbarians" of Italy, Germany, France, and England were more than willing to come to his aid. A new spirit of religious chivalry and papal dominion had arisen, Gibbon noted, and during the two centuries following 1095, thousands of Europeans, emperors and kings included, left Europe to undertake a great Crusade to recover the Holy Places of Christianity from the Mohammedans. Without this European intervention the Byzantine Empire would have been doomed.

CHAPTER LVIII

About twenty years after the conquest of Jerusalem by the Turks, the holy sepulchre was visited by a hermit of the name of Peter, a native of Amiens, in the province of Picardy* in France. His resentment and sympathy were excited by his own injuries and the oppression of the Christian name; he mingled his tears with those of the patriarch, and earnestly inquired if no hopes of relief could be entertained from the Greek emperors of the East. The patriarch exposed the vices and weakness of the successors of Constantine. "I will rouse," exclaimed the hermit, "the martial nations of Europe in your cause;" and Europe

*Whimsical enough is the origin of the name of *Picards,* and from thence of *Picardie,* which does not date earlier than A.D. 1200. It was an academical joke, an epithet first applied to the quarrelsome humour of those students, in the University of Paris, who came from the frontier of France and Flanders . . .

was obedient to the call of the hermit. The astonished patriarch dismissed him with epistles of credit and complaint; and no sooner did he land at Bari than Peter hastened to kiss the feet of the Roman pontiff. His stature was small, his appearance contemptible; but his eye was keen and lively, and he possessed that vehemence of speech which seldom fails to impart the persuasion of the soul. He was born of a gentleman's family (for we must now adopt a modern idiom), and his military service was under the neighbouring counts of Boulogne, the heroes of the first crusade. But he soon relinquished the sword and the world; and if it be true that his wife, however noble, was aged and ugly, he might withdraw with the less reluctance from her bed to a convent, and at length to a hermitage. In this austere solitude his body was emaciated, his fancy was inflamed; whatever he wished, he believed; whatever he believed, he *saw* in dreams and revelations. From Jerusalem the pilgrim returned an accomplished fanatic; but as he excelled in the popular madness of the times, Pope Urban the Second received him as a prophet, applauded his glorious design, promised to support it in a general council, and encouraged him to proclaim the deliverance of the Holy Land. Invigorated by the approbation of the pontiff, his zealous missionary traversed, with speed and success, the provinces of Italy and France. His diet was abstemious, his prayers long and fervent, and the alms which he received with one hand, he distributed with the other: his head was bare, his feet naked, his meagre body was wrapped in a coarse garment; he bore and displayed a weighty crucifix; and the ass on which he rode was sanctified, in the public eye, by the service of the man of God. He preached to innumerable crowds in the churches, the streets, and the highways: the hermit entered with equal confidence the palace and the cottage; and the people, for all was people, was impetuously moved by his call to repentance and arms. When he painted the sufferings of the natives and pilgrims of Palestine, every heart was melted to compassion; every breast glowed with indignation when he challenged the warriors of the age to defend their brethren, and rescue their Saviour: his ignorance of art and language was compensated by sighs, and tears, and ejaculations; and Peter supplied the deficiency of reason by loud and frequent appeals to Christ and his mother, to the saints and angels of paradise, with whom he had personally conversed. The most perfect orator of Athens might have envied the success of his eloquence: the rustic enthusiast inspired the passions which he felt, and Christendom expected with impatience the counsels and decrees of the supreme pontiff.

The magnanimous spirit of Gregory the Seventh had already embraced the design of arming Europe against Asia; the ardour of his zeal and ambition still breathes in his epistles; from either side of the Alps fifty thousand Catholics had enlisted under the banner of St. Peter; and his successor reveals *his* intention of marching at their head against the impious sectaries of Mohammed. But the glory or reproach of executing, though not in person, this holy enterprise, was reserved for Urban the Second, the most faithful of his disciples. He undertook the conquest of the East, whilst the larger portion of Rome was possessed and fortified by his rival Guibert of Ravenna, who contended with Urban for the name and honours of the pontificate. He attempted to unite the powers of the West, at a time when the princes were separated from the church, and the people from their princes, by the excommunication which himself and his predecessors had thundered against the emperor and the king of France. Philip the First of France supported with patience the censures which he had provoked by his scandalous life and adulterous marriage. Henry the Fourth of Germany asserted the right of investitures, the prerogative of confirming his bishops by the delivery of the ring and crosier. But the emperor's party was crushed in Italy by the arms of the Normans and the countess Mathilda; and the long quarrel had been recently envenomed by the revolt of his son Conrad and the shame of his wife,* who, in the synods of Constance and Placentia, confessed the manifold prostitutions to which she had been exposed by a husband regardless of her honour and his own. So popular was the cause of Urban, so weighty was his influence, that the council which he summoned at Placentia† was composed of two hundred bishops of Italy, France, Burgundy, Swabia, and Bavaria. Four thousand of the clergy and thirty thousand of the laity attended this important meeting; and, as the most spacious cathedral would have been inadequate to the multitude, the session of seven days was held in a plain adjacent to the city. The ambassadors of the Greek emperor, Alexius Comnenus, were introduced to plead

*She is known by the different names of Praxes, Eupræcia, Eufrasia, and Adelais; and was the daughter of a Russian prince, and the widow of a margrave of Brandenburg. . . .

†See the narrative and acts of the synod of Placentia, Concil. tom. xii. p. 821, etc.

the distress of their sovereign, and the danger of Constantinople, which was divided only by a narrow sea from the victorious Turks, the common enemies of the Christian name. In their suppliant address they flattered the pride of the Latin princes; and, appealing at once to their policy and religion, exhorted them to repel the barbarians on the confines of Asia, rather than to expect them in the heart of Europe. At the sad tale of the misery and perils of their Eastern brethren the assembly burst into tears: the most eager champions declared their readiness to march; and the Greek ambassadors were dismissed with the assurance of a speedy and powerful succour. The relief of Constantinople was included in the larger and most distant project of the deliverance of Jerusalem; but the prudent Urban adjourned the final decision to a second synod, which he proposed to celebrate in some city of France in the autumn of the same year. The short delay would propagate the flame of enthusiasm; and his firmest hope was in a nation of soldiers still proud of the pre-eminence of their name, and ambitious to emulate their hero Charlemagne, who, in the popular romance of Turpin,* had achieved the conquest of the Holy Land. A latent motive of affection or vanity might influence the choice of Urban: he was himself a native of France, a monk of Clugny, and the first of his countrymen who ascended the throne of St. Peter. The pope had illustrated his family and province; nor is there perhaps a more exquisite gratification than to revisit, in a conspicuous dignity, the humble and laborious scenes of our youth.

It may occasion some surprise that the Roman pontiff should erect, in the heart of France, the tribunal from whence he hurled his anathemas against the king; but our surprise will vanish so soon as we form a just estimate of a king of France of the eleventh century. Philip the First was the great-grandson of Hugh Capet, the founder of the present race, who, in the decline of Charlemagne's posterity, added the regal title to his patrimonial estates of Paris and Orleans. In this narrow compass he was possessed of wealth and jurisdiction; but in the rest of France Hugh and his first descendants were no more than the feudal lords of about sixty dukes and counts, of independent and hereditary

*John Tilpinus, or Turpinus, was Archbishop of Rheims, A.D. 773. After the year 1000 this romance was composed in his name, by a monk of the borders of France and Spain; and such was the idea of ecclesiastical merit, that he describes himself as a fighting and drinking priest! Yet the book of lies was pronounced authentic by Pope Calixtus II. (A.D. 1122), and is respectfully quoted by the abbot Suger, in the great Chronicles of St. Denys . . .

power,* who disdained the control of laws and legal assemblies, and whose disregard of their sovereign was revenged by the disobedience of their inferior vassals. At Clermont, in the territories of the count of Auvergne,† the pope might brave with impunity the resentment of Philip; and the council which he convened in that city was not less numerous or respectable than the synod of Placentia. Besides his court and council of Roman cardinals, he was supported by thirteen archbishops and two hundred and twenty-five bishops; the number of mitred prelates was computed at four hundred; and the fathers of the church were blessed by the saints and enlightened by the doctors of the age. From the adjacent kingdoms a martial train of lords and knights of power and renown attended the council, in high expectation of its resolves; and such was the ardour of zeal and curiosity, that the city was filled, and many thousands, in the month of November, erected their tents or huts in the open field. A session of eight days produced some useful or edifying canons for the reformation of manners; a severe censure was pronounced against the licence of private war; the Truce of God** was confirmed, a suspension of hostilities during four days of the week; women and priests were placed under the safeguard of the church; and a protection of three years was extended to husbandmen and merchants, the defenceless victims of military rapine. But a law, however venerable be the sanction, cannot suddenly transform the temper of the times; and the benevolent efforts of Urban deserve the less praise, since he laboured to appease some domestic quarrels that he might spread the flames of war from the Atlantic to the Euphrates. From the synod of Placentia the rumour of his great design had gone forth among the nations: the clergy on their return had preached in every diocese the merit and glory of the deliverance of the Holy Land; and when the pope ascended a lofty scaffold in the market-place of Clermont, his eloquence was addressed to a well-prepared and impatient audience. His topics were obvious, his exhortation was vehement, his success inevitable. The orator was

*In the provinces to the south of the Loire, the first *Capetians* were scarcely allowed a feudal supremacy. On all sides, Normandy, Bretagne, Aquitain, Burgundy, Lorraine, and Flanders, contracted the name and limits of the *proper* France. . . .

†These counts, a younger branch of the dukes of Aquitain, were at length despoiled of the greatest part of their country by Philip Augustus. The bishops of Clermont gradually became princes of the city. . . .

**The Truce of God (Treva, or Treuga Dei) was first invented in Aquitain, A.D. 1032; blamed by some bishops as an occasion of perjury, and rejected by the Normans as contrary to their privileges . . .

interrupted by the shout of thousands, who with one voice, and in their rustic idiom, exclaimed aloud, "God wills it, God wills it!" "It is indeed the will of God," replied the pope; "and let this memorable word, the inspiration surely of the Holy Spirit, be for ever adopted as your cry of battle, to animate the devotion and courage of the champions of Christ. His cross is the symbol of your salvation; wear it, a red, a bloody cross, as an external mark, on your breasts or shoulders, as a pledge of your sacred and irrevocable engagement." The proposal was joyfully accepted; great numbers, both of the clergy and laity, impressed on their garments the sign of the cross,* and solicited the pope to march at their head. This dangerous honour was declined by the more prudent successor of Gregory, who alleged the schism of the church, and the duties of his pastoral office, recommending to the faithful, who were disqualified by sex or profession, by age or infirmity, to aid with their prayers and alms the personal service of their robust brethren. The name and powers of his legate he devolved on Adhemar, bishop of Puy, the first who had received the cross at his hands. The foremost of the temporal chiefs was Raymond, count of Toulouse, whose ambassadors in the council excused the absence, and pledged the honour, of their master. After the confession and absolution of their sins, the champions of the cross were dismissed with a superfluous admonition to invite their countrymen and friends; and their departure for the Holy Land was fixed to the festival of the Assumption, the fifteenth of August, of the ensuing year.

So familiar, and as it were so natural to man, is the practice of violence, that our indulgence allows the slightest provocation, the most disputable right, as a sufficient ground of national hostility. But the name and nature of a *holy war* demands a more rigorous scutiny; nor can we hastily believe that the servants of the Prince of Peace would unsheathe the sword of destruction unless the motive were pure, the quarrel legitimate, and the necessity inevitable. The policy of an action may be determined from the tardy lessons of experience; but before we act, our conscience should be satisfied of the justice and propriety of our enterprise. In the age of the crusades, the Christians,

*Most commonly on their shoulders, in gold, or silk, or cloth, sewed on their garments. In the first crusade all were red; in the third the French alone preserved that colour, while green crosses were adopted by the Flemings, and white by the English. Yet in England the red ever appears the favourite, and, as it were, the national colour of our military ensigns and uniforms.

both of the East and West, were persuaded of their lawfulness and merit; their arguments are clouded by the perpetual abuse of Scripture and rhetoric; but they seem to insist on the right of natural and religious defence, their peculiar title to the Holy Land, and the impiety of their Pagan and Mohammedan foes.* I. The right of a just defence may fairly include our civil and spiritual allies: it depends on the existence of danger; and that danger must be estimated by the twofold consideration of the malice and the power of our enemies. A pernicious tenet has been imputed to the Mohammedans, the duty of *extirpating* all other religions by the sword. This charge of ignorance and bigotry is refuted by the Koran, by the history of the Musulman conquerors, and by their public and legal toleration of the Christian worship. But it cannot be denied that the Oriental churches are depressed under their iron yoke; that, in peace and war, they assert a divine and indefeasible claim of universal empire; and that, in their orthodox creed, the unbelieving nations are continually threatened with the loss of religion or liberty. In the eleventh century the victorious arms of the Turks presented a real and urgent apprehension of these losses. They had subdued in less than thirty years the kingdoms of Asia, as far as Jerusalem and the Hellespont; and the Greek empire tottered on the verge of destruction. Besides an honest sympathy for their brethren, the Latins had a right and interest in the support of Constantinople, the most important barrier of the West; and the privilege of defence must reach to prevent, as well as to repel, an impending assault. But this salutary purpose might have been accomplished by a moderate succour; and our calmer reason must disclaim the innumerable hosts and remote operations which overwhelmed Asia and depopulated Europe. II. Palestine could add nothing to the strength or safety of the Latins; and fanaticism alone could pretend to justify the conquest of that distant and narrow province. The Christians affirmed that their inalienable title to the promised land had been sealed by the blood of their divine Saviour; it was their right and duty to rescue their inheritance from the unjust possessors, who profaned his sepulchre, and oppressed the pilgrimage of his disciples. Vainly would it be alleged that the pre-

*If the reader will turn to the first scene of the First Part of Henry the Fourth, he will see in the text of Shakspeare the natural feelings of enthusiasm; and in the notes of Dr. Johnson the workings of a bigoted, though vigorous, mind, greedy of every pretence to hate and persecute those who dissent from his creed. (Gibbon's Note) See Introduction. (P.W.)

eminence of Jerusalem and the sanctity of Palestine have been abolished with the Mosaic law; that the God of the Christians is not a local deity, and that the recovery of Bethlehem or Calvary, his cradle or his tomb, will not atone for the violation of the moral precepts of the Gospel. Such arguments glance aside from the leaden shield of superstition; and the religious mind will not easily relinquish its hold on the sacred ground of mystery and miracle. III. But the holy wars which have been waged in every climate of the globe, from Egypt to Livonia, and from Peru to Hindostan, require the support of some more general and flexible tenet. It has been often supposed, and sometimes affirmed, that a difference of religion is a worthy cause of hostility; that obstinate unbelievers may be slain or subdued by the champions of the cross; and that grace is the sole fountain of dominion as well as of mercy. Above four hundred years before the first crusade, the eastern and western provinces of the Roman empire had been acquired about the same time, and in the same manner, by the barbarians of Germany and Arabia. Time and treaties had legitimated the conquests of the *Christian* Franks; but in the eyes of their subjects and neighbours the Mohammedan princes were still tyrants and usurpers, who, by the arms of war or rebellion, might be lawfully driven from their unlawful possession.

As the manners of the Christians were relaxed, their discipline of penance was enforced; and with the multiplication of sins the remedies were multiplied. In the primitive church a voluntary and open confession prepared the work of atonement. In the middle ages the bishops and priests interrogated the criminal, compelled him to account for his thoughts, words, and actions, and prescribed the terms of his reconciliation with God. But as this discretionary power might alternately be abused by indulgence and tyranny, a rule of discipline was framed to inform and regulate the spiritual judges. This mode of legislation was invented by the Greeks; their *penitentials* were translated, or imitated, in the Latin church; and in the time of Charlemagne the clergy of every diocese were provided with a code, which they prudently concealed from the knowledge of the vulgar. In this dangerous estimate of crimes and punishments each case was supposed, each difference was remarked, by the experience or penetration of the monks; some sins are enumerated which innocence could not have suspected, and others which reason cannot believe; and the more ordinary offences of fornication and adultery, of perjury and sacrilege, of rapine and murder, were expiated by a penance which, according to the various circumstances, was prolonged from forty days to seven years. During this term of mortification the patient was healed, the criminal was absolved, by a salutary regimen of fasts and prayers: the disorder of his dress was expressive of grief and remorse; and he humbly abstained from all the business and pleasure of social life. But the rigid execution of these laws would have depopulated the palace, the camp, and the city; the barbarians of the West believed and trembled; but nature often rebelled against principle; and the magistrate laboured without effect to enforce the jurisdiction of the priest. A literal accomplishment of penance was indeed impracticable: the guilt of adultery was multiplied by daily repetition; that of homicide might involve the massacre of a whole people; each act was separately numbered; and, in those times of anarchy and vice, a modest sinner might easily incur a debt of three hundred years. His insolvency was relieved by a commutation or *indulgence:* a year of penance was appreciated at twenty-six *solidi* of silver, about four pounds sterling, for the rich; at three solidi, or nine shillings, for the indigent: and these alms were soon appropriated to the use of the church, which derived from the redemption of sins an inexhaustible source of opulence and dominion. A debt of three hundred years, or twelve hundred pounds, was enough to impoverish a plentiful fortune; the scarcity of gold and silver was supplied by the alienation of land; and the princely donations of Pepin and Charlemagne are expressly given for the *remedy* of their soul. It is a maxim of the civil law, that whosoever cannot pay with his purse must pay with his body; and the practice of flagellation was adopted by the monks—a cheap though painful equivalent. By a fantastic arithmetic, a year of penance was taxed at three thousand lashes;* and such was the skill and patience of a famous hermit, St. Dominic of the Iron Cuirass, that in six days he could discharge an entire century by a whipping of three hundred thousand stripes. His example was followed by many penitents of both sexes; and as a vicarious sacrifice was accepted, a sturdy disciplinarian might expiate on his own back the sins of his benefactors. These compensations of the purse and the person introduced, in the eleventh century, a more

*Each century of lashes was sanctified with the recital of a psalm; and the whole Psalter, with the accompaniment of 15,000 stripes, was equivalent to five years.

honourable mode of satisfaction. The merit of military service against the Saracens of Africa and Spain had been allowed by the predecessors of Urban the Second. In the council of Clermont, that pope proclaimed a *plenary indulgence* to those who should enlist under the banner of the cross; the absolution of *all* their sins, and a full receipt for *all* that might be due of canonical penance. The cold philosophy of modern times is incapable of feeling the impression that was made on a sinful and fanatic world. At the voice of their pastor, the robber, the incendiary, the homicide, arose by thousands to redeem their souls by repeating on the infidels the same deeds which they had exercised against their Christian brethren; and the terms of atonement were eagerly embraced by offenders of every rank and denomination. None were pure; none were exempt from the guilt and penalty of sin; and those who were the least amenable to the justice of God and the church were the best entitled to the temporal and eternal recompense of their pious courage. If they fell, the spirit of the Latin clergy did not hesitate to adorn their tomb with the crown of martyrdom;* and should they survive, they could expect without impatience the delay and increase of their heavenly reward. They offered their blood to the Son of God, who had laid down his life for their salvation: they took up the cross, and entered with confidence into the way of the Lord. His providence would watch over their safety; perhaps his visible and miraculous power would smooth the difficulties of their holy enterprise. The cloud and pillar of Jehovah had marched before the Israelites into the promised land. Might not the Christians more reasonably hope that the rivers would open for their passage; that the walls of the strongest cities would fall at the sound of their trumpets; and that the sun would be arrested in his mid-career to allow them time for the destruction of the infidels?

Of the chiefs and soldiers who marched to the holy sepulchre, I will dare to affirm that *all* were prompted by the spirit of enthusiasm, the belief of merit, the hope of reward, and the assurance of divine aid. But I am equally persuaded that in *many* it was not the sole, that in *some* it was not the leading, principle of action. The use and abuse of religion are feeble to stem, they are strong and irresistible to impel,

*Such at least was the belief of the crusaders, and such is the uniform style of the historians . . . ; but the prayers for the repose of their souls are inconsistent in orthodox theology with the merits of martyrdom.

the stream of national manners. Against the private wars of the barbarians, their bloody tournaments, licentious loves, and judicial duels, the popes and synods might ineffectually thunder. It is a more easy task to provoke the metaphysical disputes of the Greeks, to drive into the cloister the victims of anarchy or despotism, to sanctify the patience of slaves and cowards, or to assume the merit of the humanity and benevolence of modern Christians. War and exercise were the reigning passions of the Franks or Latins; they were enjoined, as a penance, to gratify those passions, to visit distant lands, and to draw their swords against the nations of the East. Their victory, or even their attempt, would immortalise the names of the intrepid heroes of the cross; and the purest piety could not be insensible to the most splendid prospect of military glory. In the petty quarrels of Europe they shed the blood of their friends and countrymen for the acquisition, perhaps, of a castle or a village. They could march with alacrity against the distant and hostile nations who were devoted to their arms; their fancy already grasped the golden sceptres of Asia; and the conquest of Apulia and Sicily by the Normans might exalt to royalty the hopes of the most private adventurer. Christendom, in her rudest state, must have yielded to the climate and cultivation of the Mohammedan countries; and their natural and artificial wealth had been magnified by the tales of pilgrims and the gifts of an imperfect commerce. The vulgar, both the great and small, were taught to believe every wonder, of lands flowing with milk and honey, of mines and treasures, of gold and diamonds, of palaces of marble and jasper, and of odoriferous groves of cinnamon and frankincense. In this earthly paradise each warrior depended on his sword to carve a plenteous and honourable establishment, which he measured only by the extent of his wishes.* Their vassals and soldiers trusted their fortunes to God and their master: the spoils of a Turkish emir might enrich the meanest follower of the camp; and the flavour of the wines, the beauty of the Grecian women, were temptations more adapted to the nature, than to the profession, of the champions of the cross. The love of freedom was a powerful incitement to the multitudes who were oppressed by feudal or ecclesiastical

*The same hopes were displayed in the letters of the adventurers ad animandos qui in Francia resederant. Hugh de Reiteste could boast that his share amounted to one abbey and ten castles, of the yearly value of 1500 marks, and that he should acquire a hundred castles by the conquest of Aleppo . . .

tyranny. Under this holy sign, the peasants and burghers, who were attached to the servitude of the glebe, might escape from a haughty lord, and transplant themselves and their families to a land of liberty. The monk might release himself from the discipline of his convent, the debtor might suspend the accumulation of usury and the pursuit of his creditors, and outlaws and malefactors of every cast might continue to brave the laws and elude the punishment of their crimes.

These motives were potent and numerous: when we have singly computed their weight on the mind of each individual, we must add the infinite series, the multiplying powers of example and fashion. The first proselytes became the warmest and most effectual missionaries of the cross: among their friends and countrymen they preached the duty, the merit, and the recompense of their holy vow, and the most reluctant hearers were insensibly drawn within the whirlpool of persuasion and authority. The martial youths were fired by the reproach or suspicion of cowardice; the opportunity of visiting with an army the sepulchre of Christ was embraced by the old and infirm, by women and children, who consulted rather their zeal than their strength; and those who in the evening had derided the folly of their companions were the most eager, the ensuing day, to tread in their footsteps. The ignorance which magnified the hopes, diminished the perils, of the enterprise. Since the Turkish conquest, the paths of pilgrimage were obliterated; the chiefs themselves had an imperfect notion of the length of the way and the state of their enemies; and such was the stupidity of the people, that, at the sight of the first city or castle beyond the limits of their knowledge, they were ready to ask whether that was not the Jerusalem, the term and object of their labours. Yet the more prudent of the crusaders, who were not sure that they should be fed from heaven with a shower of quails or manna, provided themselves with those precious metals which, in every country, are the representatives of every commodity. To defray, according to their rank, the expenses of the road, princes alienated their provinces, nobles their lands and castles, peasants their cattle and the instruments of husbandry. The value of property was depreciated by the eager competition of multitudes; while the price of arms and horses was raised to an exorbitant height by the wants and impatience of the buyers. Those who remained at home, with sense and money, were enriched by the epidemical disease: the sovereigns acquired at a cheap rate the domains of their vassals, and the ecclesiastical purchasers completed the payment by the assurance of their prayers. The cross, which was commonly sewed on the garment, in cloth or silk, was inscribed by some zealots on their skin: an hot iron, or indelible liquor, was applied to perpetuate the mark; and a crafty monk, who showed the miraculous impression on his breast, was repaid with the popular veneration and the richest benefices of Palestine.

The fifteenth of August had been fixed in the council of Clermont for the departure of the pilgrims; but the day was anticipated by the thoughtless and needy crowd of plebeians; and I shall briefly despatch the calamities which they inflicted and suffered before I enter on the more serious and successful enterprise of the chiefs. Early in the spring, from the confines of France and Lorraine, above sixty thousand of the populace of both sexes flocked round the first missionary of the crusade, and pressed him, with clamorous importunity, to lead them to the holy sepulchre. The hermit, assuming the character, without the talents or authority, of a general, impelled or obeyed the forward impulse of his votaries along the banks of the Rhine and Danube. Their wants and numbers soon compelled them to separate, and his lieutenant, Walter the Penniless, a valiant though needy soldier, conducted a vanguard of pilgrims, whose condition may be determined from the proportion of eight horsemen to fifteen thousand foot. The example and footsteps of Peter were closely pursued by another fanatic, the monk Godescal, whose sermons had swept away fifteen or twenty thousand peasants from the villages of Germany. Their rear was again pressed by a herd of two hundred thousand, the most stupid and savage refuse of the people, who mingled with their devotion a brutal licence of rapine, prostitution, and drunkenness. Some counts and gentlemen, at the head of three thousand horse, attended the motions of the multitude to partake in the spoil: but their genuine leaders (may we credit such folly?) were a goose and a goat, who were carried in the front, and to whom these worthy Christians ascribed an infusion of the divine spirit. Of these, and of other bands of enthusiasts, the first and most easy warfare was against the Jews, the murderers of the Son of God. In the trading cities of the Moselle and the Rhine their colonies were numerous and rich, and they enjoyed, under the protection of the emperor and the bishops, the free exercise of their religion.* At

*Benjamin of Tudela describes the state of his Jewish brethren from Cologne along the Rhine: they were rich, generous, learned, hospitable, and lived in the eager hope of the Messiah . . . In seventy years (he wrote about A.D. 1170) they had recovered from these massacres.

Verdun, Trèves, Mentz, Spires, Worms, many thousands of that unhappy people were pillaged and massacred, nor had they felt a more bloody stroke since the persecution of Hadrian. A remnant was saved by the firmness of their bishops, who accepted a feigned and transient conversion; but the more obstinate Jews opposed their fanaticism to the fanaticism of the Christians, barricadoed their houses, and, precipitating themselves, their families, and their wealth into the rivers or the flames, disappointed the malice, or at least the avarice, of their implacable foes.

Between the frontiers of Austria and the seat of the Byzantine monarchy the crusaders were compelled to traverse an interval of six hundred miles, the wild and desolate countries of Hungary and Bulgaria. The soil is fruitful, and intersected with rivers; but it was then covered with morasses and forests, which spread to a boundless extent whenever man has ceased to exercise his dominion over the earth. Both nations had imbibed the rudiments of Christianity: the Hungarians were ruled by their native princes, the Bulgarians by a lieutenant of the Greek emperor; but, on the slightest provocation, their ferocious nature was rekindled, and ample provocation was afforded by the disorders of the first pilgrims. Agriculture must have been unskilful and languid among a people whose cities were built of reeds and timber, which were deserted in the summer season for the tents of hunters and shepherds. A scanty supply of provisions was rudely demanded, forcibly seized, and greedily consumed, and on the first quarrel the crusaders gave a loose to indignation and revenge. But their ignorance of the country, of war, and of discipline exposed them to every snare. The Greek præfect of Bulgaria commanded a regular force; at the trumpet of the Hungarian king, the eighth or the tenth of his martial subjects bent their bows and mounted on horseback; their policy was insidious, and their retaliation on those pious robbers was unrelenting and bloody. About a third of the naked fugitives, and the hermit Peter was of the number, escaped to the Thracian mountains; and the emperor, who respected the pilgrimage and succour of the Latins, conducted them by secure and easy journeys to Constantinople, and advised them to await the arrival of their brethren. For a while they remembered their faults and losses, but no sooner were they revived by the hospitable entertainment, than their venom was again inflamed; they stung their benefactor, and neither gardens, nor palaces, nor churches, were safe from their depredations. For his own safety, Alexius allured them to pass over to the Asiatic side of the Bosphorus; but their blind impetuosity soon urged them to desert the station which he had assigned, and to rush headlong against the Turks, who occupied the road of Jerusalem. The hermit, conscious of his shame, had withdrawn from the camp to Constantinople; and his lieutenant, Walter the Penniless, who was worthy of a better command, attempted without success to introduce some order and prudence among the herd of savages. They separated in quest of prey, and themselves fell an easy prey to the arts of the sultan. By a rumour that their foremost companions were rioting in the spoils of his capital, Soliman tempted the main body to descend into the plain of Nice: they were overwhelmed by the Turkish arrows, and a pyramid of bones informed their companions of the place of their defeat. Of the first crusaders, three hundred thousand had already perished before a single city was rescued from the infidels, before their graver and more noble brethren had completed the preparations of their enterprise.

None of the great sovereigns of Europe embarked their persons in the first crusade. The emperor Henry the Fourth was not disposed to obey the summons of the pope; Philip the First of France was occupied by his pleasures; William Rufus of England by a recent conquest; the kings of Spain were engaged in a domestic war against the Moors; and the northern monarchs of Scotland, Denmark, Sweden, and Poland were yet strangers to the passions and interests of the South. The religious ardour was more strongly felt by the princes of the second order, who held an important place in the feudal system. Their situation will naturally cast under four distinct heads the review of their names and characters; but I may escape some needless repetition, by observing at once that courage and the exercise of arms are the common attribute of these Christian adventurers. I. The first rank both in war and council is justly due to Godfrey of Bouillon; and happy would it have been for the crusaders, if they had trusted themselves to the sole conduct of that accomplished hero, a worthy representative of Charlemagne, from whom he was descended in the female line. His father was of the noble race of the counts of Boulogne: Brabant, the lower province of Lorraine, was the inheritance of his mother; and by the emperor's bounty he was himself invested with that ducal title, which has been improperly transferred to his lordship of Bouillon in the Ardennes. In the service of Henry the Fourth he bore the great standard of the empire, and pierced with his lance the breast of Rodolph, the rebel king: Godfrey was the first who ascended the walls of Rome; and his sickness, his vow, perhaps his remorse for bearing arms against the pope, confirmed an early resolution of visiting the holy sepulchre, not as a pilgrim, but a deliverer. His valour was matured by prudence and moderation; his piety, though blind, was sincere; and, in the tumult of a camp, he practised the real and fictitious virtues of a convent. Superior to the private factions of the chiefs, he reserved his enmity for the enemies of Christ; and though he gained a kingdom by the attempt, his pure and disinterested zeal was acknowledged by his rivals. Godfrey of Bouillon was accompanied by his two brothers, by Eustace the elder, who had succeeded to the county of Boulogne, and by the younger, Baldwin, a character of more ambiguous virtue. The duke of Lorraine was alike celebrated on either side of the Rhine: from his birth and education, he was equally conversant with the French and Teutonic languages: the barons of France, Germany, and Lorriane assembled their vassals; and the confederate force that marched under his banner was composed of fourscore thousand foot and about ten thousand horse. II. In the parliament that was held at Paris, in the king's presence, about two months after the council of Clermont, Hugh, count of Vermandois, was the most conspicuous of the princes who assumed the cross. But the appellation of *the Great* was applied, not so much to his merit or possessions (though neither were contemptible), as to the royal birth of the brother of the king of France. Robert, duke of Normandy, was the eldest son of William the Conqueror; but on his father's death he was deprived of the kingdom of England, by his own indolence and the activity of his brother Rufus. The worth of Robert was degraded by an excessive levity and easiness of temper: his cheerfulness seduced him to the indulgence of pleasure; his profuse liberality impoverished the prince and people; his indiscriminate clemency multiplied the number of offenders; and the amiable qualities of a private man became the essential defects of a sovereign. For the trifling sum of ten thousand marks he mortgaged Normandy during his absence to the English usurper; but his engagement and behaviour in the holy war announced in Robert a reformation of manners, and restored him in some degree to the public esteem. Another Robert was count of Flanders, a royal province, which, in this century, gave three queens to the thrones of France, England, and Denmark: he was surnamed the Sword and Lance of the Christians; but in the exploits of a soldier he sometimes forgot the duties of a general. Stephen, count of Chartres, of Blois, and of Troyes, was one of the richest princes of the age; and the number of his castles has been compared to the three hundred and sixty-five days of the year. His mind was improved by literature; and, in the council of the chiefs, the eloquent Stephen was chosen to discharge the office of their president. These four were the principal leaders of the French, the Normans, and the pilgrims of the British isles: but the list of the barons who were possessed of three or four towns would exceed, says a contemporary, the catalogue of the Trojan war. III. In the south of France the command was assumed by Adhemar, bishop of Puy, the pope's legate, and by Raymond count of St. Giles and Toulouse, who added the prouder titles of duke of Narbonne and marquis of Provence. The former was a respectable prelate, alike qualified for this world and the next. The latter was a veteran warrior, who had fought against the Saracens of Spain, and who consecrated his declining age, not only to the deliverance, but to the perpetual service, of the holy sepulchre. His experience and riches gave him a strong ascendant in the Christian camp, whose distress he was often able, and sometimes willing, to relieve. But it was easier for him to extort the praise of the Infidels than to preserve the love of his subjects and associates. His eminent qualities were clouded by a temper, haughty, envious, and obstinate; and, though he resigned an ample patrimony for the cause of God, his piety, in the public opinion, was not exempt from avarice and ambition. A mercantile, rather than a martial, spirit prevailed among his *provincials,* a common name, which included the natives of Auvergne and Languedoc,* the vassals of the kingdom of Burgundy or Arles. From the adjacent frontier of Spain he drew a band of hardy adventurers; as he marched through Lombardy, a crowd of Italians flocked to his standard, and his united force consisted of one hundred thousand horse and foot. If Raymond was the first to enlist and the last to depart, the delay may be excused

*The town of his birth, or first appanage, was consecrated to St. Ægidius, whose name, as early as the first crusade, was corrupted by the French into St. Gilles, or St. Giles. It is situate in the Lower Languedoc, between Nismes and the Rhône, and still boasts a collegiate church of the foundation of Raymond . . .

by the greatness of his preparation and the promise of an everlasting farewell. IV. The name of Bohemond, the son of Robert Guiscard, was already famous by his double victory over the Greek emperor: but his father's will had reduced him to the principality of Tarentum, and the remembrance of his Eastern trophies, till he was awakened by the rumour and passage of the French pilgrims. It is in the person of this Norman chief that we may seek for the coolest policy and ambition, with a small allay of religious fanaticism. His conduct may justify a belief that he had secretly directed the design of the pope, which he affected to second with astonishment and zeal: at the siege of Amalphi his example and discourse inflamed the passions of a confederate army; he instantly tore his garment to supply crosses for the numerous candidates, and prepared to visit Constantinople and Asia at the head of ten thousand horse and twenty thousand foot. Several princes of the Norman race accompanied this veteran general; and his cousin Tancred* was the partner, rather than the servant, of the war. In the accomplished character of Tancred we discover all the virtues of a perfect knight, the true spirit of chivalry, which inspired the generous sentiments and social offices of man far better than the base philosophy, or the baser religion, of the times.

Between the age of Charlemagne and that of the crusades, a revolution had taken place among the Spaniards, the Normans, and the French, which was gradually extended to the rest of Europe. The service of the infantry was degraded to the plebeians; the cavalry formed the strength of the armies; and the honourable name of *miles,* or soldier, was confined to the gentlemen† who served on horseback, and were invested with the character of knighthood. The dukes and counts, who had usurped the rights of sovereignty, divided the provinces among their faithful barons: the barons distributed among their vassals the fiefs or benefices of their jurisdiction; and these military tenants, the peers of each other and of their lord, composed the noble or equestrian order, which disdained to conceive the peasant or burgher as of the same species with themselves. The dignity of their

*The mother of Tancred was Emma, sister of the great Robert Guiscard; his father, the marquis Odo the Good. . . .

†Of the words *gentilis, gentilhomme, gentleman,* two etymologies are produced: 1. From the barbarians of the fifth century, the soldiers, and at length the conquerors, of the Roman empire, who were vain of their foreign nobility; and, 2. From the sense of the civilians, who consider *gentilis* as synonymous with *ingenuus.* Selden inclines to the first, but the latter is more pure, as well as probable.

birth was preserved by pure and equal alliances; their sons alone, who could produce four quarters or lines of ancestry, without spot or reproach, might legally pretend to the honour of knighthood; but a valiant plebeian was sometimes enriched and ennobled by the sword, and became the father of a new race. A single knight could impart, according to his judgment, the character which he received; and the warlike sovereigns of Europe derived more glory from this personal distinction than from the lustre of their diadem. This ceremony, of which some traces may be found in Tacitus and the woods of Germany, was in its origin simple and profane: the candidate, after some previous trial, was invested with the sword and spurs; and his cheek or shoulder was touched with a slight blow, as an emblem of the last affront which it was lawful for him to endure. But superstition mingled in every public and private action of life: in the holy wars it sanctified the profession of arms; and the order of chivalry was assimilated in its rights and privileges to the sacred orders of priesthood. The bath and white garment of the novice were an indecent copy of the regeneration of baptism: his sword, which he offered on the altar, was blessed by the ministers of religion: his solemn reception was preceded by fasts and vigils; and he was created a knight in the name of God, of St. George, and of St. Michael the archangel. He swore to accomplish the duties of his profession; and education, example, and the public opinion were the inviolable guardians of his oath. As the champion of God and the ladies (I blush to unite such discordant names), he devoted himself to speak the truth; to maintain the right; to protect the distressed; to practise *courtesy,* a virtue less familiar to the ancients; to pursue the infidels; to despise the allurements of ease and safety; and to vindicate in every perilous adventure the honour of his character. The abuse of the same spirit provoked the illiterate knight to disdain the arts of industry and peace; to esteem himself the sole judge and avenger of his own injuries; and proudly to neglect the laws of civil society and military discipline. Yet the benefits of this institution, to refine the temper of barbarians, and to infuse some principles of faith, justice, and humanity, were strongly felt, and have been often observed. The asperity of national prejudice was softened; and the community of religion and arms spread a similar colour and generous emulation over the face of Christendom. Abroad in enterprise and pilgrimage, at home in martial exercise, the warriors of every country were perpetually associated; and impartial taste must prefer a Gothic tournament to the Olympic games of classic antiquity.* Instead of the naked spectacles which corrupted the manners of the Greeks, and banished from the stadium the virgins and matrons, the pompous decoration of the lists was crowned with the presence of chaste and high-born beauty, from whose hands the conqueror received the prize of his dexterity and courage. The skill and strength that were exerted in wrestling and boxing bear a distant and doubtful relation to the merit of a soldier; but the tournaments, as they were invented in France, and eagerly adopted both in the East and West, presented a lively image of the business of the field. The single combats, the general skirmish, the defence of a pass, or castle, were rehearsed as in actual service; and the contest, both in real and mimic war, was decided by the superior management of the horse and lance. The lance was the proper and peculiar weapon of the knight: his horse was of a large and heavy breed; but this charger, till he was roused by the approaching danger, was usually led by an attendant, and he quietly rode a pad or palfrey of a more easy pace. His helmet and sword, his greaves and buckler, it would be superfluous to describe; but I may remark, that, at the period of the crusades, the armour was less ponderous than in later times; and that, instead of a massy cuirass, his breast was defended by a hauberk or coat of mail. When their long lances were fixed in the rest, the warriors furiously spurred their horses against the foe; and the light cavalry of the Turks and Arabs could seldom stand against the direct and impetuous weight of their charge. Each knight was attended to the field by his faithful squire, a youth of equal birth and similar hopes; he was followed by his archers and men-at-arms, and four, or five, or six soldiers, were computed as the furniture of a complete *lance*. In the expeditions to the neighbouring kingdoms or the Holy Land, the duties of the feudal tenure no longer subsisted; the voluntary service of the knights and their followers was either prompted by zeal or attachment, or purchased with rewards and promises; and the numbers of each squadron were measured by the power, the wealth, and the fame of each independent chieftain. They were distinguished by his banner, his armorial coat, and his cry of war; and the most ancient families of Europe must seek in these achieve-

*The athletic exercises, particularly the cestus and pancratium, were condemned by Lycurgus, Philopœmen, and Galen, a lawgiver, a general, and a physician. . . .

ments the origin and proof of their nobility. In this rapid portrait of chivalry I have been urged to anticipate on the story of the crusades, at once an effect and a cause of this memorable institution.

Such were the troops, and such the leaders, who assumed the cross for the deliverance of the holy sepulchre. As soon as they were relieved by the absence of the plebeian multitude, they encouraged each other, by interviews and messages, to accomplish their vow, and hasten their departure. Their wives and sisters were desirous of partaking the danger and merit of the pilgrimage: their portable treasures were conveyed in bars of silver and gold; and the princes and barons were attended by their equipage of hounds and hawks to amuse their leisure and to supply their table. The difficulty of procuring subsistence for so many myriads of men and horses engaged them to separate their forces: their choice or situation determined the road; and it was agreed to meet in the neighbourhood of Constantinople, and from thence to begin their operations against the Turks. From the banks of the Meuse and the Moselle, Godfrey of Bouillon followed the direct way of Germany, Hungary, and Bulgaria; and, as long as he exercised the sole command, every step afforded some proof of his prudence and virtue. On the confines of Hungary he was stopped three weeks by a Christian people, to whom the name, or at least the abuse, of the cross was justly odious. The Hungarians still smarted with the wounds which they had received from the first pilgrims: in their turn they had abused the right of defence and retaliation; and they had reason to apprehend a severe revenge from a hero of the same nation, and who was engaged in the same cause. But, after weighing the motives and the events, the virtuous duke was content to pity the crimes and misfortunes of his worthless brethren; and his twelve deputies, the messengers of peace, requested in his name a free passage and an equal market. To remove their suspicions, Godfrey trusted himself, and afterwards his brother, to the faith of Carloman, king of Hungary, who treated them with a simple but hospitable entertainment: the treaty was sanctified by their common Gospel; and a proclamation, under pain of death, restrained the animosity and licence of the Latin soldiers. From Austria to Belgrade, they traversed the plains of Hungary, without enduring or offering an injury; and the proximity of Carloman, who hovered on their flanks with his numerous cavalry, was a precaution not less useful for their safety than for his own. They reached the banks of the Save; and no sooner had they passed the river than the king of Hungary restored the hostages, and saluted their departure with the fairest wishes for the success of their enterprise. With the same conduct and discipline Godfrey pervaded the woods of Bulgaria and the frontiers of Thrace; and might congratulate himself that he had almost reached the first term of his pilgrimage without drawing his sword against a Christian adversary. After an easy and pleasant journey through Lombardy, from Turin to Aquileia, Raymond and his provincials marched forty days through the savage country of Dalmatia and Sclavonia. The weather was a perpetual fog; the land was mountainous and desolate; the natives were either fugitive or hostile: loose in their religion and government, they refused to furnish provisions or guides; murdered the stragglers; and exercised by night and day the vigilance of the count, who derived more security from the punishment of some captive robbers than from his interview and treaty with the prince of Scodra. His march between Durazzo and Constantinople was harassed, without being stopped, by the peasants and soldiers of the Greek emperor; and the same faint and ambiguous hostility was prepared for the remaining chiefs, who passed the Adriatic from the coast of Italy. Bohemond had arms and vessels, and foresight and discipline; and his name was not forgotten in the provinces of Epirus and Thessaly. Whatever obstacles he encountered were surmounted by his military conduct and the valour of Tancred; and if the Norman prince affected to spare the Greeks, he gorged his soldiers with the full plunder of an heretical castle. The nobles of France pressed forwards with the vain and thoughtless ardour of which their nation has been sometimes accused. From the Alps to Apulia the march of Hugh the Great, of the two Roberts, and of Stephen of Chartres, through a wealthy country, and amidst the applauding Catholics, was a devout or triumphant progress: they kissed the feet of the Roman pontiff; and the golden standard of St. Peter was delivered to the brother of the French monarch. But in this visit of piety and pleasure they neglected to secure the season and the means of their embarkation: the winter was insensibly lost: their troops were scattered and corrupted in the towns of Italy. They separately accomplished their passage, regardless of safety or dignity; and within nine months from the feast of the Assumption, the day appointed by Urban, all the Latin princes had reached Constantinople. But the count of

Vermandois was produced as a captive; his foremost vessels were scattered by a tempest; and his person, against the law of nations, was detained by the lieutenants of Alexius. Yet the arrival of Hugh had been announced by four-and-twenty knights in golden armour, who commanded the emperor to revere the general of the Latin Christians, the brother of the king of kings.

In some Oriental tale I have read the fable of a shepherd who was ruined by the accomplishment of his own wishes: he had prayed for water; the Ganges was turned into his grounds, and his flock and cottage were swept away by the inundation. Such was the fortune, or at least the apprehension, of the Greek emperor Alexius Comnenus, whose name has already appeared in this history, and whose conduct is so differently represented by his daughter Anna, and by the Latin writers. In the council of Placentia his ambassadors had solicited a moderate succour, perhaps of ten thousand soldiers; but he was astonished by the approach of so many potent chiefs and fanatic nations. The emperor fluctuated between hope and fear, between timidity and courage; but in the crooked policy which he mistook for wisdom, I cannot believe, I cannot discern, that he maliciously conspired against the life or honour of the French heroes. The promiscuous multitudes of Peter the Hermit were savage beasts, alike destitute of humanity and reason: nor was it possible for Alexius to prevent or deplore their destruction. The troops of Godfrey and his peers were less contemptible, but not less suspicious, to the Greek emperor. Their motives *might* be pure and pious; but he was equally alarmed by his knowledge of the ambitious Bohemond, and his ignorance of the Transalpine chiefs: the courage of the French was blind and headstrong; they might be tempted by the luxury and wealth of Greece, and elated by the view and opinion of their invincible strength; and Jerusalem might be forgotten in the prospect of Constantinople. After a long march and painful abstinence, the troops of Godfrey encamped in the plains of Thrace; they heard with indignation that their brother, the count of Vermandois, was imprisoned by the Greeks; and their reluctant duke was compelled to indulge them in some freedom of retaliation and rapine. They were appeased by the submission of Alexius: he promised to supply their camp; and as they refused, in the midst of winter, to pass the Bosphorus, their quarters were assigned among the gardens and palaces on the shores of that narrow sea. But an incurable jealousy still rankled in the minds of the two nations, who despised each other as slaves and barbarians. Ignorance is the ground of suspicion, and suspicion was inflamed into daily provocations: prejudice is blind, hunger is deaf; and Alexius is accused of a design to starve or assault the Latins in a dangerous post, on all sides encompassed with the waters.* Godfrey sounded his trumpets, burst the net, overspread the plain, and insulted the suburbs: but the gates of Constantinople were strongly fortified; the ramparts were lined with archers; and after a doubtful conflict, both parties listened to the voice of peace and religion. The gifts and promises of the emperor insensibly soothed the fierce spirit of the Western strangers; as a Christian warrior, he rekindled their zeal for the prosecution of their holy enterprise, which he engaged to second with his troops and treasures. On the return of spring, Godfrey was persuaded to occupy a pleasant and plentiful camp in Asia; and no sooner had he passed the Bosphorus than the Greek vessels were suddenly recalled to the opposite shore. The same policy was repeated with the succeeding chiefs, who were swayed by the example, and weakened by the departure, of their foremost companions. By his skill and diligence Alexius prevented the union of any two of the confederate armies at the same moment under the walls of Constantinople; and before the feast of the Pentecost not a Latin pilgrim was left on the coast of Europe.

The same arms which threatened Europe might deliver Asia, and repel the Turks from the neighbouring shores of the Bosphorus and Hellespont. The fair provinces from Nice to Antioch were the recent patrimony of the Roman emperor; and his ancient and perpetual claim still embraced the kingdoms of Syria and Egypt. In his enthusiasm, Alexius indulged, or affected, the ambitious hope of leading his new allies to subvert the thrones of the East; but the calmer dictates of reason and temper dissuaded him from exposing his royal person to the faith of unknown and lawless barbarians. His prudence, or his pride, was content with extorting from the French princes an oath of homage and fidelity, and a solemn promise that they would either restore, or hold, their Asiatic conquests, as the humble and loyal

*Between the Black Sea, the Bosphorus, and the river Barbyses, which is deep in summer, and runs fifteen miles through a flat meadow. Its communication with Europe and Constantinople is by the stone bridge of the *Blachernæ,* which in successive ages was restored by Justinian and Basil . . .

vassals of the Roman empire. Their independent spirit was fired at the mention of this foreign and voluntary servitude: they successively yielded to the dexterous application of gifts and flattery; and the first proselytes became the most eloquent and effectual missionaries to multiply the companions of their shame. The pride of Hugh of Vermandois was soothed by the honours of his captivity; and in the brother of the French king the example of submission was prevalent and weighty. In the mind of Godfrey of Bouillon every human consideration was subordinate to the glory of God and the success of the crusade. He had firmly resisted the temptations of Bohemond and Raymond, who urged the attack and conquest of Constantinople. Alexius esteemed his virtues, deservedly named him the champion of the empire, and dignified his homage with the filial name and the rights of adoption. The hateful Bohemond was received as a true and ancient ally; and if the emperor reminded him of former hostilities, it was only to praise the valour that he had displayed, and the glory that he had acquired, in the fields of Durazzo and Larissa. The son of Guiscard was lodged, and entertained, and served with Imperial pomp: one day, as he passed through the gallery of the palace, a door was carelessly left open to expose a pile of gold and silver, of silk and gems, of curious and costly furniture, that was heaped in seeming disorder from the floor to the roof of the chamber. "What conquests," exclaimed the ambitious miser, "might not be achieved by the possession of such a treasure?"—"It is your own," replied a Greek attendant, who watched the motions of his soul; and Bohemond, after some hesitation, condescended to accept this magnificent present. The Norman was flattered by the assurance of an independent principality; and Alexius eluded, rather than denied, his daring demand of the office of great domestic, or general of the East. The two Roberts, the son of the conqueror of England, and the kinsman of three queens,* bowed in their turn before the Byzantine throne. A private letter of Stephen of Chartres attests his admiration of the emperor, the most excellent and liberal of men, who taught him to believe that he was a favourite, and promised to educate and establish his youngest son. In his southern province, the count of St. Giles and Toulouse faintly recognised the supremacy of the king of France, a prince of a foreign nation and language. At the head of a

*After his return Robert of Flanders became the *man* of the king of England, for a pension of four hundred marks. . . .

hundred thousand men, he declared that he was the soldier and servant of Christ alone, and that the Greek might be satisfied with an equal treaty of alliance and friendship. His obstinate resistance enhanced the value and the price of his submission; and he shone, says the princess Anna, among the barbarians, as the sun amidst the stars of heaven. His disgust of the noise and insolence of the French, his suspicions of the designs of Bohemond, the emperor imparted to his faithful Raymond; and that aged statesman might clearly discern, that, however false in friendship, he was sincere in his enmity. The spirit of chivalry was last subdued in the person of Tancred; and none could deem themselves dishonoured by the imitation of that gallant knight. He disdained the gold and flattery of the Greek monarch; assaulted in his presence an insolent patrician; escaped to Asia in the habit of a private soldier; and yielded with a sigh to the authority of Bohemond, and the interest of the Christian cause. The best and most ostensible reason was the impossibility of passing the sea and accomplishing their vow without the licence and the vessels of Alexius; but they cherished a secret hope, that, as soon as they trod the continent of Asia, their swords would obliterate their shame, and dissolve the engagement, which on his side might not be very faithfully performed. The ceremony of their homage was grateful to a people who had long since considered pride as the substitute of power. High on his throne the emperor sat mute and immovable: his majesty was adored by the Latin princes; and they submitted to kiss either his feet or his knees, an indignity which their own writers are ashamed to confess, and unable to deny.

Private or public interest suppressed the murmurs of the dukes and counts; but a French baron (he is supposed to be Robert of Paris) presumed to ascend the throne, and to place himself by the side of Alexius. The sage reproof of Baldwin provoked him to exclaim, in his barbarous idiom, "Who is this rustic, that keeps his seat while so many valiant captains are standing round him?" The emperor maintained his silence, dissembled his indignation, and questioned his interpreter concerning the meaning of the words, which he partly suspected from the universal language of gesture and countenance. Before the departure of the pilgrims he endeavoured to learn the name and condition of the audacious baron. "I am a Frenchman," replied Robert, "of the purest and most ancient nobility of my country. All that I know is, that there is a church in my neighbourhood, the resort of those who are desirous of approving their valour in single combat. Till an enemy appears, they address their prayers to God and his saints. That church I have frequently visited, but never have I found an antagonist who dared to accept my defiance." Alexius dismissed the challenger with some prudent advice for his conduct in the Turkish warfare; and history repeats with pleasure this lively example of the manners of his age and country.

The conquest of Asia was undertaken and achieved by Alexander, with thirty-five thousand Macedonians and Greeks; and his best hope was in the strength and discipline of his phalanx of infantry. The principal force of the crusaders consisted in their cavalry; and when that force was mustered in the plains of Bithynia, the knights and their martial attendants on horseback amounted to one hundred thousand fighting men, completely armed with the helmet and coat of mail. The value of these soldiers deserved a strict and authentic account; and the flower of European chivalry might furnish, in a first effort, this formidable body of heavy horse. A part of the infantry might be enrolled for the service of scouts, pioneers, and archers; but the promiscuous crowd were lost in their own disorder; and we depend not on the eyes or knowledge, but on the belief and fancy, of a chaplain of Count Baldwin, in the estimate of six hundred thousand pilgrims able to bear arms, besides the priests and monks, the women and children, of the Latin camp. The reader starts; and before he is recovered from his surprise I shall add, on the same testimony, that, if all who took the cross had accomplished their vow, above SIX MILLIONS would have migrated from Europe to Asia. Under this oppression of faith I derive some relief from a more sagacious and thinking writer, who, after the same review of the cavalry, accuses the credulity of the priest of Chartres, and even doubts whether the *Cisalpine* regions (in the geography of a Frenchman) were sufficient to produce and pour forth such incredible multitudes. The coolest scepticism will remember that of these religious volunteers great numbers never beheld Constantinople and Nice. Of enthusiasm the influence is irregular and transient: many were detained at home by reason or cowardice, by poverty or weakness; and many were repulsed by the obstacles of the way, the more insuperable as they were unforeseen to these ignorant fanatics. The savage countries of Hungary and Bulgaria were whitened with their bones: their vanguard was cut in pieces by the Turkish sultan; and the loss of the first adventure, by the sword, or climate, or fatigue, has already been stated at three hundred thousand men. Yet the myriads that survived, that marched, that pressed forwards on the holy pilgrimage, were a subject of astonishment to themselves and to the Greeks. The copious energy of her language sinks under the efforts of the princess Anna: the images of locusts, of leaves and flowers, of the sands of the sea, or the stars of heaven, imperfectly represent what she had seen and heard; and the daughter of Alexius exclaims that Europe was loosened from its foundations, and hurled against Asia. The ancient hosts of Darius and Xerxes labour under the same doubt of a vague and indefinite magnitude; but I am inclined to believe that a larger number has never been contained within the lines of a single camp than at the siege of Nice, the first operation of the Latin princes. Their motives, their characters, and their arms, have been already displayed. Of their troops, the most numerous portion were natives of France: the Low Countries, the banks of the Rhine, and Apulia sent a powerful reinforcement: some bands of adventurers were drawn from Spain, Lombardy, and England; and from the distant bogs and mountains of Ireland and Scotland issued some naked and savage fanatics, ferocious at home, but unwarlike abroad. Had not superstition condemned the sacrilegious prudence of depriving the poorest or weakest Christian of the merit of the pilgrimage, the useless crowd, with mouths but without hands, might have been stationed in the Greek empire till their companions had opened and secured the way of the Lord. A small remnant of the pilgrims, who passed the Bosphorus, was permitted to visit the holy sepulchre. Their northern constitution was scorched by the rays, and infected by the vapours, of a Syrian sun. They consumed, with heedless prodigality, their stores of water and provision: their numbers exhausted the inland country: the sea was remote, the Greeks were unfriendly, and the Christians of every sect fled before the voracious and cruel rapine of their brethren. In the dire necessity of famine, they sometimes roasted and devoured the flesh of their infant or adult captives. Among the Turks and Saracens, the idolaters of Europe were rendered more odious by the name and reputation of cannibals; the spies, who introduced themselves into the kitchen of Bohemond, were shown several human bodies turning on the spit: and the artful Norman encouraged a report which increased at the same time the abhorrence and the terror of the infidels.

I have expatiated with pleasure on the first steps of the crusaders, as they paint the manners and character of Europe: but I shall abridge the tedious and uniform narrative of their blind achievements, which were performed by strength and are described by ignorance. From their first station in the neighbourhood of Nicomedia, they advanced in successive divisions; passed the contracted limit of the Greek empire; opened a road through the hills; and commenced, by the siege of his capital, their pious warfare against the Turkish sultan. His kingdom of Roum extended from the Hellespont to the confines of Syria, and barred the pilgrimage of Jerusalem: his name was Kilidge-Arslan, or Soliman, of the race of Seljuk, and son of the first conqueror; and in the defence of a land which the Turks considered as their own, he deserved the praise of his enemies, by whom alone he is known to posterity. . . .

Jerusalem has derived some reputation from the number and importance of her memorable sieges.* It was not till after a long and obstinate contest that Babylon and Rome could prevail against the obstinacy of the people, the craggy ground that might supersede the necessity of fortifications, and the walls and towers that would have fortified the most accessible plain. These obstacles were diminished in the age of the crusades. The bulwarks had been completely destroyed and imperfectly restored: the Jews, their nation and worship, were for ever banished: but nature is less changeable than man, and the site of Jerusalem, though somewhat softened and somewhat removed, was still strong against the assaults of an enemy. By the experience of a recent siege, and a three years' possession, the Saracens of Egypt had been taught to discern, and in some degree to remedy, the defects of a place which religion as well as honour forbade them to resign. Aladin, or Iftikhar, the caliph's lieutenant, was intrusted with the defence: his policy strove to restrain the native Christians by the dread of their own ruin and that of the holy sepulchre; to animate the Moslems by the assurance of temporal and eternal rewards. His garrison is said to have consisted of forty thousand Turks and Arabians; and if he could muster twenty thousand of the inhabitants, it must be

*Having captured the Turkish capital, thus relieving Byzantium, the Crusaders, under Godfrey de Bouillon, set up the Latin Kingdom of Jerusalem. (P.W.)

confessed that the besieged were more numerous than the besieging army.* Had the diminished strength and numbers of the Latins allowed them to grasp the whole circumference of four thousand yards (about two English miles and a half), to what useful purpose should they have descended into the valley of Ben Hinnom and torrent of Kedron, or approached the precipices of the south and east, from whence they had nothing either to hope or fear? Their siege was more reasonably directed against the northern and western sides of the city. Godfrey of Bouillon erected his standard on the first swell of Mount Calvary: to the left, as far as St. Stephen's gate, the line of attack was continued by Tancred and the two Roberts; and Count Raymond established his quarters from the citadel to the foot of Mount Sion, which was no longer included within the precincts of the city. On the fifth day the crusaders made a general assault, in the fanatic hope of battering down the walls without engines, and of scaling them without ladders. By the dint of brutal force they burst the first barrier, but they were driven back with shame and slaughter to the camp: the influence of vision and prophecy was deadened by the too frequent abuse of those pious strategems; and time and labour were found to be the only means of victory. The time of the siege was indeed fulfilled in forty days, but they were forty days of calamity and anguish. A repetition of the old complaint of famine may be imputed in some degree to the voracious or disorderly appetite of the Franks; but the stony soil of Jerusalem is almost destitute of water; the scanty springs and hasty torrents were dry in the summer season: nor was the thirst of the besiegers relieved, as in the city, by the artificial supply of cisterns and aqueducts. The circumjacent country is equally destitute of trees for the uses of shade or building; but some large beams were discovered in a cave by the crusaders: a wood near Sichem, the enchanted grove of Tasso, was cut down: the necessary timber was transported to the camp by the vigour and dexterity of Tancred; and the engines were framed by some Genoese artists, who had fortunately landed in the harbour of Jaffa. Two movable turrets were constructed at the expense, and in the

*The lively scepticism of Voltaire is balanced with sense and erudition by the French author of the Esprit des Croisades (tom. iv. p. 386–388), who observes, that, according to the Arabians, the inhabitants of Jerusalem must have exceeded 200,000; that, in the siege of Titus, Josephus collects 1,300,000 Jews; that they are stated by Tacitus himself at 600,000; and that the largest defalcation that his *accepimus* can justify will still leave them more numerous than the Roman army.

stations, of the duke of Lorraine and the count of Toulouse, and rolled forwards with devout labour, not to the most accessible, but to the most neglected, parts of the fortification. Raymond's tower was reduced to ashes by the fire of the besieged, but his colleague was more vigilant and successful; the enemies were driven by his archers from the rampart; the drawbridge was let down; and on a Friday, at three in the afternoon, the day and hour of the Passion, Godfrey of Bouillon stood victorious on the walls of Jerusalem. His example was followed on every side by the emulation of valour; and about four hundred and sixty years after the conquest of Omar, the holy city was rescued from the Mohammedan yoke. . . .The Latin chiefs proceeded to the election of a king, to guard and govern their conquests in Palestine. Hugh the Great and Stephen of Chartres had retired with some loss of reputation, which they strove to regain by a second crusade and an honourable death. Baldwin was established at Edessa, and Bohemond at Antioch; and two Roberts, the duke of Normandy and the count of Flanders, preferred their fair inheritance in the West to a doubtful competition or a barren sceptre. The jealousy and ambition of Raymond were condemned by his own followers, and the free, the just, the unanimous voice of the army proclaimed Godfrey of Bouillon the first and most worthy of the champions of Christendom. His magnanimity accepted a trust as full of danger as of glory; but in a city where his Saviour had been crowned with thorns, the devout pilgrim rejected the name and ensigns of royalty; and the founder of the kingdom of Jerusalem contented himself with the modest title of Defender and Baron of the Holy Sepulchre. His government of a single year, too short for the public happiness, was interrupted in the first fortnight by a summons to the field, by the approach of the vizir or sultan of Egypt, who had been too slow to prevent, but who was impatient to avenge, the loss of Jerusalem. His total overthrow in the battle of Ascalon sealed the establishment of the Latins in Syria, and signalised the valour of the French princes, who in this action bade a long farewell to the holy wars. Some glory might be derived from the prodigious inequality of numbers, though I shall not count the myriads of horse and foot on the side of the Fatimites; but, except three thousand Ethiopians or Blacks, who were armed with flails or scourges of iron, the barbarians of the South fled on the first onset, and afforded a pleasing comparison between the active valour of the Turks and the sloth and effeminacy of the natives of Egypt. After suspending before the holy sepulchre the sword and standard of the sultan, the new king (he deserves the title) embraced his departing companions, and could retain only with the gallant Tancred three hundred knights, and two thousand foot soldiers, for the defence of Palestine. His sovereignty was soon attacked by a new enemy, the only one against whom Godfrey was a coward. Adhemar, bishop of Puy, who excelled both in council and action, had been swept away in the last plague of Antioch: the remaining ecclesiastics preserved only the pride and avarice of their character; and their seditious clamours had required that the choice of a bishop should precede that of a king. The revenue and jurisdiction of the lawful patriarch were usurped by the Latin clergy: the exclusion of the Greeks and Syrians was justified by the reproach of heresy or schism; and, under the iron yoke of their deliverers, the Oriental Christians regretted the tolerating government of the Arabian caliphs. Daimbert, archbishop of Pisa, had long been trained in the secret policy of Rome: he brought a fleet of his countrymen to the succour of the Holy Land, and was installed, without a competitor, the spiritual and temporal head of the church. The new patriarch immediately grasped the sceptre which had been acquired by the toil and blood of the victorious pilgrims; and both Godfrey and Bohemond submitted to receive at his hands the investiture of their feudal possessions. Nor was this sufficient; Daimbert claimed the immediate property of Jerusalem and Jaffa; instead of a firm and generous refusal, the hero negotiated with the priest; a quarter of either city was ceded to the church; and the modest bishop was satisfied with an eventual reversion of the rest, on the death of Godfrey without children, or on the future acquisition of a new seat at Cairo or Damascus.

Without this indulgence the conqueror would have almost been stripped of his infant kingdom, which consisted only of Jerusalem and Jaffa, with about twenty villages and towns of the adjacent country. Within this narrow verge the Mohammedans were still lodged in some impregnable castles; and the husbandman, the trader, and the pilgrim were exposed to daily and domestic hostility. By the arms of Godfrey himself, and of the two Baldwins, his brother and cousin, who succeeded to the throne, the Latins breathed with more ease and safety; and at length they equalled, in the extent of their dominions, though not in the millions of their subjects, the ancient princes of Judah and Israel. After the reduction of the maritime cities of Laodicea, Tripoli,

Tyre, and Ascalon, which were powerfully assisted by the fleets of Venice, Genoa, and Pisa, and even of Flanders and Norway, the range of sea-coast from Scanderoon to the borders of Egypt was possessed by the Christian pilgrims. If the prince of Antioch disclaimed his supremacy, the counts of Edessa and Tripoli owned themselves the vassals of the king of Jerusalem: the Latins reigned beyond the Euphrates; and the four cities of Hems, Hamah, Damascus, and Aleppo were the only relics of the Mohammedan conquests in Syria. The laws and language, the manners and titles, of the French nation and Latin church, were introduced into these transmarine colonies. According to the feudal jurisprudence, the principal states and subordinate baronies descended in the line of male and female succession: but the children of the first conquerors, a motley and degenerate race, were dissolved by the luxury of the climate; the arrival of new crusaders from Europe was a doubtful hope and a casual event. The service of the feudal tenures was performed by six hundred and sixty-six knights, who might expect the aid of two hundred more under the banner of the count of Tripoli; and each knight was attended to the field by four squires or archers on horseback. Five thousand and seventy-five *serjeants,* most probably foot-soldiers, were supplied by the churches and cities; and the whole legal militia of the kingdom could not exceed eleven thousand men, a slender defence against the surrounding myriads of Saracens and Turks.* But the firmest bulwark of Jerusalem was founded on the knights of the Hospital of St. John,† and of the temple of Solomon; on the strange association of a monastic and military life, which fanaticism might suggest, but which policy must approve. The flower of the nobility of Europe aspired to wear the cross, and to profess the vows, of these respectable orders; their spirit and discipline were immortal; and the speedy donation of twenty-eight thousand farms, or manors,** enabled them to support a regular force of cavalry and infantry for the defence of Palestine. The austerity of the convent soon evaporated in the exercise of arms: the world was scandalised

*Yet on great emergencies . . . the barons brought a voluntary aid; decentem comitivam militum juxta statum suum.

†William of Tyre . . . relates the ignoble origin and early insolence of the Hospitalers, who soon deserted their humble patron, St. John the Eleemosynary, for the more august character of St. John the Baptist . . . They assumed the profession of arms about the year 1120; the Hospital was *mater;* the Temple *filia;* the Teutonic order was founded A.D. 1190, at the siege of Acre . . .

**Matthew Paris . . . assigns to the Hospitalers 19,000, to the Templars 9000 *maneria,* a word of much higher import . . . in the English than in the French idiom. *Manor* is a lordship, *manoir* a dwelling.

by the pride, avarice, and corruption of these Christian soldiers; their claims of immunity and jurisdiction disturbed the harmony of the church and state; and the public peace was endangered by their jealous emulation. But in their most dissolute period the knights of the hospital and temple maintained their fearless and fanatic character: they neglected to live, but they were prepared to die, in the service of Christ; and the spirit of chivalry, the parent and offspring of the crusades, has been transplanted by this institution from the holy sepulchre to the isle of Malta.

The spirit of freedom, which pervades the feudal institutions, was felt in its strongest energy by the volunteers of the cross, who elected for their chief the most deserving of his peers. Amidst the slaves of Asia, unconscious of the lesson or example, a model of political liberty was introduced; and the laws of the French kingdom are derived from the purest source of equality and justice. Of such laws, the first and indispensable condition is the assent of those whose obedience they require, and for whose benefit they are designed. No sooner had Godfrey of Bouillon accepted the office of supreme magistrate than he solicited the public and private advice of the Latin pilgrims who were the best skilled in the statutes and customs of Europe. From these materials, with the counsel and approbation of the patriarch and barons, of the clergy and laity, Godfrey composed the ASSISE OF JERUSALEM,* a precious monument of feudal jurisprudence. . . .

*The Assises de Jérusalem, in old law French, were printed with Beaumanoir's Coûtumes de Beauvoisis (Bourges and Paris, 1690, in folio), and illustrated by Gaspard Thaumas de la Thaumassière with a comment and glossary. An Italian version had been published in 1535, at Venice, for the use of the kingdom of Cyprus.

PART 10

The Fall of Constantinople *(Chapter LXVIII)*

The failure of the Crusades left the remnants of the Byzantine Empire weaker than ever before—so much so that in 1439 Emperor John Palaeologus agreed to the union of Roman and Eastern Christianity established at the Council of Florence. The union was short-lived, and the Empire was reduced to *hiring* Western mercenaries. On May 29, 1453, after fifty days of siege by 160,000 Turks led by the twenty-three-year-old Mohammed II, Constantinople fell, and Byzantium was no more.

CHAPTER LXVIII

The siege of Constantinople by the Turks attracts our first attention to the person and character of the great destroyer. Mohammed the Second . . . His first education and sentiments were those of a devout Musulman; and as often as he conversed with an infidel he purified his hands and face by the legal rites of ablution. Age and empire appear to have relaxed this narrow bigotry: his aspiring genius disdained to acknowledge a power above his own; and in his looser hours he presumed (it is said) to brand the prophet of Mecca as a robber and impostor. Yet the sultan persevered in a decent reverence for the doctrine and discipline of the Koran: his private indiscretion must have been sacred from the vulgar ear; and we should suspect the credulity of strangers and sectaries, so prone to believe that a mind which is hardened against truth must be armed with superior contempt for absurdity and error. Under the tuition of the most skilful masters Mohammed advanced with an early and rapid progress in the paths of knowledge; and besides his native tongue it is affirmed that he spoke or understood five languages, the Arabic, the Persian, the Chaldæan or Hebrew, the Latin, and the Greek. . . . The history and geography of the world were familiar to his memory: the lives of the heroes of the East, perhaps of the West,* excited his emulation: his skill in astrology is excused by the folly of the times, and supposes some rudiments of mathematical science; and a profane taste for the arts is betrayed in his liberal invitation and reward of the painters of Italy.† But the influence of religion and learning were employed without effect on his savage and licentious nature. I will not transcribe, nor do I firmly believe, the stories of his fourteen pages whose bellies were ripped open in search of a stolen melon, or of the beauteous slave whose head he severed from her body to convince the Janizaries that their master was not the votary of love. His sobriety is attested by the silence of the Turkish annals, which accuse three, and three only, of the Ottoman line of the vice of drunkenness.** But it cannot be denied that his passions were at once furious and inexorable; that in the palace, as in the field, a torrent of blood was spilt on the slightest provocation; and that the noblest of the captive youth were often dishonoured by his unnatural lust. In the Albanian war he studied the lessons, and soon surpassed the example, of his father; and the conquest of two empires, twelve kingdoms, and two hundred cities, a vain and flattering account, is ascribed to his invincible sword. He was doubtless a soldier, and possibly a general; Constantinople has sealed his glory; but if we compare the means, the obstacles, and the achievements, Mohammed the Second must blush to sustain a parallel with Alexander or Timour. Under his command the Ottoman forces were always more numerous than their enemies, yet their progress was bounded by the Euphrates and the Adriatic, and his arms were

*. . . he assiduously studied the lives and actions of Alexander, Augustus, Constantine, and Theodosius. I have read somewhere that Plutarch's Lives were translated by his orders into the Turkish language. If the sultan himself understood Greek, it must have been for the benefit of his subjects. Yet these Lives are a school of freedom as well as of valour.

†The famous Gentile Bellino, whom he had invited from Venice, was dismissed with a chain and collar of gold and a purse of 3000 ducats. With Voltaire I laugh at the foolish story of a slave purposely beheaded to instruct the painter in the action of the muscles. . . .

**These Imperial drunkards were Soliman I., Selim II., and Amurath IV. The sophis of Persia can produce a more regular succession; and in the last age our European travellers were the witnesses and companions of their revels.

checked by Huniades and Scanderbeg, by the Rhodian knights, and by the Persian king.

In the reign of Amurath he twice tasted of royalty, and twice descended from the throne: his tender age was incapable of opposing his father's restoration, but never could he forgive the vizirs who had recommended that salutary measure. His nuptials were celebrated with the daughter of a Turkman emir; and, after a festival of two months, he departed from Adrianople with his bride to reside in the government of Magnesia. Before the end of six weeks he was recalled by a sudden message from the divan which announced the decease of Amurath and the mutinous spirit of the Janizaries. His speed and vigour commanded their obedience: he passed the Hellespont with a chosen guard: and at the distance of a mile from Adrianople the vizirs and emirs, the imams and cadhis, the soldiers and the people, fell prostrate before the new sultan. They affected to weep, they affected to rejoice: he ascended the throne at the age of twenty-one years, and removed the cause of sedition by the death, the inevitable death, of his infant brothers.* The ambassadors of Europe and Asia soon appeared to congratulate his accession and solicit his friendship, and to all he spoke the language of moderation and peace. The confidence of the Greek emperor was revived by the solemn oaths and fair assurances with which he sealed the ratification of the treaty: and a rich domain on the banks of the Strymon was assigned for the annual payment of three hundred thousand aspers, the pension of an Ottoman prince who was detained at his request in the Byzantine court. Yet the neighbours of Mohammed might tremble at the severity with which a youthful monarch reformed the pomp of his father's household: the expenses of luxury were applied to those of ambition, and a useless train of seven thousand falconers was either dismissed from his service or enlisted in his troops. In the first summer of his reign he visited with an army the Asiatic provinces; but after humbling the pride Mohammed accepted the submission of the Caramanian, that he might not be diverted by the smallest obstacle from the execution of his great design.

*Calapin, one of these royal infants, was saved from his cruel brother, and baptised at Rome under the name of Callistus Othomannus. The emperor Frederic III. presented him with an estate in Austria, where he ended his life; and Cuspinian, who in his youth conversed with the aged prince at Vienna, applauds his piety and wisdom . . .

The Mohammedan, and more especially the Turkish casuists, have pronounced that no promise can bind the faithful against the interest and duty of their religion, and that the sultan may abrogate his own treaties and those of his predecessors. The justice and magnanimity of Amurath had scorned this immoral privilege; but his son, though the proudest of men, could stoop from ambition to the basest arts of dissimulation and deceit. Peace was on his lips while war was in his heart: he incessantly sighed for the possession of Constantinople; and the Greeks, by their own indiscretion, afforded the first pretence of the fatal rupture. Instead of labouring to be forgotten, their ambassadors pursued his camp to demand the payment, and even the increase, of their annual stipend: the divan was importuned by their complaints; and the vizir, a secret friend of the Christians, was constrained to deliver the sense of his brethren. "Ye foolish and miserable Romans," said Calil, "we know your devices, and ye are ignorant of your own danger! the scrupulous Amurath is no more; his throne is occupied by a young conqueror whom no laws can bind, and no obstacles can resist: and if you escape from his hands, give praise to the divine clemency, which yet delays the chastisement of your sins. Why do ye seek to affright us by vain and indirect menaces? Release the fugitive Orchan, crown him sultan of Romania, call the Hungarians from beyond the Danube, arm against us the nations of the West, and be assured that you will only provoke and precipitate your ruin." But if the fears of the ambassadors were alarmed by the stern language of the vizir, they were soothed by the courteous audience and friendly speeches of the Ottoman prince; and Mohammed assured them that on his return to Adrianople he would redress the grievances, and consult the true interests of the Greeks. No sooner had he repassed the Hellespont than he issued a mandate to suppress their pension, and to expel their officers from the banks of the Strymon: in this measure he betrayed a hostile mind; and the second order announced, and in some degree commenced, the siege of Constantinople. In the narrow pass of the Bosphorus an Asiatic fortress had formerly been raised by his grandfather; in the opposite situation, on the European side, he resolved to erect a more formidable castle, and a thousand masons were commanded to assemble in the spring on a spot named Asomaton, about five miles from the Greek metropolis. Persuasion is the resource of the feeble; and the feeble can seldom persuade: the ambassadors of the emperor attempted, without success, to divert Mohammed from the execution of his design. They represented that his grandfather had solicited the permission of Manuel to build a castle on his own territories; but that this double fortification, which would command the strait, could only tend to violate the alliance of the nations, to intercept the Latins who traded in the Black Sea, and perhaps to annihilate the subsistence of the city. "I form no enterprise," replied the perfidious sultan, "against the city; but the empire of Constantinople is measured by her walls. Have you forgot the distress to which my father was reduced when you formed a league with the Hungarians, when they invaded our country by land, and the Hellespont was occupied by the French galleys? Amurath was compelled to force the passage of the Bosphorus; and your strength was not equal to your malevolence. I was then a child at Adrianople; the Moslems trembled, and for a while the *Gabours* insulted our disgrace. But when my father had triumphed in the field of Varna, he vowed to erect a fort on the western shore, and that vow it is my duty to accomplish. Have ye the right, have ye the power, to control my actions on my own ground? For that ground *is* my own: as far as the shores of the Bosphorus Asia is inhabited by the Turks, and Europe is deserted by the Romans. Return, and inform your king that the present Ottoman is far different from his predecessors, that *his* resolutions surpass *their* wishes, and that *he* performs more than *they* could resolve. Return in safety; but the next who delivers a similar message may expect to be flayed alive." After this declaration, Constantine, the first of the Greeks in spirit as in rank, had determined to unsheathe the sword, and to resist the approach and establishment of the Turks on the Bosphorus. He was disarmed by the advice of his civil and ecclesiastical ministers, who recommended a system less generous, and even less prudent, than his own, to approve their patience and long-suffering, to brand the Ottoman with the name and guilt of an aggressor, and to depend on chance and time for their own safety, and the destruction of a fort which could not long be maintained in the neighbourhood of a great and populous city. Amidst hope and fear, the fears of the wise and the hopes of the credulous, the winter rolled away; the proper business of each man and each hour was postponed; and the Greeks shut their eyes against the impending danger, till the arrival of the spring and the sultan decided the assurance of their ruin.

Of a master who never forgives, the orders are seldom disobeyed. On the twenty-sixth of March the appointed spot of Asomaton was covered with an active swarm of Turkish artificers; and the materials by sea and land were diligently transported from Europe and Asia. The lime had been burnt in Cataphrygia, the timber was cut down in the woods of Heraclea and Nicomedia, and the stones were dug from the Anatolian quarries. Each of the thousand masons was assisted by two workmen; and a measure of two cubits was marked for their daily task. The fortress was built in a triangular form; each angle was flanked by a strong and massy tower, one on the declivity of the hill, two along the sea-shore; a thickness of twenty-two feet was assigned for the walls, thirty for the towers; and the whole building was covered with a solid platform of lead. Mohammed himself pressed and directed the work with indefatigable ardour: his three vizirs claimed the honour of finishing their respective towers; the zeal of the cadhis emulated that of the Janizaries; the meanest labour was ennobled by the service of God and the sultan; and the diligence of the multitude was quickened by the eye of a despot whose smile was the hope of fortune, and whose frown was the messenger of death. The Greek emperor beheld with terror the irresistible progress of the work, and vainly strove by flattery and gifts to assuage an implacable foe, who sought, and secretly fomented, the slightest occasion of a quarrel. Such occasions must soon and inevitably be found. The ruins of stately churches, and even the marble columns which had been consecrated to Saint Michael the archangel, were employed without scruple by the profane and rapacious Moslems; and some Christians, who presumed to oppose the removal, received from their hands the crown of martyrdom. Constantine had solicited a Turkish guard to protect the fields and harvests of his subjects: the guard was fixed; but their first order was to allow free pasture to the mules and horses of the camp, and to defend their brethren if they should be molested by the natives. The retinue of an Ottoman chief had left their horses to pass the night among the ripe corn: the damage was felt, the insult was resented, and several of both nations were slain in a tumultuous conflict. Mohammed listened with joy to the complaint; and a detachment was commanded to exterminate the guilty village: the guilty had fled; but forty innocent and unsuspecting reapers were massacred by the soldiers. Till this provocation Constantinople had been open to the visits of commerce and curiosity: on the first alarm the gates were shut; but the emperor, still anxious for peace, released on the third day his Turkish captives,* and expressed, in a last message, the firm resignation of a Christian and a soldier. "Since neither oaths, nor treaty, nor submission can secure peace, pursue," said he to Mohammed, "your impious warfare. My trust is in God alone: if it should please him to mollify your heart, I shall rejoice in the happy change; if he delivers the city into your hands, I submit without a murmur to his holy will. But until the Judge of the earth shall pronounce between us, it is my duty to live and die in the defence of my people." The sultan's answer was hostile and decisive: his fortifications were completed; and before his departure for Adrianople he stationed a vigilant Aga and four hundred Janizaries to levy a tribute on the ships of every nation that should pass within the reach of their cannon. A Venetian vessel, refusing obedience to the new lords of the Bosphorus, was sunk with a single bullet. The master and thirty sailors escaped in the boat; but they were dragged in chains to the *Porte:* the chief was impaled, his companions were beheaded; and the historian Ducas beheld, at Demotica, their bodies exposed to the wild beasts. The siege of Constantinople was deferred till the ensuing spring; but an Ottoman army marched into the Morea to divert the force of the brothers of Constantine. At this era of calamity one of these princes, the despot Thomas, was blessed or afflicted with the birth of a son—"the last heir," says the plaintive Phranza, "of the last spark of the Roman empire."†

The Greeks and the Turks passed an anxious and sleepless winter: the former were kept awake by their fears, the latter by their hopes; both by the preparations of defence and attack; and the two emperors, who had the most to lose or to gain, were the most deeply affected by the national sentiment. In Mohammed that sentiment was inflamed by the ardour of his youth and temper: he amused his leisure with building at Adrianople** the lofty palace of Jehan Numa (the watchtower of the world); but his serious thoughts were irrevocably bent on the conquest of the city of Cæsar. At the dead of night, about the

*Among these were some pages of Mohammed, so conscious of his inexorable rigour, that they begged to lose their heads in the city unless they could return before sunset.

†The strong expression was inspired by his feelings.

**. . . The sultan was either doubtful of his conquest or ignorant of the superior merits of Constantinople. A city or a kingdom may sometimes be ruined by the Imperial fortune of their sovereign.

second watch, he started from his bed, and commanded the instant attendance of his prime vizir. The message, the hour, the prince, and his own situation, alarmed the guilty conscience of Calil Basha; who had possessed the confidence, and advised the restoration, of Amurath. On the accession of the son the vizir was confirmed in his office and the appearances of favour; but the veteran statesman was not insensible that he trod on a thin and slippery ice, which might break under his footsteps and plunge him in the abyss. His friendship for the Christians, which might be innocent under the late reign, had stigmatised him with the name of Gabour Ortachi, or foster-brother of the infidels; and his avarice entertained a venal and treasonable correspondence, which was detected and punished after the conclusion of the war. On receiving the royal mandate, he embraced, perhaps for the last time, his wife and children; filled a cup with pieces of gold, hastened to the palace, adored the sultan, and offered, according to the Oriental custom, the slight tribute of his duty and gratitude.* "It is not my wish," said Mohammed, "to resume my gifts, but rather to heap and multiply them on thy head. In my turn I ask a present far more valuable and important—Constantinople." As soon as the vizir had recovered from his surprise, "The same God," said he, "who has already given thee so large a portion of the Roman empire, will not deny the remnant and the capital. His providence, and thy power, assure thy success; and myself, with the rest of thy faithful slaves, will sacrifice our lives and fortunes."—"Lala" (or preceptor), continued the sultan, "do you see this pillow? all the night, in my agitation, I have pulled it on one side and the other; I have risen from my bed, again have I lain down, yet sleep has not visited these weary eyes. Beware of the gold and silver of the Romans: in arms we are superior; and with the aid of God, and the prayers of the prophet, we shall speedily become masters of Constantinople." To sound the disposition of his soldiers, he often wandered through the streets alone and in disguise; and it was fatal to discover the sultan when he wished to escape from the vulgar eye. His hours were spent in delineating the plan of the hostile city; in debating with his generals and engineers on what spot he should erect his batteries; on which side he should assault the walls;

*The Oriental custom of never appearing without gifts before a sovereign or a superior is of high antiquity, and seems analogous with the idea of sacrifice, still more ancient and universal. . . .

where he should spring his mines; to what place he should apply his scaling-ladders: and the exercises of the day repeated and proved the lucubrations of the night.

Among the implements of destruction, he studied with peculiar care the recent and tremendous discovery of the Latins; and his artillery surpassed whatever had yet appeared in the world. . . . A foundry was established at Adrianople: the metal was prepared; and at the end of three months . . . a piece of brass ordnance of stupendous and almost incredible magnitude [was produced]; a measure of twelve palms is assigned to the bore; and the stone bullet weighed above six hundred pounds. . . .*

While Mohammed threatened the capital of the East, the Greek emperor implored with fervent prayers the assistance of earth and Heaven. But the invisible powers were deaf to his supplications; and Christendom beheld with indifference the fall of Constantinople, while she derived at least some promise of supply from the jealous and temporal policy of the sultan of Egypt. Some states were too weak, and others too remote; by some the danger was considered as imaginary, by others as inevitable: the Western princes were involved in their endless and domestic quarrels; and the Roman pontiff was exasperated by the falsehood or obstinacy of the Greeks. Instead of employing in their favour the arms and treasures of Italy, Nicholas the Fifth had foretold their approaching ruin; and his honour was engaged in the accomplishment of his prophecy. Perhaps he was softened by the last extremity of their distress; but his compassion was tardy; his efforts were faint and unavailing; and Constantinople had fallen before the squadrons of Genoa and Venice could sail from their harbours. Even the princes of the Morea and of the Greek islands affected a cold neutrality: the Genoese colony of Galata negotiated a private treaty; and the sultan indulged them in the delusive hope that by his clemency they might survive the ruin of the empire. A plebeian crowd and some Byzantine nobles basely withdrew from the danger of their country; and the avarice of the rich denied the emperor, and reserved for the Turks, the secret treasures which might have raised in their defence

*The Attic talent weighed about sixty minæ, or avoirdupois pounds . . . ; but among the modern Greeks that classic appellation was extended to a weight of one hundred, or one hundred and twenty-five pounds. . . . Leonardus Chiensis measured the ball or stone of the *second* cannon: Lapidem, qui palmis undecim ex meis ambibat in gyro.

whole armies of mercenaries. The indigent and solitary prince prepared however to sustain his formidable adversary; but if his courage were equal to the peril, his strength was inadequate to the contest. In the beginning of the spring the Turkish vanguard swept the towns and villages as far as the gates of Constantinople: submission was spared and protected; whatever presumed to resist was exterminated with fire and sword. The Greek places on the Black Sea, Mesembria, Acheloum, and Bizon, surrendered on the first summons; Selymbria alone deserved the honours of a siege or blockade; and the bold inhabitants, while they were invested by land, launched their boats, pillaged the opposite coast of Cyzicus, and sold their captives in the public market. But on the approach of Mohammed himself all was silent and prostrate: he first halted at the distance of five miles; and, from thence advancing in battle array, planted before the gate of St. Romanus the Imperial standard; and on the sixth day of April formed the memorable siege of Constantinople.

The troops of Asia and Europe extended on the right and left from the Propontis to the harbour; the Janizaries in the front were stationed before the sultan's tent; the Ottoman line was covered by a deep intrenchment; and a subordinate army enclosed the suburb of Galata, and watched the doubtful faith of the Genoese. The inquisitive Philelphus, who resided in Greece about thirty years before the siege, is confident that all the Turkish forces of any name or value could not exceed the number of sixty thousand horse and twenty thousand foot; and he upbraids the pusillanimity of the nations who had tamely yielded to a handful of barbarians. Such indeed might be the regular establishment of the *Capiculi** the troops of the Porte who marched with the prince, and were paid from his royal treasury. But the bashaws, in their respective governments, maintained or levied a provincial militia; many lands were held by a military tenure; many volunteers were attracted by the hope of spoil; and the sound of the holy trumpet invited a swarm of hungry and fearless fanatics, who might contribute at least to multiply the terrors, and in a first attack to blunt the swords of the Christians. The whole mass of the Turkish powers is magnified by Ducas, Chalcocondyles, and Leonard of Chios, to the amount of three or four hundred thousand men; but Phranza was a less remote and more accurate judge; and his precise definition of two

*The palatine troops are styled *Capiculi;* the provincials, *Seratculi* . . .

hundred and fifty-eight thousand does not exceed the measure of experience and probability. The navy of the besiegers was less formidable: the Propontis was overspread with three hundred and twenty sail; but of these no more than eighteen could be rated as galleys of war; and the far greater part must be degraded to the condition of store-ships and transports, which poured into the camp fresh supplies of men, ammunition, and provisions. In her last decay Constantinople was still peopled with more than a hundred thousand inhabitants; but these numbers are found in the accounts, not of war, but of captivity; and they mostly consisted of mechanics, of priests, of women, and of men devoid of that spirit which even women have sometimes exerted for the common safety. I can suppose, I could almost excuse, the reluctance of subjects to serve on a distant frontier, at the will of a tyrant; but the man who dares not expose his life in the defence of his children and his property has lost in society the first and most active energies of nature. By the emperor's command a particular inquiry had been made through the streets and houses, how many of the citizens, or even of the monks, were able and willing to bear arms for their country. The lists were intrusted to Phranza; and after a diligent addition he informed his master, with grief and surprise, that the national defence was reduced to four thousand nine hundred and seventy *Romans.* Between Constantine and his faithful minister this comfortless secret was preserved; and a sufficient proportion of shields, crossbows, and muskets, was distributed from the arsenal to the city bands. They derived some accession from a body of two thousand strangers, under the command of John Justiniani, a noble Genoese; a liberal donative was advanced to these auxiliaries; and a princely recompense, the isle of Lemnos, was promised to the valour and victory of their chief. A strong chain was drawn across the mouth of the harbour: it was supported by some Greek and Italian vessels of war and merchandise; and the ships of every Christian nation, that successively arrived from Candia and the Black Sea, were detained for the public service. Against the powers of the Ottoman empire, a city of the extent of thirteen, perhaps of sixteen, miles was defended by a scanty garrison of seven or eight thousand soldiers. Europe and Asia were open to the besiegers; but the strength and provisions of the Greeks must sustain a daily decrease; nor could they indulge the expectation of any foreign succour or supply.

The primitive Romans would have drawn their swords in the resolution of death or conquest. The primitive Christians might have embraced each other, and awaited in patience and charity the stroke of martyrdom. But the Greeks of Constantinople were animated only by the spirit of religion, and the spirit was productive only of animosity and discord. Before his death the emperor John Palæologus had renounced the unpopular measure of a union with the Latins; nor was the idea revived till the distress of his brother Constantine imposed a last trial of flattery and dissimulation. With the demand of temporal aid his ambassadors were instructed to mingle the assurance of spiritual obedience: his neglect of the church was excused by the urgent cares of the state; and his orthodox wishes solicited the presence of a Roman legate. The Vatican had been too often deluded; yet the signs of repentance could not decently be overlooked; a legate was more easily granted than an army; and about six months before the final destruction, the cardinal Isidore of Russia appeared in that character with a retinue of priests and soldiers. The emperor saluted him as a friend and father; respectfully listened to his public and private sermons; and with the most obsequious of the clergy and laymen subscribed the act of union, as it had been ratified in the council of Florence. On the twelfth of December the two nations, in the church of St. Sophia, joined in the communion of sacrifice and prayer; and the names of the two pontiffs were solemnly commemorated; the names of Nicholas the Fifth, the vicar of Christ, and of the patriarch Gregory, who had been driven into exile by a rebellious people.

But the dress and language of the Latin priest who officiated at the altar were an object of scandal; and it was observed with horror that he consecrated a cake or wafer of *unleavened* bread, and poured cold water into the cup of the sacrament. A national historian acknowledges with a blush that none of his countrymen, not the emperor himself, were sincere in this occasional conformity. Their hasty and unconditional submission was palliated by a promise of future revisal; but the best, or the worst, of their excuses was the confession of their own perjury. When they were pressed by the reproaches of their honest brethren, "Have patience," they whispered, "have patience till God shall have delivered the city from the great dragon who seeks to devour us. You shall then perceive whether we are truly reconciled with the Azymites." But patience is not the attribute of zeal; nor can the arts of a court be adapted to the freedom and violence of popular enthusiasm. From the dome of St. Sophia the inhabitants of either sex, and of every degree, rushed in crowds to the cell of the monk Gennadius,* to consult the oracle of the church. The holy man was invisible; entranced, as it should seem, in deep meditation, or divine rapture: but he had exposed on the door of his cell a speaking tablet; and they successively withdrew, after reading these tremendous words: "O miserable Romans, why will ye abandon the truth; and why, instead of confiding in God, will ye put your trust in the Italians? In losing your faith you will lose your city. Have mercy on me, O Lord! I protest in thy presence that I am innocent of the crime. O miserable Romans, consider, pause, and repent. At the same moment that you renounce the religion of your fathers, by embracing impiety, you submit to a foreign servitude." According to the advice of Gennadius, the religious virgins, as pure as angels, and as proud as demons, rejected the act of union, and abjured all communion with the present and future associates of the Latins; and their example was applauded and imitated by the greatest part of the clergy and people. From the monastery the devout Greeks dispersed themselves in the taverns; drank confusion to the slaves of the pope; emptied their glasses in honour of the image of the holy Virgin; and besought her to defend against Mohammed the city which she had formerly saved from Chosroes and the Chagan. In the double intoxication of zeal and wine, they valiantly exclaimed, "What occasion have we for succour, or union, or Latins? far from us be the worship of the Azymites!" During the winter that preceded the Turkish conquest the nation was distracted by this epidemical frenzy; and the season of Lent, the approach of Easter, instead of breathing charity and love, served only to fortify the obstinacy and influence of the zealots. The confessors scrutinised and alarmed the conscience of their votaries, and a rigorous penance was imposed on those who had received the communion from a priest who had given an express or tacit consent to the union. His service at the altar propagated the infection to the mute and simple spectators of the ceremony: they forfeited, by the impure spectacle, the virtue of the sacerdotal character; nor was it lawful, even in danger of sudden death, to invoke the assistance of their prayers or absolution. No sooner had the church of St. Sophia been polluted by the Latin sac-

*His primitive and secular name was George Scholarius, which he changed for that of Gennadius, either when he became a monk or a patriarch. . . .

rifice than it was deserted as a Jewish synagogue, or a heathen temple, by the clergy and people; and a vast and gloomy silence prevailed in that venerable dome, which had so often smoked with a cloud of incense, blazed with innumerable lights, and resounded with the voice of prayer and thanksgiving. The Latins were the most odious of heretics and infidels; and the first minister of the empire, the great duke, was heard to declare that he had rather behold in Constantinople the turban of Mohammed than the pope's tiara or a cardinal's hat. A sentiment so unworthy of Christians and patriots was familiar and fatal to the Greeks: the emperor was deprived of the affection and support of his subjects; and their native cowardice was sanctified by resignation to the divine decree or the visionary hope of a miraculous deliverance.

Of the triangle which composes the figure of Constantinople the two sides along the sea were made inaccessible to an enemy; the Propontis by nature, and the harbour by art. Between the two waters, the basis of the triangle, the land side was protected by a double wall and a deep ditch of the depth of one hundred feet. Against this line of fortification, which Phranza, an eyewitness, prolongs to the measure of six miles,* the Ottomans directed their principal attack; and the emperor, after distributing the service and command of the most perilous stations, undertook the defence of the external wall. In the first days of the siege the Greek soldiers descended into the ditch, or sallied into the field; but they soon discovered that, in the proportion of their numbers, one Christian was of more value than twenty Turks; and, after these bold preludes, they were prudently content to maintain the rampart with their missile weapons. Nor should this prudence be accused of pusillanimity. The nation was indeed pusillanimous and base; but the last Constantine deserves the name of a hero: his noble band of volunteers was inspired with Roman virtue; and the foreign auxiliaries supported the honour of the Western chivalry. The incessant volleys of lances and arrows were accompanied with the smoke, the sound, and the fire of their musketry and cannon. Their small arms discharged at the same time either five, or even ten, balls of lead, of the size of a walnut; and, according to the closeness of the ranks and the force of the powder,

*We are obliged to reduce the Greek miles to the smallest measure which is preserved in the wersts of Russia, of 547 French *toises,* and of 104 2/5 to a degree. The six miles of Phranza do not exceed four English miles. . . .

several breastplates and bodies were transpierced by the same shot. But the Turkish approaches were soon sunk in trenches or covered with ruins. Each day added to the science of the Christians; but their inadequate stock of gunpowder was wasted in the operations of each day. Their ordnance was not powerful either in size or number; and if they possessed some heavy cannon, they feared to plant them on the walls, lest the aged structure should be shaken and overthrown by the explosion. The same destructive secret had been revealed to the Moslems; by whom it was employed with the superior energy of zeal, riches, and despotism. The great cannon of Mohammed has been separately noticed; an important and visible object in the history of the times: but that enormous engine was flanked by two fellows almost of equal magnitude: the long order of the Turkish artillery was pointed against the walls; fourteen batteries thundered at once on the most accessible places; and of one of these it is ambiguously expressed that it was mounted with one hundred and thirty guns, or that it discharged one hundred and thirty bullets. Yet in the power and activity of the sultan we may discern the infancy of the new science. Under a master who counted the moments the great cannon could be loaded and fired no more than seven times in one day. The heated metal unfortunately burst; several workmen were destroyed, and the skill of an artist was admired who bethought himself of preventing the danger and the accident, by pouring oil, after each explosion, into the mouth of the cannon.

The first random shots were productive of more sound than effect; and it was by the advice of a Christian that the engineers were taught to level their aim against the two opposite sides of the salient angles of a bastion. However imperfect, the weight and repetition of the fire made some impression on the walls; and the Turks, pushing their approaches to the edge of the ditch, attempted to fill the enormous chasm and to build a road to the assault. Innumerable fascines, and hogsheads, and trunks of trees, were heaped on each other; and such was the impetuosity of the throng, that the foremost and the weakest were pushed headlong down the precipice and instantly buried under the accumulated mass. To fill the ditch was the toil of the besiegers; to clear away the rubbish was the safety of the besieged; and, after a long and bloody conflict, the web that had been woven in the day was still unravelled in the night. The next resource of Mohammed was the practice of mines; but the soil was rocky; in every attempt he was stopped and undermined by the Christian engineers; nor had the art been yet invented of replenishing those subterraneous passages with gunpowder and blowing whole towers and cities into the air. A circumstance that distinguishes the siege of Constantinople is the reunion of the ancient and modern artillery. The cannon were intermingled with the mechanical engines for casting stones and darts; the bullet and the battering-ram were directed against the same walls; nor had the discovery of gunpowder superseded the use of the liquid and unextinguishable fire. A wooden turret of the largest size was advanced on rollers: this portable magazine of ammunition and fascines was protected by a threefold covering of bulls' hides; incessant volleys were securely discharged from the loopholes; in the front three doors were contrived for the alternate sally and retreat of the soldiers and workmen. They ascended by a staircase to the upper platform, and, as high as the level of that platform, a scaling-ladder could be raised by pulleys to form a bridge and grapple with the adverse rampart. By these various arts of annoyance, some as new as they were pernicious to the Greeks, the tower of St. Romanus was at length overturned: after a severe struggle the Turks were repulsed from the breach and interrupted by darkness; but they trusted that with the return of light they should renew the attack with fresh vigour and decisive success. Of this pause of action, this interval of hope, each moment was improved by the activity of the emperor and Justiniani, who passed the night on the spot, and urged the labours which involved the safety of the church and city. At the dawn of day the impatient sultan perceived, with astonishment and grief, that his wooden turret had been reduced to ashes: the ditch was cleared and restored, and the tower of St. Romanus was again strong and entire. He deplored the failure of his design, and uttered a profane exclamation, that the word of the thirty-seven thousand prophets should not have compelled him to believe that such a work, in so short a time, could have been accomplished by the infidels.

The generosity of the Christian princes was cold and tardy; but in the first apprehension of a siege Constantine had negotiated, in the isles of the Archipelago, the Morea, and Sicily, the most indispensable supplies. As early as the beginning of April, five great ships, equipped for merchandise and war, would have sailed from the harbour of Chios, had not the wind blown obstinately from the north. One of these ships bore the Imperial flag; the remaining four belonged to the Genoese; and they were laden with wheat and barley, with wine, oil, and vegetables, and, above all, with soldiers and mariners, for the service of the capital. After a tedious delay a gentle breeze, and on the second day a strong gale from the south, carried them through the Hellespont and the Propontis; but the city was already invested by sea and land, and the Turkish fleet, at the entrance of the Bosphorus, was stretched from shore to shore, in the form of a crescent, to intercept, or at least to repel, these bold auxiliaries. The reader who has present to his mind the geographical picture of Constantinople will conceive and admire the greatness of the spectacle. The five Christian ships continued to advance with joyful shouts, and a full press both of sails and oars, against the hostile fleet of three hundred vessels; and the rampart, the camp, the coasts of Europe and Asia, were lined with innumerable spectators, who anxiously awaited the event of this momentous succour. At the first view that event could not appear doubtful; the superiority of the Moslems was beyond all measure or account, and, in a calm, their numbers and valour must inevitably have prevailed. But their hasty and imperfect navy had been created, not by the genius of the people, but by the will of the sultan: in the height of their prosperity the Turks have acknowledged that, if God had given them the earth, he had left the sea to the infidels; and a series of defeats, a rapid progress of decay, has established the truth of their modest confession. Except eighteen galleys of some force, the rest of their fleet consisted of open boats, rudely constructed and awkwardly managed, crowded with troops, and destitute of cannon; and since courage arises in a great measure from the consciousness of strength, the bravest of the Janizaries might tremble on a new element. In the Christian squadron five stout and lofty ships were guided by skilful pilots, and manned with the veterans of Italy and Greece, long practised in the arts and perils of the sea. Their weight was directed to sink or scatter the weak obstacles that impeded their passage: their artillery swept the waters; their liquid fire was poured on the heads of the adversaries, who, with the design of boarding, presumed to approach them; and the winds and waves are always on the side of the ablest navigators. In this conflict the Imperial vessel, which had been almost overpowered, was rescued by the Genoese; but the Turks, in a distant and a closer attack, were twice repulsed with considerable loss. Mohammed himself sat on horseback on the beach, to encourage their valour by his voice and presence, by the promise of reward, and by fear more potent than the fear of the enemy. The passions of his soul, and even the gestures of his body, seemed to imitate the actions of the combatants; and, as if he had been the lord of nature, he spurred his horse with a fearless and impotent effort into the sea. His loud reproaches, and the clamours of the camp, urged the Ottomans to a third attack, more fatal and bloody than the two former; and I must repeat, though I cannot credit, the evidence of Phranza, who affirms, from their own mouth, that they lost above twelve thousand men in the slaughter of the day. They fled in disorder to the shores of Europe and Asia, while the Christian squadron, triumphant and unhurt, steered along the Bosphorus, and securely anchored within the chain of the harbour. In the confidence of victory, they boasted that the whole Turkish power must have yielded to their arms; but the admiral, or captain bashaw, found some consolation for a painful wound in his eye, by representing that accident as the cause of his defeat. Baltha Ogli was a renegade of the race of the Bulgarian princes: his military character was tainted with the unpopular vice of avarice; and under the despotism of the prince or people, misfortune is a sufficient evidence of guilt. His rank and services were annihilated by the displeasure of Mohammed. In the royal presence, the captain bashaw was extended on the ground by four slaves, and received one hundred strokes with a golden rod: his death had been pronounced, and he adored the clemency of the sultan, who was satisfied with the milder punishment of confiscation and exile. The introduction of this supply revived the hopes of the Greeks, and accused the supineness of their Western allies. Amidst the deserts of Anatolia and the rocks of Palestine, the millions of the crusades had buried themselves in a voluntary and inevitable grave; but the situation of the Imperial city was strong against her enemies, and accessible to her friends; and a rational and moderate armament of the maritime states might have saved the relics of the Roman name, and maintained a Christian fortress in the heart of the Ottoman empire. Yet this was the sole and feeble attempt for the deliverance of Constantinople: the more distant powers were insensible of its danger; and the ambassador of Hungary, or at least of Huniades, resided in the Turkish camp, to remove the fears and to direct the operations of the sultan.

It was difficult for the Greeks to penetrate the secret of the divan; yet the Greeks are persuaded that a resistance so obstinate and surprising had fatigued the perserverance of Mohammed. He began to meditate a retreat; and the siege would have been speedily raised, if the ambition and jealousy of the second vizir had not opposed the perfidious advice of Calil Bashaw, who still maintained a secret correspondence with the Byzantine court. The reduction of the city appeared to be hopeless, unless a double attack could be made from the harbour as well as from the land; but the harbour was inaccessible: an impenetrable chain was now defended by eight large ships, more than twenty of a smaller size, with several galleys and sloops; and, instead of forcing this barrier, the Turks might apprehend a naval sally and a second encounter in the open sea. In this perplexity the genius of Mohammed conceived and executed a plan of a bold and marvellous cast, of transporting by land his lighter vessels and military stores from the Bosphorus into the higher part of the harbour. The distance is about ten miles; the ground is uneven, and was overspread with thickets; and, as the road must be opened behind the suburb of Galata, their free passage or total destruction must depend on the option of the Genoese. But these selfish merchants were ambitious of the favour of being the last devoured, and the deficiency of art was supplied by the strength of obedient myriads. A level way was covered with a broad platform of strong and solid planks; and to render them more slippery and smooth, they were anointed with the fat of sheep and oxen. Fourscore light galleys and brigantines of fifty and thirty oars were disembarked on the Bosphorus shore, arranged successively on rollers, and drawn forwards by the power of men and pulleys. Two guides or pilots were stationed at the helm and the prow of each vessel: the sails were unfurled to the winds, and the labour was cheered by song and acclamation. In the course of a single night this Turkish fleet painfully climbed the hill, steered over the plain, and was launched from the declivity into the shallow waters of the harbour, far above the molestation of the deeper vessels of the Greeks. The real importance of this operation was magnified by the consternation and confidence which it inspired; but the notorious, unquestionable fact was displayed before the eyes, and is recorded by the pens, of the two nations.* A similar stratagem had been repeatedly practised by the ancients; the Ottoman galleys (I must again repeat) should be consid-

*The unanimous testimony of the four Greeks is confirmed by Cantemir . . . from the Turkish annals; but I could wish to contract the distance of *ten* miles, and to prolong the term of *one* night.

ered as large boats; and, if we compare the magnitude and the distance, the obstacles and the means, the boasted miracle has perhaps been equalled by the industry of our own times.* As soon as Mohammed had occupied the upper harbour with a fleet and army, he constructed in the narrowest part a bridge, or rather mole, of fifty cubits in breadth and one hundred in length: it was formed of casks and hogsheads, joined with rafters, linked with iron, and covered with a solid floor. On this floating battery he planted one of his largest cannon, while the fourscore galleys, with troops and scaling-ladders, approached the most accessible side, which had formerly been stormed by the Latin conquerors. The indolence of the Christians has been accused for not destroying these unfinished works; but their fire, by a superior fire, was controlled and silenced; nor were they wanting in a nocturnal attempt to burn the vessels as well as the bridge of the sultan. His vigilance prevented their approach: their foremost galliots were sunk or taken; forty youths, the bravest of Italy and Greece, were inhumanly massacred at his command; nor could the emperor's grief be assuaged by the just though cruel retaliation of exposing from the walls the heads of two hundred and sixty Musulman captives. After a siege of forty days the fate of Constantinople could no longer be averted. The diminutive garrison was exhausted by a double attack: the fortifications, which had stood for ages against hostile violence, were dismantled on all sides by the Ottoman cannon; many breaches were opened, and near the gate of St. Romanus four towers had been levelled with the ground. For the payment of his feeble and mutinous troops, Constantine was compelled to despoil the churches with the promise of a fourfold restitution; and his sacrilege offered a new reproach to the enemies of the union. A spirit of discord impaired the remnant of the Christian strength: the Genoese and Venetian auxiliaries asserted the pre-eminence of their respective service; and Justiniani and the great duke, whose ambition was not extinguished by the common danger, accused each other of treachery and cowardice.

During the siege of Constantinople the words of peace and capitulation had been sometimes pronounced; and several embassies had passed between the camp and the city. The Greek emperor was humbled by adversity; and would have yielded to any terms compatible

*I particularly allude to our own embarkations on the lakes of Canada in the years 1776 and 1777, so great in the labour, so fruitless in the event. . . .

with religion and royalty. The Turkish sultan was desirous of sparing the blood of his soldiers; still more desirous of securing for his own use the Byzantine treasures; and he accomplished a sacred duty in presenting to the *Gabours* the choice of circumcision, of tribute, or of death. The avarice of Mohammed might have been satisfied with an annual sum of one hundred thousand ducats; but his ambition grasped the capital of the East: to the prince he offered a rich equivalent, to the people a free toleration, or a safe departure: but after some fruitless treaty, he declared his resolution of finding either a throne or a grave under the walls of Constantinople. A sense of honour, and the fear of universal reproach, forbade Palæologus to resign the city into the hands of the Ottomans; and he determined to abide the last extremities of war. Several days were employed by the sultan in the preparations of the assault; and a respite was granted by his favourite science of astrology, which had fixed on the twenty-ninth of May as the fortunate and fatal hour. On the evening of the twenty-seventh he issued his final orders; assembled in his presence the military chiefs; and dispersed his heralds through the camp to proclaim the duty and the motives of the perilous enterprise. Fear is the first principle of a despotic government; and his menaces were expressed in the Oriental style, that the fugitives and deserters, had they the wings of a bird, should not escape from his inexorable justice. The greatest part of his bashaws and Janizaries were the offspring of Christian parents: but the glories of the Turkish name were perpetuated by successive adoption; and in the gradual change of individuals, the spirit of a legion, a regiment, or an *oda,* is kept alive by imitation and discipline. In this holy warfare the Moslems were exhorted to purify their minds with prayer, their bodies with seven ablutions; and to abstain from food till the close of the ensuing day. A crowd of dervishes visited the tents, to instil the desire of martyrdom, and the assurance of spending an immortal youth amidst the rivers and gardens of paradise, and in the embraces of the black-eyed virgins. Yet Mohammed principally trusted to the efficacy of temporal and visible rewards. A double pay was promised to the victorious troops; "The city and the buildings," said Mohammed, "are mine; but I resign to your valour the captives and the spoil, the treasures of gold and beauty; be rich and be happy. Many are the provinces of my empire: the intrepid soldier who first ascends the walls of Constantinople shall be rewarded with the government of the fairest and most wealthy; and my gratitude shall accumulate his honours and fortunes above the measure of his own hopes." Such various and potent motives diffused among the Turks a general ardour, regardless of life and impatient for action: the camp re-echoed with the Moslem shouts of "God is God: there is but one God, and Mohammed is the apostle of God;" and the sea and land, from Galata to the seven towers, were illuminated by the blaze of their nocturnal fires.

Far different was the state of the Christians; who, with loud and impotent complaints, deplored the guilt, or the punishment, of their sins. The celestial image of the Virgin had been exposed in solemn procession; but their divine patroness was deaf to their entreaties: they accused the obstinacy of the emperor for refusing a timely surrender; anticipated the horrors of their fate; and sighed for the repose and security of Turkish servitude. The noblest of the Greeks, and the bravest of the allies, were summoned to the palace, to prepare them, on the evening of the twenty-eighth, for the duties and dangers of the general assault. The last speech of Palæologus was the funeral oration of the Roman empire: he promised, he conjured, and he vainly attempted to infuse the hope which was extinguished in his own mind. In this world all was comfortless and gloomy; and neither the Gospel nor the church have proposed any conspicuous recompense to the heroes who fall in the service of their country. But the example of their prince, and the confinement of a siege, had armed these warriors with the courage of despair; and the pathetic scene is described by the feelings of the historian Phranza, who was himself present at this mournful assembly. They wept, they embraced: regardless of their families and fortunes, they devoted their lives; and each commander, departing to his station, maintained all night a vigilant and anxious watch on the rampart. The emperor, and some faithful companions, entered the dome of St. Sophia, which in a few hours was to be converted into a mosque; and devoutly received, with tears and prayers, the sacrament of the holy communion. He reposed some moments in the palace, which resounded with cries and lamentations; solicited the pardon of all whom he might have injured;* and mounted

*This abasement, which devotion has sometimes extorted from dying princes, is an improvement of the Gospel doctrine of the forgiveness of injuries: it is more easy to forgive 490 times than once to ask pardon of an inferior.

on horseback to visit the guards, and explore the motions of the enemy. The distress and fall of the last Constantine are more glorious than the long prosperity of the Byzantine Cæsars.

In the confusion of darkness an assailant may sometimes succeed; but in this great and general attack, the military judgment and astrological knowledge of Mohammed advised him to expect the morning, the memorable twenty-ninth of May, in the fourteen hundred and fifty-third year of the Christian era. The preceding night had been strenuously employed: the troops, the cannon, and the fascines were advanced to the edge of the ditch, which in many parts presented a smooth and level passage to the breach; and his fourscore galleys almost touched, with the prows and their scaling ladders, the less defensible walls of the harbour. Under pain of death, silence was enjoined; but the physical laws of motion and sound are not obedient to discipline or fear: each individual might suppress his voice and measure his footsteps; but the march and labour of thousands must inevitably produce a strange confusion of dissonant clamours, which reached the ears of the watchmen of the towers. At daybreak, without the customary signal of the morning gun, the Turks assaulted the city by sea and land; and the similitude of a twined or twisted thread has been applied to the closeness and continuity of their line of attack. The foremost ranks consisted of the refuse of the host, a voluntary crowd who fought without order or command; of the feebleness of age or childhood, of peasants and vagrants, and of all who had joined the camp in the blind hope of plunder and martyrdom. The common impulse drove them onwards to the wall; the most audacious to climb were instantly precipitated; and not a dart, not a bullet, of the Christians, was idly wasted on the accumulated throng. But their strength and ammunition were exhausted in this laborious defence: the ditch was filled with the bodies of the slain; they supported the footsteps of their companions; and of this devoted vanguard the death was more serviceable than the life. Under their respective bashaws and sanjaks, the troops of Anatolia and Romania were successively led to the charge: their progress was various and doubtful; but, after a conflict of two hours, the Greeks still maintained and improved their advantage; and the voice of the emperor was heard, encouraging his soldiers to achieve, by a last effort, the deliverance of their country. In that fatal moment the Janizaries arose, fresh, vigorous, and invincible. The sultan himself on horseback, with an iron mace in his hand, was the spectator and judge of their valour; he was surrounded by ten thousand of his domestic troops, whom he reserved for the decisive occasion; and the tide of battle was directed and impelled by his voice and eye. His numerous ministers of justice were posted behind the line, to urge, to restrain, and to punish; and if danger was in the front, shame and inevitable death were in the rear, of the fugitives. The cries of fear and of pain were drowned in the martial music of drums, trumpets, and attaballs; and experience has proved that the mechanical operation of sounds, by quickening the circulation of the blood and spirits, will act on the human machine more forcibly than the eloquence of reason and honour. From the lines, the galleys, and the bridge, the Ottoman artillery thundered on all sides; and the camp and city, the Greeks and the Turks, were involved in a cloud of smoke, which could only be dispelled by the final deliverance or destruction of the Roman empire. The single combats of the heroes of history or fable amuse our fancy and engage our affections: the skilful evolutions of war may inform the mind, and improve a necessary, though pernicious, science. But in the uniform and odious pictures of a general assault, all is blood, and horror, and confusion; nor shall I strive, at the distance of three centuries and a thousand miles, to delineate a scene of which there could be no spectators, and of which the actors themselves were incapable of forming any just or adequate idea.

The immediate loss of Constantinople may be ascribed to the bullet, or arrow, which pierced the gauntlet of John Justiniani. The sight of his blood, and the exquisite pain, appalled the courage of the chief, whose arms and counsels were the firmest rampart of the city. As he withdrew from his station in quest of a surgeon, his flight was perceived and stopped by the indefatigable emperor. "Your wound," exclaimed Palæologus, "is slight; the danger is pressing: your presence is necessary; and whither will you retire?"—"I will retire," said the trembling Genoese, "by the same road which God has opened to the Turks;" and at these words he hastily passed through one of the breaches of the inner wall. By this pusillanimous act he stained the honours of a military life; and the few days which he survived in Galata, or the isle of Chios, were embittered by his own and the public reproach. His example was imitated by the greatest part of the Latin auxiliaries, and the defence began to slacken when the attack was pressed with redoubled vigour. The number of the Ottomans was fifty, perhaps a hundred, times superior to that of the Christians; the double walls were reduced by the cannon to a heap of ruins: in a circuit of several miles some places must be found more easy of access, or more feebly guarded; and if the besiegers could penetrate in a single point, the whole city was irrecoverably lost. The first who deserved the sultan's reward was Hassan the Janizary, of gigantic stature and strength. With his scimitar in one hand and his buckler in the other, he ascended the outward fortification: of the thirty Janizaries who were emulous of his valour, eighteen perished in the bold adventure. Hassan and his twelve companions had reached the summit: the giant was precipitated from the rampart: he rose on one knee, and was again oppressed by a shower of darts and stones. But his success had proved that the achievement was possible: the walls and towers were instantly covered with a swarm of Turks; and the Greeks, now driven from the vantage ground, were overwhelmed by increasing multitudes. Amidst these multitudes, the emperor, who accomplished all the duties of a general and a soldier, was long seen and finally lost. The nobles, who fought round his person, sustained, till their last breath, the honourable names of Palæologus and Cantacuzene: his mournful exclamation was heard, "Cannot there be found a Christian to cut off my head?" and his last fear was that of falling alive into the hands of the infidels. The prudent despair of Constantine cast away the purple: amidst the tumult he fell by an unknown hand, and his body was buried under a mountain of the slain. After his death resistance and order were no more. The Greeks fled towards the city; and many were pressed and stifled in the narrow pass of the gate of St. Romanus. The victorious Turks rushed through the breaches of the inner wall; and as they advanced into the streets, they were soon joined by their brethren, who had forced the gate Phenar on the side of the harbour. In the first heat of the pursuit about two thousand Christians were put to the sword; but avarice soon prevailed over cruelty; and the victors acknowledged that they should immediately have given quarter, if the valour of the emperor and his chosen bands had not prepared them for a similar opposition in every part of the capital. It was thus, after a siege of fifty-three days, that Constantinople, which had defied the power of Chosroes, the Chagan, and the caliphs, was irretrievably subdued by the arms of Mohammed the Second. Her empire only had been subverted by the Latins: her religion was trampled in the dust by the Moslem conquerors.

The tidings of misfortune fly with a rapid wing; yet such was the extent of Constantinople, that the more distant quarters might prolong, some moments, the happy ignorance of their ruin. But in the general consternation, in the feelings of selfish or social anxiety, in the tumult and thunder of the assault, a *sleepless* night and morning must have elapsed; nor can I believe that many Grecian ladies were awakened by the Janizaries from a sound and tranquil slumber. On the assurance of the public calamity, the houses and convents were instantly deserted; and the trembling inhabitants flocked together in the streets, like a herd of timid animals, as if accumulated weakness could be productive of strength, or in the vain hope that amid the crowd each individual might be safe and invisible. From every part of the capital they flowed into the church of St. Sophia: in the space of an hour, the sanctuary, the choir, the nave, the upper and lower galleries, were filled with the multitudes of fathers and husbands, of women and children, of priests, monks, and religious virgins: the doors were barred on the inside, and they sought protection from the sacred dome which they had so lately abhorred as a profane and polluted edifice. Their confidence was founded on the prophecy of an enthusiast or impostor, that one day the Turks would enter Constantinople, and pursue the Romans as far as the column of Constantine in the square before St. Sophia: but that this would be the term of their calamities; that an angel would descend from heaven with a sword in his hand, and would deliver the empire, with that celestial weapon, to a poor man seated at the foot of the column. "Take this sword," would he say, "and avenge the people of the Lord." At these animating words the Turks would instantly fly, and the victorious Romans would drive them from the West, and from all Anatolia, as far as the frontiers of Persia. It is on this occasion that Ducas, with some fancy and much truth, upbraids the discord and obstinacy of the Greeks. "Had that angel appeared," exclaims the historian, "had he offered to exterminate your foes if you would consent to the union of the church, even then, in that fatal moment, you would have rejected your safety, or have deceived your God."

While they expected the descent of the tardy angel, the doors were broken with axes; and as the Turks encountered no resistance, their bloodless hands were employed in selecting and securing the multitude of their prisoners. Youth, beauty, and the appearance of wealth, attracted their choice; and the right of property was decided among themselves by a prior seizure, by personal strength, and by the authority of command. In the space of an hour the male captives were bound with cords, the females with their veils and girdles. The senators were linked with their slaves; the prelates with the porters of the church; and young men of a plebeian class with noble maids whose faces had been invisible to the sun and their nearest kindred. In this common captivity the ranks of society were confounded; the ties of nature were cut asunder; and the inexorable soldier was careless of the father's groans, the tears of the mother, and the lamentations of the children. The loudest in their wailings were the nuns, who were torn from the altar with naked bosoms, outstretched hands, and dishevelled hair; and we should piously believe that few could be tempted to prefer the vigils of the harem to those of the monastery. Of these unfortunate Greeks, of these domestic animals, whole strings were rudely driven through the streets; and as the conquerors were eager to return for more prey, their trembling pace was quickened with menaces and blows. At the same hour a similar rapine was exercised in all the churches and monasteries, in all the palaces and habitations, of the capital; nor could any place, however sacred or sequestered, protect the persons or the property of the Greeks. Above sixty thousand of this devoted people were transported from the city to the camp and fleet; exchanged or sold according to the caprice or interest of their masters, and dispersed in remote servitude through the provinces of the Ottoman empire. Among these we may notice some remarkable characters. The historian Phranza, first chamberlain and principal secretary, was involved with his family in the common lot. After suffering four months the hardships of slavery, he recovered his freedom: in the ensuing winter he ventured to Adrianople, and ransomed his wife from the *mir bashi,* or master of the horse; but his two children, in the flower of youth and beauty, had been seized for the use of Mohammed himself. The daughter of Phranza died in the seraglio, perhaps a virgin: his son, in the fifteenth year of his age, preferred death to infamy, and was stabbed by the hand of the royal lover. A deed thus inhuman cannot surely be expiated by the taste and liberality with which he released a Grecian matron and her two daughters, on receiving a Latin ode from

Philelphus, who had chosen a wife in that noble family. The pride or cruelty of Mohammed would have been most sensibly gratified by the capture of a Roman legate; but the dexterity of Cardinal Isidore eluded the search, and he escaped from Galata in a plebeian habit.* The chain and entrance of the outward harbour was still occupied by the Italian ships of merchandise and war. They had signalised their valour in the siege: they embraced the moment of retreat, while the Turkish mariners were dissipated in the pillage of the city. When they hoisted sail, the beach was covered with a suppliant and lamentable crowd; but the means of transportation were scanty; the Venetians and Genoese selected their countrymen; and, notwithstanding the fairest promises of the sultan, the inhabitants of Galata evacuated their houses, and embarked with their most precious effects.

In the fall and the sack of great cities an historian is condemned to repeat the tale of uniform calamity: the same effects must be produced by the same passions; and when those passions may be indulged without control, small, alas! is the difference between civilised and savage man. Amidst the vague exclamations of bigotry and hatred, the Turks are not accused of a wanton or immoderate effusion of Christian blood: but according to their maxims (the maxims of antiquity), the lives of the vanquished were forfeited; and the legitimate reward of the conqueror was derived from the service, the sale, or the ransom of his captives of both sexes. The wealth of Constantinople had been granted by the sultan to his victorious troops; and the rapine of an hour is more productive than the industry of years. But as no regular division was attempted of the spoil, the respective shares were not determined by merit; and the rewards of valour were stolen away by the followers of the camp, who had declined the toil and danger of the battle. The narrative of their depredations could not afford either amusement or instruction: the total amount, in the last poverty of the empire, has been valued at four millions of ducats; and of this sum a small part was the property of the Venetians, the Genoese, the Florentines, and the merchants of Ancona. Of these foreigners the stock was improved in quick and perpetual circulation: but the riches of the Greeks were

*The Commentaries of Pius II. suppose that he craftily placed his cardinal's hat on the head of a corpse which was cut off and exposed in triumph, while the legate himself was bought and delivered as a captive of no value. The great Belgic Chronicle adorns his escape with new adventures, which he suppressed . . . in his own letters, lest he should lose the merit and reward of suffering for Christ.

displayed in the idle ostentation of palaces and wardrobes, or deeply buried in treasures of ingots and old coin, lest it should be demanded at their hands for the defence of their country. The profanation and plunder of the monasteries and churches excited the most tragic complaints. The dome of St. Sophia itself, the earthly heaven, the second firmament, the vehicle of the cherubim, the throne of the glory of God, was despoiled of the oblations of ages; and the gold and silver, the pearls and jewels, the vases and sacerdotal ornaments, were most wickedly converted to the service of mankind. After the divine images had been stripped of all that could be valuable to a profane eye, the canvas, or the wood, was torn, or broken, or burnt, or trod under foot, or applied, in the stables or the kitchen, to the vilest uses. The example of sacrilege was imitated, however, from the Latin conquerors of Constantinople; and the treatment which Christ, the Virgin, and the saints had sustained from the guilty Catholic, might be inflicted by the zealous Musulman on the monuments of idolatry. Perhaps, instead of joining the public clamour, a philosopher will observe that in the decline of the arts the workmanship could not be more valuable than the work, and that a fresh supply of visions and miracles would speedily be renewed by the craft of the priest and the credulity of the people. He will more seriously deplore the loss of the Byzantine libraries, which were destroyed or scattered in the general confusion: one hundred and twenty thousand manuscripts are said to have disappeared; ten volumes might be purchased for a single ducat; and the same ignominious price, too high perhaps for a shelf of theology, included the whole works of Aristotle and Homer, the noblest productions of the science and literature of ancient Greece. We may reflect with pleasure that an inestimable portion of our classic treasures was safely deposited in Italy; and that the mechanics of a German town had invented an art which derides the havoc of time and barbarism.

From the first hour of the memorable twenty-ninth of May, disorder and rapine prevailed in Constantinople till the eighth hour of the same day, when the sultan himself passed in triumph through the gate of St. Romanus. He was attended by his vizirs, bashaws, and guards, each of whom (says a Byzantine historian) was robust as Hercules, dexterous as Apollo, and equal in battle to any ten of the race of ordinary mortals. The conqueror gazed with satisfaction and wonder on the strange though splendid appearance of the domes and palaces, so dissimilar from the style of Oriental architecture. In the hippodrome, or *atmeidan,* his eye was attracted by the twisted column of the three serpents; and, as a trial of his strength, he shattered with his iron mace or battle-axe the under jaw of one of these monsters, which in the eyes of the Turks were the idols or talismans of the city. At the principal door of St. Sophia he alighted from his horse and entered the dome; and such was his jealous regard for that monument of his glory, that, on observing a zealous Musulman in the act of breaking the marble pavement, he admonished him with his scimitar that, if the spoil and captives were granted to the soldiers, the public and private buildings had been reserved for the prince. By his command the metropolis of the Eastern church was transformed into a mosque: the rich and portable instruments of superstition had been removed; the crosses were thrown down; and the walls, which were covered with images and mosaics, were washed and purified, and restored to a state of naked simplicity. On the same day, or on the ensuing Friday, the *muezin,* or crier, ascended the most lofty turret, and proclaimed the *ezan,* or public invitation, in the name of God and his prophet; the imam preached; and Mohammed the Second performed the *namaz* of prayer and thanksgiving on the great altar, where the Christian mysteries had so lately been celebrated before the last of the Cæsars. From St. Sophia he proceeded to the august but desolate mansion of a hundred successors of the great Constantine, but which in a few hours had been stripped of the pomp of royalty. A melancholy reflection on the vicissitudes of human greatness forced itself on his mind, and he repeated an elegant distich of Persian poetry: "The spider has wove his web in the Imperial palace, and the owl hath sung her watch-song on the towers of Afrasiab."*

Yet his mind was not satisfied, nor did the victory seem complete, till he was informed of the fate of Constantine—whether he had escaped, or been made prisoner, or had fallen in the battle. Two Janizaries claimed the honour and reward of his death: the body, under a heap of slain, was discovered by the golden eagles embroidered on his shoes; the Greeks acknowledged with tears the head of their late emperor; and, after exposing the bloody trophy, Mohammed be-

*This distich, which Cantemir gives in the original, derives new beauties from the application. It was thus that Scipio repeated, in the sack of Carthage, the famous prophecy of Homer. The same generous feeling carried the mind of the conqueror to the past or the future.

stowed on his rival the honours of a decent funeral. After his decease Lucas Notaras, great duke and first minister of the empire, was the most important prisoner. When he offered his person and his treasures at the foot of the throne, "And why," said the indignant sultan, "did you not employ these treasures in the defence of your prince and country?"—"They were yours," answered the slave; "God had reserved them for your hands."—"If he reserved them for me," replied the despot, "how have you presumed to withhold them so long by a fruitless and fatal resistance?" The great duke alleged the obstinacy of the strangers, and some secret encouragement from the Turkish vizir; and from this perilous interview he was at length dismissed with the assurance of pardon and protection. Mohammed condescended to visit his wife, a venerable princess oppressed with sickness and grief; and his consolation for her misfortunes was in the most tender strain of humanity and filial reverence. A similar clemency was extended to the principal officers of state, of whom several were ransomed at his expense; and during some days he declared himself the friend and father of the vanquished people. But the scene was soon changed, and before his departure the hippodrome streamed with the blood of his noblest captives. His perfidious cruelty is execrated by the Christians: they adorn with the colours of heroic martyrdom the execution of the great duke and his two sons, and his death is ascribed to the generous refusal of delivering his children to the tyrant's lust. . . . On the eighteenth of June the victorious sultan returned to Adrianople, and smiled at the base and hollow embassies of the Christian princes, who viewed their approaching ruin in the fall of the Eastern empire.

Constantinople had been left naked and desolate, without a prince or a people. But she could not be despoiled of the incomparable situation which marks her for the metropolis of a great empire; and the genius of the place will ever triumph over the accidents of time and fortune. Boursa and Adrianople, the ancient seats of the Ottomans, sunk into provincial towns; and Mohammed the Second established his own residence and that of his successors on the same commanding spot which had been chosen by Constantine. . . . Constantinople no longer appertains to the Roman historian; nor shall I enumerate the civil and religious edifices that were profaned or erected by its Turkish masters: the population was speedily renewed, and before the end of September five thousand families of Anatolia and Romania had obeyed the royal mandate, which enjoined them, under pain of death, to occupy their new habitations in the capital. The throne of Mohammed was guarded by the numbers and fidelity of his Moslem subjects; but his rational policy aspired to collect the remnant of the Greeks, and they returned in crowds as soon as they were assured of their lives, their liberties, and the free exercise of their religion. . . .

The remaining fragments of the Greek kingdom in Europe and Asia I shall abandon to the Turkish arms; but the final extinction of the two last dynasties which have reigned in Constantinople should terminate the decline and fall of the Roman empire in the East. The despots of the Morea, Demetrius and Thomas, the two surviving brothers of the name of PALÆOLOGUS, were astonished by the death of the emperor Constantine and the ruin of the monarchy. Hopeless of defence, they prepared, with the noble Greeks who adhered to their fortune, to seek a refuge in Italy, beyond the reach of the Ottoman thunder. . . .

Part 11

Medieval Rome from the Time of the Babylonian Captivity *(Chapters LXX and LXXI)*

With the death of the Byzantine Empire and the beginning of the Renaissance, the old Rome began to emerge once again as a force in the world. In these selections Gibbon surveys the history of Europe after the return of the papacy to Rome from Avignon. In the concluding section he describes the sad state of the city of Rome towards the end of the Middle Ages and endeavors to explain the various reasons for Rome's decline and fall.

CHAPTER LXX

. . . The first and most generous wish of Petrarch was the restoration of a free republic. . . . Charles the Fourth descended from the Alps to obtain the Italian and Imperial crowns. In his passage through Milan he received the visit, and repaid the flattery, of the poet laureat; accepted a medal of Augustus; and promised, without a smile, to imitate the founder of the Roman monarchy. A false application of the names and maxims of antiquity was the source of the hopes and disappointments of Petrarch; yet he could not overlook the difference of times and characters; the immeasurable distance between the first Cæsars and a Bohemian prince, who by the favour of the clergy had been elected the titular head of the German aristocracy. Instead of restoring to Rome her glory and her provinces, he had bound himself by a secret treaty with the pope to evacuate the city on the day of his coronation; and his shameful retreat was pursued by the reproaches of the patriot bard.

After the loss of liberty and empire, his third and more humble wish was to reconcile the shepherd with his flock; to recall the Roman bishop to his ancient and peculiar diocese. In the fervour of youth, with the authority of age, Petrarch addressed his exhortations to five successive popes, and his eloquence was always inspired by the enthusiasm of sentiment and the freedom of language. The son of a citizen of Florence invariably preferred the country of his birth to that of his education; and Italy, in his eyes, was the queen and garden of the world. Amidst her domestic factions she was doubtless superior to France both in art and science, in wealth and politeness; but the difference could scarcely support the epithet of barbarous, which he promiscuously bestows on the countries beyond the Alps. Avignon, the mystic Babylon, the sink of vice and corruption, was the object of his hatred and contempt; but he forgets that her scandalous vices were not the growth of the soil, and that in every residence they would adhere to the power and luxury of the papal court. He confesses that the successor of St. Peter is the bishop of the universal church; yet it was not on the banks of the Rhône, but of the Tiber, that the apostle had fixed his everlasting throne: and while every city in the Christian world was blessed with a bishop, the metropolis alone was desolate and forlorn. Since the removal of the Holy See the sacred buildings of the Lateran and the Vatican, their altars and their saints, were left in a state of poverty and decay; and Rome was often painted under the image of a disconsolate matron, as if the wandering husband could be reclaimed by the homely portrait of the age and infirmities of his weeping spouse. But the cloud which hung over the seven hills would be dispelled by the presence of their lawful sovereign: eternal fame, the prosperity of Rome, and the peace of Italy, would be the recompense of the pope who should dare to embrace this generous resolution. Of the five whom Petrarch exhorted, the three first, John the Twenty-second, Benedict the Twelfth, and Clement the Sixth, were importuned or amused by the boldness of the orator; but the memorable change which had been attempted by Urban the Fifth was finally accomplished by Gregory the Eleventh. The execution of their design was opposed by weighty and almost insuperable obstacles. A king of

France, who has deserved the epithet of wise, was unwilling to release them from a local dependence: the cardinals, for the most part his subjects, were attached to the language, manners, and climate of Avignon; to their stately palaces; above all, to the wines of Burgundy. In their eyes Italy was foreign or hostile; and they reluctantly embarked at Marseilles, as if they had been sold or banished into the land of the Saracens. Urban the Fifth resided three years in the Vatican with safety and honour; his sanctity was protected by a guard of two thousand horse; and the king of Cyprus, the queen of Naples, and the emperors of the East and West, devoutly saluted their common father in the chair of St. Peter. But the joy of Petrarch and the Italians was soon turned into grief and indignation. Some reasons of public or private moment, his own impatience or the prayers of the cardinals, recalled Urban to France; and the approaching election was saved from the tyrannic patriotism of the Romans. The powers of heaven were interested in their cause: Bridget of Sweden, a saint and pilgrim, disapproved the return, and foretold the death, of Urban the Fifth; the migration of Gregory the Eleventh was encouraged by St. Catherine of Sienna, the spouse of Christ and ambassadress of the Florentines; and the popes themselves, the great masters of human credulity, appear to have listened to these visionary females.* Yet those celestial admonitions were supported by some arguments of temporal policy. The residence of Avignon had been invaded by hostile violence: at the head of thirty thousand robbers a hero had extorted ransom and absolution from the vicar of Christ and the sacred college; and the maxim of the French warriors, to spare the people and plunder the church, was a new heresy of the most dangerous import. While the pope was driven from Avignon, he was strenuously invited to Rome. The senate and people acknowledged him as their lawful sovereign, and laid at his feet the keys of the gates, the bridges, and the fortresses, of the quarter at least beyond the Tiber. But this loyal offer was accompanied by a declaration they they could no longer suffer the scandal and calamity of his absence; and that his obstinacy would finally provoke them to revive and assert the primitive right of election. The abbot of Mount Cassin

*I have not leisure to expatiate on the legends of St. Bridget or St. Catherine, the last of which might furnish some amusing stories. Their effect on the mind of Gregory XI. is attested by the last solemn words of the dying pope, who admonished the assistants, ut caverent ab hominibus, sive viris, sive mulieribus, sub specie religionis loquentibus visiones sui capitis, quia per tales ipse seductus, etc. . . .

had been consulted whether he would accept the triple crown* from the clergy and people: "I am a citizen of Rome," replied that venerable ecclesiastic, "and my first law is the voice of my country."

If superstition will interpret an untimely death; if the merit of counsels be judged from the event; the heavens may seem to frown on a measure of such apparent reason and propriety. Gregory the Eleventh did not survive above fourteen months his return to the Vatican; and his decease was followed by the great schism of the West, which distracted the Latin church above forty years. The sacred college was then composed of twenty-two cardinals: six of these had remained at Avignon; eleven Frenchmen, one Spaniard, and four Italians, entered the conclave in the usual form. Their choice was not yet limited to the purple; and their unanimous votes acquiesced in the archbishop of Bari, a subject of Naples, conspicuous for his zeal and learning, who ascended the throne of St. Peter under the name of Urban the Sixth. The epistle of the sacred college affirms his free and regular election, which had been inspired as usual by the Holy Ghost; he was adored, invested, and crowned, with the customary rites; his temporal authority was obeyed at Rome and Avignon, and his ecclesiastical supremacy was acknowledged in the Latin world. During several weeks the cardinals attended their new master with the fairest professions of attachment and loyalty, till the summer heats permitted a decent escape from the city. But as soon as they were united at Anagni and Fundi, in a place of security, they cast aside the mask, accused their own falsehood and hypocrisy, excommunicated the apostate the antichrist of Rome, and proceeded to a new election of Robert of Geneva, Clement the Seventh, whom they announced to the nations as the true and rightful vicar of Christ. Their first choice, an involuntary and illegal act, was annulled by the fear of death and the menaces of the Romans; and their complaint is justified by the strong evidence of probability and fact. The twelve French cardinals, above two-thirds of the votes, were masters of the election; and whatever might be their provincial jealousies, it cannot fairly be presumed that they would have sacrificed their right and interest to a foreign candidate, who

*The first crown or regnum . . . on the episcopal mitre of the popes is ascribed to the gift of Constantine, or Clovis. The second was added by Boniface VIII., as the emblem not only of a spiritual, but of a temporal kingdom. The three states of the church are represented by the triple crown, which was introduced by John XXII. or Benedict XII. . . .

would never restore them to their native country. In the various, and often inconsistent, narratives, the shades of popular violence are more darkly or faintly coloured: but the licentiousness of the seditious Romans was inflamed by a sense of their privileges, and the danger of a second emigration. The conclave was intimidated by the shouts, and encompassed by the arms, of thirty thousand rebels; the bells of the Capitol and St. Peter's rang an alarm; "Death, or an Italian pope!" was the universal cry; the same threat was repeated by the twelve bannerets or chiefs of the quarters, in the form of charitable advice; some preparations were made for burning the obstinate cardinals; and had they chosen a Transalpine subject, it is probable that they would never have departed alive from the Vatican. The same constraint imposed the necessity of dissembling in the eyes of Rome and of the world; the pride and cruelty of Urban presented a more inevitable danger; and they soon discovered the features of the tyrant, who could walk in his garden and recite his breviary while he heard from an adjacent chamber six cardinals groaning on the rack. His inflexible zeal, which loudly censured their luxury and vice, would have attached them to the stations and duties of their parishes at Rome; and had he not fatally delayed a new promotion, the French cardinals would have been reduced to a helpless minority in the sacred college. For these reasons, and in the hope of repassing the Alps, they rashly violated the peace and unity of the church; and the merits of their double choice are yet agitated in the Catholic schools. The vanity, rather than the interest of the nation, determined the court and clergy of France. The states of Savoy, Sicily, Cyprus, Arragon, Castile, Navarre, and Scotland, were inclined by their example and authority to the obedience of Clement the Seventh, and, after his decease, of Benedict the Thirteenth. Rome and the principal states of Italy, Germany, Portugal, England, the Low Countries, and the kingdoms of the North, adhered to the prior election of Urban the Sixth, who was succeeded by Boniface the Ninth, Innocent the Seventh, and Gregory the Twelfth.

From the banks of the Tiber and the Rhône the hostile pontiffs encountered each other with the pen and the sword: the civil and ecclesiastical order of society was disturbed; and the Romans had their full share of the mischiefs of which they may be arraigned as the primary authors. They had vainly flattered themselves with the hope of restoring the seat of the ecclesiastical monarchy, and of relieving their poverty with the tributes and offerings of the nations; but the separation of France and Spain diverted the stream of lucrative devotion; nor could the loss be compensated by the two jubilees which were crowded into the space of ten years. By the avocations of the schism, by foreign arms, and popular tumults, Urban the Sixth and his three successors were often compelled to interrupt their residence in the Vatican. The Colonna and Ursini still exercised their deadly feuds: the bannerets of Rome asserted and abused the privileges of a republic: the vicars of Christ, who had levied a military force, chastised their rebellion with the gibbet, the sword, and the dagger; and, in a friendly conference, eleven deputies of the people were perfidiously murdered and cast into the street. Since the invasion of Robert the Norman, the Romans had pursued their domestic quarrels without the dangerous interposition of a stranger. But in the disorders of the schism, an aspiring neighbour, Ladislaus king of Naples, alternately supported and betrayed the pope and the people; by the former he was declared *gonfalonier,* or general, of the church, while the latter submitted to his choice the nomination of their magistrates. Besieging Rome by land and water, he thrice entered the gates as a barbarian conqueror; profaned the altars, violated the virgins, pillaged the merchants, performed his devotions at St. Peter's, and left a garrison in the castle of St. Angelo. His arms were sometimes unfortunate, and to a delay of three days he was indebted for his life and crown: but Ladislaus triumphed in his turn; and it was only his premature death that could save the metropolis and the ecclesiastical state from the ambitious conqueror, who had assumed the title, or at least the powers, of King of Rome.*

I have not undertaken the ecclesiastical history of the schism; but Rome, the object of these last chapters, is deeply interested in the disputed succession of her sovereigns. The first counsels for the peace and union of Christendom arose from the university of Paris, from the faculty of the Sorbonne, whose doctors were esteemed, at least in the Gallican church, as the most consummate masters of theological science. Prudently waiving all invidious inquiry into the origin and merits of the dispute, they proposed, as a healing measure, that the

*It is supposed by Giannone . . . that he styled himself Rex Romæ, a title unknown to the world since the expulsion of Tarquin. But a nearer inspection has justified the reading of Rex Ramæ, of Rama, an obscure kingdom annexed to the crown of Hungary.

two pretenders of Rome and Avignon should abdicate at the same time, after qualifying the cardinals of the adverse factions to join in a legitimate election; and that the nations should *subtract* their obedience, if either of the competitors preferred his own interest to that of the public. At each vacancy these physicians of the church deprecated the mischiefs of a hasty choice; but the policy of the conclave and the ambition of its members were deaf to reason and entreaties; and whatsoever promises were made, the pope could never be bound by the oaths of the cardinal. During fifteen years the pacific designs of the university were eluded by the arts of the rival pontiffs, the scruples or passions of their adherents, and the vicissitudes of French factions, that ruled the insanity of Charles the Sixth. At length a vigorous resolution was embraced; and a solemn embassy, of the titular patriarch of Alexandria, two archbishops, five bishops, five abbots, three knights, and twenty doctors, was sent to the courts of Avignon and Rome, to require, in the name of the church and king, the abdication of the two pretenders, of Peter de Luna, who styled himself Benedict the Thirteenth, and of Angelo Corrario, who assumed the name of Gregory the Twelfth. For the ancient honour of Rome, and the success of their commission, the ambassadors solicited a conference with the magistrates of the city, whom they gratified by a positive declaration that the most Christian king did not entertain a wish of transporting the holy see from the Vatican, which he considered as the genuine and proper seat of the successor of St. Peter. In the name of the senate and people, an eloquent Roman asserted their desire to co-operate in the union of the church, deplored the temporal and spiritual calamities of the long schism, and requested the protection of France against the arms of the king of Naples. The answers of Benedict and Gregory were alike edifying and alike deceitful; and, in evading the demand of their abdication, the two rivals were animated by a common spirit. They agreed on the necessity of a previous interview; but the time, the place, and the manner, could never be ascertained by mutual consent. "If the one advances," says a servant of Gregory, "the other retreats; the one appears an animal fearful of the land, the other a creature apprehensive of the water. And thus, for a short remnant of life and power, will these aged priests endanger the peace and salvation of the Christian world."

The Christian world was at length provoked by their obstinacy and fraud: they were deserted by their cardinals, who embraced each other as friends and colleagues; and their revolt was supported by a numerous assembly of prelates and ambassadors. With equal justice, the council of Pisa deposed the popes of Rome and Avignon; the conclave was unanimous in the choice of Alexander the Fifth, and his vacant seat was soon filled by a similar election of John the Twenty-third, the most profligate of mankind. But instead of extinguishing the schism, the rashness of the French and Italians had given a third pretender to the chair of St. Peter. Such new claims of the synod and conclave were disputed; three kings, of Germany, Hungary, and Naples, adhered to the cause of Gregory the Twelfth: and Benedict the Thirteenth, himself a Spaniard, was acknowledged by the devotion and patriotism of that powerful nation. The rash proceedings of Pisa were corrected by the council of Constance; the emperor Sigismond acted a conspicuous part as the advocate or protector of the Catholic church; and the number and weight of civil and ecclesiastical members might seem to constitute the states-general of Europe. Of the three popes, John the Twenty-third was the first victim: he fled and was brought back a prisoner: the most scandalous charges were suppressed; the vicar of Christ was only accused of piracy, murder, rape, sodomy, and incest; and after subscribing his own condemnation, he expiated in prison the imprudence of trusting his person to a free city beyond the Alps. Gregory the Twelfth, whose obedience was reduced to the narrow precincts of Rimini, descended with more honour from the throne; and his ambassador convened the session in which he renounced the title and authority of lawful pope. To vanquish the obstinacy of Benedict the Thirteenth or his adherents, the emperor in person undertook a journey from Constance to Perpignan. The kings of Castile, Arragon, Navarre, and Scotland, obtained an equal and honourable treaty: with the concurrence of the Spaniards, Benedict was deposed by the council; but the harmless old man was left in a solitary castle to excommunicate twice each day the rebel kingdoms which had deserted his cause. After thus eradicating the remains of the schism, the synod of Constance proceeded with slow and cautious steps to elect the sovereign of Rome and the head of the church. On this momentous occasion the college of twenty-three cardinals was fortified with thirty deputies; six of whom were chosen in each of the five great nations of Christendom—the Italian, the German, the French, the Spanish, and the *English:** the interference of strangers was softened by their generous preference of an Italian and a Roman; and the hereditary, as well as personal, merit of Otho Colonna recommended him to the conclave. Rome accepted with joy and obedience the noblest of her sons; the ecclesiastical state was defended by his powerful family; and the elevation of Martin the Fifth is the era of the restoration and establishment of the popes in the Vatican.

The royal prerogative of coining money, which had been exercised near three hundred years by the senate, was *first* resumed by Martin the Fifth, and his image and superscription introduce the series of the papal medals. Of his two immediate successors, Eugenius the Fourth was the *last* pope expelled by the tumults of the Roman people, and Nicholas the Fifth, the *last* who was importuned by the presence of a Roman emperor. I. The conflict of Eugenius with the fathers of Basil, and the weight or apprehension of a new excise, emboldened and provoked the Romans to usurp the temporal government of the city. They rose in arms; elected seven governors of the republic, and a constable of the Capitol; imprisoned the pope's nephew; besieged his person in the palace; and shot volleys of arrows into his bark as he escaped down the Tiber in the habit of a monk. But he still possessed in the castle of St. Angelo a faithful garrison and a train of artillery: their batteries incessantly thundered on the city, and a bullet more dexterously pointed broke down the barricade of the bridge, and scattered with a single shot the heroes of the republic. Their constancy was exhausted by a rebellion of five months. Under the tyranny of the

*I cannot overlook this great national cause, which was vigorously maintained by the English ambassadors against those of France The latter contended that Christendom was essentially distributed into the four great nations and votes of Italy, Germany, France, and Spain; and that the lesser kingdoms (such as England, Denmark, Portugal, etc.) were comprehended under one or other of these great divisions. The English asserted that the British islands, of which they were the head, should be considered as a fifth and co-ordinate nation, with an equal vote; and every argument of truth or fable was introduced to exalt the dignity of their country. Including England, Scotland, Wales, the four kingdoms of Ireland, and the Orkneys, the British islands are decorated with eight royal crowns, and discriminated by four or five languages, English, Welsh, Cornish, Scotch, Irish, etc. The greater island from north to south measures 800 miles, or 40 days' journey; and England alone contains 32 counties and 52,000 parish churches (a bold account!) besides cathedrals, colleges, priories, and hospitals. They celebrate the mission of St. Joseph of Arimathea, the birth of Constantine, and the legatine powers of the two primates, without forgetting the testimony of Bartholemy de Glanville (A.D. 1360), who reckons only four Christian kingdoms —1, of Rome; 2, of Constantinople; 3, of Ireland, which had been transferred to the English monarchs; and, 4, of Spain. Our countrymen prevailed in the council, but the victories of Henry V. added much weight to their arguments. The adverse pleadings were found at Constance by Sir Robert Wingfield, ambassador from Henry VIII. to the emperor Maximilian I., and by him printed in 1517 at Louvain. . . .

Ghibeline nobles, the wisest patriots regretted the dominion of the church; and their repentance was unanimous and effectual. The troops of St. Peter again occupied the Capitol; the magistrates departed to their homes; the most guilty were executed or exiled; and the legate, at the head of two thousand foot and four thousand horse, was saluted as the father of the city. The synods of Ferrara and Florence, the fear or resentment of Eugenius, prolonged his absence: he was received by a submissive people; but the pontiff understood, from the acclamations of his triumphal entry, that, to secure their loyalty and his own repose, he must grant without delay the abolition of the odious excise. II. Rome was restored, adorned, and enlightened, by the peaceful reign of Nicholas the Fifth. In the midst of these laudable occupations, the pope was alarmed by the approach of Frederic the Third of Austria; though his fears could not be justified by the character or the power of the Imperial candidate. After drawing his military force to the metropolis, and imposing the best security of oaths and treaties, Nicholas received with a smiling countenance the faithful advocate and vassal of the church. So tame were the times, so feeble was the Austrian, that the pomp of his coronation was accomplished with order and harmony: but the superfluous honour was so disgraceful to an independent nation, that his successors have excused themselves from the toilsome pilgrimage to the Vatican, and rest their Imperial title on the choice of the electors of Germany. . . .

The spiritual thunders of the Vatican depend on the force of opinion; and if that opinion be supplanted by reason or passion, the sound may idly waste itself in the air; and the helpless priest is exposed to the brutal violence of a noble or a plebeian adversary. But after their return from Avignon, the keys of St. Peter were guarded by the sword of St. Paul. Rome was commanded by an impregnable citadel: the use of cannon is a powerful engine against popular seditions: a regular force of cavalry and infantry was enlisted under the banners of the pope: his ample revenues supplied the resources of war; and, from the extent of his domain, he could bring down on a rebellious city an army of hostile neighbours and loyal subjects.* Since the union of the duchies

*By the economy of Sixtus V. the revenue of the ecclesiastical state was raised to two millions and a half of Roman crowns. . . ; and so regular was the military establishment, that in one month Clement VIII. could invade the duchy of Ferrara with three thousand horse and twenty thousand foot . . .

of Ferrara and Urbino, the ecclesiastical state extends from the Mediterranean to the Adriatic, and from the confines of Naples to the banks of the Po; and as early as the sixteenth century the greater part of that spacious and fruitful country acknowledged the lawful claims and temporal sovereignty of the Roman pontiffs. Their claims were readily deduced from the genuine or fabulous donations of the darker ages: the successive steps of their final settlement would engage us too far in the transactions of Italy, and even of Europe; the crimes of Alexander the Sixth, the martial operations of Julius the Second, and the liberal policy of Leo the Tenth, a theme which has been adorned by the pens of the noblest historians of the times.* In the first period of their conquests, till the expedition of Charles the Eighth, the popes might successfully wrestle with the adjacent princes and states, whose military force was equal or inferior to their own. But as soon as the monarchs of France, Germany, and Spain contended with gigantic arms for the dominion of Italy, they supplied with art the deficiency of strength, and concealed, in a labyrinth of wars and treaties, their aspiring views and the immortal hope of chasing the barbarians beyond the Alps. The nice balance of the Vatican was often subverted by the soldiers of the North and West, who were united under the standard of Charles the Fifth: the feeble and fluctuating policy of Clement the Seventh exposed his person and dominions to the conqueror; and Rome was abandoned seven months to a lawless army, more cruel and rapacious than the Goths and Vandals. After this severe lesson the popes contracted their ambition, which was almost satisfied, resumed the character of a common parent, and abstained from all offensive hostilities, except in a hasty quarrel, when the vicar of Christ and the Turkish sultan were armed at the same time against the kingdom of Naples. The French and Germans at length withdrew from the field of battle: Milan, Naples, Sicily, Sardinia, and the seacoast of Tuscany, were firmly possessed by the Spaniards; and it became their interest to maintain the peace and dependence of Italy, which continued almost without disturbance from the middle of the sixteenth to the opening of the eighteenth century. The Vatican was swayed and protected by the religious policy of the Catholic king: his prejudice and interest disposed him in every dispute to support the

*More especially by Guicciardini and Machiavel; in the general history of the former; in the Florentine history, the "Prince," and the political discourses of the latter. . . .

prince against the people; and instead of the encouragement, the aid, and the asylum which they obtained from the adjacent states, the friends of liberty or the enemies of law were enclosed on all sides within the iron circle of despotism. The long habits of obedience and education subdued the turbulent spirit of the nobles and commons of Rome. The barons forgot the arms and factions of their ancestors, and insensibly became the servants of luxury and government. Instead of maintaining a crowd of tenants and followers, the produce of their estates was consumed in the private expenses which multiply the pleasures and diminish the power of the lord.* The Colonna and Ursini vied with each other in the decoration of their palaces and chapels; and their antique splendour was rivalled or surpassed by the sudden opulence of the papal families. In Rome the voice of freedom and discord is no longer heard; and, instead of the foaming torrent, a smooth and stagnant lake reflects the image of idleness and servitude.

A Christian, a philosopher, and a patriot, will be equally scandalised by the temporal kingdom of the clergy; and the local majesty of Rome, the remembrance of her consuls and triumphs, may seem to embitter the sense and aggravate the shame of her slavery. If we calmly weigh the merits and defects of the ecclesiastical government, it may be praised in its present state as a mild, decent, and tranquil system, exempt from the dangers of a minority, the sallies of youth, the expenses of luxury, and the calamities of war. But these advantages are overbalanced by a frequent, perhaps a septennial, election of a sovereign, who is seldom a native of the country: the reign of a *young* statesman of threescore, in the decline of his life and abilities, without hope to accomplish, and without children to inherit, the labours of his transitory reign. The successful candidate is drawn from the church, and even the convent—from the mode of education and life the most adverse to reason, humanity, and freedom. In the trammels of servile faith he has learned to believe because it is absurd, to revere all that is contemptible, and to despise whatever might deserve the esteem of a rational being; to punish error as a crime, to reward mortification and celibacy as the first of virtues; to place the saints of the calendar above the heroes of Rome and the sages of Athens; and to consider the

*This gradual change of manners and expense is admirably explained by . . . Adam Smith (Wealth of Nations) . . . who proves, perhaps too severely, that the most salutary effects have flowed from the meanest and most selfish causes.

missal, or the crucifix, as more useful instruments than the plough or the loom. In the office of nuncio, or the rank of cardinal, he may acquire some knowledge of the world; but the primitive stain will adhere to his mind and manners: from study and experience he may suspect the mystery of his profession; but the sacerdotal artist will imbibe some portion of the bigotry which he inculcates. The genius of Sixtus the Fifth burst from the gloom of a Franciscan cloister. In a reign of five years he exterminated the outlaws and banditti, abolished the *profane* sanctuaries of Rome, formed a naval and military force, restored and emulated the monuments of antiquity, and, after a liberal use and large increase of the revenue, left five millions of crowns in the castle of St. Angelo. But his justice was sullied with cruelty, his activity was prompted by the ambition of conquest: after his decease the abuses revived; the treasure was dissipated; he entailed on posterity thirty-five new taxes and the venality of offices; and, after his death, his statue was demolished by an ungrateful or an injured people. The wild and original character of Sixtus the Fifth stands alone in the series of the pontiffs: the maxims and effects of their temporal government may be collected from the positive and comparative view of the arts and philosophy, the agriculture and trade, the wealth and population, of the ecclesiastical state For myself, it is my wish to depart in charity with all mankind, nor am I willing, in these last moments, to offend even the pope and clergy of Rome.

CHAPTER LXXI

In the last days of Pope Eugenius the Fourth, two of his servants, the learned Poggius and a friend, ascended the Capitoline hill, reposed themselves among the ruins of columns and temples, and viewed from that commanding spot the wide and various prospect of desolation. The place and the object gave ample scope for moralising on the vicissitudes of fortune, which spares neither man nor the proudest of his works, which buries empires and cities in a common grave; and it was agreed that, in proportion to her former greatness, the fall of Rome was the more awful and deplorable. "Her primeval state, such as she might appear in a remote age, when Evander entertained the stranger of Troy, has been delineated by the fancy of Virgil. This

Tarpeian rock was then a savage and solitary thicket: in the time of the poet it was crowned with the golden roofs of a temple; the temple is overthrown, the gold has been pillaged, the wheel of fortune has accomplished her revolution, and the sacred ground is again disfigured with thorns and brambles. The hill of the Capitol, on which we sit, was formerly the head of the Roman empire, the citadel of the earth, the terror of kings; illustrated by the footsteps of so many triumphs, enriched with the spoils and tributes of so many nations. This spectacle of the world, how is it fallen! how changed! how defaced! the path of victory is obliterated by vines, and the benches of the senators are concealed by a dunghill. Cast your eyes on the Palatine hill, and seek among the shapeless and enormous fragments the marble theatre, the obelisks, the colossal statues, the porticoes of Nero's palace: survey the other hills of the city, the vacant space is interrupted only by ruins and gardens. The forum of the Roman people, where they assembled to enact their laws and elect their magistrates, is now enclosed for the cultivation of pot-herbs, or thrown open for the reception of swine and buffaloes. The public and private edifices, that were founded for eternity, lie prostrate, naked, and broken, like the limbs of a mighty giant; and the ruin is the more visible, from the stupendous relics that have survived the injuries of time and fortune." . . .

This melancholy picture was drawn above nine hundred years after the fall of the Western empire, and even of the Gothic kingdom of Italy. A long period of distress and anarchy, in which empire, and arts, and riches had migrated from the banks of the Tiber, was incapable of restoring or adorning the city; and, as all that is human must retrograde if it do not advance, every successive age must have hastened the ruin of the works of antiquity. To measure the progress of decay, and to ascertain, at each era, the state of each edifice, would be an endless and a useless labour; and I shall content myself with two observations which will introduce a short inquiry into the general causes and effects. I. Two hundred years before the eloquent complaint of Poggius, an anonymous writer composed a description of Rome. His ignorance may repeat the same objects under strange and fabulous names. Yet this barbarous topographer had eyes and ears; he could observe the visible remains; he could listen to the tradition of the people; and he distinctly enumerates seven theatres, eleven baths, twelve arches, and eighteen palaces, of which many had disappeared before the time of Poggius. It is apparent that many stately monuments of antiquity survived till a late period,* and that the principles of destruction acted with vigorous and increasing energy in the thirteenth and fourteenth centuries. 2. The same reflection must be applied to the three last ages; and we should vainly seek the Septizonium of Severus, which is celebrated by Petrarch and the antiquarians of the sixteenth century. While the Roman edifices were still entire, the first blows, however weighty and impetuous, were resisted by the solidity of the mass and the harmony of the parts; but the slightest touch would precipitate the fragments of arches and columns, that already nodded to their fall.

After a diligent inquiry I can discern four principal causes of the ruin of Rome, which continued to operate in a period of more than a thousand years. I. The injuries of time and nature. II. The hostile attacks of the barbarians and Christians. III. The use and abuse of the materials. And, IV. The domestic quarrels of the Romans.

I. The art of man is able to construct monuments far more permanent than the narrow span of his own existence: yet these monuments, like himself, are perishable and frail; and in the boundless annals of time his life and his labours must equally be measured as a fleeting moment. Of a simple and solid edifice it is not easy however to circumscribe the duration. As the wonders of ancient days, the pyramids attracted the curiosity of the ancients: a hundred generations, the leaves of autumn, have dropped into the grave; and after the fall of the Pharaohs and Ptolemies, the Cæsars and caliphs, the same pyramids stand erect and unshaken above the floods of the Nile. A complex figure of various and minute parts is more accessible to injury and decay; and the silent lapse of time is often accelerated by hurricanes and earthquakes, by fires and inundations. The air and earth have doubtless been shaken; and the lofty turrets of Rome have tottered from their foundations; but the seven hills do not appear to be placed on the great cavities of the globe; nor has the city, in any age, been exposed to the convulsions of nature, which, in the climate of Antioch, Lisbon, or Lima, have crumbled in a few moments the works of ages into dust. Fire is the most powerful agent of life and death: the rapid

*The Père Mabillon . . . has published an anonymous pilgrim of the ninth century, who, in his visit round the churches and holy places of Rome, touches on several buildings, especially porticoes, which had disappeared before the thirteenth century.

mischief may be kindled and propagated by the industry or negligence of mankind; and every period of the Roman annals is marked by the repetition of similar calamities. A memorable conflagration, the guilt or misfortune of Nero's reign, continued, though with unequal fury, either six or nine days. Innumerable buildings, crowded in close and crooked streets, supplied perpetual fuel for the flames; and when they ceased, four only of the fourteen regions were left entire; three were totally destroyed, and seven were deformed by the relics of smoking and lacerated edifices. In the full meridan of empire the metropolis arose with fresh beauty from her ashes; yet the memory of the old deplored their irreparable losses, the arts of Greece, the trophies of victory, the monuments of primitive or fabulous antiquity. In the days of distress and anarchy every wound is mortal, every fall irretrievable; nor can the damage be restored either by the public care of government, or the activity of private interest. Yet two causes may be alleged which render the calamity of fire more destructive to a flourishing than a decayed city. 1. The more combustible materials of brick, timber, and metals, are first melted or consumed; but the flames may play without injury or effect on the naked walls and massy arches that have been despoiled of their ornaments. 2. It is among the common and plebeian habitations that a mischievous spark is most easily blown to a conflagration; but as soon as they are devoured, the greater edifices which have resisted or escaped are left as so many islands in a state of solitude and safety. From her situation, Rome is exposed to the danger of frequent inundations. Without excepting the Tiber, the rivers that descend from either side of the Apennine have a short and irregular course; a shallow stream in the summer heats; an impetuous torrent when it is swelled in the spring or winter, by the fall of rain and the melting of the snows. When the current is repelled from the sea by adverse winds, when the ordinary bed is inadequate to the weight of waters, they rise above the banks, and overspread, without limits or control, the plains and cities of the adjacent country. Soon after the triumph of the first Punic war the Tiber was increased by unusual rains; and the inundation, surpassing all former measure of time and place, destroyed all the buildings that were situate below the hills of Rome. According to the variety of ground, the same mischief was produced by different means; and the edifices were either swept away by the sudden impulse, or dissolved and undermined by the long continuance, of the flood. Under the reign of Augustus the same calamity was renewed: the lawless river overturned the palaces and temples on its banks; and, after the labours of the emperor in cleansing and widening the bed that was encumbered with ruins, the vigilance of his successors was exercised by similar dangers and designs. The project of diverting into new channels the Tiber itself, or some of the dependent streams, was long opposed by superstition and local interests; nor did the use compensate the toil and cost of the tardy and imperfect execution. The servitude of rivers is the noblest and most important victory which man has obtained over the licentiousness of nature; and if such were the ravages of the Tiber under a firm and active government, what could oppose, or who can enumerate, the injuries of the city after the fall of the Western empire? A remedy was at length produced by the evil itself: the accumulation of rubbish and the earth that has been washed down from the hills is supposed to have elevated the plain of Rome fourteen or fifteen feet, perhaps, above the ancient level; and the modern city is less accessible to the attacks of the river.

II. The crowd of writers of every nation, who impute the destruction of the Roman monuments to the Goths and the Christians, have neglected to inquire how far they were animated by a hostile principle, and how far they possessed the means and the leisure to satiate their enmity. In the preceding volumes of this History I have described the triumph of barbarism and religion; and I can only resume, in a few words, their real or imaginary connection with the ruin of ancient Rome. Our fancy may create, or adopt, a pleasing romance, that the Goths and Vandals sallied from Scandinavia, ardent to avenge the flight of Odin; to break the chains, and to chastise the oppressors, of mankind; that they wished to burn the records of classic literature, and to found their national architecture on the broken members of the Tuscan and Corinthian orders. But in simple truth, the northern conquerors were neither sufficiently savage, nor sufficiently refined, to entertain such aspiring ideas of destruction and revenge. The shepherds of Scythia and Germany had been educated in the armies of the empire, whose discipline they acquired, and whose weakness they invaded: with the familiar use of the Latin tongue they had learned to reverence the name and titles of Rome; and, though incapable of emulating, they were more inclined to admire than to abolish the arts and studies of a brighter period. In the transient possession of a rich and unresisting capital, the soldiers of Alaric and Genseric were stimulated by the passions of a victorious army; amidst the wanton indulgence of lust or cruelty, portable wealth was the object of their search: nor could they derive either pride or pleasure from the unprofitable reflection that they had battered to the ground the works of the consuls and Cæsars. Their moments were indeed precious: the Goths evacuated Rome on the sixth, the Vandals on the fifteenth day; and, though it be far more difficult to build than to destroy, their hasty assault would have made a slight impression on the solid piles of antiquity. We may remember that both Alaric and Genseric affected to spare the buildings of the city; that they subsisted in strength and beauty under the auspicious government of Theodoric; and that the momentary resentment of Totila was disarmed by his own temper and the advice of his friends and enemies. From these innocent barbarians the reproach may be transferred to the Catholics of Rome. The statues, altars, and houses of the demons were an abomination in their eyes; and in the absolute command of the city, they might labour with zeal and perseverance to erase the idolatry of their ancestors. The demolition of the temples in the East affords to *them* an example of conduct, and to *us* an argument of belief; and it is probable that a portion of guilt or merit may be imputed with justice to the Roman proselytes. Yet their abhorrence was confined to the monuments of heathen superstition; and the civil structures that were dedicated to the business or pleasure of society might be preserved without injury or scandal. The change of religion was accomplished, not by a popular tumult, but by the decrees of the emperors, of the senate, and of time. Of the Christian hierarchy, the bishops of Rome were commonly the most prudent and least fanatic; nor can any positive charge be opposed to the meritorious act of saving and converting the majestic structure of the Pantheon.

III. The value of any object that supplies the wants or pleasures of mankind is compounded of its substance and its form, of the materials and the manufacture. Its price must depend on the number of persons by whom it may be acquired and used; on the extent of the market; and consequently on the ease or difficulty of remote exportation, according to the nature of the commodity, its local situation, and the temporary circumstances of the world. The barbarian conquerors of Rome usurped in a moment the toil and treasure of successive ages;

but, except the luxuries of immediate consumption, they must view without desire all that could not be removed from the city in the Gothic waggons or the fleet of the Vandals. Gold and silver were the first objects of their avarice; as in every country, and in the smallest compass, they represent the most ample command of the industry and possessions of mankind. A vase or a statue of those precious metals might tempt the vanity of some barbarian chief; but the grosser multitude, regardless of the form, was tenacious only of the substance; and the melted ingots might be readily divided and stamped into the current coin of the empire. The less active or less fortunate robbers were reduced to the baser plunder of brass, lead, iron, and copper: whatever had escaped the Goths and Vandals was pillaged by the Greek tyrants; and the emperor Constans, in his rapacious visit, stripped the bronze tiles from the roof of the Pantheon. The edifices of Rome might be considered as a vast and various mine; the first labour of extracting the materials was already performed; the metals were purified and cast; the marbles were hewn and polished; and after foreign and domestic rapine had been satiated, the remains of the city, could a purchaser have been found, were still venal. The monuments of antiquity had been left naked of their precious ornaments; but the Romans would demolish with their own hands the arches and walls, if the hope of profit could surpass the cost of the labour and exportation. If Charlemagne had fixed in Italy the seat of the Western empire, his genius would have aspired to restore, rather than to violate, the works of the Cæsars; but policy confined the French monarch to the forests of Germany; his taste could be gratified only by destruction; and the new palace of Aix-la-Chapelle was decorated with the marbles of Ravenna and Rome. Five hundred years after Charlemagne, a king of Sicily, Robert, the wisest and most liberal sovereign of the age, was supplied with the same materials by the easy navigation of the Tiber and the sea; and Petrarch sighs an indignant complaint, that the ancient capital of the world should adorn from her own bowels the slothful luxury of Naples. But these examples of plunder or purchase were rare in the darker ages; and the Romans, alone and unenvied, might have applied to their private or public use the remaining structures of antiquity, if in their present form and situation they had not been useless in a great measure to the city and its inhabitants. The walls still described the old circumference, but the city had descended from the seven hills into the Campus Martius; and some of the noblest monuments which had braved the injuries of time were left in a desert far remote from the habitations of mankind. The palaces of the senators were no longer adapted to the manners or fortunes of their indigent successors: the use of baths and porticoes was forgotten: in the sixth century the games of the theatre, amphitheatre, and circus had been interrupted: some temples were devoted to the prevailing worship; but the Christian churches preferred the holy figure of the cross; and fashion, or reason, had distributed after a peculiar model the cells and offices of the cloister. Under the ecclesiastical reign the number of these pious foundations was enormously multiplied; and the city was crowded with forty monasteries of men, twenty of women, and sixty chapters and colleges of canons and priests, who aggravated, instead of relieving, the depopulation of the tenth century. But if the forms of ancient architecture were disregarded by a people insensible of their use and beauty, the plentiful materials were applied to every call of necessity or superstition; till the fairest columns of the Ionic and Corinthian orders, the richest marbles of Paros and Numidia, were degraded, perhaps to the support of a convent or a stable. The daily havoc which is perpetrated by the Turks in the cities of Greece and Asia may afford a melancholy example; and in the gradual destruction of the monuments of Rome, Sixtus the Fifth may alone be excused for employing the stones of the Septizonium in the glorious edifice of St. Peter's. A fragment, a ruin, howsoever mangled or profaned, may be viewed with pleasure and regret; but the greater part of the marble was deprived of substance, as well as of place and proportion; it was burnt to lime for the purpose of cement. Since the arrival of Poggius the temple of Concord and many capital structures had vanished from his eyes; and an epigram of the same age expresses a just and pious fear that the continuance of this practice would finally annihilate all the monuments of antiquity.* The smallness of their numbers was the sole check on the demands and depredations of the Romans. The imagination of Petrarch might create the presence of a mighty people; and I

*Composed by Æneas Sylvius, afterwards Pope Pius II., and published by Mabillon. . . .

Oblectat me, Roma, tuas spectare ruinas;
Ex cujus lapsû gloria prisca patet.
Sed tuus hic populus muris defossa vetustis
Calcis in obsequium marmora dura coquit.
Impia tercentum si sic gens egerit annos
Nullum hinc indicium nobilitatis erit.

hesitate to believe that, even in the fourteenth century, they could be reduced to a contemptible list of thirty-three thousand inhabitants. From that period to the reign of Leo the Tenth, if they multiplied to the amount of eighty-five thousand, the increase of citizens was in some degree pernicious to the ancient city.

IV. I have reserved for the last the most potent and forcible cause of destruction, the domestic hostilities of the Romans themselves. Under the dominion of the Greek and French emperors the peace of the city was disturbed by accidental, though frequent, seditions: it is from the decline of the latter, from the beginning of the tenth century, that we may date the licentiousness of private war, which violated with impunity the laws of the Code and the Gospel, without respecting the majesty of the absent sovereign, or the presence and person of the vicar of Christ. In a dark period of five hundred years Rome was perpetually afflicted by the sanguinary quarrels of the nobles and the people, the Guelphs and Ghibelines, the Colonna and Ursini; and if much has escaped the knowledge, and much is unworthy of the notice, of history, I have exposed in the two preceding chapters the causes and effects of the public disorders. At such a time, when every quarrel was decided by the sword, and none could trust their lives or properties to the impotence of law, the powerful citizens were armed for safety, or offence, against the domestic enemies whom they feared or hated. Except Venice alone, the same dangers and designs were common to all the free republics of Italy; and the nobles usurped the prerogative of fortifying their houses, and erecting strong towers that were capable of resisting a sudden attack. The cities were filled with these hostile edifices; and the example of Lucca, which contained three hundred towers; her law, which confined their height to the measure of fourscore feet, may be extended with suitable latitude to the more opulent and populous states. The first step of the senator Brancaleone in the establishment of peace and justice was to demolish (as we have already seen) one hundred and forty of the towers of Rome; and, in the last days of anarchy and discord, as late as the reign of Martin the Fifth, forty-four still stood in one of the thirteen or fourteen regions of the city. To this mischievous purpose the remains of antiquity were most readily adapted: the temples and arches afforded a broad and solid basis for the new structures of brick and stone; and we can name the modern turrets that were raised on the triumphal monuments of Julius Cæsar, Titus, and the Antonines. With some slight alterations, a theatre, an amphitheatre, a mausoleum, was transformed into a strong and spacious citadel. I need not repeat that the mole of Hadrian has assumed the title and form of the castle of St. Angelo; the Septizonium of Severus was capable of standing against a royal army; the sepulchre of Metella has sunk under its outworks; the theatres of Pompey and Marcellus were occupied by the Savelli and Ursini families; and the rough fortress has been gradually softened to the splendour and elegance of an Italian palace. Even the churches were encompassed with arms and bulwarks, and the military engines on the roof of St. Peter's were the terror of the Vatican and the scandal of the Christian world. Whatever is fortified will be attacked; and whatever is attacked may be destroyed. Could the Romans have wrested from the popes the castle of St. Angelo, they had resolved by a public decree to annihilate that monument of servitude. Every building of defence was exposed to a siege; and in every siege the arts and engines of destruction were laboriously employed. After the death of Nicholas the Fourth, Rome, without a sovereign or a senate, was abandoned six months to the fury of civil war. "The houses," says a cardinal and poet of the times, "were crushed by the weight and velocity of enormous stones; the walls were perforated by the strokes of the battering-ram; the towers were involved in fire and smoke; and the assailants were stimulated by rapine and revenge." The work was consummated by the tyranny of the laws; and the factions of Italy alternately exercised a blind and thoughtless vengeance on their adversaries, whose houses and castles they razed to the ground.* In comparing the *days* of foreign with the *ages* of domestic hostility, we must pronounce that the latter have been far more ruinous to the city; and our opinion is confirmed by the evidence of Petrarch. "Behold," says the laureate, "the relics of Rome, the image of her pristine greatness! neither time nor the barbarian can boast the merit of this stupendous destruction: it was perpetrated by her own citizens, by the most illustrious of her sons; and your ancestors (he writes to a noble Annibaldi) have done with the battering-ram what the Punic hero could not accomplish with the sword." The influence of the two last principles of decay must in some degree be multiplied by each other; since

*The sixth law of the Visconti prohibits this common and mischievous practice; and strictly enjoins that the houses of banished citizens should be preserved pro communi utilitate . . .

the houses and towers which were subverted by civil war required a new and perpetual supply from the monuments of antiquity.

These general observations may be separately applied to the amphitheatre of Titus, which has obtained the name of the COLISEUM, either from its magnitude, or from Nero's colossal statue: an edifice, had it been left to time and nature, which might perhaps have claimed an eternal duration. The curious antiquaries, who have computed the numbers and seats, are disposed to believe that above the upper row of stone steps the amphitheatre was encircled and elevated with several stages of wooden galleries, which were repeatedly consumed by fire, and restored by the emperors. Whatever was precious, or portable, or profane, the statues of gods and heroes, and the costly ornaments of sculpture, which were cast in brass, or overspread with leaves of silver and gold, became the first prey of conquest or fanaticism, of the avarice of the barbarians or the Christians. In the massy stones of the Coliseum many holes are discerned; and the two most probable conjectures represent the various accidents of its decay. These stones were connected by solid links of brass or iron, nor had the eye of rapine overlooked the value of the baser metals; the vacant space was converted into a fair or market; the artisans of the Coliseum are mentioned in an ancient survey; and the chasms were perforated or enlarged to receive the poles that supported the shops or tents of the mechanic trades. Reduced to its naked majesty, the Flavian amphitheatre was contemplated with awe and admiration by the pilgrims of the North; and their rude enthusiasm broke forth in a sublime proverbial expression, which is recorded in the eighth century, in the fragments of the venerable Bede: "As long as the Coliseum stands, Rome shall stand; when the Coliseum falls, Rome will fall; when Rome falls, the world will fall." . . .

The abolition at Rome of the ancient games must be understood with some latitude; and the carnival sports, of the Testacean mount and the Circus Agonalis, were regulated by the law or custom of the city. The senator presided with dignity and pomp to adjudge and distribute the prizes, the gold ring, or the *pallium,* as it was styled, of cloth or silk. A tribute on the Jews supplied the annual expense;* and

*For these expenses the Jews of Rome paid each year 1130 florins, of which the odd thirty represented the pieces of silver for which Judas had betrayed his Master to their ancestors. . . .

the races, on foot, on horseback, or in chariots, were ennobled by a tilt and tournament of seventy-two of the Roman youth. In the year one thousand three hundred and thirty-two, a bull-feast, after the fashion of the Moors and Spaniards, was celebrated in the Coliseum itself; and the living manners are painted in a diary of the times.

This use of the amphitheatre was a rare, perhaps a singular, festival: the demand for the materials was a daily and continual want, which the citizens could gratify without restraint or remorse. In the fourteenth century a scandalous act of concord secured to both factions the privilege of extracting stones from the free and common quarry of the Coliseum; and Poggius laments that the greater part of these stones had been burnt to lime by the folly of the Romans. To check this abuse, and to prevent the nocturnal crimes that might be perpetrated in the vast and gloomy recess, Eugenius the Fourth surrounded it with a wall; and, by a charter, long extant, granted both the ground and edifice to the monks of an adjacent convent. After his death the wall was overthrown in a tumult of the people; and had they themselves respected the noblest monument of their fathers, they might have justified the resolve that it should never be degraded to private property. The inside was damaged: but in the middle of the sixteenth century, an era of taste and learning, the exterior circumference of one thousand six hundred and twelve feet was still entire and inviolate; a triple elevation of fourscore arches, which rose to the height of one hundred and eight feet. Of the present ruin the nephews of Paul the Third are the guilty agents; and every traveller who views the Farnese palace may curse the sacrilege and luxury of these upstart princes. A similar reproach is applied to the Barberini; and the repetition of injury might be dreaded from every reign, till the Coliseum was placed under the safeguard of religion by the most liberal of the pontiffs, Benedict the Fourteenth, who consecrated a spot which persecution and fable had stained with the blood of so many Christian martyrs.

When Petrarch first gratified his eyes with a view of those monuments whose scattered fragments so far surpass the most eloquent descriptions, he was astonished at the supine indifference of the Romans themselves; he was humbled rather than elated by the discovery that . . . a stranger of the Rhône was more conversant with these antiquities than the nobles and natives of the metropolis. The ignorance and credulity of the Romans are elaborately displayed in the old survey of the city which was composed about the beginning of the thirteenth century; and, without dwelling on the manifold errors of name and place, the legend of the Capitol may provoke a smile of contempt and indignation. "The Capitol," says the anonymous writer, "is so named as being the head of the world; where the consuls and senators formerly resided for the government of the city and the globe. The strong and lofty walls were covered with glass and gold, and crowned with a roof of the richest and most curious carving. Below the citadel stood a palace, of gold for the greatest part, decorated with precious stones, and whose value might be esteemed at one third of the world itself. The statues of all the provinces were arranged in order; each with a small bell suspended from its neck; and such was the contrivance of art magic, that, if the province rebelled against Rome, the statue turned round to that quarter of the heavens, the bell rang, the prophet of the Capitol reported the prodigy, and the senate was admonished of the impending danger." A second example, of less importance, though of equal absurdity, may be drawn from the two marble horses, led by two naked youths, which have since been transported from the baths of Constantine to the Quirinal hill. The groundless application of the names of Phidias and Praxiteles may perhaps be excused; but these Grecian sculptors should not have been removed above four hundred years from the age of Pericles to that of Tiberius; they should not have been transformed into two philosophers or magicians, whose nakedness was the symbol of truth and knowledge, who revealed to the emperor his most secret actions; and, after refusing all pecuniary recompense, solicited the honour of leaving this eternal monument of themselves. Thus awake to the power of magic, the Romans were insensible to the beauties of art: no more than five statues were visible to the eyes of Poggius; and of the multitudes which chance or design had buried under the ruins, the resurrection was fortunately delayed till a safer and more enlightened age. The Nile, which now adorns the Vatican, had been explored by some labourers, in digging a vineyard near the temple, or convent, of the Minerva; but the impatient proprietor, who was tormented by some visits of curiosity, restored the unprofitable marble to its former grave. The discovery of a statue of Pompey, ten feet in length, was the occasion of a lawsuit. It had been found under a partition wall: the equitable judge had pronounced, that the head should be separated from the body to satisfy the claims of the contiguous owners; and the sentence would have been executed if the intercession of a cardinal, and the liberality of a pope, had not rescued the Roman hero from the hands of his barbarous countrymen.

But the clouds of barbarism were gradually dispelled; and the peaceful authority of Martin the Fifth and his successors restored the ornaments of the city as well as the order of the ecclesiastical state. The improvements of Rome, since the fifteenth century, have not been the spontaneous produce of freedom and industry. The first and most natural root of a great city is the labour and populousness of the adjacent country, which supplies the materials of subsistence, of manufactures, and of foreign trade. But the greater part of the Campagna of Rome is reduced to a dreary and desolate wilderness: the overgrown estates of the princes and the clergy are cultivated by the lazy hands of indigent and hopeless vassals; and the scanty harvests are confined or exported for the benefit of a monopoly. A second and more artificial cause of the growth of a metropolis is the residence of a monarch, the expense of a luxurious court, and the tributes of dependent provinces. Those provinces and tributes had been lost in the fall of the empire; and if some streams of the silver of Peru and the gold of Brazil have been attracted by the Vatican, the revenues of the cardinals, the fees of office, the oblations of pilgrims and clients, and the remnant of ecclesiastical taxes, afford a poor and precarious supply, which maintains, however, the idleness of the court and city. The population of Rome, far below the measure of the great capitals of Europe, does not exceed one hundred and seventy thousand inhabitants; and within the spacious enclosure of the walls, the largest portion of the seven hills is overspread with vineyards and ruins. The beauty and splendour of the modern city may be ascribed to the abuses of the government, to the influence of superstition. Each reign (the exceptions are rare) has been marked by the rapid elevation of a new family, enriched by the childless pontiff at the expense of the church and country. The palaces of these fortunate nephews are the most costly monuments of elegance and servitude: the perfect arts of architecture, painting, and sculpture, have been prostituted in their service; and their galleries and gardens are decorated with the most precious works of antiquity, which taste or vanity has prompted them to collect. The ecclesiastical revenues were more decently employed by the popes themselves in the pomp of the Catholic worship; but it is superfluous to enumerate their pious foundations of altars, chapels, and churches, since these lesser stars are eclipsed by the sun of the Vatican, by the dome of St. Peter, the most glorious structure that ever has been applied to the use of religion. The fame of Julius the Second, Leo the Tenth, and Sixtus the Fifth, is accompanied by the superior merit of Bramante and Fontana, of Raphael and Michael Angelo; and the same munificence which had been displayed in palaces and temples was directed with equal zeal to revive and emulate the labours of antiquity. Prostrate obelisks were raised from the ground, and erected in the most conspicuous places; of the eleven aqueducts of the Cæsars and consuls, three were restored; the artificial rivers were conducted over a long series of old or of new arches, to discharge into marble basins a flood of salubrious and refreshing waters: and the spectator, impatient to ascend the steps of St. Peter's, is detained by a column of Egyptian granite, which rises between two lofty and perpetual fountains to the height of one hundred and twenty feet. The map, the description, the monuments of ancient Rome, have been elucidated by the diligence of the antiquarian and the student; and the footsteps of heroes, the relics, not of superstition, but of empire, are devoutly visited by a new race of pilgrims from the remote and once savage countries of the North.

Of these pilgrims, and of every reader, the attention will be excited by a History of the Decline and Fall of the Roman Empire; the greatest, perhaps, and most awful scene in the history of mankind. The various causes and progressive effects are connected with many of the events most interesting in human annals: the artful policy of the Cæsars, who long maintained the name and image of a free republic; the disorders of military despotism; the rise, establishment, and sects of Christianity; the foundation of Constantinople; the division of the monarchy; the invasion and settlements of the barbarians of Germany and Scythia; the institutions of the civil law; the character and religion of Mohammed; the temporal sovereignty of the popes; the restoration and decay of the Western empire of Charlemagne; the crusades of the Latins in the East; the conquests of the Saracens and Turks; the ruin of the Greek empire; the state and revolutions of Rome in the middle age. The historian may applaud the importance and variety of his subject; but, while he is conscious of his own imperfections, he must often accuse the deficiency of his materials. It was among the ruins of the Capitol that I first conceived the idea of a work which has amused and exercised near twenty years of my life, and which, however inadequate to my own wishes, I finally deliver to the curiosity and candour of the public.

LAUSANNE,
June 27, 1787.

Index